Applied Network Analysis

Applied Network Analysis

A Methodological Introduction

Ronald S. Burt / Michael J. Minor

Richard D. Alba
Ronald L. Breiger
Paul W. Dayton
Claude S. Fischer
Peter Greenwald
Paul W. Holland
David Knoke

Edward O. Laumann
Samuel Leinhardt
Nan Lin
Peter V. Marsden
Lynne S. McCallister
Gwen Moore
Philippa E. Pattison

David Prensky

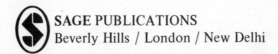
SAGE PUBLICATIONS
Beverly Hills / London / New Delhi

Burgess
HM
131
.A62
1983

The following portions of this book are reprinted from *Sociological Methods & Research:* Chapters 3, 6, 12, 13, 15, and 16 from the November 1978 issue; and Chapter 5 from the February 1981 issue.

For information address:

SAGE Publications, Inc.
275 South Beverly Drive
Beverly Hills, California 90212

SAGE Publications India Pvt. Ltd.
C-236 Defence Colony
New Delhi 110 024, India

SAGE Publications Ltd
28 Banner Street
London EC1Y 8QE, England

Printed in the United States of America

Library of Congress Cataloging in Publication Data

Main entry under title:

Applied network analysis.

   Bibliography: p.
   1. Social structure—Research. I. Burt, Ronald S.
HM131.A62 1982   302'.072   82-16849
ISBN 0-8039-1906-9
ISBN 0-8039-1907-7 (pbk.)

FIRST PRINTING

Contents

Acknowledgments

The arguments assembled here are the final product of a series of letters exchanged during the summer of 1977 with the then reigning editors of *Sociological Methods & Research,* George W. Bohrnstedt and Edgar F. Borgatta, regarding the advantages of devoting a special issue to problems in applying abstract network concepts in empirical research. There was a shared perception that developments in network analysis were creating a large interdisciplinary audience of social scientists interested in applying recently developed network concepts in empirical research. *Sociological Methods & Research* had become recognized as a journal specializing in applied methodology for a general audience, so it seemed a logical outlet for a collection of didactic papers on applied network analysis. Five of the chapters in this volume (3, 6, 12, 15, and 16) come from the special issue on applied network analysis (Volume 7, number 2), with only minor changes. Judging from the frequent citations to them in published work, they have been very well received. We are pleased to be able to offer them here through the good graces of Sage Publications, releasing this volume as an extended version of that special issue.

In extending the special issue, we have drawn on our mutual interest in research design and analysis in the context of our complementary perspectives as psychologist (Mr. Minor) and sociologist (Mr. Burt). This is most apparent in the extensive attention allocated to methods for obtaining adequate network data. Several chapters appear here for the first time (1, 2, 4, 9, 10, and 11), and others have been written for this applied methodology volume by partially or completely rewriting articles published by Burt with various colleagues in *Human Organization, Social Networks, Social Science Research, Sociological Methodology,* and *Sociological Methods & Research,* as noted in the appropriate chapters (5, 7, 8, 13, and 14).

In carrying out this work, we both received support from a National Institute on Drug Abuse grant to Mr. Minor through the Pacific Institute for Research and Evaluation (grant DA02566). In addition, secretarial and computing assistance were provided to Mr. Burt through a grant from the National Science Foundation (grant SES79-25728) and the collegial generosity of Percy H. Tannenbaum, Director, and James A. Wiley, Assistant Director, of the Survey Research Center, University of California, Berkeley.

—Ronald S. Burt
Michael J. Minor

Introduction

RONALD S. BURT and MICHAEL J. MINOR

PURPOSE AND AUDIENCE

This is a methodology reference book for research on the social environments of people, groups, or formal organizations as actors. Such research is at the heart of network analysis. Social environments are conceptualized and studied in network analysis as a structure of relations among actors in an environment. Actor attributes and behaviors are then explained in terms of the structure of relations in which they occur. There are a number of practical problems that arise when abstract concepts of network structure are applied to empirical research. This is a book on resolving and avoiding such problems— those that emerge during the design of research in which data on relations are to be obtained, and those that confront the individual wishing to analyze network data within the scope of some more general study.

In contrast to several edited volumes on network analysis, this is not an archive for classic papers published some time ago (e.g., Leinhardt, 1977), nor a collection of recent papers on diverse substantive themes (e.g., Marsden and Lin, 1982), nor a collection of technically sophisticated papers indicating the current frontiers of network analysis (e.g., Freeman et al., 1982). This volume complements the above collections as well as recent books articulating the social theory underlying what has come to be termed network analysis (e.g., Berkowitz, 1982; Burt, 1982a). The discussion here is didactic and problem-oriented, drawing on diverse substantive areas in illustrating general methodological arguments. The chapters reflect a purposive diversity in samples (from areal probability household samples to special groups such as physicians, elites, and former heroin users), in data collection procedures (from face-to-face interviews to the coding of archival records), and in analytical concepts (from simple counts of relationships up to the estimation of subtle features of network structure).

In other words, this book has been assembled for the general audience of scholars interested in social environments. We hope that people currently active in network analysis will find the book a useful reference, both for themselves and as a citation directing their students and colleagues to illustrative review discussion. However, the book is explicitly intended to provide an inexpensive reference for the wider audience of scholars who are interested in the study of social environments, who have noticed the excitement being generated by network analysis, and who would like to incorporate some of its insights into their own work.

OVERVIEW

The first half of the volume is concerned with strategies for obtaining data on relations among actors in one or more networks. The second part concerns methods by which those data can be described in terms of abstract concepts of structure. Each chapter begins with an abstract, so there is no need to summarize the forthcoming chapters here. However, there is value in giving you a general sense of the issues to be addressed.

Research Design and Network Data

First, there is the problem of deciding what to observe. How is a social environment to be defined in terms of a boundary around a system of actors? How are kinds of relations to be selected for analysis? These questions are addressed in the first two chapters. Without proposing a single best answer to the questions, Edward O. Laumann, Peter V. Marsden, and David Prensky offer a review of alternative answers in Chapter 1. Focusing on the particularly troublesome issue of relation content, Chapter 2 is an application of methods for distinguishing types of relations in a system by discovering how system actors themselves distinguish contents in their relationships. Guidelines are given for the selection of contents in the pretest stage of a study.

The design problem subsequent to deciding what to observe lies in deciding how to observe it. Relations in a network are typically measured in terms of binary, yes-no connections—direct sociometric choices between actors, and aggregate indirect connections through other actors or activities. These data are typically obtained with the familiar sociometric question, one eliciting actors or activities connected to a respondent under some criterion. Who are your best friends? To whom do you go for advice on work-related issues? What activities do you most like to do in your free time? With whom do you engage in these activities? The list of possible criteria for sociometric questions seems to be endless. Several review discussions, occasionally overlapping in content and purpose, are available in which alternative methods of measuring relations are described and compared (Bernard and Killworth, 1977; Burt, 1980b, 1982a: 20-29; Hallinan, 1974: 24-30; Holland and Leinhardt, 1973; Killworth and Bernard, 1974, 1976; Lindzey and Borgatta, 1954; Lindzey and Byrne, 1968; Rogers and Kincaid, 1981: 96-122). These reviews principally concern the use of sociometric questions to measure relations among all actors in a system.

One of the most important innovations in applied network analysis has been the development of strategies for obtaining network data in mass surveys—interviews with large numbers of respondents drawn at random to constitute a probability sample of respondents in some much larger population. These mass surveys have become one of the data collection strategies most often used in empirical social research. The incompatibility of the mass survey research design with the traditional network research design intended to obtain data on relations among all actors in a sample poses a serious barrier to substantive exchange between network analysis and more general lines of social science research. Chapters 3, 4 and 5 of this volume concern methods for obtaining network data from respondents in mass survey research designs.

The first generation of developments in this area was provided by Edward O. Laumann and colleagues describing networks of friendship, neighboring, and kinship relations in two urban areas based on interviews in 1963 and 1966 with probability samples of white adult males (see Laumann, 1966, 1973; Fischer et al., 1977; Verbrugge, 1977). This work was extended to include more detailed network data (more kinds of relations linking respondents with a larger number of others) in a second generation of developments. Particularly well known in this second generation are the descriptions based on interviews conducted in 1968 by Barry Wellman and colleagues with a probability sample of adults in an urban area (see Wellman, 1979, 1981, 1982) and the rich descriptions of roles and exchange relations that Claude S. Fischer and his colleagues generated from interviews in 1977 with survey respondents in a large probability sample of an urban and extraurban region (see Fischer, 1982a).

In Chapter 3 of this volume, Lynne McCallister and Claude Fischer describe the procedure they used to obtain extensive network data from respondents sampled in a mass survey research design. Their discussion is extended in Chapter 4 with a description of what could be termed a third generation development in obtaining network data from mass surveys. Chapter 4 describes the procedure used to obtain data on a large number of types of relations, with and among a large number of others, over time in several panels of interviews with a sample of heroin addicts. Finally, Chapter 5 is a description of a method by which patterns of relations defining role-sets in a large population could be inferred from interviews with a probability sample of population respondents.

Although a flexible methodology for obtaining network data, and an important methodology for bringing such data to bear on social science research more generally, sociometric questions in mass surveys are limited in many ways. For one thing, they are confined to descriptions of relations that have already occurred (e. g., "From whom did you borrow money if you were faced with an emergency?"). Unfortunately, every respondent need not have been involved in every type of relation, and there is no way of knowing what a respondent would in fact do when confronted with an emergency. One method for observing what respondents do when confronted with the problem of using their relations to reach other people involves chain data illustrating the "small world" phenomenon. Useful reviews of methodological issues in obtaining such data are provided by Erickson (1978) and Bernard and Killworth (1978; also see their intriguing creation of a reverse small world experiment, Killworth and Bernard, 1978). In Chapter 6 of this volume, Nan Lin, Paul W. Dayton, and Peter Greenwald provide illustrative application of the "small world" strategy.

A further problem with relying on mass surveys is the large number of interviews typically involved. A traditional response to the large budget survey is the use of informants. Although interviews with a small number of strategically selected informants can be conducted within the means of very meager research budgets, the network data obtained are suspect as hearsay evidence. The analysis in Chapter 7 shows that efficient, reliable, and valid network data can be obtained from interviews with a mere handful of informants. There are obvious limitations to the data obtained, but those limitations are tractable and readily identified.

A third problem with relying on mass surveys is the necessity of physical respondents—a person must respond to the interviewer even if the respondent is answering as the agent of a corporate actor (e.g., an interview with a corporate president about his or her firm's relations with other firms). This need for physical respondents is a problem for studies of network structure over a long period of time, studies of networks occurring a long time ago, and studies of networks involving relations among classes of actors for whom there is no physical respondent (symbolic actors, latent groups, informal collectivities, and so forth). Archival records can provide a rich source of network data for such studies. There are obvious examples in which network data have been archived explicitly to document relations (for example, input-output tables of national and regional economies). More to the point here, there are network data implicit in archival records such as historical documents, mass media accounts, books, pamphlets, and the like describing activities in which actors are involved. These implicit network data can be recovered with reasonable precision and at modest cost by content analyzing sampled archival records. Chapter 8 is a discussion of this methodology and limitations to its use.

Data Analysis and Network Structure

The second half of this volume is concerned with applying abstract structural concepts to describe network data once the data are available. The chapters in Part II each offer a comparatively nontechnical discussion of an abstract structural concept. General, but technical review of concepts describing network structure is given elsewhere (Burt, 1982a: ch. 2; see also Freeman et al., 1982). The focus here is practical. It is on structural concepts as they inform, and are operationalized in, substantive research.

Chapters 9, 10 and 11 concern individual patterns of relations. Beginning with one of the least sophisticated of network concepts, Chapter 9 is a discussion of ego-network range. The range of an actor's relations increases with the diversity of actors with whom he or she has relations. When operationalized, however, diversity can be measured in several ways according to the volume of contacts an actor has versus the quality of those contacts where contacted actors can be individuals or status groups. The measures of range distinguished by these alternative treatments of diversity are shown in Chapter 9 to refer to such different structural conditions that using them interchangeably in empirical research can result in erroneous substantive inferences.

The same kind of point is illustrated with respect to actor prominence in Chapter 10, by David Knoke and Ronald S. Burt. Prominent actors are extensively involved in relations with other actors, while peripheral actors are comparatively isolated. However, a single formal index of actor prominence can capture centrality as the extent to which an actor is involved in relations or prestige as the extent to which the actor is the object of relations. The authors describe formal similarities and substantive distinctions between several well-known prominence measures as they reflect the volume and quality of an actor's relations and his or her centrality versus prestige. The general conclusion is that erroneous inferences can be made from empirical research in which the measures are used interchangeably. Turning to the coordination of different kinds of relations, Chapter 11 is an analytical discussion of alternative manners in which the multiplexity of relations can be described—at one point in time, across multiple points in time, and at different levels of aggregation—in association with other variables.

Chapters 12, 13, and 14 concern comparisons between relational patterns, comparisons made in the interest of detecting members of network subgroups. In Chapter 12, Richard D. Alba and Gwen Moore illustrate the application of the concept of cohesion to identify and analyze network subgroups in a large system of elites. Each subgroup is a set of actors interconnected by relatively intense relationships. The discussion in Chapter 12 is continued in Chapter 13 with a comparison of network subgroups based on cohesion versus those based on structural equivalence. Two or more actors are structurally equivalent within a system of actors to the extent that they have identical patterns of relations with the other actors in the system. The equivalence offers conceptual and substantive advantages over cohesion to the extent that it is the preferable basis for defining network subgroups in all but a small class of studies. This critical examination of methods for detecting and analyzing network subgroups is continued in Chapter 14 with an illustrative discussion of how easy it is to report subgroups in computer output where subgroups do not in fact exist. The general point illustrated in Chapter 14 is at once obvious and easily overlooked: The social structure of a system is both the substance and a methodological factor in making inferences about system subgroups.

Finally, Chapters 15 and 16 concern the overall structure of relations in a system. In Chapter 15, Paul W. Holland and Samuel Leinhardt discuss network structure as patterns of relations among triads of actors and illustrate the use of a global measure of the extent to which there is nonrandom network structure present in a network at a triadic level. Building on the concept of structural equivalence, one of the more interesting developments in network analysis during the 1970s was the idea of analyzing social structure across multiple networks in terms of blockmodels. In Chapter 16, Ronald Breiger and Philippa E. Pattison offer an informative illustration of some methods by which blockmodel analysis can provide insights into the structure of multiple networks.

COMPUTER PROGRAMS

A great wealth of computer software has been written in connection with network analysis. Algorithm cognoscente are referred to two places in which blurbs on recently released software appear: *Social Networks* and *Connections,* both of which are affiliated with the International Network for Social Network Analysis (coordinated by Barry Wellman, Department of Sociology, University of Toronto, Ontario, M5S 1A1).

Many computer programs are mentioned in the forthcoming chapters, and the addresses of contributors are given at the end of the book. However, four programs would be sufficient to conduct the analyses to be described here (excluding date preparation software, in which raw data are transformed into network data): (1) A general purpose program would be required. The program STRUCTURE (Project, 1981) has been used to analyze relationship contents in Chapter 2, range in Chapter 9, path distances and prominence in Chapter 10, and cliques, structural equivalence, and density tables in Chapters 13 and 14. Other general purpose programs containing some of these options, as well as their own unique options, are SONET (Seidman and Foster, 1979), NEGOPY (Richards and Rice, 1981), and GRADAP (Mokken and van Veen, 1981). (2) A program for locating densely connected subgroups of actors in large sytems would also be required. Alba and Moore have used COMPLT (Alba, 1972) in Chapter 12 to locate social circles among 941 people. (3) A program for describing triad structure would be required. Holland and Leinhardt have written FORTRAN software for describing the triad census of a network and apply it in Chapter 15. (4) Finally, a matrix manipulation program would be required to obtain multiplication tables and homomorphisms of density tables recorded as image matrices in a blockmodel. In Chapter 16, Breiger and Pattison have used White's JNTHOM algorithm (Boorman and White, 1976) to identify the joint role structure of two systems of community elites.

Part I

NETWORK DATA

Chapter 1

The Boundary Specification
Problem in Network Analysis

EDWARD O. LAUMANN, PETER V. MARSDEN,
and DAVID PRENSKY

The problem of defining boundaries of social systems for study in a network analysis is discussed. We distinguish between nominalist and realist views of social phenomena and give three definitional foci for delimiting the component actors or nodes of a network: nodal attributes, relations, and participation in specified events or activities. A typology of boundary specification strategies is illustrated by reference to the extant network literature. Brief attention is given to formulation of inclusion rules for relations and activities or events.

In this chapter, we are concerned with an issue of central importance in the design of network studies: the problem of specifying system boundaries. From a network perspective, individual behavior is viewed as at least partially contingent on the nature of an actor's social relationships to certain key others. Likewise, the outcomes of events are seen to be partially dependent on the presence of a specific network configuration. In making use of this perspective, care must be given to specifying rules of inclusion for different network elements. Such rules pertain both to the selection of actors or nodes for the network *and* to the choice of types of social relationships to be studied. The latter issue is sometimes overlooked, but it is of enormous importance, especially with the development of methods for the analysis of multiple kinds of relationships.

In studies concerned with the explanation of particular events (e.g., Granovetter, 1973; Wheeldon, 1969), it is obviously of great

Author's Note: *This chapter is a revised version of a paper presented at a conference on Methods in Social Network Analysis, Laguna Beach, California, April 13-16, 1980, sponsored by the University of California at Irvine. Writing was supported by grant SOC77-26038 from the National Science Foundation. For helpful comments and suggestions, we are indebted to Stephen Berkowitz, Ronald S. Burt, James S. Coleman, Jean Comaroff, Joseph Galeskiewicz, David Knoke, J. Clyde Mitchell, Franz U. Pappi, Barry Wellman, and Christopher Winship.*

consequence if a key intervening actor or "bridging" tie is omitted due to oversight or use of data that are merely convenient. Such an error, because it distorts the overall configuration of actors in a system, may render an entire analysis meaningless. Carelessness in system specification is probably a more serious issue for network analysis than for much survey analysis. Survey analyses are concerned with individual level processes thought to be uniformly applicable to each unit of analysis in some population. Incorrect system specification may result in problems such as slightly biased estimates of population means, proportions, and the like or in efficiency in statistical estimation. Misspecification will not, however, cause a fundamental misrepresentation of the process under study. The latter is precisely the outcome of errors in the definition of system boundaries in a network analysis.

In view of the potential consequences of an incorrect specification of system boundaries in network analysis, it is somewhat surprising that the published literature reporting studies of social networks shows little concern for the problem of specifying the inclusion rules used in defining the membership of actors in particular networks and in identifying the types of social relationships to be analyzed. Oftentimes the sole justification for selecting a particular portion of the "total network" (Mitchell, 1969; Barnes, 1969) for the empirical focus of an investigation has been an apparent appeal to common sense. At other times the availability of data in some published form appears to be the only basis of an investigator's claim that a set of actors linked in some way possesses an apparent "entitativity" as a self-evident natural object (Campbell, 1958). Clearly, a given empirical analysis carries conviction only to the extent that such a claim can be accepted.

In this chapter, we discuss criteria that have been explicitly or implicitly employed in defining boundaries of social networks. We will attempt to trace the consequences of assuming different rules. For instance, the use of particular inclusion rules can render the results of certain analytic procedures artifactual (see Barnes, 1979). We do not advocate any particular strategy among those we discuss; the appropriate choice of rules remains contingent on the object of explanation for a given study. We do suggest, however, that, irrespective of the solution chosen, the problem of boundary definition should be given conscious attention when studies using a network approach are designed.

As noted, network analysts have, to date, been relatively mute on the matter of boundary definition. For this reason, we have been forced to adopt an inductive approach in this review, deriving metatheoretical views on the question of network closure from an inspection of published studies of social networks. In the next section, we distinguish two major approaches to boundary definition, the *nominalist* and *realist* approaches. We later distinguish several definitional foci used in the boundary specification process for delimiting the set of actors to be studied. We then illustrate a typology of approaches developed, by reference to extant network studies. We later discuss issues concerning the choice of particular social relationships to generate networks linking actors. Throughout, we comment on the implications of the different approaches considered for the use of analytic techniques, as well as on some unresolved theoretical issues that must be confronted if network analysis is to achieve the goal of providing new insights into social phenomena. To make our task manageable, we have paid little attention to egocentric approaches to network analysis that have been ably reviewed and explicated by Mitchell (1969) and Barnes (1972),[1] focusing attention instead on sociocentric or structural approaches.

APPROACHES TO BOUNDARY DEFINITION

The rules followed by investigators in establishing network closure or boundaries are quite varied. They range from highly diffuse and implicit notion to some quite self-conscious formalizations. It often appears that the matter of boundary definition is one of no particular import. The boundaries of a network are presented as so self-evident in a social situation studied as to require no comment (see the classic description of the bank wiring room in Roethlisberger and Dickson, 1939, or in Sampson's [1969] study of novitiates in a monastery). Other rules for establishing network limits appear to have solely an operational justification: limited resources constraining researchers to stop pursuing chains of contacts after a certain point (e.g., Travers and Milgram, 1969) or respondent recalcitrance preventing full disclosure of the actors in a network.

Nonetheless, our reading of the presently published studies suggests that researchers have generally bounded their studies in one of two ways. We distinguish between these two alternatives by referring to the time-honored controversy in the social sciences between nominalist and realist views of the ontological status of social phenomena (see Lenski, 1952; Ossowski, 1963). Having made this distinction, we hasten to add that many network studies do not fall neatly into one category or the other, perhaps because researchers have not been sufficiently self-conscious about the matter.

In the realist approach, the investigator adopts the presumed vantage point of the actors themselves in defining the boundaries of social entities. That is, the network is treated as a social fact only in that it is consciously experienced as such by the actors composing it. Braithwaite (1959) refers to this as a phenomenalist conception of facts. For example, in Weber's (1947: 145) classic definition of a corporate group (*Verband*) as "a social relationship which is either closed or limits the admission of outsiders by rules," stress is placed on the subjective meaningfulness to participants of the bounded nature of group membership. Thus, the 800-plus students in the high school studies by Coleman (1961) clearly recognize their common membership status when contrasting themselves with students attending any other high school. The fact that any given member may not even know, let alone sustain social relationships with, all other members of the corporate group has no significance for the specification of a network inclusion rule in terms of group membership.

The realist strategy of setting network boundaries by definition assumes the proposition that a social entity exists as a collectively shared subjective awareness of all, or at least most, of the actors who are members. This assumption is not often examined empirically.[2] This may not be problematic in the case of studies formally constituted groups with widely agreed-upon labels such as General Motors or the University of Chicago. As one examines more informally and fluidly constituted groups, such as Whyte's (1955) street corner society, tribal societies lacking fully differentiated political and social institutions (Cohen, 1969), or ethnic groupings (Barth, 1969; Cohen, 1974; Wellman, 1979), matters become more uncertain. Consider, for example, the dormitory at the University of Michigan studied by Newcomb (1961). This had no officially constituted status beyond that of being an experimental observation site in which some students had been given housing in exchange for their willingness to submit to certain testing procedures. It is difficult to be confident that the persons thus recruited had much of the "we-feeling" characteristic of a corporate group, or that the relations they maintained with others in the dormitory were imbued with much in the way of meaning or affect. As Mitchell (1969: 13) points out in discussing sociometric studies of school classrooms, there can be danger in uncritically accepting the proposition that common-sense groupings of actors possess subjective meaning to those in them: "The behavior of individuals . . . may be affected by circumstances beyond the immediate context."

The second major approach used to define network closure is the nominalist perspective on social reality. Here, an analyst self-consciously imposes a conceptual framework constructed to serve his own analytic purposes. Delineation of network boundaries is analytically relative to the purposes of the investigator, and thus

e. g.   within 3 steps from ego

network closure has no ontologically independent status. There is no assumption that reality itself will naturally conform to the analyst's distinction; the perception of reality is assumed to be mediated by the conceptual apparatus of the analyst, be he (or she) an active participant in the social scene under study or an outside observer.[3]

The theoretical treatment of the social system, and of social action more generally, by Parsons (1951, 1961) exemplifies the nominalist strategy. With such an approach, the match between the investigator's analytically drawn boundaries and the subjective awareness of these distinctions by participants becomes an empirical question rather than an assumption. Thus, with Marx's conception of social class (Bendix and Lipset, 1966), one begins with the nominalist concept of class-in-itself (*Klasse an sich*) and inquires into the conditions under which this will or will not be transformed into the realist grouping, a class-for-itself (*Klasse fur sich;* see Rosenberg, 1953; Broom and Jones, 1977).

In addition to utilizing a nominalist or realist metatheoretical approach, investigators also set boundaries on the inclusion of actors by focusing on particular components or "primitive elements" of a network. In this next section, we discuss the ways in which these definitional foci have been used in the specification of network boundaries.

DEFINITIONAL FOCI FOR THE INCLUSION OF ACTORS

In the process of choosing a set of actors as a network, analysts focus on one or more of three sets of components: actors, relations, or activities. In part inspired by the distinction between nodes and relations in graph theory (Harary et al., 1965), studies of social networks have generally stressed the sharp analytic distinction between actors and social relationships. Somewhat less common, but important, is a third approach adopted explicitly or implicitly by other investigators in which participation in some activity or event of relevance is the criterion of membership.   *contexts*

The choice of a definitional focus is of importance in that it fixes certain features of a network while leaving the remaining features free to vary. It is important that an investigator's choice of definitional focus be made explicit in order to avoid circular analytic procedures leading to tautological results referring to the features fixed by the inclusion rule. For instance, it is scarcely informative to learn that a network constructed by a snowball sampling procedure is well connected or "integrated."

✕ { actors, contexs }

The most commonly used definitional tactic is that of using a restriction based on some attribute or characteristic of the actors or nodes in the network. Actors may be persons, corporate actors, or other collective entities or groupings (for example, social classes, ethnoreligious groups) that are to be treated as unique elements. Two well-worn approaches to the determination of boundaries on the inclusion of actors in this way are the *positional* approach and the *reputational* approach. In the positional approach, the membership test refers to the presence or absence of some attribute, most commonly the occupancy of a position in a formally constituted group. The reputational approach, on the other hand, utilizes the judgments of knowledgeable informants in delimiting participant actors. The two approaches to constructing a nodal inclusion rule are, of course, sometimes combined (see Laumann and Pappi, 1976).

With the adoption of some approach restricting the number of actors in a network on the basis of nodal characteristics, the nature of the interconnectedness among those actors, as well as the participation patterns of actors in events or activities, are empirically free to vary. It is, however, of little more than descriptive interest to learn about the distribution of actors on the nodal characteristics used for boundary delimitation. A second definitional focus used to select actors in network studies is that of specifying the network such that it includes those actors participating in a social relationship of a specified type. For instance, Haas and Drabek (1973: 65) suggest that organizational boundaries be drawn on the basis of interaction frequency. The relational approach to boundary definition includes the procedure known as "snowball sampling" (Erickson, 1978). In this procedure, a study initially is concerned with a small set of individual actors; the networks or chains of contact of actors in this set are traced until some criterion of termination or network closure is satisfied.

Because the relational approach to boundary definition is used rather infrequently, there appear to be few routinized methods of applying it, comparable to the positional or reputational methods for delimiting a set of actors. Seiler and Summers (1974) propose a method of locating community boundaries on the basis of interaction frequency and other measures of the degree to which places are of common relevance to one another.

Use of a relational approach to boundary definition rules out certain questions about the morphology of a network, in that the design of the study fixes or constrains these relational features. On the other hand, issues referring to the composition of the interrelated actors in terms of individual attributes, or to the participation patterns of actors, are empirical ones in a network with a relationally defined boundary.

contexts

✗ A final element sometimes used to set boundaries is that of a defining event or activity, participation in which serves to select individual actors and the social relationships among them into a network. Pfeffer and Salancik (1978: 32) prefer this as a solution to the vexing problem of defining membership in an organization:

> When it is recognized that it is behaviors, rather than individuals, that are included in structures of coordinated behavior, then it is possible to define the extent to which any given person is or is not a member of the organization. ... The boundary is where the discretion of the organization to control an activity is less than the discretion of another organization or individual to control that activity.

The classic formulation of an inclusion rule based on participation in some activity is Dahl's (1958) decisional method for determining membership in a community elite. Of course, use of this or a related approach means that both the composition (in terms of the attributes of actors) and the relational pattern of a network are empirically at issue, while participation in the event or events on which the network is focused is predetermined.

Some investigators have stipulated inclusion rules in terms of two or more of our three definitional foci. While this may lead to theoretically elegant definitions of membership, it also has a major weakness, in that it reduces the number of problematic features to be explained given knowledge of network structure.

By cross-tabulating the distinction between nominalist and realist views with the distinctions among definitional foci drawn in this section, we arrive at an eightfold typology of boundary specification strategies. This typology is presented in Table 1.1. The cells of the typology are filled with references to empirical studies of social networks that utilize the different approaches to boundary definition. We review these in the next section.

ILLUSTRATIVE BOUNDARY
SPECIFICATION STRATEGIES

The eight boundary specification approaches located on the basis of our search of the literature have been assigned Roman numerals in Table 1.1. We shall review studies illustrative of these strategies in the order indicated.

We have already mentioned the most frequently adopted realist tactic, strategy I. Here, actors are treated as nodes in a network because they are members of a group which is closed or bounded according to

TABLE 1.1 A Typology of Boundary Specification Strategies for Delimiting Actors Within a Network, With Examples

Metatheoretical Perspective	Definitional Focus for Delimitation			
	Attributes of Nodes	Relation	Participation in Event or Activity	Multiple Foci
Realist	*I*	*III*	*V*	*VII*
	corporate group (Weber, 1947) bank wiring room (Roethlisberger and Dickson, 1939) monastery (Sampson, 1969) high school (Coleman, 1961; Fararo and Sunshine, 1964) Norwegian Island Parish (Barnes, 1954) cell room of Electrozinc Plant (Kapferer, 1969) school classroom (e.g., Davis, 1970)	primary group, clique (Cooley, 1909)	participants in a community controversy (Dahl, 1961) participants in common social events (Homans, 1950) street corner society (Whyte, 1955)	*Klasse für sich* (Marx) ethnic community (Barth, 1975; Laumann, 1973; Yancey et al., 1976)
Nominalist	*II*	*IV*	*VI*	*VIII*
	Klasse an sich (Marx) doctors in small cities (Coleman et al., 1966) formal organizations in a small city (Galaskiewicz, 1979) American business elite (Useem, 1979) community influentials (Laumann and Pappi, 1973, 1976)	small world problem (Travers and Milgram, 1969; Erickson, 1978)	Invisible College (Crane, 1972; Burt, 1978b; Breiger, 1976)	Supporters of psychotherapy (Kadushin, 1966) National elite circles (Moore, 1979)

the Weberian (1947) definition of a corporate group. The inclusion rule for actors refers to socially defined and recognized group memberships. Examples include attendance at a particular high school (Coleman, 1961; Fararo and Sunshine, 1964), employment in a particular work group in a factory (Roethlisberger and Dickson, 1939; Kapferer, 1969), residence in a monastery (Sampson, 1969) or parish (Barnes, 1954), or assignment to a particular classroom within a school (e.g., Davis, 1970). These examples should serve to indicate that strategy I is typically applied to the study of small tightly bounded groups.

In contrast to this, strategy II, in which a nominally defined group is delimited on the basis of nodal attributes, is more often applied to larger networks. These may include hundreds or even thousands of individual actors. The actors, furthermore, are sometimes corporate actors or organizations rather than individual persons. Useem's (1979: 558) definition of the American business elite provides a good illustration of strategy II. He utilizes a positional approach, defining the elite to include "those who were directors of the 797 largest U. S. corporations in 1969." This criterion yielded a set of 8623 directors. The interrelations among these members, measured most notably by membership on two or more corporate boards, were then studied empirically.

Another illustration of strategy II is given by Galaskiewicz's (1979) study of organizations in the small city of Towertown. In this study, a territorial criterion was initially used to restrict membership within a geographical area. As a second step, a functional or industry criterion was applied:

> Our target population included all industries, banks, savings and loans, newspapers, radio stations, service clubs, fraternal organizations, business associations, unions, law firms, health agencies, high schools, welfare agencies, churches, professional associations, county offices, municipal offices, and political parties. Commercial establishments, transportation facilities, public utilities, real estate offices, block clubs, community organizations, and elementary schools were excluded due to time and budget constraints [Galaskiewicz, 1979: 1350].

The rationale for including some types of organizations at the expense of others is not made explicit, but it would appear to pertain at least in part to the size of organizations.

Few empirical studies have relied exclusively on the relational nexus for determining memberships of actors in a network. We consider strategies III and IV, which use the relation as a boundary specifier, primarily for reasons of analytic completeness.

Cooley's (1909) concept of the primary group has long been a key term in small group research. The primary group is defined as a face-to-face interacting group with diffuse positive affect. This definition is essentially relational; it requires direct linkages of positive affect among all members of a group and excludes the possibility of "isolates" claiming subjective membership in the group but lacking relations with other members. Despite its time-honored place in the sociological literature, the primary group concept has rarely, if ever, served as the basis for identifying network limits. This is perhaps because analysts with a realist viewpoint have assumed a perfect correspondence among various features of such groups: complete connectedness, subjective we-feeling, diffuse positive sentiments toward all members, and multiple shared activities and interests, and then focused on one of the latter three features at the expense of connectedness. In our view, however, complete connectedness remains the litmus test for a primary group.

Of course, the connectedness criterion is frequently applied in efforts to locate subgroups or "cliques" within larger networks delimited in some other manner (see, for example, Alba, 1973; Burt, 1978a). Subgroupings identified in this way are often believed to have an ontological status distinguishing them in socially significant ways from other actors in the larger network to whom they are more loosely and indirectly connected. Here, then, we have a combination of strategies I and III, with the former being used to delineate the inclusive network and the latter to define cliques within it. Methods for locating subgroups on the criterion of structural equivalence proceed in a similar manner (Lorrain and White, 1971; White et al., 1976; Burt, 1978a).

Studies of the "small world" problem (e.g., Travers and Milgram, 1969) provide a good illustration of strategy IV. Here, arbitrarily selected "starters" serve as initiators of chains intended to reach arbitrarily selected "target" persons by way of preexisting personal relationships. The inclusion rule is thus specified in terms of an actor's presence in a chain of ties of unspecified type. Both the attributes of the individuals in the chain and the content of the relations composing it are theoretically and empirically free to vary given this inclusion rule (see Lin et al., 1978), and empirical variation in nodal characteristics may be used in efforts to discriminate between chains which are successful in reaching the intended target and those which are unsuccessful.

Strategy V, in which an actor's inclusion in a network is defined in terms of participation or interest in one or more event, activity, or concern is the primary alternative to strategy I from the realist perspective. Homans (1950: 82-86) provides a classic instance of this strategy, drawn from the field work of Davis et al. (1941, esp. 147-156). A clique structure among 18 women was induced from information about their participation in 14 informal gatherings taking place over the course of several months. Similarly, Dahl (1961), in a quite self-conscious application of strategy V, specifies three community controversies in the city of New Haven as a basis for locating community influentials. In a somewhat more implicit fashion, Whyte's (1955) description of street corner society in an Italian-American neighborhood of Boston uses the physical setting of a particular street corner as a focal observational scene or frame (see Goffman, 1974) for identifying nodal elements of the "society" (see also Leibow, 1967; Anderson, 1978).

Researchers adopting a nominalist perspective have been somewhat more reluctant than the realists to employ an event-focused approach to boundary delimitation. Most notable in illustrating strategy VI is work on "invisible colleges" of scientists (Crane, 1972; Burt, 1978b), in which network members are identified on the basis of their interest in a particular field of research, irrespective of their disciplinary label. The membership criterion in Breiger's (1976) study of biomedical researchers is publication of one or more articles in the research area on which the "invisible college" is focused.[4]

The three definitional foci for boundary delimitation can be and are combined in some cases (strategies VII and VIII). An example from the realist perspective is the Marxian concept of classes for itself (*Klasse fur sich*), which simultaneously requires occupancy of a common position relative to the means of production, relations of solidarity with those in the class, recognition of the attendant interests implied by objective position, and establishment of a self-conscious political organization in pursuit of those interests. Similarly, in delimiting an ethnic community, some investigators require both the nodal feature of a common heritage and the presence of a disproportionate level of interaction among members in terms of intimate social relations such as marriage or friendship (Laumann, 1973; Barth, 1975). Thus Yancey et al. (1976: 399) assert that

> ethnicity defined in terms of frequent patterns of association and identification with common origins . . . is generated and becomes crystallized under conditions of residential stability and segregation, common occupational positions and dependence on local institutions and services.

The discussion of social circles by Kadushin (1966, 1968) in some ways combines elements of the realist and nominalist perspectives and is therefore intermediate between the application of strategies VII and VIII. Kadushin defines social circles analytically, in terms of the sharing of certain broadly conceived social or political interests, together with the presence of indirect relational connectedness to other members. He asserts, however, that groups thus defined are real social entities. Hence, in describing a social circle called the Friends and Supporters of Psychotherapy, he writes that "like all circles, the Friends do not have a listing in the telephone book, but only in that sense are they a non-existent social unit" (Kadushin, 1966: 792).

In his actual analysis of data, Kadushin attempts to locate social circles within a group delimited on the basis of a nodal attribute (having made an application to the psychiatric clinic) using latent structure analysis of items measuring participation in certain types of cultural events and information levels concerning psychotherapy. His purpose in doing this is to "define circles empirically without necessarily having to engage in extensive and difficult sociometric analysis" (Kadushin, 1966: 792). This is obviously an important operational advantage if there is a sufficiently close correspondence between the participation and knowledge measures and the unmeasured connectedness criterion. The procedure may be problematic in the absence of a close correspondence, and others have chosen operationally to define circles otherwise (e.g., Alba and Moore, 1978).

Moore's (1979; see also Alba and Moore, 1978) study of the American national elite is more clearly representative of the application of strategy VIII. The study design for identifying this elite involved an initial selection of 545 incumbents of command positions in key institutional sectors of American society, supplemented by another 331 persons identified on the basis of a reputational survey of the initial positionally identified group, and a snowball sampling procedure (see Moore, 1979: 675-676).

Laumann and Marsden (1979) utilize multiple foci for defining "collective actors" within oppositional structures in political systems; i.e., for defining subgroups within networks delimited on some other basis. They define a collective actor in terms of individual members who "(1) share an outcome preference in some matter of common concern, and (2) are in an effective communication network with one another" (Laumann and Marsden, 1979: 717).

As mentioned earlier, the central difficulty with strategies VII and VIII is that in using two or more analytic features of networks to define membership of actors in the network, these strategies consume many theoretical degrees of freedom. Great caution must be used in drawing substantive inferences here. For instance, Moore's (1979) study concludes that the structure of the American elite is that of a large, integrated collection of interrelated actors rather than a set of fragmented groups. Despite her explicit attention to the issue (Moore, 1979: 677), the reader is left with the suspicion that her conclusion is necessitated, or at least made likely, by the boundary specification rule employed: The selection of certain institutional sectors (e.g., mass media leaders) carries strong relational implications; the use of snowball sampling requires connectedness among at least some members of the network; and the granting of discretion to respondents to select national events as discussion topics, and to give an unlimited number of responses to sociometric questions, in all likelihood encouraged the recognition of diverse and ramifying communication ties.

This concludes our review of strategies for delimiting boundaries of a network as far as actors are concerned. This is, to our minds, the most central issue in boundary specification, and it is certainly the issue that had received the most concerted attention. It is also of importance, however, to consider rules of inclusion for the other two analytic foci we have mentioned: relations and events or activities.

ON INCLUSION RULES FOR RELATIONS

The identification of the social relationship as a definitional focus, together with the development of analytic techniques permitting consideration of multiple types of relationships (White et al., 1976; Burt, 1977b) points to the need for developing rules of inclusion for relationships studied, as well as actors. A major barrier in this enterprise is the current lack of any well-articulated typology of social relationships that could lead to the development of explicit selection strategies parallel to those reviewed earlier for actors. Probably the best guidance we have available in this regard is derived from Parson's (1951) set of five pattern variables. Particular attention has been given to the distinction between instrumental and expressive social relations; somewhat more implicit is a focus on the diffuseness-specificity dimension.

Even with a suitable classification of relationships, however, an analyst is left with the problem of selecting types to be analyzed. Rather little self-conscious attention appears to have been given to this matter; implicit appeals to common-sense justifications for the use of particular relations as generators of a social structure or analyses of any available relational data run rampant. Probably the most serious consequence of such neglect is what we shall term the *partial system fallacy*. This is present wherever a set of relationships connecting a subset of the actors to which the relations are relevant is analyzed without prior attention to the entire set of actors. The result of such a procedure may be a seriously misleading description of network structure.

To clarify this point, we refer to an illustrative case with which we have some familiarity, pertaining to the social structure of a community defined in terms of interorganizational relations (see Laumann et al., 1978). Consider two specific types of interorganizational relations: transfer of money and transfer of information pertinent to local community affairs. If the boundary for inclusion of organizations has been drawn on the basis of geography, then the analysis of social structure in terms of intracommunity money flows may be uninformative. This is because many of the central organizations in the total network of money flows would be excluded from the network by virtue of the geographically based nodal inclusion rule. Examples of the excluded organizations would be state and federal government agencies, extralocal banks, headquarters or subsidiary organizations located elsewhere, and supplier and consumer organizations. For many, or even most, local organizations, these might be more important sources or destinations of money than other organizations in the locality. Their omission from the network of money flows makes the analysis of such flows subject to the partial system fallacy. We would be more comfortable with an analysis based on information flows pertinent to community affairs. Because these relationships are defined with explicit reference to a criterion of common relevance to the organizations delimited on the basis of the nodal inclusion rule, it is plausible to treat the patterns of information flow analytically as a closed system, while such a treatment is implausible for the money flows.

Two other issues raised when we consider inclusion rules for relations are of special concern to multiple network studies using structural equivalence as a central concept. The procedures outlined by White et al. (1976) are premised on the idea that social roles can be understood by simultaneously considering, or "stacking," several different relations or generators. Blockmodels of roles and positions are either induced by clustering nodes on the basis of the profile similarities across the multiple relations (Breiger et al., 1975) or deduced by searching for "empty places" in the network (Heil and White, 1976). This approach has led to some interesting analyses of social structure (e.g., Breiger, 1976; Snyder and Kick, 1979). This approach does, however, place an obligation on investigators to be explicit regarding the rationale for merging different generators in a single analysis—that is, to indicate *why* these particular relations ought to be seen as jointly definitive of social roles in a given population. In some applications it appears that the social positions induced by the procedures mentioned have been arbitrarily determined by the happenstance availability of particular generators. This appearance is accentuated by the inability of some analysts to find a meaningful substantive interpretation of the partitions of actors identified.

In our view, some potential generators ought not to be used at all in the definition of social positions or roles, because to use them is to commit the partial system fallacy discussed above. In other cases, it may be preferable to utilize multiple network strategies like those advocated by Burt (1977b). In this approach, several different sets of social positions or roles are induced on the basis of social relationships considered separately; the intersections among the different partitionings of actors into positions are then analyzed empirically.

One final point pertaining to multiple network approaches and the setting of boundaries on the inclusion of relations is of particular importance to those approaches and techniques assigning special weight to the absence of social ties as a criterion for locating social structure in networks. When applied to small, closed groups, these methods have been quite successful. As increasingly large networks are analyzed, however, the fact that any given actor is capable of maintaining only a limited number of ties, together with the well-known generalization that the total number of ties increases as the square of the number of actors, creates a fundamental ambiguity about the absence of relations. Absent ties may appear either because of active avoidance or limited opportunity for contact. The implication of this is that in efforts to apply techniques resting on the notion of structural equivalence to large networks, care should be taken to obtain multiple measures that permit the analyst to discriminate between avoidance and lack of contact (see, for example, Breiger's [1976] study of awareness relations among biomedical scientists, or the analysis by White et al., 1976, of positive and negative relations of affect, influence, and so forth in a monastery studied by Sampson [1969]).

BOUNDARY SPECIFICATION FOR ACTIVITIES

We shall comment briefly on the question of setting limits on the inclusion of events, activities, or interests in network studies. It is obvious that the network boundaries for the inclusion of actors obtained using strategies V and VI are entirely dependent on the selection of particular events or activities as ones of focal interest. An analytic rationale for event selection is generally *not* given by those applying these strategies.[5] It is often assumed that the relevant events are self-evident to any well-informed observer. This gives an unfortunate impression of arbitrariness, which leaves the reader to inquire what shape the leadership and power structure of New Haven might have taken had Dahl (1961) and his associates chosen to study additional or other issues, or what changes in the clique structure of women in Old City might have emerged if other social gatherings that doubtless occurred during the observation period of Davis et al. (1941) had been mentioned in the newspapers or noticed by the participant observers.

Part of the issue here is whether an analyst is intrinsically interested in the events under study, or whether their selection is an intermediate step in an effort to obtain a description of a regularized structure of social relations among actors. In the former case, a rationale for event selection is straightforward and obvious. We are more concerned with latter case. When the goal is to obtain a description of a presumably enduring social structure using an event-base strategy for boundary delimitation, steps should be taken to carefully delineate the event space to be explored.

Unfortunately, this problem is more easily posed than solved. As in the case of boundary specification for relations, the development of a workable typology of issues or activities that might be used for sampling or selection of focal events would be a useful first step toward a solution. Aside from referring to our previously published commentary addressing this problem (Laumann et al., 1977), and to some efforts in the literature to develop classification schemes for issues (Barth and Johnson, 1959; Freeman, 1968; Molotch, 1976), we have little guidance to offer on it.

CONCLUSION

In this chapter we have reviewed approaches to the problem of setting network boundaries. While we feel that network analysis has a great deal to offer social scientists seeking to study social systems, we think it important to emphasize the point that *there is no sense in which social networks must "naturally" correspond to social systems.* Freeman (1980) gives elegant formal criteria, in terms of nodes, relations, and attributes, for defining social networks. Adopting a nominalist view, we define a social system as "a plurality of actors interacting on the basis of a shared symbol system" (Parsons, 1951: 19). The problem of boundary specification in efforts to adapt network analysis to the study of social systems is essentially that of specifying the standard of common relevance (Newcomb, 1961: 12-23)—that is, the basis of mutual orientation for actors—which circumscribes membership in the system. Given a suitable definition of this standard, the network boundaries for actors, relations, and activities or events may be specified such that they can be plausibly equated to those of the social system under study.

Boundary specification also lays a basis for the identification of sets of social roles in that system, with respect to both its internal organization and its environment.

The question of boundary specification has received comparatively little attention in the past decade during which network analysis has largely come into its own, partly because of the preoccupation of the field with the development of novel strategies for analysis of relational data. It is a much less tractable sort of problem than those addressed by some of the chapters concerned with analytic methods included elsewhere in this volume, and one on which there are few objective criteria that may be used to resolve conflicting positions. We have argued here, however, that networks can be meaningfully understood only in terms of the elements of focal interest used to define membership, whether that usage is explicit or inadvertent. We feel that more explicit attention to boundary specification will contribute to the success of network methods in the study of social structures and systems as new studies are designed and new data collected.

NOTES

1. Because they anchor a network on a focal individual or set of individuals of interest to an investigator, egocentric approaches to network analysis avoid some of the problems of boundary delimitation that we note for sociocentric approaches. Even here, issues arise about the lengths to which an investigator must go in identifying relevant indirect ties that might affect the attitudes or behavior of the focal actor. The problems are pragmatic as well as theoretical: Boissevain (1974), for example, enumerated a set of over 1000 persons related in some fashion to an "ordinary" person in the island society of Malta. Mitchell (1969) and Barnes (1969) suggest that in practice it is rarely necessary to inquire into indirect ties involving more than one intermediary. In Barnes's terminology, inspection of the "primary" and "second-order" zones is usually sufficient. Thus, a "stopping rule" used to establish network closure is obviously a necessity for egocentric as well as structural approaches, but we shall not consider such problems here.

2. For research strategies relevant to assessing this hypothesis, see Laumann and Senter (1976), Broom and Jones (1977), or Gurin et al. (1980).

3. What we have called here the *nominalist* approach to boundary definition appears to correspond to Braithwaite's (1959) *realist* view of social facts as things accessible to some falsifiable method of observation, irrespective of whether they are experienced as facts by participants. It also reflects Kaplan's (1964) *instrumentalist* view of the nature of theories and concepts, seeing these as the investigator's tools of inquiry rather than as necessarily accurate pictures or maps of the world.

4. The researchers actually studied by Breiger were sampled from a population delimited by the criterion given here.

5. Consider, for instance, the advice given to those wishing to apply a decisional method of locating leaders by Polsby (1960: 495), who suggests that issues "which are generally agreed to be significant" be studied.

Chapter 2

Distinguishing Relational Contents

RONALD S. BURT

Before gathering network data, specific relational contents must be selected for analysis. The selection can be informed significantly by pretest data and readily available network models of relational form. This chapter is a methodological discussion of using survey interview data to distinguish the content, the substantive meaning, of relations in the multiple network social system from which survey respondents were drawn. Two contents are defined as distinct to the extent that they are used by respondents in a nonsubstitutable way and with different levels of ambiguity. Illustrative data are taken from personal interviews conducted in 1977 with a cross-section of adults living in Northern California. Guidelines are offered for selecting contents as a pretest activity in a network study.

Let me begin by distinguishing naturally occurring relations from analytical relations—the first being the relations in which people are actually involved, the second being the re-creation of relations for a network analysis. For example, when I go to a colleague for advice, that interaction occurs in the context of other activities for which I have sought her out: lunch, cocktails, dinner, committee work, colloquia, leads to new acquaintances, and so on. My naturally occurring relation to my colleague, my relation to her as it exists in fact, is a bundle of specific interaction activities. Similarly, my naturally occurring relations to other people, other actors, are bundles of specific interaction activities, some consisting of many specific activities, others containing very few.

With the notable exception of ethnographers, network analysts rarely capture the complexity of naturally occurring relations. Their concern is less the complexity of the relationship between pairs of actors than it is

Author's Note: *The work reported here is a byproduct of support from the National Science Foundation (grant SES79-25738) and has received direct support from the National Institute on Drug Abuse through the Pacific Institute for Research and Evaluation (grant DA02566). Claude S. Fischer graciously provided data for this analysis. Molly Haggard and Davida Weinberg provided able research assistance in the data analysis. Portions of this chapter were presented in a 1980 colloquium at the University of California, Irvine, and at the 1982 Sun Belt Network Conference at Tampa, Florida. I appreciate the helpful comments of Edward O. Laumann, Peter V. Marsden, and Michael J. Minor on drafts of this material.*

the complexity of the structure of relations among many actors as a system. The relations described are analytical constructs, with a relation's form being its intensity or strength as a tendency to occur and its content being its substance as reason for occurring. The form of a friendship relation, for example, would refer to the intensity or strength of the relation, while its content, or substantive meaning, would be friendship. Network models of social structure typically describe the form of relations while taking the content of those relations as a given, an item exogenous to the model. The most general of these models purport to describe formal structure in multiple networks among actors in a system where each network consists of relations having the same content. The questions of why certain networks are to be distinguished in a system, how actors within the system interpret their interaction activities, and how they distinguish different types of such activities are assumed to be resolved a priori.

Unfortunately, these unasked questions are quite unresolved; not only in general, but in the particular. When someone poses a sociometric question to me asking for the names of people to whom I go for such-and-such, I must disentangle the welter of interaction activities in my naturally occurring relations and classify some as such-and-such activities before I can answer the question. If I am asked to name my friends, for example, I must decide which of my activities fall under the label of friendship. If I am asked to name the people with whom I engage in leisure activities, I must decide which of my activities fall under the label of leisure. If I am asked to name the people who most influence my thinking with their personal comments, I must decide which of my activities fall under the label of influence. Obviously, people can differ in their interpretation of specific interaction activities as manifestations of more general types of activities, with some viewing as intimate, for example, what others view as no more than friendly. More obviously, people in different social contexts, systems, and cultures often differ in their interpretation of specific activities as types of more general activities.

The necessary distinctions between contents required in order to formulate sociometric questions before collecting network data are thus unsettlingly ad hoc. The sociometric questions finally selected can be no more than a compromise between the theoretical extreme of initial hunches regarding significant dimensions of interaction stratifying a system—this determining a minimum number of different contents to be described, e.g., social relations versus economic relations—versus the empirical impossibility of gathering data on the full range of specific activities possibly stratifying the system—this determining a maximum number of contents to be distinguished as a function of the number of different sociometric questions respondents will tolerate.

This problem in data definition creates problems in data analysis. Ad hoc distinctions among relational contents make it difficult to analyze the coordination of different types of interaction activities. But such analysis is integral, almost by definition, to a description of social structure in a multiple network system. Consider the concept of multiplexity. The relation of one person to another is multiplex to the extent that there is more than one type of relation between the first person and the second. For example, I have a multiplex relation to the person I described above. I have social, economic, and collegial ties to the person. My relation to my colleague would be uniplex if I had only one of these types of ties.

But who is to say when one type of relational content stops and another begins? When does a colleague relation become a friendship relation? One observer might decide each of the above classes of interaction activities constitutes a different relational content, whereupon the described relation is multiplex. Another observer might only distinguish two types of relations, kinship versus nonkinship, whereupon the described relation is uniplex. It consists of multiple examples of nonkinship interaction activities. Without empirical guidance regarding relational contents, these alternative distinctions between contents are ad hoc, raising an important analytical question: When is a uniplex relation mistakenly discussed as a multiplex relation merely because a network analyst has treated various aspects of a single relational content as if they were different contents? Consequential as a clear understanding of relational content is for accurate description of social structure by network models ranging in sophistication from ego-network multiplexity to multiple network role structures, very little is known about it. Research inferences are correspondingly ambiguous.

My purpose in this chapter is to illustrate methods by which a network analyst can understand how actors in a system themselves distinguish relational contents in their naturally occurring relations. Armed with this understanding, obtained from pretest interviews, the analyst can formulate sociometric questions so that they elicit information efficiently and accurately from the full sample of respondents: efficiently in the sense that redundant relational contents are minimized, and accurately in the sense that the analyst knows how respondents are interpreting the questions. Three sections of discussion follow. Concepts are introduced. An illustrative application is discussed. I conclude with comments on the selection of contents as a pretest activity in a network study and on the analysis of relationship content more generally.

CONTENT SUBSTITUTABILITY AND AMBIGUITY

I employ a perspective on relational contents in which the meaning of relations is inferred from patterns of content in much the same way that social structure itself has been inferred from patterns of relational form. The perspective turns on three concepts, elaborated in detail elsewhere (Burt, 1982c) and illustrated below: confusion between contents, substitutability of contents, and content ambiguity. A content has a high tendency to be confused with another to the extent that every naturally occurring relation containing the one contains the other. In other words, content A has a high tendency to be confused with content B to the extent that the conditional probability of observing content B in a naturally occurring relation is high, given the knowledge that the relation contains content A. Two contents are substitutable to the extent that they tend to be similarly confused with the same other contents. In other words, substitutable contents are structurally equivalent in a network of tendencies for contents to be confused with one another. A content is ambiguous to the extent that it is used in a great diversity of naturally occurring relations in which a great many other contents occur. In other words, an ambiguous content is prominent in a network of confusion tendencies among contents. Finally, and most pertinent to this chapter, two relational contents are substantively distinct to the extent that they are used by actors in a system in such a way as to be nonsubstitutable and differentially ambiguous. These ideas can be defined in a usefully more rigorous way with a concrete example.

RELATIONS AMONG NORTHERN CALIFORNIANS

In the fall of 1977, personal interviews were conducted with a cross-section of people living in a northern region of California, a region stretching from San Francisco to Sacramento. Survey respondents were representative of predominantly white urban locations (although dense urban populations were undersampled). Minority ethnicities are conspicuously absent as part of the research design. Adult respondents (ages 21 and over) who have lived in their current city of residence for at least a year have been selected for this analysis as people likely to have developed stable adult relationships. There were 858 such respondents (192 children, recent arrivals, and students were omitted).

Let a respondent be ego and let alter be a person named by a respondent as the object of some kind of relation from ego. Each of the 858 egos could have named from one to five alters in this analysis. Alters were selected as the first person named in response to sociometric questions concerning house care, work, informal socializing, personal problems, obtaining advice on family or work-related issues, and borrowing money. These alters were selected to be among the most active, intimate, and central members of a respondent's ego network. The alters most likely to fall outside the sampled alters are those who were the object of uniplex relations. My concern in this chapter is with confusions between coincident contents, so this bias against uniplex alters is less troubling than it would be in a more general study. Moreover, there is a wealth of information only available on the sampled alters that can be used to advantage here. The data collection strategy is described in detail in the project final report (Fischer, 1982a, esp. pp. 267-350), and in brief by McCallister and Fischer in the next chapter of this volume.

This is obviously a much larger sample than would be drawn for a study pretest; however, the conclusions to be reached here could have been reached with a mere 10-20 strategically selected interviews —a point to which I shall return in concluding the chapter.

Networks of Confusion Relations

Tendencies for each respondent to confuse one content with another were computed. In response to multiple questions, a respondent names N alters; n_i of those alters are named as the object of a relation with content i, and n_{ij} are named as the object of a relation with content i as well as content j. The numbers n_i and n_{ij} could range from zero to five in the subsample data. The ratio of n_i over N is the proportion of all ego's alters who are the object of relations having content i:

$$c_{ii} = n_i/N \qquad [2.1]$$

and the ratio of n_{ij} over n_i is the proportion of alters receiving content i that also receive content j:

$$c_{ij} = n_{ij}/n_i \qquad [2.2]$$

Focusing on ego's relations to the subsample alters as his or her most important naturally occurring relations, c_{ii} is the probability of content i occurring in one of those relations, and c_{ij} is the conditional probability of content j occurring in one of those relations given the knowledge that the relation contains content i. Equations 2.1 and 2.2 thus define a network of tendencies for ego to confuse contents with one another in his or her most important naturally occurring relations.

Mean values of these confusion relations across all 858 respondents are presented in Table 2.1 as a confusion matrix among five specific contents: friendship, acquaintance, work, kinship, and intimacy. The specific questions eliciting data on these contents are given in the note to the table. Average values of c_{ii} are given in parentheses and indicate the probability that a naturally occurring relation contained one of the contents. For example, two out of three relations contained friendship as a content ($c_{11} = .67$), one out of four relations contained some form of kinship as a content ($c_{44} = .26$), and one out of three relations contained intimacy as a content in the sense that the object of the one relation was someone with whom ego discussed personal matters ($c_{55} = .35$). Average values of c_{ij} are given in the off-diagonal elements of Table 2.1. Each column describes the tendency for a content to be perceived in a naturally occurring relation, given a knowledge of some other type of content being in the relation. For example, the elements in column one are the highest in each row, showing that friendship content has a high tendency to be perceived in all of these important naturally occurring relations, although the tendency drops noticeably for relations containing work or kinship contents. The average tendency for a relation to contain friendship is .67, and this tendency drops slightly given a knowledge of acquaintance or intimacy content in the relation (.59 and .56, respectively), but it drops much more if the relation contains work or kinship contents (to .22 and .23, respectively). At the other end of the table, in column five, intimacy in one of these important naturally occurring relations is not uncommon ($c_{55} = .35$), and that tendency is not affected by knowing that the relation contains friendship content ($c_{15} = .34$); however, the likelihood of intimacy in a relation is decreased if the relation contains acquaintance, work, or kinship content (to .21, .18, and .20, respectively).

Content Ambiguity

These tendencies for contents to be confused with one another define the relative ambiguity with which they are used by the typical respondent. Ambiguity has no absolute meaning here. A content i is used with high ambiguity to the extent that it is used with greater ambiguity than some other content k, k being a numeraire content in the sense of providing a criterion level of ambiguity. Where g_i is the ambiguity of content i, in other words, g_i is defined as the ratio of g_i over the ambiguity of the numeraire content g_k:

$$g_i = g_i/g_k \qquad [2.3]$$

TABLE 2.1 Summary Confusion Matrix among Content Domain
Indicators

Content Domains	Mean Confusion Relations					Ambiguity
	F	A	W	K	I	
Friendship	(.67)	.37	.10	.11	.34	1.81
Acquaintance	.59	(.26)	.06	.00	.21	.69
Work	.22	.06	(.10)	.03	.18	.30
Kinship	.23	.00	.03	(.26)	.20	.69
Intimacy	.56	.20	.13	.21	(.35)	1.00

NOTE: Confusion relations are defined in equations 2.1 and 2.2 and have been averaged across 858 respondents. The relational contents are taken from the data described
by McCallister and Fischer in the next chapter. Work and Intimacy refer to specific
sociometric questions. The following question elicited work ties: "Some people
never talk to anyone, either on or off the job, about how to do their work. Other
people do discuss things like decisions they have to make, work problems they have
to solve, and ways to do their work better. Is there anyone you talk with about how
to do your work? Who do you talk with about how to do your work?" The following question elicited intimates: "When you are concerned about a personal matter—
for example, about someone you are close to or something you are worried about
—how often do you talk about it with someone—usually, sometimes, or hardly ever?
When you *do* talk with someone about personal matters, who do you talk with?"
After a long list of alters had been composed for each respondent, a variety of characteristics were asked about each alter. The respondent was handed a list of different
relational contents and told: "This is a list of some of the ways people are connected
with each other. Some people will be related in more than one way. So, when I read
you a name, please tell me *all* the ways that person is connected with you right now."
"Friend" and "acquaintance" and "relative" were three of the possible responses
and define the above contents of friendship, acquaintance, and kinship, respectively.
Kin refers only to adult relatives (parent, sibling, uncle, aunt, cousin, parent-in-law,
other in-law, grandparent, stepparent).

which means that the numeraire content will always have an ambiguity of
one.

In reference to tendencies for contents to be confused with one
another, content i is used with high ambiguity to the extent that it has a
high probability of being perceived in all naturally occurring relations
(that is, $c_{ii} >> 0$) and a high tendency to be confused with other
ambiguous contents (that is, $c_{ji}g_j >> 0$). The same conditions define
actor prestige within a network. The prestige of actor i, p_i, is high to the
extent that he is the object of intense relations from other actors j,
measured as z_{ji}, who are themselves prestigious (that is, $z_{ji}p_j >> 0$; see
equation 10.2 in Chapter 10, this volume). The advantage of this
equivalence between concepts of actor prestige and content ambiguity is
that easily available computer programs generating prestige scores from
a network of relations between actors can be used to generate ambiguity
scores from a network of confusion relations between contents. I have
obtained content ambiguities as prestige scores output from the

computer program STRUCTURE when the network of mean confusion relations among contents is program input.[1]

Content ambiguities are presented at the far right of Table 2.1 for the five contents listed. Any of the contents could be selected as a numeraire. I have selected intimacy. This means, as stated in equation 2.3, that the ambiguity of each content will be defined in terms of the relative extent to which it is used more ambiguously than intimacy.[2] The ambiguities in Table 2.1 show that friendship is used almost twice as ambiguously as intimacy (g_1 = 1.81), acquaintance and kinship contents are used with two-thirds the ambiguity of intimacy (g_2 = g_4 = .69), and work content is used with about one-third the ambiguity of intimacy (g_3 = .30). These relative ambiguities can be discerned in the structure of confusion relations among the five contents in Table 2.1. The most ambiguous content, friendship, occurs in most of the naturally occurring relations and has high probabilities of being found in the relations containing other ambiguous contents: acquaintance (with ambiguity .69) and intimacy (with ambiguity 1.00). The next most ambiguous content, intimacy, occurs in about half as many relations as friendship but has a high tendency to be found in relations containing the ambiguous content friendship. Acquaintance has the same tendency to be found in relations containing friendship, but acquaintance occurs less often than intimacy in these important relations and so has a lower level of ambiguity when it does occur. Work is the least ambiguous content in Table 2.1. It is found in few of these important naturally occurring relations and has no particularly high tendency to be found in relations containing ambiguous contents.

Substitutability Within Content Domains in a Cognitive Map of Association

More than describing the structure of confusion relations among specific contents, the results in Table 2.1 describe the structure of relations among content domains. Friendship, acquaintance, work, and kinship were more than specific contents for respondents; they were indicators of general domains of relational content. These four content domains have been located in an analysis of the network of mean confusion relations among 33 contents. Corresponding to the (5,5) confusion matrix in Table 2.1, the whole (33,33) confusion matrix is given in Table 2.2 with c_{ij} rounded to the nearest decimal and multiplied by ten to eliminate decimal points. The table is blocked by content domain in the same order of contents given in Table 2.1.

The first content domain is friendship, with content 1 in Table 2.1 being listed in Table 2.2 as content 1. When the value of c_{11} in Table 2.1 (.67) is rounded to the nearest decimal (.7) and multiplied by ten, it equals the 7 reported as c_{ll} in Table 2.2. The second content domain is acquaintance, with content 2 in Table 2.1 being listed in Table 2.2 as content 8. The third content is work, with content 3 in Table 2.1 being listed in Table 2.2 as content 13. Kinship is the fourth content domain, with content 4 in Table 2.1 being listed in Table 2.2 as content 17. The remaining contents are residual in the sense of not falling within any of the four identified content domains and not combining with two or more other contents to form their own content domain. In addition to actual relations between ego and alters, I have included attributes of alters in Table 2.2 as contents under the belief that these features of alters affect the meaning of the relation ego has with them—a friendship with an elderly person, for example, being qualitatively different from a friendship with a young person.

The various contents listed within a single domain of content in Table 2.2 were used as substitutable contents by the typical respondent. By this I mean that respondents, on average, perceived these contents as alternative aspects of the same naturally occurring relations. For example, socializing with alter and feeling especially close to alter were substitutable contents within the friendship content domain. When typical respondents named an alter as a friend, they could just as well have named the alter as someone with whom they frequently socialized or someone to whom they felt especially close. These contents were used in a substitutable way by typical respondents.

More specifically, contents within a content domain were structurally equivalent within the network of confusion relations. The concept of structural equivalence as a basis for network subgroups and its implementation in empirical research are discussed in detail in Chapter 13 of this volume. In terms of a network of confusion relations, contents i and j are substitutable in the eyes of respondents to the extent that: respondents have an equal tendency to perceive them in their naturally occurring relations (that is, $c_{ii} = c_{jj}$), they have an equal tendency to confuse one with the other (that is, $c_{ij} = c_{ji}$), and they tend to confuse them to the same extent with other types of contents (that is, $c_{ik} = c_{jk}$ and $c_{ki} = c_{kj}$ for all contents k, $i \neq k \neq j$). Adopting a spatial representation of ego's perceptions of multiple contents, contents i and j are substitutable in the above sense to the extent that ego perceives the following distance between them to be zero (where $i \neq k \neq j$):

$$d_{ij} = [(c_{ii}-c_{jj})^2 + (c_{ij}-c_{ji})^2 + \Sigma_k(c_{ik}-c_{jk})^2 + \Sigma_k(c_{ki}-c_{kj})^2]^{1/2} \qquad [2.4]$$

which increases to the extent that ego perceives the two contents as entirely different kinds of relations, each occurring in different naturally occurring relations.

TABLE 2.2 Confusion Matrix and Ambiguity Among 33 Relational Contents

	FRIENDSHIP 1 2 3 4 5 6 7	ACQUAINT-ANCE 1 1 1 8 9 0 1 2	WORK 1 1 1 1 3 4 5 6	KINSHIP 1 1 1 2 2 2 2 2 7 8 9 0 1 2 3 4	RESIDUAL 2 2 2 2 2 3 3 3 3 5 6 7 8 9 0 1 2 3	RELATIVE AMBIGUITY	RELATIONAL CONTENTS
							friendship content domain
1	7 7 4 5 6 5 6	4 3 2 2 3	1 2 2 3	1 2 2 1 2 2 2 1	3 3 1 4 4 0 1 1 1	1.81	1 ego cites alter as a friend
2	8 6 5 6 7 6 6	3 3 3 2 2	1 2 2 2	2 1 2 1 3 2 3 1	4 3 1 4 4 0 1 1 1	1.66	2 ego socializes with alter (going out, visiting, gossiping)
3	6 5 5 5 6 5 5	2 2 2 2 1	1 1 1 1	3 3 4 2 3 2 3 2	4 2 2 3 2 0 1 1 0	1.39	3 ego feels especially close to alter
4	6 6 5 5 6 5 5	2 2 2 2 2	1 2 1 2	2 2 2 0 3 2 2 1	4 4 1 3 4 0 1 0 0	1.40	4 ego meets alter frequently (one or more times a week)
5	7 7 5 5 6 6 6	3 3 2 2 2	1 2 1 2	2 3 2 3 2 3 3 2	4 3 2 4 4 0 1 1 0	1.75	5 ego and alter are the same sex
6	6 5 5 5 6 6 6	2 1 2 1 2	1 1 1 2	3 2 3 2 3 3 3 2	3 3 2 4 3 0 1 0 1	1.65	6 alter is married
7	6 6 5 5 6 6 6	3 3 2 2 2	1 2 1 2	2 2 3 2 3 2 3 1	3 3 2 5 3 0 0 1 1	1.71	7 alter is employed
							acquaintance content domain
8	6 5 3 3 4 3 4	3 2 2 1 2	1 1 1 2	0 1 1 1 1 1 1 0	2 1 1 2 3 0 1 1 1	.69	8 ego cites alter as an acquaintance or just a friend
9	4 4 3 3 4 2 4	2 3 3 2 2	1 1 1 2	1 1 1 1 2 1 2 1	2 2 1 1 2 1 1 1 0	.75	9 no children in alter household
10	4 4 3 3 3 2 4	2 3 2 2 1	1 1 1 0	1 1 1 1 1 0 2 0	1 2 0 2 3 0 0 0 0	.60	10 alter is a young adult (protest cohorts 1967, 1972; ages 21-30)
11	3 3 1 3 3 2 3	2 2 2 2 0	1 1 1 2	0 0 0 0 1 1 0 0	1 2 0 2 3 0 0 0 1	.43	11 ego first met alter very recently (during 1977 cohort; less than 3 years ago)
12	5 4 2 3 4 3 4	2 2 2 0 2	1 1 1 2	0 1 1 1 1 1 0 0	2 2 1 2 3 0 0 0 1	.56	12 ego first met alter recently (during 1972 cohort; 3-7 years ago)
							work content domain
13	2 2 2 2 2 2 2	1 1 1 1 1	1 2 1 1	0 1 1 0 1 0 1 0	2 1 0 1 1 0 0 0 0	.30	13 ego discusses work with alter
14	3 3 2 3 3 2 4	1 1 1 1 1	2 1 2 1	0 1 1 0 1 1 1 0	2 1 1 2 1 0 0 0 0	.43	14 alter is a co-worker or ego thinks of alter as doing same kind of work
15	3 3 2 3 2 3 2 3	1 1 1 1 1	1 2 1 1	0 1 1 0 0 1 1 0	2 1 0 2 0 0 0 0 0	.36	15 ego first met alter at work
16	5 4 2 3 4 3 4	2 2 2 0 2	1 1 1 2	0 1 1 1 1 1 0 0	2 1 1 2 3 0 0 0 1	.30	16 ego first met alter some time ago (during 1967 cohort; 8-12 years ago)

kinship content domain

#	matrix row	ambiguity	content
17	2342453 01100 0000 3243333 212200100	.69	alter is one of ego's adult relatives
18	3343334 11101 1111 22212121 3111210000	.56	ego relies on alter's judgment for important (e.g., family or work) decisions
19	4353455 12101 1101 42333333 212310101	.81	ego would borrow money from alter if ego needed money
20	3230343 11101 0101 31332222 101210100	.49	alter lives more than an hour away from ego
21	3333343 11111 0101 21213122 222210100	.80	ego and alter have the same religion
22	3333443 11001 0110 31322222 221020001	.59	alter is a mature adult (depression cohorts 1942, 1937, 1932; ages 51-65)
23	4443454 12200 0110 32322230 222210100	.78	ego first met alter during the cold war years (postwar cohorts; 13-32 years ago)
24	2232332 01000 0000 31322202 211100100	.45	ego first met alter before the cold war years (war and depression cohorts; more than 32 years ago)

residual contents

#	matrix row	ambiguity	content
25	6565655 22212 1212 22213222 321320110	1.00	ego discusses personal matters with alter (NUMERAIRE CONTENT)
26	6546655 13223 1113 21102231 331351101	.83	ego would ask alter to care for house while ego was out of town
27	2221222 01100 0000 21212211 112100000	.47	ego perceives alter has having ego's ethnicity (however ego defines ethnicity)
28	5544556 21012 1112 22212021 321430000	.99	alter is an adult (cold war cohorts 1962, 1957, 1950; ages 31-50)
29	7534554 32223 0103 01113110 241340100	.89	ego first met alter through social ties (friends, neighbors, groups)
30	1101100 01000 0000 00000000 010010100	.06	alter is a child (1977 cohort; ages less than 21)
31	2222220 11000 0000 21110111 110010100	.28	alter is elderly (predepression cohorts; ages over 65)
32	2111111 11100 0000 00000010 100100010	.15	ego first met alter in school or grew up with alter
33	1111121 10001 0001 10101110 010100001	.15	ego first met alter through ego's spouse

NOTE: Each element c_{ij} is the mean for 858 adults who have lived in their current city for at least a year. The element has been multiplied by 10 and rounded to the nearest whole number in order to eliminate decimals in the matrix (e.g., c_{11} = .669 but is reported as 7). Ambiguity is a content's ambiguity relative to the ambiguity of intimacy ties (content 25).

The advantage of this connection between structurally equivalent actors and substitutable contents is that easily available computer programs locating structurally equivalent actors in networks of relations can be used to locate substitutable contents in a network of confusion relations. Following the methods outlined in Chapter 13 of this volume, I have located substitutable contents by analyzing the distances in equation 2.4 as output from the computer program STRUCTURE obtained when the network of mean confusion relations in Table 2.2 is program input.[3] The ambiguity scores in Table 2.1 and 2.2 were also obtained in this run.

Figure 2.1 is a two-dimensional representation of distances among the 33 relational contents listed in Table 2.2.[4] Content domains are indicated by circled areas. The distribution of contents in the space provides a cognitive map of the typical respondent's perception of contents in his important naturally occurring relations. Contents close together in the space were used in a substitutable way to refer to the same relations. Contents far apart in the space were clearly distinguished as features of separate relations. A sociometric question requesting the names of persons to whom the respondent has a such-and-such relation would be interpreted in terms of this map. The respondent could be expected to search through Figure 2.1 for the content most similar to such-and-such. His sociometric choices would then be the people with whom he had relations containing that content. What Figure 2.1 provides, in other words, is a basis for anticipating how a typical respondent would have responded to sociometric questions. Two hypothetical response mechanisms can be distinguished, both based on the cognitive map in Figure 2.1.

A respondent could have interpreted naturally occurring relations in terms of general dimensions of content. When confronted with a sociometric question, such a respondent would make sociometric choices based on the dimensions of content he understood the question to be eliciting. The typical Northern Californian in 1977 had at least two global dimensions of content. The vertical axis in Figure 2.1 distinguishes weak relations at the top of the space (e.g., acquaintance) from strong relations at the bottom of the space (e.g., kinship). This differentiation occurs within content domains as well as across them. Within the friendship domain to the far left of Figure 2.1, for example, "informal socializing" (content 2) appears near the top of the space as a relatively weak content, while "feels especially close to" (content 3) appears near the bottom of the space as a relatively strong content. The horizontal axis in Figure 2.1 distinguishes ambiguous relations at the far left of the space (e.g., friendship) from unambiguous relations at the far right of the space (e.g., work).

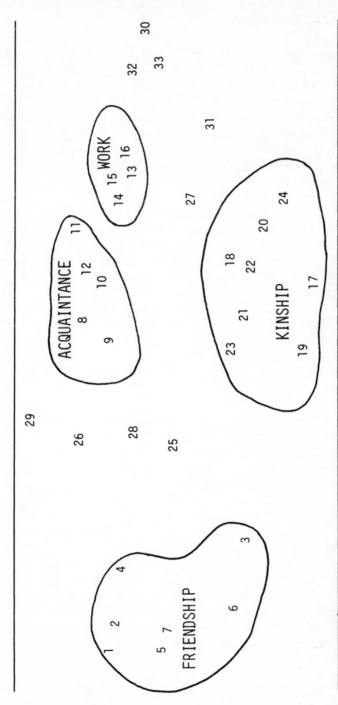

Figure 2.1: Spatial Representation of Substitutability Among the Relational Contents Listed in Table 2.2 (contents are proximate in the space to the extent that they were used substitutably by survey respondents; content domains are circled)

A respondent also could have interpreted naturally occurring relations in terms of specific bundles of contents within content domains. When confronted with a sociometric question, such a respondent would first interpret the question as eliciting a specific content domain. Sociometric choices would then be made to the people with whom the respondent had relations particularly characterized by that content domain. As indicated by the circled areas in Figure 2.1 and the blocked contents in Table 2.2, the typical respondent in this survey had at least four content domains from which to draw sociometric choices.

The most ambiguous content domain was friendship.[5] Contents in this domain were found in the greatest number of naturally occurring relations and in relations with the greatest diversity of other contents. The relations characterized by this content domain could have been elicited by several different sociometric questions (see contents under "friendship" in Table 2.2) asking the respondent to name friends, people with whom he or she socialized, people to whom he felt especially close, or the people the respondent saw often. The people named in response to these questions would have been very similar to the respondent: married, employed, and of the same sex.

Acquaintance was a much less ambiguous content domain [6]. This content characterized relations to alters on the social periphery of ego's network. In contrast to the typical respondent, who was married, employed, and matured during the early 1960s or before, acquaintances were people who matured in the late 1960s or after, had no children living with them, and had only recently met ego.

Least ambiguous of all was the content domain concerned with work.[7] This content was found in few of the typical respondent's important naturally occurring relations and rarely found in combination with other contents. Questions that would elicit relations with a work content would ask the respondent to name the people with whom he or she discussed work, co-workers, or people first met at work.

Finally, there is a domain of kinship contents.[8] These contents spanned a variety of naturally occurring relations indicating strong ties between ego and alter. Relations with kinship content tended to reach adults whom the respondent had known for a long time and who shared the respondent's religious affiliation. These were people who lived more than an hour away from the respondent, yet who were influential in important decisions the respondent had to make and who were perceived to be potential sources of money in an emergency.

There is no way of knowing whether respondents interpreted sociometric questions in terms of the dimensions of the cognitive map in Figure 2.1, the content domains distinguished in the map, or both;

however, one thing is clear. Typical respondents distinguished at least four domains of content in their important naturally occurring relations: friendship, work, acquaintance, and kinship. If the 1977 social structure of Northern Californians were to be described, in other words, at least four distinct networks of relations would define the structure: a friendship or social network, an acquaintance network, a work-related network, and a kinship network. Table 2.2 and Figure 2.1 indicate how alternative wordings of sociometric questions would reflect the relations in these four networks that the respondents themselves distinguished.

Identifying Subcultural Differences

To say that the typical respondent distinguished four content domains as described in Table 2.2 and Figure 2.1 is not the same as saying that each respondent made those distinctions. On the contrary, it seems likely that there would be subcultures within which people understood relations in a similar way, but across which a single word or phrase could refer to quite different qualities of interaction. The problem for a network analyst planning to study a social system rich in subcultures would be to interpret words and phrases to be used to elicit relational data.

There are a great many social categories of respondents in the Northern California survey that could be treated as if they were subcultures in 1977. For the purposes of describing variations in relational content, however, my own concern with these possibilities is to identify respondents who were maximally different in their interpretations of relations. The initial studies by Laumann (1966, 1973) were helpful in suggesting categories across which respondents were likely to be different in their interpretation of relations. On the basis of Laumann's analyses, and unsystematic hunches on my part, 58 social categories of respondents have been defined so as to represent the range of respondents likely to be different in their interpretation of relations. A (33,33) network of mean confusion relations has been computed for each category of respondents, just as a mean network was computed for all adult respondents and presented in Table 2.2. Figure 2.2 is a smallest space representation of differences in these confusion networks across the 58 categories of respondents. Two categories are close together in Figure 2.2 to the extent that the network of mean confusion relations for each is identical—i.e., to the extent that respondents in the two categories had identical patterns of confusion among the 33 contents in Table 2.1.[9]

I am looking for social categories at opposite extremes of the space in Figure 2.2. Respondents typical of these contrasting social categories were maximally different in their interpretation of relations. Three pairs

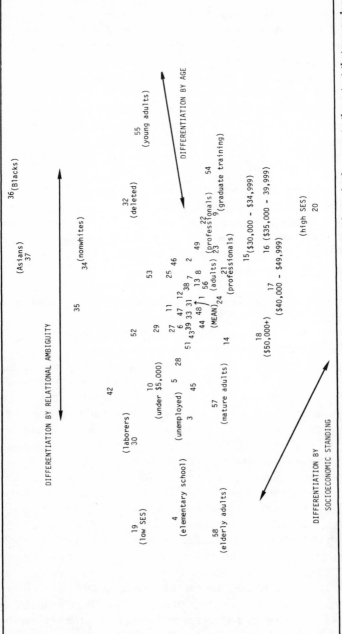

Figure 2.2: Social Differentiation by Use of Relational Contents (two categories are proximate in the space to the extent that respondents in the categories have identical patterns of using the relational contents in Table 2.2)

SOCIAL CATEGORIES REFERENCED IN THE SPACE

1 self-employed
2 employed by someone else
3 unemployed (includes those looking, laid off, retired, unable to work, keeping house, or something else)

4 elementary schooling
5 some high school
6 high school graduate
7 some college
8 college graduate
9 graduate training

10 family income is less than $5,000
11 family income is $5,000 but not $12,000
12 family income is $12,000 but not $20,000
13 family income is $20,000 but not $25,000
14 family income is $25,000 but not $30,000
15 family income is $30,000 but not $35,000
16 family income is $35,000 but not $40,000
17 family income is $40,000 but not $50,000
18 family income is $50,000 or more

19 low SES (family income under $5,000 and respondent did not graduate from high school)
20 high SES (family income over $40,000 and respondent had some graduate school training)

21 culture workers (professionals in education, religion, or the arts)
22 personal maintenance workers (professionals in medicine, law, or personal therapy)
23 data workers (professionals in engineering, accounting, computer processing, assorted technicians)
24 managers and administrators (nonfarm)
25 sales workers
26 clerical workers
27 craftsmen and kindred workers
28 operatives
29 service workers (includes full time housekeepers who claim no occupation)
30 laborers (farm and nonfarm)

31 all adult residents (described in table 1 and figure 1)
32 deleted respondents (nonadults and recent arrivals)
33 Whites
34 nonwhites
35 Brown (Arab, Am. Indians, Mex. American, other Sp. American)
36 Black
37 Asian
38 males
39 females
40 respondents for whom work is the one most important activity with which they identify themselves
41 respondents for whom spare time activities are the actions with which they identify themselves
42 respondents for whom religion is the one most important activity with which they identify themselves
43 respondents for whom there is no one most important activity with which they identify themselves
44 married to a working spouse
45 married to a nonworking spouse
46 unmarried
47 respondents with no children living in the house
48 respondents with children living in the house
49 respondents with no adult relatives in the area
50 respondents with one or more adult relatives in the area

51 Protestants
52 Catholics
53 respondents with some other religion or religion unknown
54 respondents explicitly claiming no religious preference
55 young adults (respondents maturing in the late 1960s through the early 1970s; ages 21-30 in 1977)
56 adults (respondents maturing in the cold war years after World War II; ages 31-50 in 1977)
57 mature adults (respondents maturing during the Depression or World War II, ages 51-65 in 1977)
58 elderly adults (respondents maturing before the Depression, ages 66 and higher in 1977)

Figure 2.2 (Continued)

of contrast groups seem to span the space in Figure 2.2. One contrast is between various minority races at the top of Figure 2.2 and whites at the bottom of the figure. To the extent that there were differences among respondents in their interpretations of relations, in other words, some of those differences can be described by comparing the meaning of relations for whites with the meaning of relations for nonwhites. There are also two axes of differentiation indicated in Figure 2.2: age and socioeconomic standing (SES). Along the age axis in Figure 2.2, respondent age increases as one moves from right to left. Along the SES axis, respondent education and income increase as one moves from the upper left in the figure down to the lower right. In sum, the sharpest differences in respondent interpretations of relations can be found in three contrasts: whites versus nonwhites, the young versus the elderly, and the wealthy and highly educated versus the poor with little education. Summary differences among these contrast groups are presented in Table 2.3 and Figure 2.3.

Table 2.3 lists mean confusion relations for the whole sample and for each contrast group. The first column of the table contains the mean c_{ij} across all different contents. The higher this mean is for a group, the more that respondents in the group perceived all contents in the same naturally occurring relations—in other words, the more ambiguously they used relational contents. There was little difference between whites and nonwhites on this criterion (mean c_{ij} of .18 and .17, respectively); however, youth and high socioeconomic standing are clearly associated with content ambiguity. Young adults and adults with high SES used contents more ambiguously (mean c_{ij} of .19) than did elderly adults and adults with low SES (mean c_{ij} of .13 and .14, respectively). These differences suggest a point that will become increasingly clear: The horizontal axis in Figure 2.2 appears to be a relational ambiguity axis, and persons to the far right of the figure (the young, high-SES, and to some extent, nonwhite respondents) interpreted their relations more ambiguously than did persons to the far left of the figure (the elderly, low-SES respondents). The classic stratification dimensions of age and socioeconomic standing are imperfectly, but strongly, correlated with this dimension of relational ambiguity. Table 2.2 also reports tendencies for each domain of content to be used by the whole sample and each contrast group. There are specific group differences to be described for each content domain.

Figure 2.3 will help illustrate these differences. The ambiguity with which respondents in each pair of contrast groups used the 33 contents in Table 2.2 is indicated in Figure 2.3. For example, Figure 2.3a compares the ambiguity with which low (vertical axis) versus high (horizontal axis)

TABLE 2.3 Contrasting Confusion Matrix Elements across Maximally Different Types of Respondents

	Mean Off-Diagonal c_{ij}	Mean Diagonal Element				
		all c_{ii}	friend c_{11}	acquaint. c_{88}	work $c_{13,13}$	kinship $c_{17,17}$
all adult residents (N = 858)	.17	.29	.67	.26	.10	.26
whites (N = 739)	.17	.29	.67	.25	.10	.25
nonwhites (N = 119)	.18	.30	.64	.30	.09	.31
low socioeconomic standing (N = 34)	.14	.28	.43	.14	.01	.25
high socioeconomic standing (N = 19)	.19	.30	.70	.29	.13	.20
young adults (N = 234)	.19	.31	.73	.30	.14	.35
elderly adults (N = 131)	.13	.26	.56	.19	.01	.14

NOTE: Types of respondents correspond to social categories at opposite ends of the space in Figure 2.2. Category 31 consists of all adult residents. The mean confusion matrix for this category is presented in Table 2.2. The remaining categories are: whites (#33), nonwhites (#34), low SES (#19), high SES (#20), young adults (#55), and elderly adults (#58).

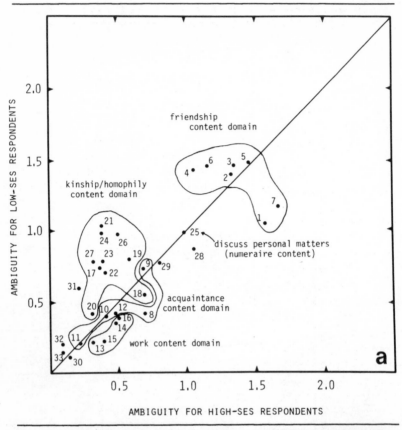

Figure 2.3a: Contrasts in the Relative Ambiguity with Which Types of Respondents Used Relational Contents (contents are referenced in each graph by the identification numbers in Table 2.2)

socioeconomic standing respondents interpreted their relations. If respondents in the two contrast groups used a content with identical levels of ambiguity, that content appears on the diagonal line drawn in each box. For example, the numeraire content "discussing personal matters" is defined to have ambiguity of 1.0 for each contrast group. If respondents in two contrast groups used a content with very different levels of ambiguity, that content appears far away from the diagnonal line. For example, friendship was used more ambiguously by high socioeconomic standing people than by people with low socioeconomic standing. Note in Figure 2.3a that content 1 appears below the diagonal—higher in ambiguity on the horizontal axis than it is in

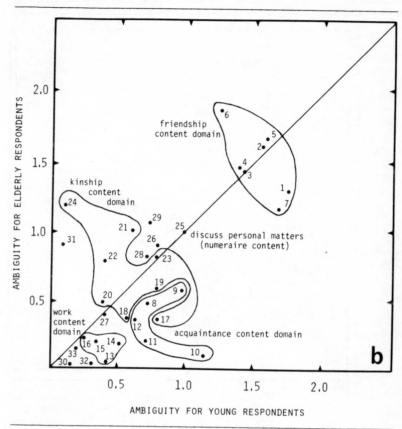

Figure 2.3b

ambiguity on the vertical axis. More generally, a content far from the diagonal was used more ambiguously by the group toward which it deviates from the diagonal (e.g., content 1 in Figure 2.3a deviating toward the horizontal axis, the high-SES axis).

Figure 2.3 thus provides a visual guide to detecting relations for more detailed analysis. The more that a content deviates from the diagonal lines in Figure 2.3, the more interesting a subject the relation will be for more detailed analysis—more interesting in the sense of revealing significant differences between respondent perceptions of relations. I have drawn a circle around contents within each content domain. To the extent that respondents in separate contrast groups used relations within a domain in very different ways, the circled elements will cover a wide area to either side of the diagonal lines in Figure 2.3. I will describe each content domain separately.

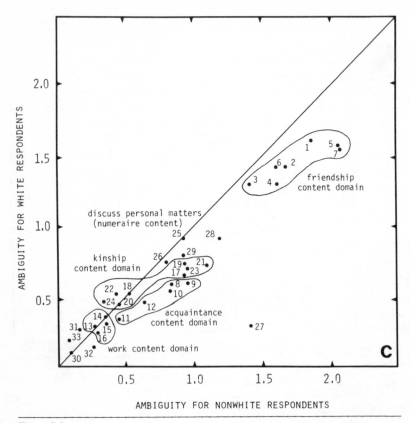

Figure 2.3c

The Friendship Content Domain

Friendship is consistently the most ambiguous of all content domains. It appears in the upper right-hand corner of each graph in Figure 2.3. Specific contents within the domain, however, were not used in a consistent fashion by respondents in all of the contrast groups.

The content domain does hold together across racial differences. Figure 2.3c illustrates white/nonwhite differences in ambiguity, but similar results are obtained if whites are contrasted with specific types of nonwhites: Browns, Asians, or Blacks. Whites and nonwhites had very similar, and high, ambiguity in their friendship relations, but nonwhites had slightly more ambiguity in theirs—the domain lies below the diagonal in Figure 2.3c.

This slight difference is not a result of the different extent to which whites and nonwhites used the friendship label to describe their relations. Note in Table 2.3 that two of three alters named by whites or nonwhites were cited as friends (c_{11} is .67 and .64, respectively). This similar tendency for whites and nonwhites to name alters is repeated for each kind of friendship content (contents 1 through 7). Quite negligible correlations are obtained between race dummy variables and the probability of a respondent naming an alter as the object of one of the friendship contents (e.g., the correlation between c_{11}, probability of alter being named a friend, and a white/nonwhite contrast is -.03 across the 858 egos).

Racial differences in friendship ambiguity stem less from friendship contents per se than from the importance of alter ethnicity for friendships. While the probability of citing alter as a friend is uncorrelated with ego having a minority (nonwhite) race (r = .03), the same probability—given the fact that ego recognized alter as having ego's ethnicity, $c_{27,1}$—is strongly correlated with ego having a minority ethnicity (r = .28, p < .001). Nonwhites are five times as likely as whites to recognize ethnicity homophily with alters named as friends ($c_{1,27}$ is .07 and .36 for whites and nonwhites respectively). Roughly one in two persons with whom a nonwhite socializes are recognized as having ego's ethnicity ($c_{2,27}$ = .46). This proportion drops to one in ten for whites ($c_{2,27}$ = .09). In general, nonwhites had more alters recognized to share ego's ethnicity than did whites ($c_{27,27}$ is .48 and .11, respectively). This tendency increased across types of nonwhites—Browns to Asians to Blacks ($c_{27,27}$ is .38, .52 and .69, respectively)—and accordingly increased the ambiguity of their friendships.

The rank order of types of nonwhites can be observed in Figure 2.2, with Blacks being furthest from the center and most likely to cite same ethnicity alters. This greater tendency for nonwhites to cite same ethnicity alters was facilitated by the manner in which citations were elicited from respondents. However, the fact remains that nonwhites were recognizing an ethnicity bond to alters not found among whites.[10] When interpreting their friendship relations, nonwhites thus had the additional complication of ethnicity to consider. This created the slightly greater ambiguity in friendship contents for nonwhites that is illustrated in Figure 2.3c.

The spread of the friendship content domain across the diagonal line in Figure 2.3a and 2.3b indicates that respondents extremely different in age and socioeconomic standing tended to differ in the ambiguity with which they used specific contents within the friendship domain. Putting aside two rather obvious differences in the life-cycle activities of alters,[11] the principal differences associated with respondent age and socioeconomic standing concern two contents: the tendency to interpret a relation as a friendship (content 1) and the tendency to interpret it as a frequently occurring relation (content 4). The remaining contents are quite similar across age and socioeconomic differences in respondents.

Young and highly educated respondents tended to have more ambiguous friendships than elderly and poorly educated respondents. This greater ambiguity resulted from the tendency young and highly educated respondents had to perceive friendship in all of the core naturally occurring relations considered here. Ambiguity differences are illustrated in Figures 2.3a and 2.3b by the fact that content 1, friendship, is well below the diagonal line in each figure, closer to the young and high-SES axes in these figures. The ambiguity of the friend label is 1.1 for low-SES respondents and 1.2 for elderly respondents (respondents over 65 years of age). These ambiguities are to be compared to the 1.8 reported in Table 2.2 for respondents generally, the 1.6 for high-SES respondents, and the 1.8 for young respondents (respondents 21-30 years of age).

The higher ambiguity of friendship for young and high-SES respondents is illustrated by the mean confusion relations in the first two columns of Table 2.4. Selected elements in the confusion network for low- versus high-SES respondents are presented. Elements are taken from the column leading to the label "friend" (corresponding to column 1 of Table 2.2). High-SES respondents had a much higher tendency to label alters as friends (c_{11} is .70 for high-SES respondents and .43 for low). This affects the conditional probabilities of an alter being cited as a friend. Given any type of relation to an alter, the conditional probability of the alter also being perceived as a friend is higher for high-SES respondents than for low-SES respondents. If the alter was someone with whom the respondent socialized or met frequently, then a high-SES respondent was little less than twice as likely as a low-SES respondent to cite the alter as a friend (.78 versus .45 and .68 versus .38, respectively). The strongest contrast is in work relations. No respondent with low SES cited an alter as a friend if the alter was someone with whom the respondent discussed work ($c_{13,1}$ is .00). Among the respondents with high socioeconomic standing, almost half of the alters with whom work was discussed were also considered friends ($c_{13,1}$ is .42).

In short, high-SES respondents used friendship more ambiguously than low-SES respondents because they used the label to refer to a larger number of alters and used it more often in combination with other types of relational contents. The ambiguity of the content was determined by the extent to which it was used. The differences illustrated in Table 2.4 between high- and low-SES respondents hold across respondents more generally. Across the four age cohorts distinguished in Figure 2.2, the

TABLE 2.4 Low- Versus High-SES Respondent Tendencies to Cite
Alters as Friends and Frequently Met Persons

	Alter is a Friend		Alter is Met Frequently	
Row Content	*low SES*	*high SES*	*low SES*	*high SES*
1 friend	(.43)	(.70)	.51	.51
2 socialize	.45	.78	.63	.61
3 close to	.38	.42	.60	.42
4 frequent	.38	.68	(.58)	(.50)
5 same sex	.51	.75	.61	.55
8 acquaintance	.29	.66	.18	.34
13 work discussion	.00	.42	.03	.42
17 adult relative	.11	.21	.26	.11

NOTE: Contents are referenced by their identification numbers given in Table 2.2,
and diagonal elements are enclosed in parentheses. Elements are the probability of
an alter being the column type given the knowledge that he is the row type, e.g.,
the conditional probability of an alter being a friend, given the knowledge that he is
an adult relative, is .11 for low-SES respondents and .21 for high-SES respondents.

probability of an alter being named a friend (c_{11}) systematically decreases
as respondent age cohort increases ($r = -.21$, $p < .001$). The same
probability increases systematically across the categories of income and
education distinguished in Figure 2.2; however, the increase is much
clearer as respondent education increases (respective correlations of .12
and .24).

Just the opposite association with socioeconomic standing occurs
with respect to frequently occurring relations. The higher ambiguity of
frequent relations for low-SES respondents is illustrated by the last two
columns of Table 2.4 (corresponding to column 4 in Table 2.2). It is also
apparent in Figure 2.3 by the fact that content 4 is well above the diagonal
in graph a and below its positions in graphs b and c. The ambiguity of this
content for high-SES respondents is 1.1, a level below the 1.4 reported for
all respondents in Table 2.2 and the 1.5 for low-SES respondents. Table
2.4 shows that high- and low-SES respondents had very similar
tendencies to cite alters as frequently met people, although the tendency
was slightly high for low-SES respondents (c_{44} is .58 versus .50 for low-
versus high-SES respondents). There are no differences across the age
cohorts in Figure 2.2 with respect to citing alters as frequent contacts ($r =
-.07$).

To continue, high- and low-SES respondents had similar tendencies to
cite an alter as a frequent contact, given some other type of friendship

content to the alter. In Table 2.4, for example, half of the alters cited as friends by either type of respondent were also cited as frequent contacts; c_{14} is .51 for both high- and low-SES respondents.

There are circumstances in which high-SES respondents actually tended to name more alters as frequent contacts. Given an alter as an acquaintance, for example, high-SES respondents were twice as likely as low to cite the alter as a frequent contact (c_{84} is .34 versus .18, respectively). Given an alter as someone with whom work was discussed, high-SES respondents were more than ten times as likely to cite alter as a frequent contact. However, there were circumstances in which low-SES respondents were more likely to cite alters as frequent contacts, and these circumstances involved highly ambiguous contents. Low-SES respondents were about twice as likely as high-SES respondents to cite relatives as frequent contacts ($c_{17,4}$ in Table 2.4 is .26 versus .11, respectively). The same difference between extremes in socioeconomic standing is observed with respect to other kinship content domains.

As a result of the slightly higher tendency for respondents with low SES to cite frequently met alters and the tendency for those alters to have been the object of relations with kinship domain content, frequency of contact had more ambiguity for the poor and uneducated respondents. The naturally occurring relations in which frequency was perceived contained highly ambiguous kinship contents. High-SES respondents had a much higher tendency to cite work discussion alters as frequent contacts; however, discussing work was a very low ambiguity content, so its mixture with frequency did not greatly increase the ambiguity of frequent contacts for high-SES respondents.

The Acquaintance Content Domain

Acquaintance was less ambiguous than friendship for each contrast group, although, like friendship, it was used more ambiguously by young, high-SES respondents than it was by elderly, low-SES respondents. Age in particular was associated with differences in the meaning of acquaintance.

The content domain appears as a snakelike cluster close to the diagonal in the lower left-hand corner of each graph in Figure 2.3. The snakelike appearance of the cluster indicates the variable (albeit consistently low) ambiguity with which contents within the domain were used. The proximity of the cluster to the diagonal and its distribution parallel to the diagonal indicate the similarity with which respondents in contrast groups used each content.

Differences in the perception of acquaintance concerned respondents of different ages and socioeconomic standing. Note in Table 2.3 that young respondents were one and a half times as likely as elderly respondents to name an alter as an acquaintance (c_{88} is .30 versus .19, respectively). High-SES respondents were twice as likely as low-SES respondents to name an alter as an acquaintance. These differences appear in Figures 2.3a and 2.3b in content 8 lying below the diagonal in each graph. The difference between extremes of socioeconomic standing was more a result of differences in education than income.

The following standardized results are obtained if the probability of naming an alter as an acquaintance is regressed over the education (E), income (I), and age (A) categories distinguished in Figure 2.2, as well as a dummy variable (NW) distinguishing nonwhites from whites:

$$c_{88} = .12E + .01I - .10A + .06NW + r_{88}$$
$$(3.1) \quad (0.4) \quad (2.6) \quad (1.6)$$

where t-tests are given in parentheses, r_{88} is a residual term, and the standardized coefficients have been computed across the 858 respondents. The probability of naming an alter as an acquaintance increased most clearly with increasing respondent education and decreasing respondent age. Respondent youth, in particular, is associated with tendency for acquaintance to have been a substitutable content for recency. Let c_{8r} be the conditional probability that an alter was someone ego had met recently (contents 11 or 12 in Table 2.2), given the alter acquaintance (content 8). The following standardized regression results are obtained when c_{8r} replaces c_{88} in the above prediction:

$$c_{8r} = .07E - .07I - .37A - .00NW + r_{8r}$$
$$(1.9) \quad (2.1) \quad (10.6) \quad (0.1)$$

Respondent age is the clearly dominant effect. This does not mean that increasing age decreased the number of people a respondent named as recently met acquaintances. It means that the five core naturally occurring relations sampled for this analysis tended to occur with recently met acquaintances for young respondents.

The Work Content Domain

Work was the least ambiguous of content domains for each contrast group, occurring infrequently in general and rarely with other contents. Its stability as a content domain is indicated in Figure 2.3 by the fact that the four contents in the domain are close together and close to the diagonal in the lower left-hand corner of each graph.

At the same time, work content ambiguity was strongly associated with respondent age and socioeconomic standing. Work contents appear below the diagonal in Figures 2.3a and 2.3b, indicating their greater ambiguity for the young, high-SES respondents. The mean $c_{13,13}$ elements in Table 2.3 show that young, high-SES respondents were more than ten times as likely to have work discussion content in their important naturally occurring relations. More significantly, these respondents tended to mix work contents into all relations. Given an alter named as a friend, for example, the conditional probability of discussing work with the person, $c_{1,13}$, systematically increased with respondent income and education while systematically decreasing with respondent age:

$$c_{1,13} = .13E + .11I - .21A - .02NW + r_{1,13}$$
$$(3.4) \quad (3.1) \quad (5.9) \quad (0.5)$$

where the predictors are the same as those in the above equations, and standardized results across the 858 respondents are presented with t-tests in parentheses.

Turning this point around, work was a context in which diverse relations were developed for young, high-SES respondents. Comparing the two extremes of socioeconomic standing in Table 2.3, for example, high-SES respondents were more likely to name alters first met at work as friends ($c_{15,1}$ is .53 versus .12, respectively) as people with whom they often socialized ($c_{15,2}$ is .36 versus .09, respectively), as people to whom they felt especially close ($c_{15,3}$ is .41 versus .03, respectively), as people on whose judgment they relied in making important decisions ($c_{15,18}$ is .36 versus .00, respectively), and as people with whom they discussed personal matters ($c_{15,25}$ is .29 versus .03, respectively). *The general point illustrated is that work was increasingly a source of important, multiplex relations across respondents with increasing income and education and decreasing age.* The frequency and multiplexity of these work-connected relations increased the ambiguity of work contents for young, high-SES respondents.

The Kinship Content Domain

Of the four content domains, kinship is the least stable across the kinship groups. Contents within the domain vary extensively across respondents in terms of the ambiguity with which they were used. Nonwhites had a slightly higher tendency than whites to cite relatives as alters in important naturally occurring relations ($c_{17,17}$ in Table 2.3 is .31 and .25, respectively), so there is slightly more ambiguity in kinship contents for nonwhites. This slighter greater ambiguity appears in Figure 2.3c, with a portion of the kinship content domain lying below the diagonal in the graph. By and large, however, the domain lies along the diagonal in the graph, indicating that whites and nonwhites used kinship contents with similar levels of ambiguity. In contrast, there are striking differences in the manner with which respondents of different ages and socioeconomic standing used kinship contents. Table 2.5 provides an illustration of these differences. Selected mean confusion relations are presented for low- versus high-SES respondents (the first two columns) and for young versus elderly respondents (the last two columns). The relations correspond to relations in column 17 of Table 2.2. They indicate the probability of an alter being an adult relative. For example, the mean probability of a high-SES-respondent citing an adult relative as an alter ($c_{17,17}$) is .20 in Table 2.5, and this probability increases to .40 if the alter is someone from whom the respondent would borrow money if necessary ($c_{19,17}$).

There is a general tendency for respondents of low socioeconomic standing to have had more ambiguous kinship relations in comparison to wealthy, well-educated respondents. The bulk of the kinship domain lies above the diagonal line in Figure 2.3a, indicating the greater ambiguity it had for low-SES respondents. Focusing on alter being an adult relative, kinship was about one and a half times as ambiguous for low-SES respondents as it was for high-SES respondents (g_{17} is .7 and .4, respectively). More severe differences in kinship contents between high- and low-SES respondents can be seen in Figure 2.3a.

This greater ambiguity is not determined by a greater tendency for low-SES respondents to name relatives as alters in the important naturally occurring relations considered here. They did have a higher tendency to name relatives, but the difference from high-SES respondents was slight. One in every four alters were relatives of low-SES respondents ($c_{17,17}$ is .25 in Tables 2.3 and 2.5). One in five alters were relatives of high-SES respondents ($c_{17,17}$ is .20 in Tables 2.3 and 2.5). Further, the probability of naming a relative as an alter in one of these important naturally occurring relations, $c_{17,17}$, does not vary significantly across the categories of increasing income distinguished in Figure 2.2 ($r = -.06$) or across categories of increasing education in the figure ($r = -.06$).

The greater ambiguity of kinship for low-SES respondents stemmed from the multiplexity of relations to kin for these respondents. For one thing, low-SES respondents were more likely to mix friendship contents with kinship. In comparison to high-SES respondents, low-SES respondents were more likely to have an adult relative as a friend ($c_{1,17}$ is .12 versus .09 for low- and high-SES, respectively, in Table 2.5), someone with whom he or she socialized ($c_{4,17}$ is .22 versus .14), and someone met frequently (c_{2+17} is .22 versus .14). The first two differences are more pronounced than the third; however, the third content, frequent contact,

TABLE 2.5   Contrasting Tendencies for Adult Relatives to be Cited as Alters by Respondents of Different Ages and Socioeconomic Standing

Row Content	low SES	high SES	young adult	elderly adult
1 friend	.12	.07	.18	.04
8 acquaintance	.00	.00	.00	.00
13 work discussion	.00	.05	.07	.01
17 adult relative	(.25)	(.20)	(.35)	(.14)
18 rely on judgment	.11	.16	.31	.07
$c_{18,18}$	(.14)	(.29)	(.23)	(.14)
19 borrow money from	.21	.40	.62	.17
$c_{19,19}$	(.30)	(.25)	(.34)	(.20)
20 over an hour away	.09	.32	.36	.14
$c_{20,20}$	(.11)	(.15)	(.17)	(.19)
21 same religion	.18	.16	.31	.12
$c_{21,21}$	(.43)	(.20)	(.25)	(.32)
27 same ethnicity	.18	.04	.23	.05
$c_{27,27}$	(.22)	(.13)	(.17)	(.13)

NOTE: Contents are referenced by their identification numbers given in Table 2.2, and diagonal elements are enclosed in parentheses. Elements not in parentheses indicate the probability of an alter being cited as an adult relative, given the knowledge that he is the row type, e.g., the conditional probability of an alter being an adult relative, given the knowledge that he is someone from whom the respondent could borrow money, is .21 for low-SES respondents and .40 for high-SES respondents.

was particularly ambiguous for low-SES respondents because of its mixture with kinship, as discussed above with reference to Table 2.4. Further, this mixture of kinship and friendship contents was facilitated by the physical proximity of relatives for low-SES respondents. As reported in Table 2.5, the probability of an alter who lives more than an hour away being a relative is more than three times smaller for low-SES respondents than it is for those with high socioeconomic standing, even though both high- and low-SES respondents had roughly equal tendencies to name alters who lived more than an hour away from them.

In addition to mixing social activities with kinship, low-SES respondents had a greater tendency to perceive religious and ethnic homophily between themselves and their adult relatives. As reported in Table 2.5, low-SES respondents had a greater overall tendency to perceive religious and ethnic homophily with alters they named ($c_{21,21}$ is .43 for low-SES and .20 for high-SES; $c_{27,27}$ is .29 for low-SES and .13 for high-SES). This greater ambiguity of religious and ethnic homophily, occurring in relations with adult relatives, increased the ambiguity of relations with relatives.

With decreasing income and education, in short, a respondent would have found kinship within multiplex relations of social homophily; relations also composed of friendship, informal socializing, frequent contact, and a recognition of shared religion and ethnicity. Despite the lack of difference between high- and low-SES respondents in their tendencies to name relatives as alters, the mixture of kinship with highly ambiguous contents by low-SES respondents resulted in kinship being more ambiguous for them. In other words, the task of interpreting naturally occurring relations with relatives would have been a much more difficult task for poor respondents with little education, not because they were less able to understand relations relative to high-SES respondents, but rather because of the greater diversity of contents found in their relations to kin.

Differences in respondent age break the kinship content domain into two separate contents, with elderly respondents perceiving more social homophily with alters, and with young respondents perceiving a greater diversity of contents in their relations specifically with adult relatives. The contents used more ambiguously by elderly respondents appear above the diagonal line in Figure 2.3b, including tendencies to perceive alter as sharing ego's religious affiliation (content 21) and for alter to be a mature adult close to ego's age (note contents 22 and 31 in Figure 2.3b), where alter was first met by the respondent sometime before World War II (content 24).

Putting these alter attributes to one side, kinship itself was much more ambiguous for the young respondent than it was for the elderly. Note that kinship, content 17, lies below the diagonal line in Figure 2.3b. The reason for its greater ambiguity for young respondents is clear from the last two columns in Table 2.5: Young respondents relied more on their adult relatives for everything. Young respondents were more than twice as likely as the elderly to name an adult relative as an alter ($c_{17,17}$ is .35 versus .14 in Table 2.5). This difference carried over in a greater tendency for relatives to be the object of other contents. Each element in the third column of Table 2.5 is larger than the corresponding element in the fourth column. This holds despite a much stronger tendency for elderly respondents to cite alters sharing their religious affiliation. Sharply illustrating the dependence of young respondents on their adult relatives, the conditional probability of a source of emergency money being an adult relative and of an influential alter being an adult relative are more than three times as great for young respondents as they are for the elderly ($c_{18,17}$ and $c_{19,17}$ in Table 2.5). In fact, age is the principal determinant of differences between respondents in the conditional probability of a source of emergency money being an adult relative; $c_{19,17}$ decreases systematically across the age cohorts distinguished in Figure 2.2 ($r = -.27$, $p < .001$), even if respondent differences in socioeconomic standing and nonwhite ethnicity are held constant.[12]

In short, young respondents used kinship more ambiguously than elderly respondents because they relied more on adult relatives for important naturally occurring relations. The greater ambiguity of kinship for the young resulted from the extent to which it occurred in a diversity of important relations. This stands in marked contrast to the manner in which kinship was ambiguous for low-SES respondents. Instead of the extent of relying on kin, it was the combination of kinship with friendship and social homophily that made kinship ambiguous for low-SES respondents. Further, the ambiguous kinship relations of young respondents reached over longer distances than those of the low-SES respondents. Given an hour or more of travel necessary to reach an alter, the conditional probability of that alter being an adult relative is four times greater for young respondents than it is for low-SES respondents ($c_{20,17}$ in Table 2.5).

METHODOLOGICAL CONCLUSIONS

A new class of research opportunities has been created with the availability of network data in mass survey intervews. Beginning with a small number of alters and a few contents (Laumann, 1966, 1973) and expanding to many alters and a rich diversity of contents (e.g., Wellman, 1979, 1982; Fischer, 1982a; McCallister and Fischer in Chapter 3, this volume; Minor in Chapters 4, 11), the prospect of burgeoning survey data on multiple content relationships casts into bold relief the typically ad hoc quality of distinctions among contents in network analyses. Analyses of relational content must be brought closer to the center of network methodology than has been the case in the past. In particular, the study of manners in which different kinds of relations are coordinated requires methodology for distinguishing different kinds of relations—as relations are understood by the people being studied.

Analyzing the Content of Relationships

I have illustrated some methods by which existing models of relational form can be used to lay open for inspection differences in relational content. Given a set of alters named by a respondent (or multiple respondents representative of a social category of respondents) in response to multiple sociometric questions, tendencies for interaction activities to be confused for one another can be stated as a network of confusion relations. The structure of this network holds insights into the meaning of relations in the same way that the form of relations in a network holds insights into social structure itself. Given a network of confusion relations, these insights into the meaning of relations can be obtained with network concepts in readily available computer programs used to describe relational form.[13] I have used two formal concepts here: structural equivalence (to describe the substitutability of contents) and prestige (to describe the ambiguity of contents). Of course, there is a great wealth of formal models available that could prove useful in analyzing content. Moreover, the connection with linguistic models is obvious and yet to be exploited.

Selecting Contents in the Pretest Stage of Research

More to the point of collecting network data, the results presented here from a cross-section of Northern Californians illustrate a strategy by which contents can be distinguished efficiently and accurately in the pretest phase of a study. Selections typically occur in an ad hoc way, with contents in a network analysis being determined by an arbitrary selection of questions long before any information is obtained on respondent understandings of relations. Were I planning a study of social structure in Northern California, however, I would now know that I could recover the principal outlines of that structure with five sociometric questions rather than the many questions posed in the study providing the data for this analysis. Moreover, I would know what respondents meant when they gave me names in response to those questions.

First, I would need two questions to represent a friendship content domain. For example, the question: "Who are your closest personal friends?" would represent the friendship domain. It would elicit the names of people to whom the respondent felt especially close and with whom the respondent frequently visited, gossiped, or socialized more generally (see the items listed under friendship in Table 2.2). At the same time, I know that low-SES respondents would use the friendship label less ambiguously than high-SES respondents. In order to map out the friendship domain for low-SES respondents, I would need to include a question explicitly focused on frequent contacts, such as : "Who are the people with whom you socialize or visit more than once a week?"

I would need a question to represent the acquaintance content domain. For example: "Have you met any people within the last five years who are very important to you but not close friends? Who are they?" People named on this question would be more involved in core naturally occurring relations with young, highly educated people than with elderly people having little education. For the young respondents especially, the acquaintances elicited by this question, alters who are not quite friends, would be an important source of interaction.

I would also need a question to represent the work content domain. For example, the question: "With whom do you discuss your work?" would represent the domain. People named on this question would be individuals first met at work and with whom the respondent shares a common line of work. For young respondents with high socioeconomic standing, this question is likely to elicit the names of friends as well as work contacts.

Finally, I would need a question to represent the kinship content domain. For example: "Have you spent any time during the last year with any of your adult relatives; relatives who are over the age of 21? Who are they?" For respondents of low socioeconomic standing, people named on this question would be the object of strong bonds of social homophily and frequent interaction. Adult relatives would be a prominent source of advice and financial security for young respondents.

Two points regarding these five sociometric questions should be stressed. First, I am not saying that the five questions exhaust the range of interesting sociometric questions that could be asked of Northern Californians. I am saying that the high cost of interviews and limited respondent patience put constraints on the number of questions that can be asked. These five questions would span the domain of relational contents in the social structure of a cross-section of Northern Californians and would provide data on the social structure that is the backdrop for any interaction activity to be studied in detail. If I were studying the process of obtaining a job, for example, I would ask these five questions and then ask a sociometric question specifically eliciting names of people from whom a respondent obtained information leading to his or her current job. If I were studying social support, I would ask these five questions and then ask a sociometric question specifically concerned with the discussion of personal problems. Second, I am not saying that all social systems will be differentiated in terms of these five relational contents. In 1977, these five contents were distinguished in relations involving a cross-section of adult Northern Californians. Fewer or more contents could be distinguished by people in other systems, or even by Northern Californians observed at a later time.

While the empirical results obtained here need not generalize to other systems, the illustrated methodology for distinguishing contents does generalize. In particular, the relational contents could be distinguished during the pretest phase of research. To be more specific, one pretest strategy for identifying contents distinguished by people in a study population is the following five-step process:

(1) A list of all concrete interaction activities (e.g., visiting, getting advice, discussing work, and so forth) and all relationship labels (e.g., friend, co-worker, relative) pertinent to the study population would be compiled in sociometric questions. This is the usual wish list of questions that would be asked of respondents if their patience and our funding were inexhaustible.

(2) The two or three most important axes of social differentiation in the study population would be identified to the extent that identification is possible prior to gathering network data. For example, age and socioeconomic standing were two such axes exhibited in the data on the Northern Californians (Figure 2.2). Racial differences were little more than a greater tendency for nonwhites to mix ethnic homophily with contents generally. It seems likely that age and socioeconomic standing will be principal axes of differentiation in most social systems, so they might be used as general axes to be anticipated in a study, axes to be augmented by the special focus of the study.

(3) A pretest sample of three or four respondents would be selected from the opposite ends of the identified axes.[14] Using the Northern California data as an example, a pretest sample of 12-16 persons would be composed equally of young educated persons, elderly educated persons, uneducated young persons, and uneducated elderly persons. The pretest sample need not represent the distribution of people in the study population so much as it should represent extreme differences in the interpretation of relations likely to be encountered in interviews with study respondents.

(4) Intensive interviews would be conducted with the pretest respondents. Each respondent would be asked the full range of sociometric questions compiled as pertinent to the study and asked about the attributes of alters they name. Obviously, it would be important to pose sociometric questions just as they would be posed in the actual study interviews (so as to maximize consistent interpretation of pretest and study questions).[15] However, the small number of pretest interviews required is an opportunity to augment the standardized questions with open-ended, detailed descriptions of naturally occurring relations. This would be an especially valuable opportunity in studies of deviant populations.[16]

(5) Networks of confusion relations would be analyzed to locate domains of substitutable contents and to discover the relative ambiguity

with which each content is used. This analysis could be carried out on the entire sample of pretest respondents to describe the content distinctions made by the typical respondent (see Tables 2.1, 2.2; Figure 2.1). The analysis could be carried out on the subsets of pretest respondents drawn from extremes of social differentiation to describe variations in the content distinctions made by respondents (see Tables 2.3, 2.4, 2.5; Figures 2.2, 2.3). The analysis could even be carried out on the confusion network of an individual respondent in order to describe in detail the contents a particularly interesting person distinguishes in his or her naturally occurring relations. In the same manner that five sociometric questions were selected here as representative of contents in the social structure of Northern Californians, a set of sociometric questions would be selected from the analysis of the pretest data. The selected questions would then provide an efficient and accurate basis for eliciting relational data in the study proper.

NOTES

1. As defined in the article proposing content ambiguity, ambiguity scores are given by the left-hand eigenvector for a confusion matrix (Burt, 1982c: equation 13). Given a confusion matrix, therefore, ambiguity scores are readily available in most university computer centers. By using the computer program STRUCTURE (Project, 1981) to obtain ambiguities, I have ignored differences in the row sums of the confusion matrix because the program normalizes rows of an input matrix to equal one before it solves for the left-hand eigenvector of the matrix as a prestige index. This means that g_i is defined here as the following linear composite:

$$g_i = c^*_{i1}g_1 + c^*_{i2}g_2 + \ldots + c^*_{ii}g_i + \ldots + c^*_{iK}g_K$$

where the starred confusion matrix elements have been normalized to be row stochastic (i.e., $\Sigma_k c^*_{ik} = 1$). The ambiguity of content i is high to the extent that the content tends to be confused for other ambiguous contents (i.e., to the extent that $c^*_{ik}g_k >> 0$).

2. I have selected intimacy as the numeraire for three reasons, anticipating the forthcoming discussion. First, the content is located in the middle of the typical respondent's cognitive map of all 33 contents, apart from each of the four content domains (Figure 2.1). Second, it is one of the questions on the basis of which alters were selected for the subsample data. Therefore, it will be represented in these data for its own sake rather than because of its association with one of the questions actually used to select subsample data because of their association with subsample contents are kinship, friend, and acquaintance (see note to Table 2.1). Third, intimacy is roughly equally ambiguous for the contrast groups to be described (Figure 2.3), so it provides a convenient basis for comparing content ambiguity across groups.

3. The distances in equation 4 are obtained when one network is being considered and relations to self are arbitrary constants. The detection of content domains is based on the hierarchical cluster of analysis of distances produced by STRUCTURE, followed by repeated tests of the structural equivalence of contents hypothesized to be substitutable (see Table 2.2 in Chapter 13, this volume and notes 5, 6, 7 and 8 below).

4. The distribution of contents in the figure is based on a two-dimensional smallest space analysis (SSA-I, Lingoes, 1965). Distances between contents in Figure 2.1 almost perfectly reflect actual distances between them, inasmuch as the .04 coefficient of alienation is close to zero.

5. As explained in Chapter 13, this volume, the hypothesis that a set of network nodes are structurally equivalent can be tested by fitting a single factor covariance model to the matrix of covariances among distances to the nodes. There are 33 distances defined by equation 2.4 for each of the contents specified as falling within the friendship domain in Table 2.2. Correlating these distances generates a (7,7) correlation matrix among the contents listed as friendship contents. A single principal component can account for 95 percent of the variance in distances to these contents, with loadings on the component ranging from .93 up to .99 across the seven specific contents. In other words, the seven contents hold together quite well as a single content domain.

6. A single principal component can account for 90 percent of the variance in distances to the five contents listed as acquaintance contents. The loadings on this component range from .91 up to .98 across the five specific contents.

7. A single principal component can account for 98 percent of the variance in distances to the four contents listed as work contents. The loadings on this component range from .99 to 1.00 across the four specific contents.

8. A single principal component can account for 84 percent of the variance in distances to the eight contents listed as kinship contents. The loadings on this component range from .79 up to .98 across the eight specific contents. This is the weakest of the rank tests for structural equivalence across the four content domains, but a principal component accounting for 84 percent of variance in distances clearly indicates redundancy among the contents. If a second domain were to be distinguished among the kinship contents, it would be a financial content. The second principal component accounted for 12 percent of the variance in distances to the eight contents and was principally associated with content 19, alter being a source of money in an emergency. I have not distinguished money as a separate content domain both because this second principal component is so weak in comparison to the first and because borrowing money is closely associated with kinship in the confusion matrix.

9. The distances represented in Figure 2.2 are Euclidean distances between corresponding mean confusion relations for respondents in two social categories. Where $\overline{c}_{ijk}$ and $\overline{c}_{ijk}$ are mean confusion relations $\overline{c}_{ij}$ for respondents in social categories k and m respectively, the distance between the two categories is computed as:

$$d_{km} = \left[\Sigma_i \Sigma_j (\overline{c}_{ijk} - \overline{c}_{ijm})^2 \right]^{1/2}$$

where summation is across all 33 contents in Table 2.2. Distances in Figure 2.2 were obtained as a two-dimensional smallest space representation with SSA-I (Lingoes, 1965). The spatial representation in Figure 2.2 is being used here merely to locate extremely different social categories; however, the space is moderately accurate in representing actual distances among the categories (coefficient of alienation is .14).

10. Respondents were asked the following question: "Some people describe themselves by their race, ethnicity, or national background. [Here] are some examples of those descriptions. How would you describe yourself?" For those respondents who did think of themselves in terms of a specific social group, the list of names compiled from multiple sociometric questions was returned and the following question posed: "Are any of the people on the list of names also [the respondent's ethnicity]? Which ones are they?" The more narrow the ethnic group with which the respondent identified, the more unlikely that any alter would be a same-ethnicity citation. If the respondent did not think of him- or

herself as a member of a particular race, ethnicity, or nationality, he or she had no same-ethnicity citations. For the purposes of this analysis, the same-ethnicity citations would have been better elicited by asking the respondent merely to indicate which alters shared the respondent's race, ethnicity, or national origin and then asking for a description of that shared ethnicity.

11. These differences concern the marital status and employment status of alters. Alters cited by the young, high-SES respondents had a lower tendency to be married than did alters cited by respondents generally, and those cited by the elderly and low-SES respondents in particular. The greater ambiguity of relations to married alters for elderly and low-SES respondents is indicated in Figures 2.3a and 2.3b by content 6 being above the diagonal lines in each figure. Assuming a tendency for friendship ties to occur between similar people, this difference in ambiguity merely reflects a life-cycle phase, a tendency for young, high-income, well-educated people to be unmarried. Similarly, elderly, low-income, less-educated people had a lower tendency to have friendships with employed alters. The elderly are retired, so it is especially likely that they will develop friendships with others who are out of the labor force. The greater ambiguity of relations to employed alters for young and high-SES respondents is indicated in Figures 2.3a and 2.3b by content 7 being below the diagonal lines in each figure.

12. The mean difference between high- and low-SES respondents in Table 2.5 with respect to $c_{19,17}$ shows that high-SES respondents were more likely to rely on adult relatives for emergency money. This tendency does not increase systematically across the categories of income distinguished in Figure 2.2 ($r = .02$), but it does across the categories of education ($r = .18$). This tendency notwithstanding, the effect of age on the tendency for sources of emergency money to have been adult relatives is strong after respondent differences in socioeconomic standing are held constant, and a nonwhite versus white dummy variable is used to hold race constant. The standardized partial regression coefficient for age predicting $c_{17,19}$ is only slightly less than the zero-order correlation: $b = -.26$ with a t-test of 8.4, $p < .001$.

13. Even where network analysis programs are not readily available, applications of formal concepts can be carried out on a network of confusion relations with routine data analysis programs such as SPSS or SAS—a point developed in other chapters of this volume. There is even a precedent of analyzing relational content with correlation and regression models. The precedent, however, is not well developed and can be quite misleading. Consider the routine multiple regression strategies invoked by Wellman (1979) and Fischer (1982b). Wellman presents equations predicting the probability of an alter being named as a source of assistance, given other kinds of relations to the alter (kinship, physical proximity, emotional closeness, and so on). Fischer presents equations predicting the probability of an alter being named as a friend, given other kinds of relations to the alter (several of which are given in Table 2.2).

There are at least two reasons why this multiple regression strategy is undesirable as a methodology for analyzing the content of relationships:

(1) It invalidates the use of statistical inference—traditionally a strength of mass survey data. This occurs because alters are used as units of analysis rather than egos. Egos are independently sampled observations; alters are not. The 3,930 alters analyzed by Wellman in fact refers to interviews with 845 sampled respondents. The 3,804 alters analyzed by Fischer are sampled from the total of 19,417 alters named in interviews with 1,050 sampled respondents. The use of alters as units of analysis obviously exaggerates sample size so that test statistics grossly exaggerate statistical significance. But more detrimental to making inferences, respondents are not equally weighted in these analyses. In determining statistical effects, the respondent citing one alter, for example, has one-tenth the weight given to a respondent citing ten alters (ceteris paribus) because the latter respondent

appears as ten alters in the data, while the former only appears once. In sum, using alters as units of analysis exaggerates the statistical significance of findings and biases inferences toward data on respondents citing many alters. If two contents are significantly correlated, one has to ask if the significance is only a result of the exaggerated sample size. If two contents are not significantly correlated, one has to ask if the lack of association is only true of respondents citing many alters. In contrast, the analysis of confusion relations aggregates alters by respondent to generate a network of confusion relations for each respondent. This means that each respondent is weighted equally in the analysis so that routine statistical inferences can be made from analyses of the content data.

(2) As a second limitation, multiple regression equations are likely to be misspecified so as to be misleading. Wellman predicts the likelihood of an alter being named as a source of assistance, and Fischer predicts the likelihood of an alter being named as a friend. Were these predictions stated at the level of respondents, they would correspond to columns in a matrix of confusion relations. The column headed "17" in Table 2.2, for example, is a list of the conditional probabilities of the typical respondent naming an adult relative as an alter, given any one of the other kinds of connections between alter and ego. The analysis of subgroups in Figures 2.2 and 2.3, however, shows that these mean effects are aggregations of clearly distinct subculture effects. In other words, contents have different tendencies to be combined by respondents in different subcultures. For example, high- and low-SES respondents had roughly equal tendencies to cite adult relatives as alters and to cite alters as sources of emergency money, but the probability of sources of emergency money being adult relatives was twice among high-SES respondents what it was among low-SES respondents (see Table 2.5 for details). These subcultural differences among respondents would be specified as interaction effects in a multiple regression model. In an equation predicting a kinship tie to alters, for example, there would be a positive, direct effect from alter being a source of emergency money, and there would be a positive interaction effect from the product variable "alter a source of emergency money" multiplied by "ego a high-SES respondent." This is an analysis of covariance form of multiple regression. Although multiple regression equations are easily modified to include such interaction effects (e.g., Hanushek and Jackson, 1977: 101-108; Allison, 1977; Marsden, 1981b), these modifications become cumbersome as the number of interactions increases and require a knowledge of important interactions prior to estimating effects. In other words, a correctly specified multiple regression equation predicting a type of content would require an analysis such as that illustrated in Figures 2.2 and 2.3 in order to identify social categories of respondents extremely different in their interpretation of contents so that interaction effects could be correctly specified. Social categories likely to yield significant interaction effects would be categories on opposite sides of a space, such as the one in Figure 2.2. Based on the analysis here, age and socioeconomic standing would define subcultures likely to evidence significant interaction effects. Neither age nor SES of respondents showed significant effects in Wellman's (1979: 1217n) analysis. Fischer (1982b: 297, 299, 301-303) reports significant age effects, but negligible effects of respondent SES. The effects that Wellman and Fischer estimate, however, are only direct effects—not the subculture interaction effects illustrated here.

The general methodological point is that routine data analysis strategies such as multiple regression across alters as units of analysis can be extremely misleading.

14. The number of pretest respondents has not been selected at random. The standard error of a mean confusion relation for a set of pretest respondents representing an extreme social category (e.g., "poor and uneducated" respondents) refers to a t-distribution with degrees of freedom equal to one less than the number of independent observations drawn from the category. In the interest of placing informative confidence intervals around these mean estimates, it is advantageous to interview at least three or four pretest respondents in

each extreme social category for which a network of mean confusion relations might be constructed. The .95 confidence interval around a mean confusion relation for two respondents decreases by 66 percent when based on three respondents, by 75 percent when based on four respondents, and by 78 percent when based on five respondents. The largest increase in precision for unit cost of another pretest interview is obtained with four respondents, but a large increase is obtained even if three, rather than two, people can be interviewed.

15. Of particular note here is the difference between contents obtained in response to a sociometric question eliciting alter names versus those obtained after a list of alters has been compiled. With respect to Table 2.1, for example, the "work" and "intimacy" contents generated alter names in response to sociometric questions, but the "friendship," "acquaintance," and "kinship" contents were labels respondents assigned to alters after names had been compiled from multiple sociometric questions (see the note to Table 2.1 for exact wordings). The confusion relation, substitutability and ambiguity concepts describe words or phrases in general that people use to interpret naturally occurring relations. In other words, the ambiguity and substitutability of words or phrases descriptive of interaction could be analyzed with respect to generating names or labeling names generated. However, the difference between contents generating names and those labeling names could have nontrivial empirical consequences. For example, asking a person to name all of her relatives is likely to generate a longer list of alters than asking her first to list people with whom she actually interacts and then asking her to identify those of these often-met alters who are relatives. Other examples are easily imagined, but the important point here is that there is no published research on the consequences of obtaining relation citations as name-generators versus name labels. Until such research is available, it seems safest to maintain consistent question styles between pretest and final questionnaire under the assumption that they need not be identical, i.e., the ambiguity and substitutability of a content generating names in one questionnaire need not match the ambiguity and substitutability of the same content when used to label names in another questionnaire.

16. Relation labels can emerge from an analysis of content as unanticipated content domains. People should have a colloquial label for each content domain distinguished in their naturally occurring relations. In reference to Table 2.2, for example, the content domains refer to well-known kinds of relations: friend, acquaintance, co-worker, kin. In more esoteric populations, populations such as delinquent youths, drug addicts, ghetto residents, or any self-conscious subculture, it is likely that respondents will have in-group labels for relationships unfamiliar to a network analyst prior to gathering data. These unknown labels will appear as unanticipated content domains of substitutable interaction activities. When a person in the study population is asked to name the kind of relation that contains the activities identified as substitutable, he should be able to provide the colloquial term immediately.

Chapter 3

A Procedure for Surveying Personal Networks

LYNNE McCALLISTER
and CLAUDE S. FISCHER

The application of network analysis to certain issues in sociology requires measurement of individuals' personal networks. These issues generally involve the impact of structural locations on persons' social lives. One such case is the Northern California Community Study of the personal consequences of residential environments. This article describes and illustrates the methodology we have developed for studying personal networks by mass survey. It reviews the conceptual problems in network definition and measurement, assesses earlier efforts, presents our technique, and illustrates its applications.

Although mass survey data are often used in network analysis, the methods available for generating such data have received relatively little attention. In this chapter, we present a survey technique that we believe produces more accurate and efficient descriptions of personal social networks than the procedures currently in use. We go on to discuss one of the most important aspects of methodological choice in network analysis—the impact of the operational definition of network on substantive research findings.

The methodology and research this chapter presents will be most useful to researchers concerned with studying the "social worlds" of individuals and their connections to social structure. Because mass surveys produce data on individual members of the general population, the survey methods we discuss are less appropriate for "structural" network analysis (à la White, Breiger, and Burt) or traditional sociometry than for research in the tradition of the British

Authors' Note: *this work was supported by grant ROI-MH26802, "Effects of Urbanism on Social Networks and Mental Health" from the National Institute of Mental Health, Center for Studies of Metropolitan Problems, to the second author. The procedures described in this article were developed in discussion with Charlotte Ann Stueve, Robert Max Jackson, and Charlotte Coleman. Helpful comments were made on an earlier draft by Ron Burt, but we remain solely responsible for the contents. A full report of this project is available elsewhere (Fischer, 1982a). This chapter first appeared in* Sociological Methods & Research, *November 1978.*

anthropologists such as Mitchell, Bott, and Gutkind, who use the network metaphor to understand individuals' social milieux. Research in the latter tradition proceeds on the assumption that individuals are influenced by and integrated into society through their personal networks (see Fischer et al., 1977: ch. 2). Mass surveys in general, and the procedures offered here in particular, permit researchers to supplement the qualitative, in-depth research on which this tradition has relied with data on more varied and representative populations. Therefore, it is especially useful to those working in the "social world" tradition of network analysis. (The discussion may also be useful to researchers who study egocentric networks for other purposes.)

The bulk of this chapter describes the procedure we have developed and illustrates its application in data from a small pilot survey. Our discussion is organized as follows: (1) a brief outline of the theoretical purposes to which the method is being put; (2) a review of the limitations of earlier techniques; (3) the conceptual assumption underlying our procedure; (4) an outline of the method; (5) two illustrations of applications, one on the topic of homophily, the other on community differences. We hope that the procedure we present here can be usefully modified to serve other network analysts' research. (A much fuller presentation of the method, its rationale, and its empirical properties is available in Jones and Fischer, 1978.)

THEORETICAL CONCERNS AND PRACTICAL NEEDS

The methodology presented in this chapter was developed for the Northern California Community Study (NCCS) to study the personal consequences of residential environments.[1] Network analysis is used in the NCCS to ask two questions: How do the communities people live in affect aspects of their social milieux such as supportiveness, homogeneity, cohesion, and geographical dispersal? And, how do the attributes of social milieux affect psychological well-being? To answer these questions, we use a mass survey that permits us to compare the environmental experiences, social relations, and feelings of well-being of respondents in many communities of various types, controlling for other structural variables such as age and occupation. We have chosen to think of respondents' social milieux as personal social networks composed of actors linked to egos and of the relations involved in those links. The method presented here was designed to elicit descriptions of the members of these egocentric networks and of their relations with respondents.[2]

In order to address questions about respondents' social milieux, we needed to study respondents' whole network (and not just limited sectors of the network such as kin, friends, or neighbors). The restrictions of the mass survey format—the high cost of household interviews and respondents' limited patience—forced us to develop a technique for eliciting descriptions of respondents' networks in 20 minutes of interview time. Therefore, a primary concern was to elicit information as efficiently as possible and to consider carefully the trade-offs between the accuracy and extent of the data.

EARLIER METHODS

Several previous mass survey studies have elicited information on respondents' social networks, notably Laumann's Altneustadt study, Laumann (1973), Wellman (1979), Erickson and Yancey (1976), and Kleiner and Parker (1976). Typically, they ask one basic question that calls on the respondent to name his or her "best friends" (e. g., Laumann, 1973) or the people he or she "feels closest to" (Wellman, 1979). Or the investigator might (as Kleiner and Parker, 1976, do) ask the respondent to name people in each of a few roles, such as friend or co-worker.

We follow their general strategy—asking respondents to name people and then having them describe these people and how they are related. We developed new techniques, however, for eliciting the names of the people in respondents' networks. This, in our minds, is the critical issue in network surveys: the techniques used to elicit names determines what kinds of people are included in the network membership and, therefore, the operational definition of "network" used in the subsequent analysis.

We rejected the name-eliciting methods used in previous studies for two major reasons. First, they tend to sample certain sectors of networks at the expense of the rest. For example, asking for "friends" tends to undersample significant associates who are kin; or, asking for the people respondents "see socially" (Irving, 1977) loses significant others who live far away. Second, these questions seem especially vulnerable to measurement error. People interpret terms such as "best friend" and "close" in varying ways. Some think of kin as friends, others do not; some define closeness in terms of behavior, such as sharing confidences, others in terms of roles, such as kinship. Error also results from the poor recall respondents have of the people they know; without extensive probing they are likely to forget important network members. Finally, error is likely to result from respondents' exaggeration when they lengthen lists of associates to avoid seeming unpopular. These sorts of errors are especially troublesome when they are unlikely to be randomly distributed. For example, lonely people probably exaggerate more; well-educated people are probably more able or willing to separate affective feelings from role expectations.[3]

No mass survey of networks is likely to be immune from such problems. However, we felt that some significant improvements could be made that would minimize the difficulties.

UNDERLYING ASSUMPTIONS

Most people know hundreds of other people in very many different ways—from intimate kin to nodding acquaintances to vaguely familiar store clerks. Survey researchers can only hope to learn about a fraction of that population. *Which* fraction will determine the decriptions of networks that are ultimately obtained. Data show that if it is the fraction involving frequent face-to-face meetings, the description will disproportionately include neighbors; if it is the fraction respondents think of often, it will lean toward kin. Therefore, one ought to be explicit about the part of the network to be described.[4]

We wanted, for our own purposes, to tap the part of respondents' networks that most influenced their attitudes, behavior, and well-being. We call this the "core" network.

Based on both methodological and theoretical considerations, we define the core network as the set of people who are most likely to be sources of a variety of rewarding interactions, such as discussing a personal problem, borrowing money, or social recreation. Thus, we elicited the names of members of repondents' networks with questions such as the following:

> Often people rely on the judgement of someone they know in making *important* decisions about their lives—for example decisions about their family or their work. Is there anyone whose opinion you consider *seriously* in making important decisions? (IF YES:) Whose opinion do you consider?

An exchange theory of relations (Homans, 1974; Thibaut and Kelley, 1959) leads us to believe that people who are sources of rewarding interactions will be particularly important in shaping respondents' attitudes and behavior. In addition, we found in informal pretesting that questions about such behavior elicited more consistent and complete sets of names than questions about categories of relations (such as requests from lists of "relatives" or "people you feel close to").

This operational measure of respondents' networks follows a decision to define "relation" as an *exchange*: an interdependence between two actors where the actions of each directly affect the outcomes (rewards or punishments) of the other. In choosing an exchange definition of relation, we rejected two other commonly used bases for defining relation: (1) *affective content*— a subjective orientation, or feeling (Laumann, 1973; Wellman, 1979); and (2) *normative content*—a specific, culturally defined set of expectations, obligations, and rights between incumbents of two reciprocal social positions, such as father-son (see Kleiner and Parker, 1976). Thus we chose to exclude relations with purely affective or normative content, no matter how important respondents perceived them to be.[5]

In one hour-long pilot survey devoted exclusively to network questions, we tested about 30 items that were designed to identify respondents' core networks. In a second pilot, we tested about half that many. In the final survey of 50 communities, we used ten items that analysis of the pilots indicated would elicit a major and representative subset of the larger "core network" (see the next section).[6]

THE PROCEDURE

Based on the consideration discussed above, we attempted to design a survey procedure that would, in 20 minutes, identify and elicit descriptions of respondents' associates who were likely to be sources of rewarding exchanges.[7]

Our solution to this problem has four parts: first, we developed questions asking the respondent to give the first names of people with whom they were likely to engage in highly valued interactions. For example, we ask, "When you are concerned about a personal matter— for example, about someone you are close to or something you are worried about—how often do you talk about it with someone—usually, sometimes, or hardly ever? When you do talk with someone about personal matters, whom do you talk with?"

Second, we selected a set of questions that identified network members from a full variety of social contexts (such as work, the neighborhood, and the family) as efficiently as possible. That is, we tried to choose a question that produces (1) as many names as possible; (2) a substantial number of names that were not elicited from other questions in the set; and (3) names from context that were not tapped by other questions in the set. The ten name-eliciting questions we used cover the following topics:

(1) who would care for the respondents' homes if they went out of town:
(2) if they work, with whom they talk about work decisions;

(3) who, if anyone, had helped with household tasks in the last three months;

(4) with whom they engaged in social activities (like inviting home for dinner, or going to a movie);

(5) who they talk with about hobbies;

(6) if unmarried, who their fiancé(e) or "best friend" is;

(7) with whom they talk about personal worries;

(8) whose advice they consider in making important decisions;

(9) from whom they would or could borrow a large sum of money;

(10) enumeration of adult members of the respondents' households.

Respondents can name as many people as they wish in response to each question. However, interviewers record only the first eight names for each (actually, ten for question 4 and four for question 9).

Third, we obtained descriptions of respondents' networks by asking them to look at a list the interviewer had compiled of all the names elicited in the interview and to select those people who fit a series of criteria. The process of making a list of all the people the respondent named permitted the interviewer to check for redundancies (for example, the same person called by two names) and to supplement the list of names by giving the respondent a copy of the list and asking: "Is there anyone who is important to you who doesn't show up on this list?" (In the end, most respondents had between 10 and 30 names on their lists.)

With these lists, the interview finds out:

(1) the sex of each person;

(2) all the role relations of ego with the named people (e. g., cousin, co-worker, fellow union member, "friend");

(3) which persons respondents "feel especially close" to;

(4) which persons live within a five-minute drive;

(5) which live more than an hour's drive away;

(6) which they see at a favorite "hang-out";

(7) (for homemakers) which are also full-time homemakers;

(8) (for workers) which are in the same line of work;

(9) (for respondents with an ethnic identity) which are of the same ethnicity;

(10) (for respondents with a religious affiliation) which share the same religion;

(11) (for respondents with a favorite pastime) which share the favorite pastime.

In addition, we know from the name-eliciting question which exchanges the respondents claim to receive from each person named. The technique of asking respondents to select names from a list permits us to obtain a much great variety of descriptions than would be permitted by asking about each name directly (the usual procedure in network surveys). We chose to accept the potential inaccuracies of this approach (in the form of names the respondents may fail to mention) in return for its greater efficiency.

Finally, we obtained further information about a subsample of elicited names (up to five names, and usually no less than three),[8] by having respondents fill out self-administered questionnaires about each person. (The respondent was asked to fill out the questionnaire while the interviewer was involved in compiling the entire list of names.) The questionnaires asked respondents:

(1) how they had met the person;
(2) how many years they have known each other;
(3) what city the person lives in;
(4) how often they "get together";
(5) the person's age;
(6) the person's employment status;
(7) the person's marital status; and
(8) whether the person has children and how old they are.

In addition, the interviewer obtained a crude index of network density for this subsample by asking respondents, for each pair of names, whether the two "know each other well."

The primary advantage of this procedure is that it permits us to focus on the segment of respondents' networks that is most appropriate for our theoretical concerns—the full variety of people who are important sources of valued exchanges. Our evaluation of the method suggests that it identifies these people reliably (Jones and Fischer, 1978). If respondents had selected the names for a complete list of their network membership, they would have replaced a maximum of one in five names. (The names we missed tend to be "specialists," sources of only one kind of exchange.) As a result, we are confident that the networks we identified are comparable across respondents. The illustrations of the method presented in the next section demonstrate the importance the definition of network has in determining research findings.[9]

APPLICATIONS

By generating data about the individuals in respondents' networks, our survey procedure permits us to conduct analyses at two levels: the level of dyadic relations, in which each respondent-nominee pair is treated as a unit of analysis; and the level of whole networks, in which the set of relations is the unit of analysis. The first level of analysis speaks primarily to social-psychological concerns, while the second permits us to look at relationships between personal and structural variables.

Relations as the Unit of Analysis

A perennial topic in the study of dyadic relations is homophily: the similarity between two persons in a relation tends to be far greater than chance. Verbrugge's (1977) reanalysis of the Laumann (1973) Altneustadt data provides the latest statement of the topic. She writes of two principles that underlie homophily: "meeting"—the structural circumstances that influence who will meet—and "mating" the social psychological factors that influence the choice of associates from among available pools. However, she cannot, in her analysis, distinguish between the two processes. (For an analysis of the Laumann data that does distinguish somewhat between the two, see Jackson, 1977.) One limitation Verbrugge faced was the data: each respondent provided up to only three names of these people loosely called "best friends." Perhaps our method can do better.

We will present results from our second pilot program. Although the sample of respondents is small (N = 78) and not very representative of the general population, the survey can serve as an illustration. Respondents were randomly selected from four neighborhoods in the San Francisco Bay Area: an inner-city district, a working-class suburb, a planned suburban community, and a very affluent "ex-urb."[10]

The "dependent variables" in the analysis are the percentage of respondent-associate pairs who are similar (according to respondent report) on each of several dimensions. Respondents were asked to characterize all named associates on five dimensions: sex, ethnicity, religion, line of work, and favorite leisure activity. (The last four were asked only of respondents who claimed such an identity; see notes to Table 3.1) In addition, we asked about four other characteristics—age, marital status, child-rearing status, and labor-force status—on the self-administered questionnaires concerning a subsample of the networks.

The analysis presented in Table 3.1 shows that the method used affects findings about homophily. Column one displays the percentages of respondent-alter pairs who are similar—*only for the names elicited by the question, "Who do you think of as your closest friend?"*[11] This question resembles the one that generated Verbrugge's network data. We observe high rates of similarity, no doubt higher than chance. Column two displays the same data for *all the names* elicited on *all the questions*. Rates of similarity are still high, but notably lower than those in column one, especially with respect to sex and life-cycle attributes. We draw the implication that a single, "best friends" probe is likely to

TABLE 3.1   Percentage of Network Members Similar to
Respondents, for "Closest Friends" and Overall

Similarity Dimension	Only Names Elicited on "Closest Friends"		All Names		Difference
Same Sex	77%	(308)	59%	(1306)	18
Same Age (±5 yrs.)[a]	62	(143)	44	(308)	18
Same Marital Status[b]	68	(148)	61	(324)	7
Same Child Status[c]	61	(148)	53	(324)	8
Same Ethnicity[d]	44	(139)	47	(592)	−3
Same Religion[e]	49	(230)	44	(996)	5
Same Labor Force Status[f]	53	(148)	49	(324)	4
Same Line of Work[g]	22	(222)	17	(943)	5
Same Leisure Activity[h]	31	(203)	20	(876)	11

a. Asked only of subsample names.
b. Asked only of subsample names; three categories: married; separate, divorced, or widowed; never married.
c. Asked only of subsample names; two categories: has no children or has children.
d. Asked only of respondents who profess a (non-American) ethnicity.
e. Asked only of respondents who profess a religion; for Protestants, read "Same Denomination."
f. Asked only of subsample names; three categories: full-time, part-time, not working.
g. Asked only of respondents who are currently employed, looking for work, or retired.
h. Asked only of respondents who have one special hobby or activity.

overestimate systematically ego-alter similarity compared to a more diversified method of eliciting network membership.[12]

The reason for this becomes evident when we look at Table 3.2. In that table, the respondent-alter relations are distinguished by the primary "social context" in which they exist. This categorization is based on the reported role-relations between the respondent and each person he or she named. Since any link could involve more than one role-relation (e.g., neighbor and friend), a hierarchical rule was applied, with primacy running from left to right across the table.[13] This variable is strongly related to the answers to the question, "How did you meet this person?" and might therefore be read as a proxy for the origin of the relation (see Fischer, 1982a, for discussion of "context").

The differences in degrees of similarity across contexts are striking. For example, over 80 percent of co-workers named are of the same sex as ego, but only about 50 percent of kin are; the latter figure does not differ from chance. Almost 60 percent of named neighbors are the same age as respondents, but less than 10 percent of them share an ethnicity or a line of work with respondents. These variations reflect the differential

TABLE 3.2 Percentage of Network Members Similar to Respondents on Nine Dimensions, by Social Context of Relations

				Social Context of Relation					
Similarity Dimension	Spouse/ Surrogate[a]	Parent/Child	Other Kin	Neighbor	Coworker	Organization	Just Friend	Other	Total
Same Sex	02% (54)	49% (150)	51% (326)	66% (82)	82% (92)	86% (58)	68% (502)	41% (32)	59% (1306)
Same Age (±5 yrs.)[b]	–	02 (41)	32 (69)	59 (34)	–	–	59 (133)	–	44 (308)
Same Marital Status[b]	–	51 (43)	58 (71)	71 (35)	–	–	65 (141)	–	61 (324)
Same Child Status[b]	–	51 (43)	39 (71)	63 (35)	–	–	58 (141)	–	53 (324)
Same Ethnicity[c]	52 (21)	73 (62)	67 (170)	09 (33)	20 (41)	19 (26)	42 (214)	–	47 (592)
Same Religion[c]	56 (39)	62 (122)	55 (255)	38 (66)	16 (61)	64 (55)	33 (361)	10 (30)	44 (996)
Same Labor Force St.[b]	–	58 (43)	45 (71)	57 (35)	–	–	45 (141)	–	49 (324)
Same Line of Work[c]	08 (38)	09 (104)	06 (231)	08 (60)	68 (91)	20 (46)	15 (351)	–	17 (943)
Same Leisure Activ.[c]	21 (38)	13 (97)	09 (205)	20 (44)	07 (55)	70 (37)	25 (371)	–	20 (876)

NOTE: N under 20.

a. Spouses or "living together" spouse-surrogate; includes one gay couple.
b. Asked only of subsample names; total N = 324.
c. Asked only of respondents who have an ethnic, religious, occupational, or hobby identity; N varies.

segregations of social settings in American society. Neighborhoods, for example, are much more stratified by life-cycle than by specific occupation or white ethnicity (this was not true of preindustrial cities). With regard to Verbrugge's concern over "meeting and mating," these data suggest that much homophily is produced by the social structuring of meeting contexts before homophilitic "mating" processes (e.g., "like is attracted to like") even begin.

Networks and Units of Analysis

While the ability to study the social psychology of interpersonal relations is a major benefit of this method, our main purpose in developing it was to be able to categorize the *networks* of respondents. Since the Northern California Community Study is focused on intercommunity differences, it is fitting to draw an illustration from that area of study: How do the four neighborhoods we interviewed in vary in the "local-*Gemeinschafty*-ness" of their residents' networks?

The independent variable is composed of the four locales: "Barrio," "Old Suburb," "New Suburb," "Elite Suburb." The dependent variables fall into two categories generally associated with the concept of Gemeinschaft: (1) how local the network is, in terms of the residences of the network members, and (2) the network density of the subsample network. Table 3.3 presents the results. Note first that there is little difference among the four locales in geographic dispersal of the network. An average of 27 percent of each respondent's network members live within a five-minute drive of him or her, and an average of 30 percent of those members live over one hour's drive away, irrespective of community. (There does seem to be, however, some difference between the lower- and higher-status locales in individual variability on these dimensions.) Second, there is still a notable difference in the percentage of network members who are called "neighbors," with New Suburb residents including more neighbors in the networks than other respondents. From readings of the interview protocols, we might attribute this to the fervent organizational activity in this "semiplanned" community, a phenomenon common to new suburbs (see Gans, 1967). Yet, third, the data on network density seem to contradict this pattern. Typical Gemeinschaft formulations imply that neighbor involvement and network density go together. But the New Suburbanites have the *lowest* average (perceived) density, while Barrio residents, whose percentage of neighbors is the least of the four locales, have the *highest* average (perceived) density—probably because of the high representation of kin in their networks.

TABLE 3.3 Local Gemeinschaft Measures by Neighborhood

| | | Neighborhood | | | |
| | | Lower Status | | Upper Status | | |
Measures		Barrio	Old Suburb	New Suburb	Elite Suburb	
	(N =)	(20)	(20)	(19)	(19)	
(1) Percentage Neighbors[a]	M = (SD =)	02% (±04)	06% (±08)	10% (±14)	06% (±09)	F = 2.5
(2) Percentage within 5 min.[b]		28 (±24)	28 (±29)	24 (±17)	27 (±13)	F = 0.2
(3) Percentage over 1 hr. away[c]		34 (±25)	26 (±19)	29 (±17)	29 (±13)	F = 0.6
(4) Network Density[d]		.64 (±.30)	.46 (±.33)	.31 (±.24)	.51 (±.31)	F = 4.2
[Total Network Size]		14.4 (±5.6)	15.2 (±7.9)	19.8 (±4.9)	17.9 (±7.5)	F = 2.8

a. Of all names provided by each respondent, the percentage called "neighbor."
b. The percentage the respondent identifies as living within a five-minute drive.
c. The percentage living over an hour away.
d. Density = $T \div (N(N-1)/2)$, where N equals the number of subsample names and T equals the number of ties ("knows each other well") among the names identified by the respondent.

This is not the place to unravel and explain the pattern of data reported in Table 3.3. We note that the method we have described permits elaborations of the analysis in various directions. For example, we could distinguish among respondents by controlling for class. The Barrio group is composed of both working-class, middle-aged Mexican-Americans and of upper-middle-class, young Anglos. Or, we could elaborate the analysis by distinguishing among network members in creating other network measures. For instance, some clarification might be achieved by recalculating the indices for kin and nonkin separately. It may be that localization of nonkin ties conforms more closely to the density pattern. In any case, we have great flexibility in aggregating descriptions of separate relations into descriptions of whole networks.

CONCLUSION

The method we have presented and illustrated here was designed to elicit and describe respondents' "social worlds." However, it is flexible enough to be adapted to other purposes. For example, a researcher interested in interpersonal influence on political behavior might do the following: define a relation as a connection between two persons in which politically relevant information is regularly passed; identify a set of questions that elicit the names of many people who may have such a relation with respondents (e.g., the questions might ask for those persons who "you argue politics with," "you watch the evening news with," "you see at neighborhood meetings," "belong to the same organizations you do," and the like); and with the compiled list ask the respondents detailed questions about the named people's personal and political characteristics. This would yield descriptions, at the relational level, of the characteristics of respondents' political ties, and at the network level, of respondents' political milieux.

The method we have presented is adaptable in many such ways. But we would stress one conceptual issue that applies to any technical adaptation: It is important that network researchers consciously and clearly specify what they need to know about networks and what they mean theoretically by "relation." The findings of network research can be strongly influenced by the measures of "relation" used to define the network. Therefore, researchers should pay as much attention to the methods they use to identify network memberships as they do to the analysis of data describing those networks.

NOTES

1. Reports from the project are available, at cost, from Publications, Institute of Urban and Regional Development, University of California, Berkeley 94720.

2. We have concluded from our analysis of the Laumann (1973) network data that the structure of relations *among* respondents' primary ties has little influence on intimacy once the specific content of their relations has been taken into account (Fischer et al., 1977; see also Wellman, 1979). Therefore, we have not focused very much attention on second-order relations, excepting a rough measure of network density.

3. These conclusions are based on our reanalysis of the network survey used by Laumann (1973)—see Fischer et al. (1977)— and on extensive pretesting of our own method.

4. A researcher might, for heuristic purposes, wish to sample the whole network proportionately. Could that task be accomplished—it would require a "census" of all relations—it would likely be filled with trivial acquaintances.

5. In practice, we used a few questions about roles and emotions to elicit names when we found them to be efficient substitutes for questions about sources of rewarding exchanges.

6. The first pilot elicited an average of 20.3 names, while the final survey elicited an average of 18.5 names.

7. The procedure described here is the one used in the final, full survey of the NCCS; the data presented later are from our *second* pilot survey (the questions there differed somewhat).

8. The procedure used to sample the list tends to yield names with the same distribution of traits as the entire set (Jones and Fischer, 1978).

9. In terms of administering such an instrument, our experience suggests that people can answer almost an hour's worth of questions about their networks, but many do tire of the need to think of names and the repetitiveness of the names. It seems that the 20-minute version suffices to capture most of what we have called the "core network."

10. Sampling and interviewing were done by the Survey Research Center, University of California, Berkeley.

11. The question was asked only in the pilots, not in the final survey.

12. A different way to interpret this finding is that the "best friends" network is more homophilous than other networks. We do not see it in such terms because it reifies "best friend," treats friendship as if everyone knew and agreed about what it was, which is not the case. Instead, we see "best friend" probes as crude efforts to measure the core network.

13. The major impact of using this procedure, one that creates mutually exclusive categories, and using the multiple classification categorization where the relation can appear twice, is to distribute about 200 "friends" into other categories, leaving about 500 "just friends" for whom no context was identified.

Chapter 4

Panel Data on Ego Networks

A Longitudinal Study of Former Heroin Addicts

MICHAEL J. MINOR

This chapter describes a field methodology used to measure ego networks over time. Strategies for asking about ego-alter relations, alter attributes, and alter-alter relations are discussed. Preliminary findings are presented which show that egos will disclose information about sensitive relations and that missing data about alters do not appear to be a substantial problem. Future directions for methodological research on longitudinal studies of ego networks are mentioned.

Systematic studies of personal relations over time have been carried out for over 40 years. The statistical sophistication of analytic techniques employed in these investigations has increased dramatically. For example, compare Davis et al.'s (1941) study of 18 women with Runger and Wasserman's (1980) reanalysis of Hallinan's (1978) data on classrooms. In the bulk, though, these over-time studies have focused only on "closed" networks, such as students in a residential hall (Newcomb, 1961), factory workers in a production unit (Kapferer, 1972), and participants in a telecommunication experiment (Rice, 1982). The adjective "closed" denotes that the system boundaries are a priori defined and that the scope of data collection and analysis involves only those actors (and their relations) specified at the initial point of the investigation. Thus, although temporal dynamics have played diverse roles in applied network analyses, from studies of the diffusion of innovation (Coleman et al., 1966; Burt, 1982b; and Rogers and Kincaid, 1981) to acquaintance processes (Newcomb, 1961), there is a paucity of methodological discussions about measuring open ego networks over time.

Author's Note: *This research is supported by grant DA02566-03 from the National Institute on Drug Abuse. I would like to thank Bob Saltz, Chris Beard, and Carol Taylor for their assistance in carrying out the computational work and also for their valuable comments. Ron Burt also provided helpful comments on drafts of this chapter.*

In the following pages I discuss a field methodology we are using in a panel study of the ego networks of former heroin addicts. This methodology builds directly on Laumann's (1966, 1973) techniques for measuring relations among three best friends and on subsequent developments by Fischer and his associates (Chapter 3, this volume, and Fischer, 1982a) for assessing theoretically positive exchange relations. The basic strategy uses the respondent (ego) as an informant to provide four types of data at each interview point: (1) a psychosocial profile of ego; (2) a description of ego-alter relations; (3) a psychosocial profile of alters; and (4) a description of alter-alter relations. The procedure is "open" because it does not restrict the focus of ego-alter or alter-alter relations to those measured at a prior point in time.

The next section discusses the key conceptual and operational issues in designing the panel study. Some preliminary findings on selective methodological questions and on the stability of ego-alter relations are then presented. The final section reviews the role of time in network analysis and suggests some future directions for methodological studies in this area.

STUDY DESIGN: CONCEPTUAL AND OPERATIONAL ISSUES

The panel study was motivated by interest in the changing social environments of persons who are attempting to disengage from a lifestyle of heroin addiction and establish a stake in conventional society. In brief, we set out to measure the over-time characteristics of social networks and their influence on psychosocial functioning in a group of persons who were in a difficult life transition stage. The sample consists of approximately 200 persons residing in the San Francisco Bay Area who were selected as reasonably "good bets" for reentry. In other words, from our judgments or the judgments of referral sources, they appeared to have a relatively good prognosis for achieving a nonaddiction status. Sample selection followed an orthogonal quota scheme that was stratified by sex, race (White, Black, and Hispanic), age (five-year groupings from 20 years old to 45 years old), and drug treatment status at the first interview wave (methadone, therapeutic community, and none).

Ego-Alter Relations

At the core of the study design were decisions about which ego-alter relations to measure. Notable previous survey investigations of ego networks had focused on three best friends outside of the respondent's household (Laumann, 1966, 1973); six close friends, again outside of the respondent's household (Wellman, 1979), and alters who were involved in theoretically positive exchanges with the respondent (Fischer, 1982b). These data sets are very useful for mapping close primary positive ties but shed minimal light on other network sectors, such as weak ties (Granovetter, 1973), that have significant influence on psychosocial status.

Building on findings from these previous studies, and drawing from the social-psychological literature on personal relations (particularly Kurt Lewin's work, as in Cartwright, 1951), we developed a conceptual framework that suggested sampling ego-alter relations along five dimensions. One dimension is supply-receipt. Most ego-network studies ask about relations in which an alter supplied something (e.g., advice, affect, or direct help) to the respondent, but rarely the converse. Aggregate social interaction, though, consists of both receipt and supply. Characterization of ego's "supply" relations may indeed be a very sensitive indicator of his or her social well-being. The positive-negative feature of relations is a second dimension. Although some theorists place primary importance on positive relations as key guideposts (e.g., Thibaut and Kelly, 1959), negative relations in particular circumstances may, in fact, be the most important determinant of behavior. Evaluations of relations as positive and negative, of course are relativistic and can change over time.

A third dimension is relational content. Our strategy here was to span the familiar contents of affect, advice, and direct help across various life domains, such as finances, health, and employment. Relational form is a fourth dimension. We wanted to include a spectrum of ties from strong primary (such as spouse) to weak secondary (such as transitory professional contacts). Finally, a mix of actual and hypothetical exchanges was desired. This mix would yield data about ego-alter events during the specified period before the interview and also ego's perception of his or her ability to mobilize collective network resources.

Turning this conceptual framework into a feasible field methodology was our next task. Because of the comprehensiveness in the strategy for measuring ego-alter relations, we decided that face-to-face interviews were necessary. Following Fischer's (1982b) procedures, our questions about ego-alter relations were formatted to ask for the first name and last initial of alters with regard to specific exchanges and roles. Respondents were probed to cite as many alters as he or she thought pertinent to each question. To minimize the effects of memory decay (see Sudman and Bradburn, 1974), most of the ego-alter event questions

TABLE 4.1   Ego-Alter Relational Items: Waves I, II, III

How found place to live	*Best friend
How found previous places to live	Anyone asked your opinion about
Names of people living with	decision
Short-term place to stay	Anyone talked about their worries
Alters who stayed with respondent	Regular partners in free time activities
*Friends to help when sick	Someone special
Family members with serious health	People socialized with in last month
problem	Persons arrested with respondent
Friends who helped when sick	Friends in jail
*How found out about job	*Who bailed respondent out of jail
Someone to talk to about work	*Persons to talk to about legal problems
*Friends at work	Anyone talked about their legal
*How found out about other jobs	problems
*How found out about vocational	Drinking partners
counseling	Binge partners
*How found out about classes	Persons who suggested respondent has
To whom have you loaned car	drinking problem
*From whom borrow car	How found out about alcohol program
Household members who give money	Persons who suggested respondent has a
Family or relatives not in household	drug problem
who give money	Persons whose drug use affected
Friends who give money	respondent
*Borrow large sums of money	Friends in treatment program
To whom loaned money	*Persons involved in most positive event
*Spouse or intimate living with	Persons talked to about positive event
*Spouse or intimate not living with	*Persons involved in most negative event
Children	Persons talked to about negative event
Who children live with	*Important persons not already
Who babysit children	mentioned
Advice about handling children	
*Persons to depend on in emergency	
*Persons to talk to about personal	
matters	
*Persons to help with decisions	

referred to the six-month period prior to the interview point.[1] These items are spaced throughout the questionnaire (which takes about two hours to administer) to reduce the chances of response sets; that is, citing same alters across items. Table 4.1 displays the 54 ego-alter relational questions used in the first three waves of the panel study. These items produced a median of 17 and a range of 3 to 48 alters in Wave I, which was carried out during the period January-December 1981.

Alter Attributes

Once alters have been enumerated by the ego-alter relational items, there are decisions regarding what attributes of which alters should be

TABLE 4.2 Alter Attributes Asked About in Panel Study

Alter Attributes

- how long known ego
- age
- where usually get together with ego
- frequency of contact with ego
- race
- distance of residence from ego
- current living arrangement
- means of support
- typical occupation
- alter-ego involvement in heroin use
- is alter an ex-addict
- been in drug treatment program
- been arrested
- how well ego knows alter

asked of the respondent. The primary goal here is to provide data for analysis of the effects of homophily and heterophily. We ask about three characteristics for all alters cited: sex, kin/nonkin relation to ego, and co-worker status with regard to ego. In addition, we ask for in-depth data (Table 4.2) on up to 15 alters (excluding children under seven years) cited on the subset of items marked by asterisks in Table 4.1. We view these items as the key relations in the addict's struggle for a straight life.

We found through extensive pretesting that respondents could not easily report on more than 15 alters. Thus, if more than 15 alters are cited on the key items, a random number table is used to eliminate the appropriate number of alters for the in-depth descriptions. If less than 15 alters are cited on the key items, the random number table is used to select the appropriate number of alters from the pool of those not cited on the key items.

Data from the Wave I interviews show that about 72 percent of the alters cited are described in depth. We ask respondents to give us these descriptions of selected alters at each interview wave, regardless of prior data collected. These data will facilitate the first thorough examination of across-time reliability in reports of alter attributes.

Alter-Alter Relations

Extending ego-based survey analysis beyond the relational to the network level requires collecting data about the relations among the alters. Such data are typically gathered by asking the respondent a binary question about whether alter i knows alter j. In our study we asked respondents to use a fine-point scale (not at all to very well) to describe the interconnections between the 15 alters cited on the key items or selected randomly. Responses to these questions in Wave I show that 18,775 alter-alter relations were described with the following distribution: 22 percent were rated to know each other very well, 9 percent moderately well, 10 percent so-so, 6 percent not so well, and 52 percent not at all. Like the alter attribute data, respondents were asked to describe alter-alter relations at each interview point, regardless of prior data collected. The over-time consistency in selective parts of this data set will supply a new perspective on the reliability of reports of alter-alter relations.

A second component to the alter-alter data is the subsample of 44 egos who form 22 couples. The couples vary in length of relationship (from 2 months to 16 years at Wave I), and both members of each couple are former heroin addicts. By mapping together alter-alter matrices from each member of the couple, we can investigate several important concepts in network analysis, such as role strain (Bott, 1957). Descriptions of same alters from a couple will also provide an opportunity to examine across-rater reliability in reports of alter attributes and alter-alter relations.

SOME FINDINGS

The Six-Month Time Frame

A crucial design question in any panel study is the appropriate interval between interview waves. The answer to this question rests on both theoretical and methodological considerations. From a theoretical perspective, the panel interval should be designated to optimize the detection of true change in the variables or system of variables that are of substantive interest.[2] Measurement of true change is the heart and soul of panel studies. If change cannot be reliably measured, or if the variables are constant (the system is in equilibrium), there is little justification for a panel investigation. From a methodological perspective, the panel interval should usually be regular and operationally cost-effective. Cost effectiveness includes trade-offs between such factors as memory decay, intrusiveness, interviewer management, and tracking problems. Despite these complex considerations, the interval of interviewing in most panel studies is, unfortunately, determined by funding level.

We have selected a six-month panel interval in our study of former addicts as the balance between theoretical and methodological concerns. We found this period to be optimal in terms of field

TABLE 4.3   Three-Way Cross-Classification of Alters Cited During Three Waves of Pilot Study (# of Egos = 181)

			Time 2	Time 3		
				Cited	Not Cited	
	Cited	Cited		812	271	1083
		Not Cited		199	987	1186
Time 1	Not Cited	Cited		377	741	1118
		Not Cited		810	--	810
				2198	1999	4197

management, and findings from a three-wave pilot study showed considerable change in ego-alter relations (using a somewhat smaller item pool) across the six-month intervals. Table 4.3 shows the distribution of alters cited in the three waves of interviews for the sample of 181 egos who were interviewed at each point. In all, 4197 alters were cited in three waves, an average of about 23 alters per ego (with a range of 9 to 40). Of these alters, 54 percent were cited at Time 1, 50 percent at Time 2, and 52 percent at Time 3. In all, 19 percent were cited at all three time points, 20 percent at two points, and 61 percent at one time point. Thus, about a third (36 percent at Time 1, 37 percent at Time 2, and 37 percent at Time 3) of the alters cited at any one time point were also cited at the other two time points. In all, 51 percent of the alters cited at Time 2 (N = 2202) and 37 percent of those cited at Time 3 (N = 2198) were first-time mentions.

Table 4.4 displays the interrelationships among the three distributions of alter citations. Surprisingly, citation at one time point has only a negligible effect on the probability of being cited at another time point. (Note that the probabilities in the $T_1, T_2, T_3 \times T_1, T_2, T_3$ submatrix are all close to .5.) If an alter was cited at one point, there was about a .37 probability that he or she was also cited on the other two waves. Conversely, if an alter was cited on any two waves, there was about a three in four chance that he or she was also cited at the other time point.

The regularity in these data is interesting. The findings can be summarized succinctly by a model that postulates that an alter had a 50-50 chance of being cited at any point, and that in the aggregate, alter citation was independent across time. This independence model states that the joint probability of an alter being cited at two time points is .25 $(.5 \times .5) = (.25)$. The observed proportions were .26 (T_1T_2), .24 (T_{1T3}), and .28 (T_2T_3). A pretty good fit! The independence model also postulates that the proportions of alters cited in all three time points

TABLE 4.4 Conditional Probabilities of Alter Being Cited–
            Column Status Given Row Status
            (main diagonal entries are marginal probabilities)

	T_1	T_2	T_3	T_1T_2	T_1T_3	T_2T_3	$T_1T_2T_3$
T_1	.54	.48	.45	.48	.45	.36	.36
T_2	.49	.52	.54	.49	.37	.54	.37
T_3	.46	.54	.52	.37	.46	.54	.37
T_1T_2	1.00	1.00	.75	.26	.75	.75	.75
T_1T_3	1.00	.80	1.00	.80	.24	.80	.80
T_2T_3	.68	1.00	1.00	.68	.68	.28	.68
$T_1T_2T_3$	1.00	1.00	1.00	1.00	1.00	1.00	.19

should be .13 ($.5 \times .5 \times .5$). The observed proportion was .19. Thus, the model slightly underestimates this proportion.

Although specific ego-alter ties appear to come and go across the three waves, there is remarkable similarity in the cross-sectional composition of alter groupings (Table 4.5). T_1 is somewhat different from T_2 and T_3 in three regards: more immediate kin, fewer friends, and fewer professional contacts. These differences across waves can probably be attributed to both changes in the questionnaire (primarily dropping items about family background after T_1) and also life events (e.g., the clinical interventions). In sum, the "typical" network of size 12 (the sample average) would consist of 4.3 immediate kin, .6 distant kin, .48 in-law kin, .36 ex-spouse, 4.2 friends, and two professional contacts. Note that about 5 percent of the alters cannot be placed in a single alter group across the three waves. That is, their relational status vis-à-vis ego changes over time.

Another perspective on change in ego-alter relations is available from data on 74 egos who were interviewed at all three points during the pilot study and also at the first wave of the panel study. The 74 egos cited 279 alters who appeared at all four interview points, a median of about 4 alters per ego, with a range of 1-11 alters. Thus, on the average, it appears that over this two-year period only about one-third of the ego network remained intact. In sharp contrast to the cross-sectional profile of alter groups shown in Table 4.5, 73 percent of these longitudinally stable alters were immediate kin, 15 percent were friends, and each of the other four groups contained less than 5 percent of these alters.

Alter Names

Measuring changes in ego-alter relations requires reliable identification of alters. We have encountered the following problems

TABLE 4.5 Distribution of Six Alter Groups in Pilot Study Data (based on the 181 egos interviewed at all three interview points)

Alter Group*	Time 1 (N = 2174)	Time 2 (N = 2092)	Time 3 (N = 2075)	Total (N = 3990)
	%	%	%	%
Immediate kin	59	38	37	36
Distant kin	4	4	4	5
In-law kin	2	4	5	4
Ex-spouse	3	4	4	3
Friend	22	31	35	35
Professional contact	9	18	15	17

*"Other" and "changing spouse" alters are missing from this table. The number of alters in these two categories were: at T_1 = 95, at T_2 = 110, at T_3 = 123, Total = 207. Thus, such alters are about 5 percent of the data base.

with regard to this task: (1) absence of full first name or last initial; (2) the use of sobriquets; (3) misspellings of names; and (4) changing alter roles. These problems arise because of the complexity of the field work, interviewer and coder errors, respondent misreporting (both purposive and unintentional), and changes in actual life circumstances. The extent of these problems cannot be accurately estimated without carrying out interviews with all the alters cited. A review of alter lists generated from the first three waves, though, shows that 85 percent of the egos have at least two alters with the same first name, and that 30 percent have at least two alters with the same first name and last initial. Thus, errors in misidentifying alters can have a significant influence on the panel analysis.

Sensitive Ego-Alter Relations

A fundamental issue in asking a comprehensive set of ego-alter relational items is whether egos will disclose the presence and name of alters in sensitive or negative relations. Although there has been considerable heat generated by this issue, few empirical data have been collected to substantiate patterns of underreporting. Findings from five items in the Wave I interviews suggest that egos in our panel study are willing to describe such relations:

—30 percent of alters cited on key items were described as current or former heroin addicts;

—20 percent of the egos cited an alter who made it difficult for them to "stay clean" during the six-month period prior to the interview;

—26 percent of those egos arrested during the preceding six-month period gave the name of an alter they were arrested with;

—21 percent of those who had been in jail during this six-month period cited an alter they became friends with; and

—44 percent of those egos who went on an alcohol binge cited a drinking partner.

Of course, it is impossible to gauge the amount of underreporting in these items. However, the relatively high degree of demonstrated disclosure is encouraging.

Alter Attributes

Once one assumes that egos are willing to disclose information about alters, the next issue is what egos can inform us about alters. As described in Table 4.2, we asked egos a long list of questions about a subset of up to 15 alters. One indication of what egos can tell us about alters is the distribution of missing data across these items.[3] Of the egos, 82 percent had at least one alter with missing data on these items, but only 16 percent of the alters were missing data. Interestingly, there was only about a 3 percent increase in missing data (15-18 percent) with decreased ego-alter familiarity (as measured by the how-well-know item). Nonkin alters were about one and one-half times more likely to have missing data than kin alters. The majority of these alters missing data had only one item missing.

With regard to distributions for specific items, the largest proportions missing are for alter's occupation (10 percent), alter's means of support (8 percent), alter's living arrangement (6 percent), and how far from ego alter lives (5 percent). The rest of the items show less than 5 percent missing data. Thus, overall, the amount of missing data for alter attributes is not substantially greater than that found in typical cross-sectional household surveys.

CLOSING REMARKS

Recent developments in statistical modeling and computational algorithms (for example, Singer and Spilerman, 1976; Kessler and Greenberg, 1981), are paving the way for advanced analysis of temporal dynamics in ego networks. Concomitant developments in field methodology for panel studies, however, are currently lacking. Our experience with the former heroin addict study, described briefly here, suggests that a comprehensive item set that asks about many forms and contents of ego-alter relations can be successfully used to enumerate alters. When respondents are dealt with in a respectful fashion and remunerated for their efforts (we paid $20 for each completed interview), they appear willing to disclose information about sensitive relations and provide detailed descriptions of selected alters. Although only about 60 percent of the alters described in depth were known "very well" by respondents, missing data on alter attributes were overall not much more than might be expected in a typical household survey. Keeping track of specific alters and minimizing ego attrition across interviews are important challenges for the panel investigator, but they do not appear to be insurmountable obstacles. Besides instrumentation and field management, the major decision in carrying out a panel study is specifying the time interval between interview waves. We have found that a six-month interval is optimal for the former heroin addict sample; however, other samples may experience less short-term change, and thus an appropriate interval may be longer.

Numerous important questions about networks can only be addressed by longitudinal studies. The cost of panel investigations, however, will probably limit future opportunities for such studies. Thus, an important area of methodological research in network analysis will be the development of inexpensive techniques for measuring ego networks over time. Careful experimental work with diaries, mail, and telephone survey strategies will provide much needed guidance for the design and implementation of future longitudinal studies of ego networks.

NOTES

1. Another factor determining our choice of a six-month interview period was tracking concerns. Although former heroin addicts are notoriously difficult to track over time, we experienced only about a 10 percent attrition rate across each wave of interviews.

2. True change refers here to change that is inherent in the phenomenon independent of the methodology used to measure it.

3. Missing data, of course, can arise from interviewer coding and data transfer procedure errors. Careful review of these sources of error, however, suggests that the bulk of missing data stem from respondent reluctance or inability to answer those questions.

Chapter 5

Studying Status/Role-Sets Using Mass Surveys

RONALD S. BURT

A method is described for interviewing a random sample of persons drawn from a large population so as to describe role-sets defining statuses in the population social structure. The key to the method is a connection between the concept of an actor's network position in social structure and combinations of attributes that define statuses in the social structure. With data obtained in a survey interview with a randomly selected respondent, it is possible to describe the relational pattern defining his "ersatz network position" in the population social structure from which he has been drawn. Given ersatz network positions for a representative sample, it is possible to test hypotheses concerning status/role-sets in terms of which the population is stratified.

The single factor most restricting structural theory employing network concepts to small systems of actors is the realpolitik of data processing. Network concepts typically, although not always, call for data on relations among all actors in a system. In order to meet this need, the typical network study involves fewer than 100 distinct actors; children in a classroom, employees in a small bureaucracy, a small number of large corporations within a geographical region, a small number of nations in some type of exchange system.[1] Unfortunately, the number of relations to be estimated for each of the networks within a system increases expotentially with system size. Where there are N(N-1) relations to be estimated within a network among N actors, there are 9,900 relations to be estimated in a network among 100 persons, 249,500 relations to be estimated in a network among 500 persons, 6,247,500 relations to be estimated in a network among 2,500 persons, and so on. Even a vague

Author's Note: *This chapter was a byproduct of support from the National Science Foundation (grants SOC77-22938, SOC79-25728) and received direct support from the the Pacific Institute for Research and Evaluation under a grant from the National Institute on Drug Abuse (DA 02566-01). The chapter is abbreviated from a working paper written during a leave of absence spent in the Department of Sociology, State University of New York at Albany. The discussion has benefited from comments from H. R. Bernard, P. M. Blau, M. Granovetter, D. R. Heise, N. Lin, and J. A. Wiley, all of whom are absolved of the uses to which I have put their sage advice. An earlier version appeared in* Sociological Methods & Research, *February, 1981.*

familiarity with data processing is sufficient to know that it would be difficult to obtain such extensive data from respondents, and no easy task to analyze them.

But who lives in an area occupied by only 2,500 persons? In seeking network data on a single network in such a system, a system the size of a small rural hamlet, we have outstripped our data analysis capabilities, as well as the patience of the typical survey respondent. If a rural hamlet is too large for analysis, what about cities, states, regions, or the nation? It is in these larger systems that the typical citizen resides.

System size is not the only problem. Structural theory makes statements about perceptions and behaviors in terms of network context of actors. This context is lost for a random sample of actors. Within the hypothetical hamlet of 2,500 persons, 100 could be randomly selected to be interviewed concerning their relations to other persons. But there is no method of knowing how those respondents are connected within the system. In a random sample of N* respondents drawn from a system of N actors, information can be obtained on relations among the respondents and to others in the system—a total of N(N*-1) relations. Information on relations among the noninterviewed actors and relations from the noninterviewed actors to the sampled respondents is not obtained—a total of N(N-1)-NN* relations. The network data ignored in a random survey of k percent of a population is roughly (l-k) percent, so that a random sample of 10 percent of a population ignores 90 percent of its network data, a random sample of 25 percent ignores 75 percent, and so on.[2] These lost data are significant. To what extent do the nonsampled persons reciprocate relations directed to them from the sampled respondents? Are respondents the object of strong relations from the system as a whole, or are they relatively isolated within the system? How are the nonsampled persons interconnected, apart from the respondents? Answers to these questions define the network context of the random sample, but the typical survey research design obliterates that context from our view.

In theory, new research designs could be proposed so that network concepts could inform survey data. Beginning with accolades for the theoretical significance of network concepts, for example, Granovetter (1976: 1287) writes that most discussions of network concepts "have had practical application only to small groups." Striving to bring such discussions "more squarely into the mainstream of sociological research," he builds on work estimating the total number of persons and relations in a large population (Frank, 1975) to propose a sample estimate of network density in a large population—density being a scalar estimate of overall interaction in the population. As Granovetter takes pains to point out, these are clearly "some first steps." But even though density is among the more primitive of network concepts, there are practical problems in data collection that make even density estimates difficult (Morgan and Rytina, 1977).

Of course, there is always the short-term solution of gathering what network data a survey research design permits and making the severely limited inferences such data allow. Concomitant with the increasing popularity of the term "network," for example, an increasing number of articles have appeared as "network studies," in which the author refers to a survey respondent's sociometric citations as a network. To the extent that "networks" have an effect on some dependent variable under study, the number of citations a respondent makes is expected to strongly predict the dependent variable. This measure of ego-network range is perhaps the least presumptuous of all network concepts, yet even it has been useful in research, particularly research on social stress. Researchers accustomed to the subtlety and depth of structural theory applied to typical network data can certainly frown on the ostensible naivete of research in which network structure is reduced to frequency counts of contacts. But with the need to make inferences about persons in large populations, and therefore a need to use traditional survey research designs ruling out designs in which typical network data are obtained, how can more sophisticated network concepts be invoked?

One kind of answer to this question is the use of what I shall term "ersatz network positions" in survey data. A connection exists between the usual concept of an actor's network position in social structure and combinations of attributes defining statuses in that social structure. Survey data on a randomly sampled respondent can be used to describe the relational pattern defining his "ersatz" network position in the social structure from which he has been drawn. In proposing the idea of an ersatz network position, I draw on the data collection strategy developed by Edward Laumann and Claude Fischer, with their respective colleagues, for studying respondent ego networks (Laumann, 1966, 1973; McCallister and Fischer, 1978; Fischer, 1982a), the macrolevel conception of parameters defining positions in social structure developed by Peter Blau (1974, 1977a, 1977b), and my own work on network models of status/role-sets in social structure (Burt, 1975, 1976a, 1977b, 1982a: chs. 2, 3). The next section defines status/role-sets as network positions. The connection between positions and attributes is then described, and in the third section, I use that connection to propose ersatz network positions.

THE STATUS/ ROLE-SET
AS A NETWORK POSITION

The classic status/role-set duality is captured in network models as a network position jointly occupied by structurally equivalent actors, with their pattern of relations defining the role-set and the rights and obligations of performing those relations defining the status. The key concepts in this representation are position, distance, and equivalence (see Burt, 1982a: 40-49, for detailed review). Since the extension of these concepts from a single network to multiple networks is obvious (compare Burt, 1976a, 1977b, and the review in Burt, 1982a), I shall focus on single network systems throughout this discussion. The network of relations among N actors is given by an (N,N) matrix Z_{NN}, in which element z_{ji} is the strength of j's relation to actor i. Actor j's network position in the system of N actors is given by his relations to and from actors. This 2N vector of relations, Z_j, is given by the elements in row and column j of the matrix Z_{NN} as j's relational pattern:

$$Z_j = (z_{j1}, z_{j2}, \ldots z_{jN}, z_{1j}, z_{2j}, \ldots z_{Nj}) \qquad [5.1]$$

A set of actors jointly occupy a position to the extent that they have identical relational patterns within the system. Two actors are separated by high distance to the extent that they have very different relational patterns and by zero distance to the extent that they have the same relational pattern. This distance between actors j and i can be estimated by comparing each corresponding relation involving them:

$$d_{ij} = d_{ji} = (\Sigma_k^N[(z_{ik} - z_{jk})^2 + (z_{ki} - z_{kj})^2])^{1/2}$$
$$= ((Z_i - Z_j) (Z_i - Z_j))^{1/2} \qquad [5.2]$$

To the extent that they are separated by zero distance, actors j and i are structurally equivalent and jointly occupy a single network position. Social structure in the system can now be described in terms of role relations among jointly occupied statuses. The (N,N) matrix of relations among actors, Z_{NN}, can be used to compute an (M,M) matrix of role relations among M statuses jointly occupied by structurally equivalent actors, Z_{MM}, where element z_{ab} is the mean relation, or density, from occupants of status S_a to occupants of status S_b:

$$z_{ab} = (\Sigma_h \Sigma_k z_{hk})/(n_a n_b) \qquad [5.3]$$

where summation is across all n_a actors h occupying S_a and all n_b actors k occupying S_b. The matrix Z_{MM} is a density table.

Figure 5.1 illustrates the logic of this operation in a manner that will be useful. There are two mapping operations in computing an interstatus role relation as a density of relations between individuals. It is assumed that each individual actor occupies only a single status; actors i and h occupy status S_a in Figure 5.1. This means that the relation from one actor to another corresponds to one and only one role relation between statuses. In consequence of these assumptions, the role relation

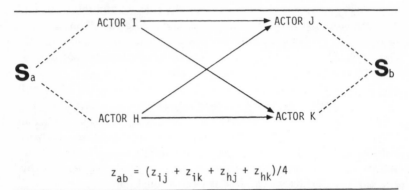

$$z_{ab} = (z_{ij} + z_{ik} + z_{hj} + z_{hk})/4$$

Figure 5.1:   The Relation from Status S_a to Status S_b in Terms of Relations Between Individual Occupants (occupancy given by dashed lines and relations given by arrows, z_{ab} defined in equation 5.3)

from S_a to S_b is equally reflected in any relation from an occupant of S_a to an occupant of S_b so the four estimated interactor relations in Figure 5.1 are merely variations on the interstatus relation, and that relation is assumed to be their expected value, i.e., $z_{ab} = (z_{ij} + z_{ik} + z_{hj} + z_{hk})/4$. Of course, since occupants of each status are structurally equivalent, the four interactor relations will be very similar in magnitude by definition. The role-set defining status S_a is now given by the 2M relations in row and column a of the density table Z_{MM}:

$$Z_a = (z_{a1}, z_{a2}, \ldots z_{aM}, z_{1a}, z_{2a}, \ldots z_{Ma}) \qquad [5.4]$$

Given role-sets defining statuses in a system and the relational patterns defining the network positions of individual actors, a variety of hypotheses can be tested regarding actor perceptions and behavior (see Burt, 1982a, for review and discussion).

Unfortunately, data on role-sets defining statuses in the social structure of large systems cannot be obtained in the typical survey research design. Such designs are not suited to estimating relations among all actors in a system. Without these elements for Z_{NN}, routine network analysis strategies for locating statuses as jointly occupied positions and assigning individual actors to specific statuses cannot be invoked.

THE ASYMMETRIC CONNECTION BETWEEN ACTOR ATTRIBUTES AND STATUSES

It is well known that actors jointly occupying a status tend to be homophilous in regard to one or more attributes such as race, sex, beliefs, occupation, religion, political affiliations, and so on. I have elsewhere discussed the social homophily of status occupants in detail (Burt, 1982a: chs. 5, 6) but take it as given for the purposes here.

Some persons have suggested that actor attributes can be used directly as a surrogate for defining structural equivalence—that is, actors homophilous on key attributes can be treated as jointly occupying a single status. With various colleagues, Laumann (1966, 1973) has made major advances in developing this line of research so as to describe relations between racial, religious, and particularly occupational statuses in the United States. While not backing his arguments with the same extent of data, Blau (1974, 1977a, 1977b) has more systematically developed the analysis of actor attributes as "parameters" of social structure. In an analogue to the stratification space defined by distances between positions in network analysis (d_{ij} in equation 5.2), Blau (1977a: 30) suggests that:

> the structure of societies and communities are delineated by parameters. Structural parameters are the axes in the multidimensional space of social positions among which the population is distributed. They are attributes of people that underlie the distinctions they themselves generally make in their social relations, such as age, race, education, and socioeconomic status. . . . In short, a parameter is a variable that characterizes individuals and differentiates their role relations and social positions.

Blau then derives hypotheses concerning intergroup relations in stratified society from data on relations between persons with different attributes, hypotheses testable with data obtained in a typical survey research design.

This use of actor attributes as a surrogate definition of positions in social structure, a surrogate for direct investigation of interactor relations, is limited by the asymmetric connection between actor attribute homophily and structural equivalence. While all status occupants can be expected to share some common parameters in Blau's sense, all persons sharing common parameters need not be structurally equivalent. For example, consider a classroom of students stratified across four very cohesive cliques, each constituting a set of structurally equivalent children; two cliques composed of boys and two composed of girls. The four cliques are homophilous with regard to sex, but each boy is not in a clique with each other boy and each girl is not in a clique with each other girl. More generally, hypotheses derived from actor attribute homogeneity as a surrogate for actor structural equivalence will always have an initial empirical link in the chain of deductions leading to hypotheses. If attributes are incorrectly selected as parameters on which actors are homophilous, incorrect in the sense that parameters are selected which do not accurately differentiate jointly occupied statuses, then empirical tests of structural hypotheses stated in terms of the selected attributes are meaningless.[3] Accordingly, Blau (1977a: 30) requires that actor attributes only be considered as parameters when they differentiate:

> People can be classified on the basis of innumerable attributes any of which may be a parameter. But if a classification made by an investigator does not influence social relations at all, or exerts only idiosyncratic influence on the personal relations of some individuals, it is not meaningful to consider it indicative of social positions. Hence, the double criterion of a parameter circumscribing social positions is that it is an attribute by which a population is classified and that the social relations among persons similarly classified differ on the average from the relations between persons in widely different categories.

This is a necessary—but not sufficient—condition for an attribute being a parameter in the sense of defining a position jointly occupied by structurally equivalent actors. In the four-clique example above, sex as a parameter does classify and differentiate children in the classroom. However, it also obscures classroom differentiation. Separating boys and girls as two groups would show higher within-group relations than between-group relations, since each group would contain two cohesive cliques and no clique would cut across the two groups. But each group homophilous on sex is differentiated into two completely separate cliques that are capriciously combined by the sex parameter.

Suppose that in addition to knowing the sex of children in the hypothetically cliqued classroom, data are also available on their involvement in the Little League and their intelligence as IQ scores. The following distribution of attributes across the four cliques is observed: Clique A is composed of *boys* with *high* involvement in the Little League and *low* IQ scores. Clique B is composed of *boys* with *low* involvement in the Little League and *low* IQ scores. Clique C is composed of *girls* with *low* involvement in the Little League and *low* IQ scores. Clique D is composed of *girls* with *low* involvement in the Little League and *high* IQ scores.

With these three variables—sex, involvement in the Little League, and IQ score—actor attributes can be used to define structural equivalence. The first male clique is composed of sports enthusiasts, while the second is composed of boys not involved in sports. The first female clique is composed of unintelligent girls, while the second is composed of intelligent girls. Note that any one of the variables alone would differentiate the children in the sense that there would be zero interaction across groups and some interaction within groups—but it would also group together separate cliques. Intelligence erroneously groups together the first three cliques, and involvement in sports erroneously groups together the last three cliques. Similarly, no two variables together are able to accurately differentiate cliques, even though any two variables taken together would distinguish separate cliques. It is only when all three variables are considered simultaneously that they are able to capture accurately the four classroom cliques.

This illustrates what will be a useful concept: Refer to the set of structural parameters sufficient to accurately distinguish the status/role-sets in a system as the system's "parameter set." Each parameter in the set need not define structurally equivalent actors. However, some combination of values on the parameters in the set must define each status jointly occupied by structurally equivalent actors. Sex, involvement in sports, and intelligence constitute the example classroom's parameter set. Any one of the three variables is unable to accurately distinguish the four cliques; however, each clique has a unique pattern of values on the three variables. At the same time, all combinations of parameter values need not define a status. In the four-clique classroom, for example, there are no groups composed of intelligent boys, nor any groups composed of sports-minded girls. The key to using actor attributes as structural parameters defining jointly occupied statuses is to detect which combinations of values in a system's parameter set actually define statuses. This requires some initial information on relations as they are associated with actor attributes in a system's parameter set.

THE STATUS/ROLE-SET AS AN ERSATZ NETWORK POSITION

Two types of information are required in order to construct a survey instrument for eliciting data sufficient to define what I shall term ersatz network positions: an enumeration of the variables in the parameter set for the population from which respondents will be sampled, and an enumeration of types of relations that define networks in the population. For the purposes here, I focus on relations within a single network and let Q refer to the number of possible different combinations of values on variables in the population's parameter set, i.e., Q equals the product across variables in the set of the number of values on each variable. The purpose of the survey instrument will be to obtain data from each respondent on the attributes of persons to whom he goes for each type of relation to be studied. Such data have been obtained successfully in several surveys to date (e.g., Laumann, 1966,

1973; Wellman, 1979), but the most extensive study to date is the Northern California Community Study conducted by Claude Fischer (1982a) and his colleagues. Each respondent was asked to name persons who were contacts for 20 important types of social exchange, ranging from discussing personal worries, to borrowing a large sum of money, to discussing hobbies. On average, respondents named 19 different persons across all 10 types of exchange relations, some persons being the source of only a single type of exchange, while others were the source of multiple types. Given a list of persons named as the object of relations from a respondent, it is a simple matter to obtain attribute data on each person named where attributes are taken from the parameter set for the population under study.[4] Focusing on a single network for the purposes here, let r_j be the number of persons to whom respondent J gives a sociometric citation during his interview. Also obtained during the interview are parameter attributes for each person cited and for the respondent himself.

Theoretically, some combination of attributes in the population parameter set defines each jointly occupied status in the population. Instead of locating statuses directly by analyzing relations among individual actors, as is usually done in network analysis, it should be possible to locate them indirectly by detecting those combinations of attributes which are associated with structurally equivalent respondents.

Relations Between Combinations of Attributes

Consider a population with a parameter set composed of two variables, each with some number of values for a total of Q^* different possible combinations in the population (Q^* equals the number of values of variable one, times the number of values of variable two). The extent to which respondent j goes to persons with attribute i on the first variable in the parameter set and attribute t on the second variable (goes to persons with attribute combination it, in other words) is given as:[5]

$$z_{j,it} = f_{j,it}/r_j \qquad [5.5]$$

where r_j is the number of citations j makes (his network range) and $f_{j,it}$ is the number of those citations he directs to persons with the attribute combination it. The relation $z_{j,it}$ is the proportion of respondent j's citations directed to persons who have attributes i and t.[6] There will be Q^* possible relations defined for respondent j by equation 5.5, one relation from him to each of the Q^* different combinations of attributes in the population's parameter set.

There are two further features of equation 5.5 that merit special mention. First, since each respondent and each cited person corresponds to a single combination of attributes, respondent j's relations sum to 1 across the Q^* combinations of attributes in the parameter set: $1 = \Sigma_q z_{j,q}$. The fact that each person maps into a single combination of attributes also limits the number of the Q^* possible attribute combinations actually observed. The number of attribute combinations to which respondent j has nonzero relations will be lower than this maximum to the extent that he cites some persons with the same attributes.

Let Q equal the number of different attribute combinations observed in a sample. This would include respondent attributes, as well as those of persons cited. The maximum value of Q would be the sample size plus the total number of different persons cited by respondents in the sample. In the typical network study, for example, Q would equal N, the order of the network under study, Z_{NN}. In practice, of course, Q will be much smaller than this maximum. It would only reach its maximum if every respondent and every person cited by any respondent had a unique combination of attributes. Since relations tend to occur among socially homophilous persons, the likelihood of Q reaching its maximum seems low. At the other extreme, if all respondents have the same attributes and all of their citations are to persons with those attributes, then Q equals its minimum of one, indicating that the respondents are members of a completely homophilous system.

The respondent-to-attribute combination relations defined by 5.5 can be used to generate a Q by Q matrix of attribute combination to attribute combination relations. First, relations can be summed across respondents with identical attributes:

$$f_{(i't',it)} = \Sigma_j (z_{j,it})(\delta_{j,i't'}) \qquad [5.6]$$

where $\delta_{j,i't'}$ is a dummy variable equal to zero unless respondent j has attribute combination i't', whereupon it equals one. Element $f_{(i't',it)}$ ranges from zero (if no respondent with attribute combination i't' cites any person with attribute combination it) up to a maximum equal to the number of respondents who have attribute combination i't' (which occurs if every respondent with that combination of attributes only cites persons with attribute combination it). Then dividing equation 5.6 by its maximum, $n_{i't'}$, the number of respondents with attribute combination i't' yields, as the mean proportion of their citations, persons with attribute combination i't' direct toward persons with combination it:[7]

$$z_{(i't',it)} = f_{(i't',it)} / n_{i't'} \qquad [5.7]$$

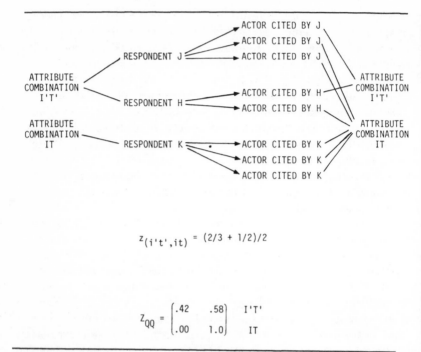

$$z_{(i't',\,it)} = (2/3 + 1/2)/2$$

$$Z_{QQ} = \begin{bmatrix} .42 & .58 \\ .00 & 1.0 \end{bmatrix} \begin{matrix} I'T' \\ IT \end{matrix}$$

Figure 5.2: The Relation from Attribute Combination I′T′ to Attribute Combination IT in Terms of Citations by Survey Respondents to Unknown Actors (actors' attributes indicated by solid lines and citations given by arrows, $z_{(i't',\,it)}$ defined in equation 5.7)

Figure 5.2 illustrates the logic of the above operation as a modification of the typical procedure illustrated in Figure 5.1. Each respondent and each person cited by a respondent maps into a single combination of attributes; respondents j and h have attribute combination i′t′ in Figure 5.2. According to the definition of a system's parameter set, actors with identical attributes within the set are structurally equivalent. Therefore, a respondent's citations to persons with identical attributes can be aggregated in 5.5 as citations to structurally equivalent actors. Similarly, relations from respondents with identical attributes can be aggregated in 5.7 as relations from structurally equivalent actors. In Figure 5.2, respondent j cites 3 persons, 2 of whom have attribute combination it, so that the proportion of his citations given to persons with that combination is 2/3. Similarly, respondent h gives 1 of his 2 citations to persons with that attribute combination. Respondents j and h have attribute combination i′t′, so that the average of their individual relations to persons with attribute combination it gives the mean proportion of citations persons with attribute combination i't' direct toward persons with combination it: $58 = (2/3 + 1/2)/2$. The matrix of relations among attribute combinations, Z_{QQ}, is given in the diagram.

Respondent Ersatz Network Positions

Respondent j corresponds to a single row and column of the matrix Z_{QQ} as defined by equation 5.7, the row and column containing his combination of attributes in the parameter set. I refer to respondent j's ersatz network position as his pattern of relations with each of the Q attribute combinations; Q relations from him to persons with each combination of attributes, and Q relations to persons with his attributes from respondents generally

$$Z_j = (z_{ji}, z_{j2}, \ldots z_{jQ}, z_{1j}, z_{2j}, \ldots z_{Qj})$$ [5.8]

where relations from the respondent are given by the $z_{j,q}$ in 5.5 and relations to him (as a person with attribute combination it) are given by the z_{qj} in 5.7. A respondent's ersatz network position corresponds to the idea of a position defined for typical network data by equation 5.1, except that instead of containing relations to and from other actors, the ersatz relational pattern consists of relations to and from attribute combinations in a parameter set. Given a relational pattern for each respondent, the distance between respondents i and j can be computed from equation 5.2. This provides a check on the assumption that actors with the same attribute combination are structurally equivalent. The (n_{it}, n_{it}) covariance matrix computed from the N distances to each of the n_{it} respondents having attribute combination it should have a rank of one where N is the number of respondents interviewed (see Burt, 1982a: 73-78, for references and detailed discussion). This test only considers differences in the relations respondents direct toward other actors, since differences in relations to respondents with the same attribute combination are identical by definition in 5.7. If the hypothesis of structurally equivalence is rejected, then the parameter set has not been correctly specified. In order to accurately differentiate statuses in the population, either more variables or more distinctions on the variables already specified are needed.[8]

Status Role-Sets

A status in the population social structure is jointly occupied by structurally equivalent actors, actors with similar relations to every other status and similar relations from those statuses. In terms of the parameter set, statuses are defined as structurally equivalent combinations of attributes; attribute combinations that are similarly the object of relations from respondents with each combination of attributes and that are found in respondents who have similar relations to each attribute combination.

Consider the interattribute relations defined by equation 5.7. The extent to which attribute combinations i't' and it are similarly the object of relations is given by the sum of squared differences in their respective column elements of Z_{QQ}; $d_c^2 = \Sigma_q(z_{q,i't'} - z_{q,it})^2$. The extent to which respondents with these two combinations of attributes have the same tendency to cite persons with each different attribute combination is given by the sum of squared differences in corresponding elements of rows in the matrix; $d_r^2 = \Sigma_q(z_{i't',q} - z_{it,q})^2$. A status can now be defined as a set of attribute combinations separated by zero distance; i.e., for all pairs of attribute combinations i't' and it proposed as defining the same status, $0 = d_{(i't',it)} = d_{(it,i't')} = (d_c^2 + d_r^2)^{1/2}$.

In fact, relations are likely to be measured with error so that some search procedure in the form of a computer algorithm will be needed in order to locate structurally equivalent attribute combinations. If Q is sufficiently small, standard network analysis algorithms can be employed. I have reviewed these elsewhere (Chapter 13, this volume). Also, the matrix F defined by 5.6 can be analyzed as a Q by Q frequency table in order to determine which categories can be collapsed into one another, e.g., Duncan, 1975; Goodman, 1979. When Q is very large, an iterative data analysis would be necessary (see next section).

Fortunately, statuses proposed by any algorithm can be statistically tested. Distances from each of the N respondents to the ersatz network position of each of the n_a respondents proposed as occupying S_a can be computed via equations 5.2 and 5.8. Under the hypothesis that these n_a actors are structurally equivalent as occupants of S_a, the (n_a, n_a) covariance matrix among distances to the n_a occupants will have a rank of one (e.g., Burt, 1982a: 73-78). Since the distances being correlated are computed for individual respondents, this test simultaneously assesses the extent to which status occupants with identical attributes are structurally equivalent and to which occupants with different attributes are structurally equivalent.

An (M,M) matrix of ersatz role relations can now be computed where M is the number of different statuses defined by the matrix Z_{QQ} and element (a,b) is the mean relation from occupants of status S_a to occupants of status S_b:

$$z_{ab} = \Sigma_{i't'} \Sigma_{it} (z_{(i't',it)}) (n_{i't'} n_{it}) / n_a n_b \qquad [5.9]$$

where z is defined by 5.7, $n_a = \Sigma_{i't'} (n_{i't'})$, $n_b = \Sigma_{it}(n_{it})$, and summation is across all attribute combinations i't' that define status S_a and all attribute

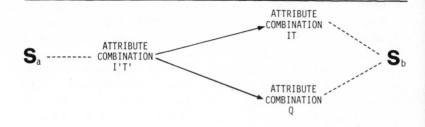

$$z_{ab} = \frac{z_{(i't', it)} n_{it} n_{i't'}}{n_a n_b} + \frac{z_{(i't', q)} n_q n_{i't'}}{n_a n_b}$$

$$n_a = n_{i't'}$$

$$n_b = n_{it} + n_q$$

Figure 5.3: The Relation from Status S_a to Status S_b in Terms of Relations Between Attribute Combinations (occupancy given by dashed lines and interatribute relations given by arrows, $z_{(i't', \; it)}$ illustrated in Figure 5.2, z_{ab} defined in equation 5.9)

combinations it that define S_b. Where $n_{i't'}$ and n_{it}, respectively, are the numbers of respondents with attribute combinations i't' and it, n_a and n_b, respectively, are the numbers of respondents occupying S_a and S_b. The density in 5.9 corresponds to that in 5.3, in the sense that both are average relations between sets of structurally equivalent actors. Building on Figure 5.2, Figure 5.3 illustrates the logic of the operation in 5.9 so as to be comparable to Figure 5.1 illustrating equation 5.3. Figures 5.1 and 5.3 differ in two ways. Figure 5.1 shows actors being mapped into unique statuses—each actor mapping into a single status, while Figure 5.3 shows actor attribute combinations being mapped— each attribute combination mapping into a single status. Second, Figure 5.1 shows each pair of actors being weighted equally in determining the interstatus relation, that weight being $1/n_a n_b$. It would not be appropriate to weigh attribute combinations equally in determining interstatus relations, since the combinations need not occur with equal frequency in the population. Therefore, equation 5.9 weights the pair of attribute combinations i't' and it by the extent to which they are observed in the sample; the extent to which all respondents in status S_a have attributes i't' ($n_{i't'}/n_a$), and the extent to which all respondents in status S_b have attributes it (n_{it}/n_b). Given the citations made by occupants of status S_a, z_{ab} in equation 5.9 is the mean proportion they give to occupants of S_b. The role-set defining S_a as an ersatz network position is now given by the 2M relations in row and column a of the density table defined by 5.9, as is the case in a typical network analysis (equation 5.4). With these data on status/role-sets for population social structure and data on the relational patterns for actors representative of population (equation 5.8), the wide range of hypotheses regarding network positions can be used to predict respondent attitudes and behaviors.

COMMENTS

I have argued that in theory, data obtained in a standard survey research design can be used to describe the network positions of each respondent in the social structure of a large population from which each is randomly drawn. Of course, these are ersatz representations of the positions typically captured by models of network structure. Relations to and from a respondent are not estimated with equal precision. As captured by 5.5, relations from a respondent to status occupants in the population are based on ties involving him personally. However, relations to him from status occupants are aggregate relations to his combination of attributes rather than to him personally (equation 5.7). Respondents with identical attributes are therefore the object of identical relations by fiat. This aggregate quality in equation 5.8 as a representation of a respondent's relational pattern makes it an ersatz representation of his pattern as it exists (equation 5.1). Its ersatz character notwithstanding, the availability of relational patterns defining respondent positions and statuses in large population social structures means that structural theory stated in terms of network concepts can be used to inform standard survey data.

Of course, theory and practice are not the same thing. I do not expect ersatz network positions to be used in practice in the same manner that I have introduced them in theory. In practice, a good deal of iterative data analysis will be required in order to specify the parameter set.

I have assumed that the Q attribute combinations specified as the parameter set for a population accurately distinguish statuses in the sense that each status in the population social structure corresponds to at least one of the Q attribute combinations. In practice, the variables defining these Q attribute combinations will be selected and coded according to hunches an investigator has about attributes likely to be associated with jointly occupied statuses in the population under study.

Since these hunches can be wrong, it is quite possible that a system's a priori specified parameter set is misspecified.

There is a serious problem with underspecifying the parameter set, i.e., failing to consider one or more attributes that actually do stratify the population. Some statuses in the final model would then refer to structurally nonequivalent actors. These actors stratified by deleted parameters would appear to be structurally equivalent (see note 8).

However, there is no problem with overspecifying the parameter set, i.e., including more attributes in the set than are actually necessary to distinguish population statuses. When in doubt about the importance of an attribute as what Blau terms a structural parameter, therefore, it is wisest to err on the side of including too many attributes rather than too few. These additional parameters will merely be deleted from the final model in much the same manner that insignificant predictors are deleted from a regression equation. If an attribute is negligible, it will not affect the structural equivalence of respondents; respondents homophilous on the attribute will be as likely to be structurally equivalent as are respondents heterophilous on the attribute. It might appear that overspecifying the parameter set would lead to problems in data processing. A necessary, but not sufficient, condition for Q increasing is an increasing number of distinctions in the parameter set. As more combinations of attributes become possible, more combinations could be observed in fact. Since the matrix of interattribute relations defined by 5.7 is a Q by Q matrix, overspecifying the parameter set could result in the matrix F (equation 5.6) and the matrix Z (equation 5.7) being too large to analyze with routine computer packages.

This potential problem is easily circumvented by iteratively analyzing the ersatz relational patterns in order to discover those combinations of attributes actually defining statuses. The ersatz network positions of respondents can be computed for each respondent (equation 5.8), where Q refers to all observed combinations of attributes in the possibly overspecified parameter set. The extent to which specific combinations are actually stratifying the population can now be tested by testing the structural equivalence of respondents homophilous on the combination. For example, suppose race is assumed to be the key variable stratifying a population under study, where race is coded into four attribute categories; Black, Asian, Chicano, and White. Under the hypothesis that race defines statuses in the population, respondents homophilous on the variable should be structually equivalent. Consider the Asian respondents. The hypothesis that all Asians are structurally equivalent can be statistically tested by computing the rank of the covariance matrix among distances to them from each respondent. If this hypothesis is rejected, then Asians are themselves stratified in terms of further attributes.

Either of the two strategies could be adopted in order to correctly respecify the attribute category "Asian." The investigator could guess at the missing attributes and then test the hypothesis that Asians homophilous on these further attributes are structurally equivalent. Alternatively, distances among the ersatz network positions of the Asians could be computed and subjected to an exploratory network analysis in order to locate structurally equivalent Asians. I have reviewed this work elsewhere (Burt, 1982a: chs. 2, 3). Given groups of structurally equivalent Asians, discriminant function analysis or one-way analysis of variance could be used to locate attributes most homophilous among structurally equivalent Asians (within groups) and most heterophilous between structurally nonequivalent Asians (across groups). Once a set of attributes has been located as the basis for stratification among Asians, the hypothesis of structural equivalence can be tested for each set of Asians homophilous in regard to each attribute combination. The same procedure could be repeated for the other racial groups. Of course, any attribute combination could be used as an initial parameter set, depending on one's initial hunches, some systems obviously being stratified by race, some being stratified by occupation, some being stratified by race and occupation jointly, and so on. By successively testing the structural equivalence of respondents homophilous on attributes in a tentative parameter set, attribute combinations actually stratifying the population can be uncovered.

In other words, the parameter set in terms of which ersatz network positions are estimated need not be known prior to conducting a survey (although all possible attributes in the set must be known), and there need not be a single parameter set distinguishing statuses in all subgroups of the population, e.g., Blacks, Asians, Chicanos, and Whites. Statuses in one subgroup might be defined by attributes different than those defining statuses in another subgroup. The parameter set for the population from which a specific sample has been drawn can be uncovered by iterative data analysis, first hypothesizing a specific parameter set, then testing the structural equivalence of respondents homophilous in regard to attribute combination distinguished in the set, then respecifying the initial parameter set so that it accurately defines structurally equivalent respondents.

NOTES

1. The phrase "distinct actors" is important here. If individual actors are aggregated in some manner so that the number of distinct actors being studied is small, then network

studies can be conducted on large populations such as actors in a community (Laumann, 1966; Laumann and Pappi, 1976: ch. 12; Burt et al., 1980), manufacturing establishments in the American economy (Pfeffer, 1972; Burt et al., 1980), or persons and corporations in the United States during the last century (Burt, 1975; Burt and Lin, 1977). This aggregation, of course eliminates the possibility of analyzing networks at the level of individual actors.

2. Specifically, the proportion of a network ignored by interviewing k percent of the actors in the network is: $1 - kN^2/N(N-1)$. As system size increases, the term $N^2/N(N-1)$ approaches 1, so the proportion ignored is roughly 1-k. To be sure, most of the relations in this network will be absent; a small number of residents are actually connected to any one resident (see Wellman, 1979). The problem is knowing where those few actual relations occur in the network as a whole.

3. It might seem that this argument can be turned back on theory based on structural equivalence, since, a priori to observing a system, one does not know who is structurally equivalent to whom. Once relations are observed, however, there are explicit conditions under which a set of actors are structurally equivalent occupants of a single position. At this point, falsifiable hypotheses are stated in terms of role-sets defining statuses. In contrast, the observation that a set of actors is homophilous in terms of one or more attributes as a surrogate for structural equivalence demonstrates no more than the fact that actors in the set share attributes. Thus, theory derived from attribute homophily is not deductive theory concerned with positions as statuses in social structure. It is deductive theory concerned with attribute homophily which can be extended with uncertainty (and thereby transformed into inductive theory) to hypotheses regarding positions in social structure.

4. In order to obtain more complete information on the link between respondent and the named persons, e.g., how did you meet this person, how long have you known this person, how often do you get together with this person, and so on, Fischer focuses on three to five of the persons cited by a respondent. The information required here is less extensive on each cited person, but is required for all persons cited.

5. I wish to make a special acknowledgement to James A. Wiley here for suggesting the ratio in equation 5.5 in lieu of an inelegant formulation I had used, based on the geometric mean.

6. At this point, multiple networks require special mention. The relation from respondent j to persons with attribute combination it across multiple networks can be given as: $z_{j,it} = (\Sigma_k f_{j,it,k})/(\Sigma_k r_{jk})$, where summation is across the K different networks (types of relations) in which citations are obtained, r_{jk} is the number of persons respondent j cites within network k, and $f_{j,it,k}$ is the number of those persons who have attribute combination it. As is typically done in multiple network models, each network is given equal weight. This representation further gives equal weight to the number of persons cited with attribute combination it and the number of different types of relations directed at that combination. If one person with attributes i and t is cited in regard to each type of relation (K citations), for example, the above relation would be the same as if K persons with attributes i and t were cited in regard to only one type of relation. Alternatively, it seems reasonable to estimate $z_{j,it}$ across multiple networks as the number of persons j cites who have attributes i and t divided by the total number of persons he cites. This measure has an uncomplicated substantive meaning as the proportion of j's ego network that has the attributes i and t. The above representation seems preferable, however, because a person who is a source of multiple types of exchanges should be a more significant part of j's network than a person who is a source for only one type of exchange (see Burt, 1982a, for references and further discussion).

7. Although equation 5.7 divides the frequency of citations made by the maximum possible, it is not—strictly speaking—a density measure, since it cannot take into account

the number of persons who could have possibly been cited. Equation 5.7 is quite correct as a proportion measure of relationship, but provides a biased density measure. If there are few actors in the population with attribute combination it, then there can be few citations to that attribute combination from any one respondent, so 5.7 will be low. In this case, a density measure of the same relation would adjust the mean upward by taking into account the few actors available to be cited. Similarly, 5.7 overestimates the density of citations to an attribute combination that is often observed in the population.

8. On the other hand, failure to reject the hypothesis of structural equivalence does not verify the parameter set as specified. If a significant attribute is deleted from the set, then respondents who differ only on the deleted attribute would appear to be structurally equivalent, when in fact they are not. As is the case when structural equivalence is tested in typical network studies, the equivalence of ersatz network positions can never be proven. Rather, it can only be rejected for a given set of relational patterns.

Chapter 6

Analyzing the Instrumental Use of Relations in the Context of Social Structure

NAN LIN, PAUL W. DAYTON, and PETER GREENWALD

Employing a variation of the small world technique for tracing social relations in the context of a larger social structure, the instrumental uses of social relations are examined in terms of the prestige and types of relations characteristic of participants in the search process. The results show that successful chains tend to involve participants of higher occupational prestige as the chains progress before "dipping" down toward the target prestige level at the last link. Also, the successful chains tend to utilize weak and infrequent social relations rather than strong and frequent ones.

The purpose of this discussion is to outline methodology and some findings in an analysis of what can be termed the "instrumental" uses of social relations in the context of macrolevel urban social structure. More detailed discussion of the points raised here, in particular with regard to the substantive implications of our findings, is given elsewhere (Lin et al., 1978). The methodology we have used is based on the "small world" technique. The reported findings are concerned with the manner in which an individual's prestige and relations within an urban social structure are used to affect his likelihood of successfully searching for a stranger in a social structure. The task of searching for a stranger is the goal of the "instrumental" use of relations, and the search procedure discussed below requires the use of social relations maintained by the respondents. When relations are being used instrumentally, we discuss them here as "instrumental relations."

Prestige is defined as an attribute or value attached to an actor's social position. Such attributes and values usually have normative

Author's Note: *An earlier version of this chapter was presented at the annual meetings of the American Sociological Association, 1976. The chapter benefited from Robert K. Merton's helpful comments on an earlier draft. The study was first published in* Sociological Methods & Research, *November, 1978.*

meanings for the rankings of the actors in a society. Central in the examination of the instrumental use of social relations is the test of heterophily-homophily (or, in this case, the "prestige" and "like-me") principle (Laumann, 1966; Laumann and Senter, 1976; Rogers and Bhowmik, 1970). The limited empirical evidence on hand suggests that the "prestige" principle tends to operate in instrumental relations; actors seek out others whose statuses are higher in prestige for instrumental reasons. Granovetter's (1974: 7) work on the strength of weak ties, for example, suggests that, at least among the professional, technical, and managerial workers he studied, actors in job-seeking activities bypass strong ties with people having presumably similar or adjacent statuses as the actors themselves to seek contacts with weak ties with people having presumably dissimilar statuses.

In addition to the respondent's use of prestige, itself derivative from relations in the urban social structure, is his or her direct use of the relations themselves. Prescribed relations include kinship ties which are either consanguineous or affinal. Constructed relations include friends, co-workers, and so forth. Indicators of social relations here include types of contacts (relatives, friends, or acquaintances) and strength of contacts (frequency and recency of contacts). These social relations can be considered a respondent's "resources" in the sense that they provide a means for reaching the goal of a stranger within the respondent's geographical area. Types of relations as resources are to be expected to interact with respondent prestige. Based on the above-cited work on heterophily-homophily and strong-weak ties, the instrumental use of relations should follow a weak tie principle when "prestige" principle holds for a social status. In other words, instrumental relations should tend to occur among weak ties for the actors ocupying the status; i.e., among contacts who are not intimately related to the actors or who are not the actor's frequent or recent contacts. On the other hand, when the "like-me" or homophily principle holds for a social status, the reverse linkage should be true. In this latter case instrumental relations should tend to occur among strong ties for the status occupants, i.e., among contacts who are intimately related to the actors and/or who are in frequent and recent contact with the actors.

THE SMALL WORLD TECHNIQUE

The small world technique maps chains of communications by tracing the forwarding processes involved in the delivery of a packet to a described target person. In this technique, a target is selected and described (name, address, age, sex, occupation, and so on) in a packet which is then sent to a starter. The starter is asked to send the packet

either directly to the target (if the target is an acquaintance
or to a person who may know the target or a friend of tl
keeping track of the persons (links) who send and receive
until the packet either successfully reaches the target or tel...ninates, it
becomes possible to gather data on the intermediaries as well as the
starters and to map the communication flow and the characteristics of
the participants.

The small world technique has been used to forward packets to a
target in one part of the country, Boston, from starters in another part of
the country, Nebraska (Milgram, 1967). In the past, this technique has
helped estimate the average number of links in chains which successfully
forwarded the packets to the target (about 7, including the starter and
the target) and the probability of reaching the targets (about 25-30
percent of the packets), and so forth.

For our purposes, the small world techniques is useful for examining
the instrumental task of searching for a stranger vis a vis the prestige and
relational characteristics of the participants. For example, Korte and
Milgram (1970) found that in the searching task, participants
immediately preceding the targets tended to have higher prestige than
the targets. They also found that when the starter group was
predominantly white, a white target had a greater likelihood of being
reached than a black target. Similarly, Milgram (1967) and Beck and
Cadamagnani (1968) found that participants tend to send packets to
persons of similar sex. Travers and Milgram (1969) found that selection
of the next link is differentiated in terms of acquaintance and friendhip,
resident of the target, and occupation of the target.

STUDY DESIGN

Our methodology differs from previous small world investigations in
several respects. First and most importantly, it employs the small world
technique as a means to examine the instumental uses of prestige and
social relations, rather than to describe the success rate of reaching the
targets and its correlates or to ascertain the uses of the technique as a
tool for inferring the entire interpersonal network. To do so, we selected
a study site within one urbanized area, rather than cross-country as is
the usual case in such studies. We assumed that restricting both starters
and targets to the same urbanized community would mean that most of
the forwarding activities would take place within the same area and that
the mapping would therefore approximate the networks within and
across certain socioeconomic strata. The study site selected was a tri-city
area in the Northeast, classified as a single urbanized area by the U.S.
Census Bureau.

The target characteristics and the pack information describing the targets is controlled and manipulated. Both male and female, as well as white and black targets, were used. The four types of targets were selected and matched in terms of their length of residence in the community, age, marital status, and social involvement (participation in religious and civic activities). However, the targets were cross-classified on the variables of sex and race; namely, the four targets were white-male, black-male, and white-female, and black-female. This enables us to ascertain the effect these major ascribed statuses have on communication flow. All four targets resided in one of the three cities in the tri-city area.

For each target, information in the packets regarding his/her race and occupation was varied: (1) race and occupation of the target both given, (2) race but not occupation of the target given, (3) occupation, but not race of the target given, and (4) neither race nor occupation of the target given.

This appears to be the first empirical small world study in which the target characteristics and packet types are experimentally controlled and manipulated for the purpose of investigating the effect of prestige and social relations on the communication flow. The effects of target characteristics and packet information on the searching task has been reported elsewhere (Lin et al., 1977).[1] It is probably also the first such study conducted in a single urban area.

DATA COLLECTION

A random sample of the households in the largest city of the tri-city area (different from the one in which the targets resided) was drawn from the city directory. A letter soliciting participation in the study was sent to each household, with an attached business reply postcard to indicate whether the head of the household, the spouse, or both would be willing to participate as starters in the study. The final list of starter households included the first 300 voluntary households whose returned postcards reached us. The starter group is therefore not necessarily representative of the city households—to obtain such a sample would be prohibitively expensive and would call for involuntary participation. Analysis showed that the voluntary participants are of slightly higher social status than the population in the area, with ethnic minorities underrepresented. This trend is consistent with earlier findings of relationships between social class and voluntary participation in a small world study (Beck and Cadamagnani, 1968).

Past research found that the success rate (number of packets reaching the target over the number of packets initiated) in American communities ran about 25-30 percent. Given 300 volunteers, we anticipated that about 60 percent would actually initiate (start), or about 180 volunteers would forward the packets. If each volunteer were to send one packet, the anticipated number of successful packets (namely $180 \times .30$) would have been between 50 and 60 packets. Since there were 16 packet types involved, the anticipated number of successful packets for each type would have been reduced to 3 or 4 packets—much too small a number for comparative analysis. It was therefore decided that each volunteer would receive two packets describing two different targets. The 300 volunteers received 600 packets, and each packet type was delivered to 37 or 38 volunteers. The usual success rate should result in at least 6 successes for each packet type.

The decision to send two packets to each volunteer raised several conceptual and methodological issues. First, would this cause the volunteer to forward both packets indiscriminately? For example, would the volunteer send both packets to the same next link? Table 6.1 examines this possibility by analyzing the volunteers' forwarding behavior and shows that 92 percent of the started packets were sent to different persons initially.[2]

The packet sent to each volunteer identified the sponsoring university and department on the cover. Attached to the inside of the cover page were 10 stamps and address labels to be used on the envelope to forward the packet. The next page consisted of a roster of the names and addresses (city and state) of those who had previously forwarded the packet. A description of the projects preceded the description of the target. Described characteristics of the target included: name, address, marital status, number of children, first name of spouse, religion and church affiliation, social and professional organization affiliations, and education (school and year). Depending on the packet type, information on race and/or occupation (including name and location of employer) was not provided. The next three pages gave the detailed procedure for participation. On the inside backcover page were stapled 10 business reply postcards. Each sender was requested to detach a postcard, fill it out, and send it to the investigator. The postcard contained a brief questionnaire requesting information about the sender and the person he was sending it to (next link). For the sender, the information included name, address, education of self and spouse, occupation of self and spouse, age, sex, race, number of years residing in the community, number of affiliated clubs and organizations, and number of persons

TABLE 6.1   Forwarding Behavior of Initial Volunteers

	Percentage of volunteers (N = 298)		*Percentage of packets sent (N = 596)*	
Sent neither	35	(104)	——————	
Sent one	4	(13)	2	(13)
Sent two to the same person	5	(14)	5	(28)
Sent two to different persons at the same address	1	(3)	1	(6)
Sent two to different addresses	55	(164)	55	(328)

known on a first-name basis (best guess). For the next link, information requested included name, address, occupation, age, sex, race, date when the sender last saw the intended receiver, nature of relationship between the sender and the receiver, and reasons for selecting the receiver.

As soon as each postcard was received, information was entered into a computer file for both the sender and receiver, each sender being identified as an observation. A week after each observation was entered in the file, a search was made to ascertain whether the intended receiver had returned the postcard—whether the intended receiver had been entered as an observation. If not, a follow-up note was sent to the intended receiver, reminding him of the packet which was forwarded to him and requesting his participation.

In the event that participants needed additional stamps, address labels, or postcards or had any questions regarding the study, they were asked to contact the investigator by phone.

In the end only 3 chains exceeded 10 links, requiring additional materials, and relatively few persons called for clarification of the procedure.

As shown in Table 6.1, of 596 packets sent to the 298 volunteers, 375 packets were forwarded. Of the 375 packets initiated, 112 packets successfully reached the targets within four and a half months when the field work was terminated. The result was a completion rate of 30 percent, slightly higher than response rates reported in previous small world studies conducted in communities.

MEASUREMENT

Prestige was indexed by Siegel's (1971) occupational prestige scale. For participants without regular occupation, but with the wage earner of the household (the spouse) not retired or unemployed, the occupational prestige of the spouse was used to estimate the relative prestige of the participant. This decision was made in order not to exclude a large number of female participants from the data analysis. Also, it was felt that the prestige of a nonworking participant is, to a substantial extent, affected by the wage-earning spouse.

It must be pointed out that while an effort was made to find targets with matched characteristics (with the exception of sex and race, which were controlled), the effort was not entirely successful in terms of their occupational statuses. The white female target had a higher occupational prestige than the other three targets (the occupational prestige scores were 40, 52, 35, and 42, respectively for the white male, white female, black male, and black female targets.) The four targets were all middle-aged (37-47), married, high school graduates, and Protestant with annual incomes ranging from \$8,000 to \$12,500.

DATA ANALYSIS

This study identified positions and chains. Two types of positions were examined: the terminal and nonterminal positions. The terminal position is one in a chain leading to either the target as the next link in the chain or another person who failed to forward the packet further. Thus, the terminal person represents the final forwarding participant in the chain. The nonterminal position is one in a chain which forwarded the packet to another nontarget participant, who eventually forwarded the packet to at least one other participant. Thus, each participant at each link could be classified as either a terminal or nonterminal participant.

Two types of chains were also identified: the successful chain and the unsuccessful chain. A successful chain consists of all the participants linked by a single packet leading successfully to the defined target. An unsuccessful chain consists of all the participants linked by a single packet which did not reach the defined target within the period of time allowed.

Thus, at each link, four types of participants could be identified: (1) the successful terminals, (2) the successful nonterminals, (3) the unsuccessful terminals, and (4) the unsuccessful nonterminals.

Table 6.2 presents the frequency counts of participants defined by the type of the position and the chain and by the link in the chain. The average length of the successful chains involved four intermediary links between the starter and the target. By the sixth link, the probability of chains staying alive was reduced to 12 percent and the probability of eventual successful terminations (reaching the target) was reduced to 12 percent.

TABLE 6.2   Frequency of Participation by Type of Participant and Position (Link) in Chain

Link	Type of Participants			
(Intermediary)	Successful Chains		Unsuccessful Chains	
	Terminals	Nonterminals	Terminals	Nonterminals
0 (starters)	0	112	90	173
1	6	106	60	113
2	21	85	30	83
3	29	56	23	60
4	17	39	20	40
5	13	26	11	29
6	12	14	10	19
7	8	6	10	9
8	2	4	5	4
9	1	3	4	0
10	2	1	0	0
11	1	0	0	0

Because of the the low probabilities of continuation and successful termination beyond the sixth link and of the low reliability of aggregated data because of the small number of participants, the subsequent analayses were limited to the first seven links in each chain— the starter and the first six links. Since all analyses are based on comparisons of the seven links, there are too few categories for meaningful statistical inference. While nonparametric analysis is possible (e.g., the sign test or the rank-order test), we would rather entrust testing the substantive validity of the research findings to future replications using the same technique and to cross-method replications from other types of studies of the instrumental uses of social relations.

The Use of Prestige

The status variable examined was the occupational prestige of the participants. Recall that the occupational prestige of the targets ranged from the middle 30s to the low 50s, with an average of about 42. Two strategies were available to participants in an effort to reach the targets in the specific occupational status strata: either to forward the packet to someone whose status was similar to the target's or to forward it to someone whose status was much dissimilar to the target's. The former strategy would indicate the operation of the homophily (or "like-me")

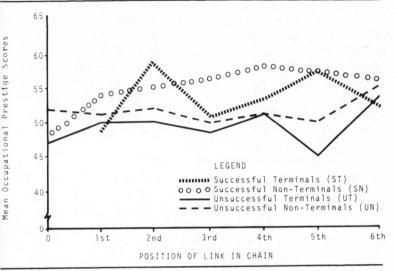

Figure 6.1: Occupational Prestige by Position in Chain for the Four Types of Chains

principle and the latter the heterophily (or "prestige") principle. As shown in Figure 6.1, the starters tend to have higher occupational prestige than the targets. The participants in the successful chains and the unsuccessful chains are distinguished quite clearly in that the former, especially the nonterminals, tended to forward the packets to others higher in prestige than themselves and much higher than the targets. The latter, on the other hand, tended to forward the packets to persons occupying statuses of prestige similar to their own (note the different patterns of the two nonterminal lines.)

Two explanations can be proposed for the different patterns in Figure 6.1; either the participants in the successful chain were themselves of high occupational prestige, thus having the capability of reaching persons of even higher prestige, or they made a more conscientious effort to choose persons of higher prestige. The first explanation must be rejected by the fact that among the starters, participants in the successful chains did not have higher prestige than those in the unsuccessful chain. In fact, the group with the highest occupational prestige were the unsuccessful nonterminal starters. Thus the participants in the successful chains would probably not have had better access to others of high occupational prestige. The second explanation, that the participants made a more conscientious effort to reach up, seems more plausible. The data suggest the operation of the "prestige" principle in successful instrumental relations.

Why, then, does the strategy of reaching up to higher status tend to lead to success in the searching task? One clue provided by past research is that as social prestige increases, the extensiveness and heterogeneity of the actor's social contacts also increases (Shotland, 1970; Lin, Ensel, et al., 1981; Lin, Vaughn, et al., 1981). *If a given social structure is viewed a pyramidal, then the higher the prestige of an actor's position in the pyramid, the more panoramic view he has of the structure, especially the levels below him.* Thus, as the packet is forwarded upward on the pyramid, the likelihood of eventually locating the target with a relatively low position is increased.

This suggestion is further confirmed by the patterns exhibited between the nonterminals and terminals of the successful chains. With the exception of the first two steps (the starter and the first link), the occupational prestige of the nonterminal tended to be higher than that of the terminals of the next link. For example, the successful nonterminals at the second link had higher occupational prestige than the successful terminals at the third link. The "dipping" relationship between the nonterminals and the subsequent terminals in the successful chains holds consistently from the second link on. It suggests that the up-the-status-slope effort paid off when the packet reached a participant of sufficiently high prestige to be able to identify someone below himself and to be certain that this someone could deliver the packet to the target. Only then did the forwarding take a dip on the pyramidal slope.

The Use of Social Relations

The second series of variables concerns the participants' social relations. First examined was the extent of social contacts, as indicated by the number of friends each participant claimed to have. The data can only be considered as rough outlines of patterns, in view of the great variability of the distribution. However, as shown in Figure 6.2, the general pattern is clear: the participants in the successful had more contacts than those in the unsuccessful chains. The differences became quite clear beyond the third link in the chains.

Does the extensity of social contacts imply that participants in the successful chains will forward the packets to someone they intimately know? Past literature on the extensity versus intensity of social relations (Laumann, 1973), as well as the strength of weak ties (Liu and Duff, 1972; Granovetter, 1973, 1974) suggests that weak ties or extensive ties rather than strong or intensive ties are more useful in obtaining new information, such as searching for a job. In light of the finding that the prestige principle operates for instrumental use of prestige, it was expected that weak ties would contribute more to the likelihood of

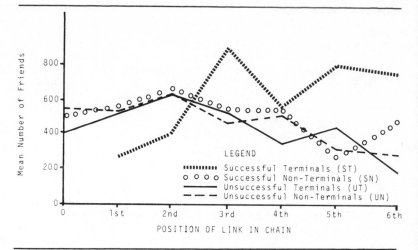

Figure 6.2: Number of Friends by Position in Chain for the Four Types of Chains

instrumental success. To determine the extent to which this principle applies to the search task defined for the participants, we examined the recency of last contact between each participant and the person next in the chain ("How many days ago did you last see this person?"). Figure 6.3 presents the data for the four groups of participants.

In general, the participants in successful chains tended to forward the packets to persons of less recent contact, as compared to those in the unsuccessful chains (note the consistent patterns between the two nonterminal lines and the terminal lines). The successful strategy was to reach persons who were not strong ties to the senders but were thought to have access to extensive social relations. In other words, the participants (nonterminals) in the successful chains tended to turn to weak ties (see the successful terminal line in Figure 6.3). These successful terminals uniformly have a large reservoir of social relations (note the mean number of friends for the successful terminals in Figure 6.2) and were able to reach the targets, even though they had only weak ties with the targets.

To verify the hypothesis that weak ties were more useful, we examined the relations between each pair of consecutive links in each chain. Each sender was asked to indicate the relationship between himself and the persons to whom he forwarded the packet. We computed the percentage of mentions of strong ties (relatives, friends, neighbors) and present the results in Figure 6.4. The patterns confirmed the strength of weak ties. For both nonterminals and terminals, *the participants in the successful chains tended to utilize fewer strong ties in*

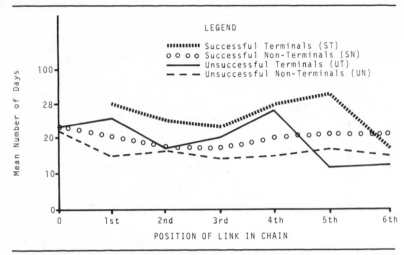

Figure 6.3: Recency of Last Contact with Next Person in Chain, by Position in Chain for the Four Types of Chains

their forwarding effort. The successful terminals dramatically showed that they had weak ties with the targets.

COMMENTS

A methodological question arising from the reported study has to do with making inferences based on data generated from a small world study. Ideally, an examination of the social relations should map (1) all members, (2) overall ties, (3) those involving free and unlimited choices, (4) over all relevant characteristics or criteria, and (5) for representative sampled structures of that society. Being realistic, however, we must proceed to modify these ideal conditions in order to collect data for furthering theoretical work. Social scientists have made modifications in the (1) restriction on the size of the group, (2) restriction on the number of choices, (3) restriction on the characteristics or criteria used, and (4) restriction on the number of structures studied. In most cases of large-scale relational studies, all the above restrictions are applied with varying degrees. For larger social systems, "pseudo-networks" are constructed. These include: (1) forward tracing (e.g., snowball sampling), (2) backward tracing (e.g.,adoption of innovations), and (3) anypoint tracing (e.g., random walk and news diffusion). Erickson (1978) has considered the shortcomings of all these modifications. The

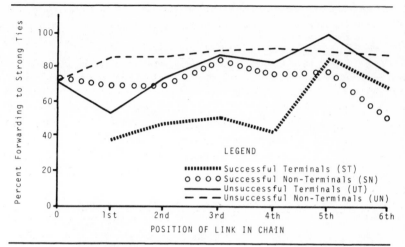

Figure 6.4:   Strength of Tie with Next Person by Position in Chain for the Four
Types of Chains

small world technique we have used restricts the number of choices (in
fact, each participant, except the starter, has only one choice). However,
it has no restriction on the size of the group studied (be it a city or a
country), on the characteristics or criteria used for choosing (in fact, the
freely chosen criteria by the participants constituted the central focus of
analysis in the reported study), or on the boundary of the relations (there
were a couple of chains in our study which extended to several states
before they returned to the research site.)

Given these limitations, generalization of any finding must be
confirmed with data from the other small world studies (method-
specific validity) and from other types of studies (multimethod validity).
Our findings are consistent with those from all small world studies
available to us. We are encouraged by similar results uncovered with
other methodologies such as surveys and direct observation (e.g.,
Laumann, 1966, 1973; Granovetter, 1973, 1974).

NOTES

1. Suffice it here to indicate that for the mostly white participants, it was easier to
reach female than male targets, white rather than black targets, and participants with
higher occupational status. It was theorized that critical communication flows downward,
that social status is positively related to the ability to search the status hierarchy, and that

social status is negatively related to the willingness to manipulate social resources in communication flow toward a person of relatively low social status.

2. That is, the total number of packets sent was $(13) + (14 \times 2) + (3 \times 2) + (164 \times 2) = 375$, and the total number of packet sent by each starter to two different persons was $(13) + (3 \times 2) + (164 \times 2) = 347$. However, this does not mean that all next links were different persons. Different senders could send packets to the same persons. In fact, as the packets approached the targets, fewer and fewer persons would be involved as receivers. This funneling phenomenon was discussed by Korte and Milgram (1970).

Chapter 7

Network Data from Informant Interviews

RONALD S. BURT

Relations between actors can be inferred from interviews with a small number of strategically chosen informants. This chapter is a methodological discussion of gathering and assessing the adequacy of the resultant network data. The methods are described with respect to comparative network analyses of community power. Drawing on interviews with a handful of informants within each of 51 American cities during the late 1960s, the network data are shown to be efficient, reliable, and substantively valid despite their low cost.

At some point in planning any research project, a compromise is made between the extremes of a case study—describing one unit of analysis in great detail—and a comparative analysis of many cases in relatively little detail. These extremes are nicely illustrated with respect to structural analyses in two traditions of research on community power— one in which individual communities are studies in detail, and a second tradition in which many communities are studied relative to one another.

Most, if not all, community researchers would agree that the study of a community's power structure is best accomplished when data are available on the multiple networks of relations among significant actors in the community (where significant actors could be individuals, groups, or formal organizations). Intensive studies of community power such as Hunter's (1953) analysis of Atlanta, Banfield's (1961) analysis of Chicago, Dahl's (1961) analysis of New Haven, or Laumann and Pappi's (1976) analysis of Julich all rely on extensive information on multiple relations among significant community actors.

Author's Note: *This research was facilitated by grant SOC77-22938 from the National Science Foundation. Research assistance in various stages of the work was provided by the University of Chicago by J. Orthman and R. Roman, and the University of California, Berkeley, by M. G. Fischer, and at the State University of New York, Albany, by K. Lieben. Portions of this chapter were presented in 1979 at a "Conference on Comparative Urban Policy Research" coordinated by Terry N. Clark at the University of Chicago, in 1979 at the East-West Center's "Seminar of Communication Network Analysis" coordinated by D. Lawrence Kincaid, in 1977 at the American Sociological Association's seminar on "Comparative Analyses of Metropoli" coordinated by Herman Turk at the*

Recent work has compromised the substantive richness of these studies in order to enhance the generalizability of research findings. The structure of relations among actors in a community is summarized in a single score—that is, a matrix of ties is expressed as a scalar—measuring some significant structural property in terms of which communities can be informatively compared. This scalar usually corresponds in some manner to centralization or hierarchy within a community. In order to access the effect of community decision-making structure on community policy, for example, Clark (1971) analyzes the network of ties among community actors as a score measuring "decentralization" in community decision making. In a similarly pace-setting study, Turk (1970) analyzes the network of relations among a community's corporate actors as a centralization score calculated from the incidence of communitywide civic associations. Related to these efforts are analyses of community power in terms of its concentration in the hands of a minority of community actors. For example, Smith (1976) and Lincoln (1976) utilize Hawley's (1963) "MPO ratio" as an index of the extent to which power over a community's labor force is concentrated in the hands of a small number of managers, proprietors, and officials (MPO). Smith finds that communities in which power is concentrated tend to enact communitywide, as opposed to special interest, policies. Lincoln finds a strong association across communities in power concentration and the ability of a community to mobilize so as to act on community policy. Different from these studies in number of dimensions of community structure, if not in spirit, Grimes et al. (1976) describe community structure in their review of comparative research on community leadership in terms of a score on each of three dimensions: centralization, visibility, and legitimacy.

The wide range of comparative studies illustrated by these examples has enabled community research to escape the lack of generalizability characteristic of the earlier case study research. In the process—and this is the reason for some researchers returning to the earlier case study approach (e.g., Laumann and Pappi, 1973: 213)—community research has lost the substantive richness of its early descriptions of the network structure of power.

University of Chicago, and in 1975 with Terry N. Clark at the annual meetings of the American Sociological Association. The informant data for the 51 cities in the Permanent Community Sample were kindly provided by Terry Clark, and the discussion benefited from his comments on initial drafts. For their comments on previous drafts, I am also grateful to J. Galaskiewicz, D. Knoke, P. V. Marsden, H. Turk, and several anonymous referees. This chapter has been abstracted from material appearing in Human Organization *and* Social Science Research *(Burt et al., 1980; Burt, 1981b).*

Designing research to bridge the gap between the substantive richness of case studies and the generalizability of comparative structural analyses is yet another problem in applied network analysis. The problem is one of engineering more than theory, of tactics more than strategy. Cost is the key; cost in time, in data collection, and in data analysis. Network data are extremely expensive to collect using traditional sociometric or other interpersonal methodologies. In order to accomplish across a large number of communities what Hunter or Dahl accomplished in their case studies, significant resources would be required to gather data (not to mention the subsequent costs of data analysis). A thorough structural analysis of a single community with population less than 50,000 can easily cost two or three years of research time and tens of thousands of research dollars. It is quite simply impractical to contemplate extending this case study research design to a large sample comparative study.

My purpose in this chapter is to propose one method of circumventing the data collection impediment to large sample, comparative structural analyses. Short interviews with two to five informants in a community should be sufficient to infer the "ersatz" network structure of power in the community. Considering the low cost of these ersatz power structures, they are surprisingly efficient, reliable, and substantively valid—judging from the results reported here using interviews with up to seven informants in each of 51 communities representative of American places of residence in the late 1960s. This is not to say that the proposed ersatz structures could ever replace the detailed information obtained in a case study. While too limited for a case study network analysis such as those conducted by Hunter (1953) or Laumann and Pappi (1976), the data are far richer than the usual scalar measures typically employed in comparative studies. It is in the spirit of compromising between generalizable (but grossly simplified) comparative analyses and substantively rich (but nongeneralizable and prohibitively expensive) case studies that the ersatz structures seem promising. I first define relation in an ersatz network, describe the ersatz network data obtained in the sample American cities, discuss the sampling variability, the reliability and validity of the data, and close with comments on selecting informants.

NETWORK STRUCTURE REFLECTED IN INFORMANT PERCEPTIONS

Suppose that a single informant in one community is interviewed and asked to evaluate the control different types of actors in the community have over the outcome of a specific issue. Is the support of the Democratic party essential for determining the outcome of a municipal bond referendum? Is the support of the leading newspapers essential for determining such a referendum? A leading network structure of power in the community—as perceived by this one informant in regard to the one issue considered—could be studied now in terms of two kinds of variables. To the extent that a type of actor (e.g., the Democratic party) exercises control over the outcome of an issue in the community, an informant should perceive the actor as powerful. The more that a pair of actors (e.g., the Democratic party and the leading newspapers) oppose or support one another in controlling the issue outcome, the more likely that an informant should perceive the two actors as simultaneously powerful. This interview can be extended to multiple issues (Q), multiple actors (N), and repeated with multiple informants (K) so as to increase the adequacy of estimation. An (N,N) symmetric matrix, Z, representing the community's power structure could be generated as the weighted sum of each informant's perceptions in regard to each issue:

$$Z = \{z_{ij}\} = \left\{ \sum_{k=1}^{K} p_k \left[\sum_{q=1}^{Q} p_q (m_{ikq} m_{jkq})^{\frac{1}{2}} \right] \right\} \qquad [7.1]$$

where m_{jkq} is informant k's perception of the control of actor j over the outcome of issue q. If signed ratings are requested from informants with m_{jkq} being positive if k perceives j as supporting q, negative if he perceives the actor as opposed to the issue, then positive z_{ij} could indicate support between actors i and j, while negative z_{ij} could indicate opposition. The weights p_k and p_q, respectively, assign relative importance to informants and issues so that the Z in one community can be compared to those in other communities.

The jth diagonal element, z_{jj}, would be high—greater than 0.0, close to 1.0—to the extent that all informants perceive actor j as controlling all community issues. While any set of persons, formal organizations, or informal collectivities (e.g., ethnic groups) could be treated as an actor, equation 7.1 is based on the assumption that each actor j refers to a single structural position in each community to be compared. In other words, persons and groups aggregated into a single actor for equation 7.1 are assumed to be structurally equivalent in all communities in the sense of having similar relations with other actors in their community (see Chapter 13, this volume, for details on structural equivalence). Failure to meet this assumption means that the ersatz network elements are obscuring distinct relations in a community (see Chapter 8, this volume, for more detailed discussion).

An off-diagonal element, z_{ij}, would be high to the extent that all informants perceived actors j and i as controlling all community issues. This element could be low for either of two reasons: (1) actor j or actor i is perceived by all informants as having no control over any community issues; (2) informants differ in their perception of who controls specific issues, such that some informants perceive actor j as controlling some community issues, while other informants perceive actor i as controlling those isues, or most informants perceive actors i and j as controlling different community issues.

The manner in which z_{ij} captures a relation between actors i and j is thus quite indirect. Actors i and j are not being assessed in terms of their power over one another, nor are they being assessed in terms of their relative control over valuable community resources, nor are they being assessed in terms of their relations with one another. A review and discussion of these approaches to describing power is given elsewhere (Burt, 1977a). Actors j and i are being assessed here in terms of their tendency to be perceived by the same informants as powerful in regard to the same issues, the inference being that persons controlling the same issues are more likely to have relations with one another than persons controlling different issues. In this sense, the z_{ij} as network elements are clearly inferior to the usually sociometric-type data and deserve to be discussed as ersatz network elements.

Nevertheless, data similar to those generated by equation 7.1 have been the basis for previous structural analyses. Interviewing a sample of community residents concerning their willingness to trust each of the most elite persons in the community, the network of associations among the elite has been studied in terms of the extent to which pairs of elites are trusted to the same extent by the same groups of community residents (Laumann and Pappi, 1976: 217-253).[1] Focusing on "interorganizational leaders" as persons holding high positions in four or more community organizations, Perrucci and Pilisuk (1970) build on earlier work (Freeman, 1968) to describe power in the community as a network of associations between pairs of interorganizational leaders, leaders being connected to the extent that they hold positions in the same organizations.

Case study precedents notwithstanding, the data generated by equation 7.1 are ersatz network data in a strict sense and will be discussed as such here. In order to assess the adequacy of the ersatz network data, I have drawn on interviews conducted with informants in the well-known Permanent Community Sample.

ERSATZ POWER STRUCTURES IN AMERICAN COMMUNITIES

In January of 1967, personal interviews were conducted with informants in 51 communities representative of American places of residence (Clark, 1968: 463-478, 1971; Rossi and Crain, 1968). In each community, interviews were conducted with up to seven informants regarding fifteen types of potentially significant actors and their control over five issues. For equation 7.1, these data have the following parameters: $N = 15$, $K = 7$, and $Q = 5$. The actors were selected so as to represent the different sectors of a community likely to be involved in resolving one or more of the five issues (see Table 7.1).[2] The five issues (school board election, air pollution project, municipal bond referendum, urban renewal project, and mayoral election) were chosen to represent significant issues during the late 1960s that activated different sectors of a community (Clark, 1971: 296-297). The seven informants (head of the chamber of commerce, head of the labor council, publisher/editor of leading newspaper, head of bar association, head of Democratic party, head of Republican party, leading banker) represented different community sectors and described actor power as:

$$m_{jkq} = \begin{cases} 1.0, \text{ if support from actor j is perceived by informant k as essential for} \\ \quad \text{successfully determining issue q,} \\ 0.5, \text{ if support from actor j is perceived by informant k as important} \\ \quad \text{but not essential for successfully determining issue q,} \\ 0.0, \text{ if support from actor j is perceived by informant k as unimportant} \\ \quad \text{for successfully determining issue q.} \end{cases}$$

Of the total set of 357 interviews (7 informants in 51 communities), all but 31 informants were contacted (96 percent). The completion rate for interviews was unequal across communities and well below the overall contact rate.[3] In order to take these intercommunity differences into account, the weights in equation 7.1 have been set equal to one over the number of observations made in a community. In a community with seven informants discussing five issues, for example, $p_k = 1/7$ and $p_q = 1/5$.

Interpretations of the ersatz network elements are now defined. The score z_{jj} will equal one if all informants perceive support from actor j to be essential for determining the outcomes of all five issues. The score z_{ji} will be one if all informants perceive support from both actors i and j to be essential for determining the outcome of all five issues. This score will be close to zero to the extent that informants perceive support from actors i and j to be essential for determining the outcomes of different issues (some determined by actor i, while others are determined by actor j) or informants vary in their perception of actors i and j (some perceiving actor i as determining community issues, while others perceive actor j as determining community issues).

As a heuristic example, consider three actors (newspapers, Democratic party, chamber of commerce) as perceived by two informants concerning two issues. Informant 1 perceives support from the Democratic party and newspapers to be essential for determining issue 1 but unimportant for determining issue 2, and perceives support from the chamber of commerce to be essential for determining issue 2 but unimportant for issue 1. Where rows 1, 2, and 3 of Z refer to newspapers, Democratic party, and chamber of commerce, respectively, informant 1 perceives the following structures in issues 1 and 2 respectively:

$$\begin{bmatrix} 1 & 1 & 0 \\ & 1 & 0 \\ & & 0 \end{bmatrix} \text{ and } \begin{bmatrix} 0 & 0 & 0 \\ & 0 & 0 \\ & & 1 \end{bmatrix}$$

Informant 2 also perceives support from the Democratic party and newspapers to be essential for determining the first issue. In addition, this informant perceives their support to be important, although not essential, for determining issue 2. Informant 2's perception of the power of the chamber of commerce is the same as informant 1's perception. Informant 2 therefore perceives the following structures in issues 1 and 2, respectively:

$$\begin{bmatrix} 1 & 1 & 0 \\ & 1 & 0 \\ & & 0 \end{bmatrix} \text{ and } \begin{bmatrix} .5 & .5 & .7 \\ & .5 & .7 \\ & & 1. \end{bmatrix}$$

Across the two issues and two informants, the following (3,3) matrix Z is given by equation 7.1:[4]

$$Z = \begin{bmatrix} .63 & .63 & .18 \\ & .63 & .18 \\ & & .50 \end{bmatrix} \begin{array}{l} \text{newspapers} \\ \text{Democratic party} \\ \text{chamber of commerce} \end{array}$$

This structure indicates that all three actors tend to be powerful; all three z_{ij} are .5 or more. The Democratic party and community newspapers, however, tend to be powerful to the same extent and over the same issues, issues which are different from those over which the chamber of commerce is powerful. The different issues over which the actors are powerful are indicated by z_{12} being .63, while the associations between the chamber of commerce with the other two actors, z_{13} and z_{23}, are much lower: .18.

Although signed ratings were not obtained from informants in the 51 cities, there is heuristic value in considering how the z_{ij} might differ if such data had been obtained. Suppose the ratings solicited from informants, the m_{jkq}, had been 1, .5, 0, -.5 and -1, where positive values indicate actor j's support for an issue outcome, while negative values indicate the actor's opposition to the issue outcome. The rating m_{jkq} would have the same relative meaning it is given above, but it would have the additional meaning of opposition or support.

Referring to the above hypothetical example, suppose that both informants perceived the chamber of commerce to be the principal source of support for issue 1 against opposition from newspapers and the Democratic party. Suppose further that both informants perceived newspapers and the Democratic party as supporting issue 2 against opposition from the chamber of commerce. In this case, there would be no change in informant 1's perception of community power from the structure given above; the chamber of commerce and the other two actors are not perceived as being powerful in regard to the same issues. Informant 2's perceptions would be changed, but only with respect to issue 1, which would now be perceived as:

$$\begin{bmatrix} .5 & .5 & -.7 \\ & .5 & -.7 \\ & & 1. \end{bmatrix}$$

where $.5 = (.5 \times .5)^{1/2}$, $1 = (-1 \times -1)^{1/2}$, and $-.7 = -1[(.5 \times 1)^{1/2}]$. Note that the square root of a negative product is only taken with respect to the magnitude of the product, leaving the negative sign to indicate opposition (e.g., z_{13} is now defined as $-.7 = (.5 \times -1)^{1/2}$). As pointed out just below equation 7.1, the negative z_{ij} can indicate products of rating with opposite signs.[5] The final ersatz network structure would be identical to that generated above, except that it would show that the chamber of commerce opposed both the newspapers and Democratic party when it became embroiled in the same issues with them:

$$Z = \begin{bmatrix} .63 & .63 & -.18 \\ & .63 & -.18 \\ & & .50 \end{bmatrix} \begin{matrix} \text{newspapers} \\ \text{Democratic party} \\ \text{chamber of commerce} \end{matrix}$$

In the same manner that a (3,3) ersatz network structure was generated in this simple example, a (15,15) structure has been generated for each of the 51 communities.[6] Table 7.1 gives the ersatz power structure obtained for Albany, New York. Standard deviations of the z_{ij} are given in parentheses. The higher the standard deviation of z_{ij} across issues and informants, the more informants disagreed in their perceptions of the power of actors i and j concerning different issues.[7]

With Table 7.1 as data, a network analysis of Albany could locate cliques and prominent actors in the community or sets of structurally equivalent actors in the community. These two alternatives are illustrated for a small West German community by Laumann and Pappi (1976) and Burt (1976a, 1977c), respectively. In the case of Albany, both approaches are likely to result in a single conclusion: Albany is dominated by the Democratic party. Note in Table 7.1 that each actor, to the extent of having power in the community, tends to exercise power jointly with the Democratic party. The z_{ij} are high relative to the z_{jj} for every actor j. The most powerful actor in the community is the Democratic party, for which z_{ij} equals .95, almost a maximum estimate of power, with a standard deviation of .52. Albany is an example of what will be discussed shortly as MACHINE power structure. In this structure, the Democratic party is a structurally unique, central, and dominant actor. Other actors in the structure occupy a peripheral position.

More important to the concern here with comparative analysis is the fact that any network analysis conducted on Albany's ersatz power structure could be replicated in each of the other 50 communities, since the same network elements in Z are estimated for each community. Before doing so, however, it would be convenient to have at least tentative answers to some questions concerning the adequacy of ersatz network data.[8]

ARE THE DATA REASONABLY EFFICIENT?

As given in equation 7.1, an estimated z_{ij} is a mean computed across combinations of issues and informants. Across the sampled informants

TABLE 7.1 Ersatz Power Structure for Albany, New York, as of 1967

Actors	1	2	3	4	5	6	7	8	9	10	11	12	13	14	15
1. Democratic party	.95 (.52)	.15 (.33)	.51 (.43)	.30 (.35)	.40 (.42)	.22 (.30)	.22 (.31)	.33 (.38)	.32 (.36)	.17 (.29)	.17 (.29)	.35 (.39)	.32 (.37)	.42 (.40)	.29 (.36)
2. Republican party		.14 (.33)	.08 (.23)	.06 (.16)	.13 (.30)	.04 (.10)	.04 (.10)	.04 (.10)	.04 (.10)	.02 (.10)	.02 (.10)	.08 (.23)	.04 (.10)	.04 (.10)	.07 (.21)
3. Chamber of Commerce			.41 (.37)	.19 (.25)	.28 (.34)	.17 (.24)	.15 (.23)	.26 (.31)	.25 (.28)	.13 (.23)	.13 (.23)	.29 (.34)	.25 (.29)	.31 (.32)	.24 (.30)
4. Church leaders				.21 (.25)	.16 (.23)	.16 (.22)	.16 (.23)	.14 (.22)	.14 (.22)	.13 (.21)	.13 (.21)	.15 (.23)	.14 (.22)	.18 (.23)	.14 (.22)
5. Newspapers					.32 (.36)	.14 (.22)	.14 (.22)	.20 (.28)	.19 (.25)	.13 (.21)	.13 (.21)	.25 (.31)	.21 (.27)	.23 (.29)	.20 (.28)
6. Bar Association						.16 (.22)	.16 (.22)	.14 (.22)	.14 (.22)	.13 (.21)	.13 (.21)	.15 (.23)	.14 (.22)	.16 (.22)	.14 (.22)
7. Labor unions							.16 (.23)	.14 (.22)	.14 (.22)	.13 (.21)	.13 (.21)	.15 (.23)	.14 (.22)	.16 (.23)	.14 (.22)
8. Ethnic groups								.25 (.30)	.24 (.27)	.13 (.21)	.13 (.21)	.19 (.27)	.18 (.25)	.20 (.29)	.14 (.22)
9. Neighborhood groups									.23 (.26)	.13 (.21)	.13 (.21)	.19 (.25)	.18 (.24)	.20 (.26)	.14 (.22)
10. Heads of local government agencies										.13 (.21)	.13 (.21)	.13 (.23)	.13 (.21)	.13 (.21)	.13 (.21)
11. City and county employees											.13 (.21)	.13 (.23)	.13 (.21)	.13 (.21)	.13 (.21)
12. Industrial leaders												.29 (.33)	.25 (.28)	.25 (.28)	.24 (.30)
13. Retail merchants													.25 (.30)	.25 (.28)	.20 (.25)
14. Bankers and executives of financial institutions														.32 (.32)	.20 (.24)
15. Other businessmen															.23 (.29)

and issues in a community, the variance of z_{ij} increases to the extent that z_{ij} changes from informant to informant and from issue to issue.[9] The link between this sampling variance and the magnitude of its corresponding ersatz network element has important analytical consequences. If z_{ij} varies so much across issues and informants that its sampling variance is much greater than z_{ij} itself, then there is little incentive to analyze z_{ij} as an estimate of a single power structure underlying issues raised in a community and perceived by informants. Rather, if estimated z_{ij} are in a sense "swamped" by sampling variance, community power should be analyzed issue by issue and informant by informant.

Deferring to the next section, a disaggregation of issue and information biases, my concern here is to describe the connection between the magnitude of z_{ij} and its sampling variance. As a mean across issues and informants, the standard error of z_{ij} is the ratio of its standard deviation across issues and informants, s_{ij}, divided by the square root of the number of independent observations used to estimate z_{ij}, i.e., the square root of the number of informants whose ratings are used to estimate z_{ij}, K:

$$s_{z_{ij}} = s_{ij}/K^{\frac{1}{2}} \qquad [7.2]$$

To what extent is an estimated z_{ij} insignificant in comparison to its sampling variance? The ratio of z_{ij} over its standard error has a t distribution with K-1 degrees of freedom. At the .05 level of confidence under a two-tail test with six ($6 = K-1$) degreees of freedom, an estimated z_{ij} cannot be distinguished from zero if it is less than 2.45 times the magnitude of its standard error, that is, if the ratio of $s_{z_{ij}}$ over z_{ij} exceeds .41. It is unlikely that every actor exercises power jointly with every other actor, and it is certainly unlikely that all actors are powerful over each issue in each community. There should be some z_{ij} that are negligible simply because they estimate a genuine absence of community power. However, to the extent that all z_{ij} are negligible in the sense that $s_{z_{ij}}/Z_{ij}$ exceeds .41, there is too much sampling variability in the ersatz network elements to be able to use them in studies of community power.

Figure 7.1 presents a graph of the estimated ersatz network elements (the z_{ij}) against the ratio of standard error to estimate (the $s_{z_{ij}}/z_{ij}$) across all communities. There are 6120 ersatz network elements represented in Figure 7.1; each of the 51 communities contributing $15(15+1)/2$, or 120 elements to the graph.[10]

A line has been drawn in Figure 7.1 corresponding to the .41 criterion for significance. Points below the line refer to estimated z_{ij} that are statistically greater than zero. Points above the line are negligible in the

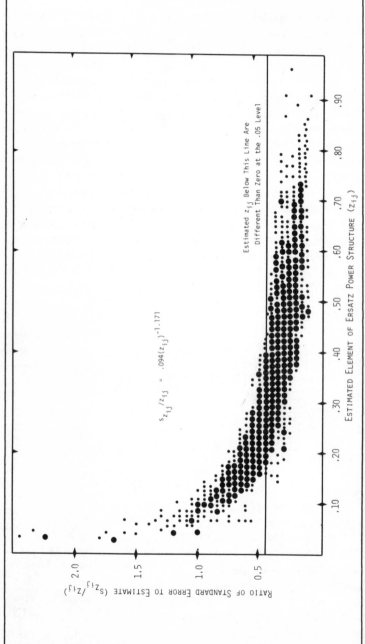

Figure 7.1: Ratio of Standard Error to Network Element Graphed Against the Elements Magnitude (large circles refer to more, small circles to fewer than five z_{ij})

sense that the sampling variability of z_{ij} is so large that it is impossible to distinguish z_{ij} from zero. Of the 765 z_{jj}, elements indicating the power of individual actors, 208 or 27 percent cannot be distinguished from zero at the .05 level of confidence. Of the 5355 z_{ij} , elements indicating the tendency for pairs of actors to exercise power simultaneously, 49 percent cannot be distinguished from zero at the .05 level of confidence. It is impossible to determine how many z_{ij} should be significant; however, the fact that 48 percent of the estimated z_{ij} are significant clearly demonstrates that it is possible to estimate a single ersatz power structure within a community that cannot be attributed to variation in the z_{ij} across issues and informants in the community.

The functional form of the data distribution in Figure 7.1 corroborates this conclusion. If the variation in z_{ij} across issues and informants is random, then it should be constant within communities as a function of the number of independent observations used to compute z_{ij} —the more observations, the lower the random error in z_{ij} . But what if z_{ij} varies as a result of genuine differences in the power of actors over specific issues? In some cities, of course, there migh be a concentration of power such that a single actor or set of actors dominates all issues (e.g., the Democratic party in Albany, NY, as given in Table 7.1), but across all communities one would expect different actors to be powerful in regard to different issues. To the extent that z_{ij} is high on a specific issue, therefore, its low value on other issues would create high variation in z_{ij} across issues. The lowest variation in the z_{ij} would occur when actors i and j have no power over any issues. In consequence, the standard error of z_{ij} should increase as the magnitude of z_{ij} increases, the most powerful actors having the greatest tendency to have variable power across issues. This same argument extends to genuine differences between informant perceptions.

Consider these two interpretations of variation in z_{ij} in terms of the ratio of standard error to estimated network element. If s_{ij} increases with the magnitude of z_{ij}, as would be expected to the extent that variation in z_{ij} across issues and informants is a result of genuine differences in actor power across issues and/or informants, then the ratio $s_{z_{ij}} / z_{ij}$, should be approximately constant across levels of z_{ij} depending on the rate at which s_{ij} increases with z_{ij}. In a regression of $s_{z_{ij}} / z_{ij}$ over z_{ij}, a negligible slope coefficient would be expected. On the other hand, if s_{ij} is a constant determined by K, as would be expected to the extent that variation in z_{ij} across issues and informants is merely random, then the ratio $s_{z_{ij}} / z_{ij}$ should decrease at increasing magnitudes of z_{ij}. The more rapidly the ratio declines, the more adequately efficient the estimation of z_{ij} in the sense that moderate to high z_{ij} are discernible from sampling variance.

As can be seen from Figure 7.1, the ratio of standard error to estimated network element is definitely not a constant across levels of z_{ij}. Not only is there a strong negative correlation between this ratio and the magnitude of z_{ij} ($r = -.745$), there is an increased ability to predict the ratio from the magnitude of z_{ij} if one assumes an exponential rather than linear decrease in the proportion at increasing magnitudes of z_{ij}. The squared correlation for the linear model is .56 but increases to .67 for the exponential model. The exact function predicting the ratio from the magnitudes of z_{ij} is given in Figure 7.1 as:[11]

$$s_{z_{ij}} / z_{ij} = .094(z_{ij})^{-1.171} \qquad [7.3]$$

When z_{ij} is .28, for example, this function predicts that the standard error $s_{z_{ij}}$ will be .42 as large as z_{ij} itself. With six degrees of freedom, this is the point at which the function crosses the line in Figure 7.1 marking significance beyond the .05 level of confidence. Based on the function in Equation 7.3, any estimated ersatz network element that is equal to or greater than .28 can be expected, on average, to be significantly greater than zero. Note in Figure 7.1 that some elements of only moderate strength, as low as $z_{ij} \simeq .2$, are significantly greater than zero at the .05 level of significance.

I conclude that it is not only possible to estimate an ersatz power structure, a structure visible in spite of variation across issues and informants, but that the efficiency with which each ersatz network element is estimated can be adequate to distinguish even moderately strong elements from sampling variance. Of course, this is only a first step. To say that elements in a community's ersatz power structure cannot be attributed to random variation or variation in structure across issues and informants is not to say that differences in the structure across issues and informants are themselves negligible. Such a statement requires a consideration of the ersatz network data's reliability over issue and informant biases.

ARE THE DATA RELIABLE DESPITE INFORMANT AND ISSUE BIASES?

Not all issues and informants are equally useful sources of information (see Burt, Lieben, et al., 1980: 124). Of the seven informants, the head of the bar association was most often missing or gave "don't know" ratings to all actors on all issues. In contrast, the leading banker gave very few "don't know" answers and rarely said that everyone was unimportant in determining any of the five issues.

Similarly, the issues varied in usefulness. The mayoral election and urban renewal were good issues at the time of the survey, since few informants said that none of the 15 actors was unimportant for determining these issues (only 1 and 4 actors, respectively), and few informants gave "don't know" ratings to all actors for these issues (only 6 and 4 informants, respectively). The air pollution issue, in contrast, was quite poor. Ten informants said that no one was important for determining the issue, and twelve informants gave "don't know" ratings to all actors for this issue. This variability in the data provided by different issues and informants raises the question of reliability. To what extent are the estimated z_{ij} affected by the selection of informants and issues?

One method of addressing this question is to assess the reliability of estimated ersatz network elements when computed from different combinations of informants and issues. Corresponding to the multitrait-multimethod model of reliability, where informants and issues are traits and methods, an ersatz network element is reliable to the extent that similar values of z_{ij} are obtained using different informants and issues.

Four estimates of each z_{ij} have been computed from a different combination of informants and issues. After deleting the air pollution issue as the least informative, the remaining four issues were randomly assigned to two categories. The school board election and the mayoral election constitute set I, while the municipal bond referendum and urban renewal project constitute set II. After deleting the head of the bar association as the least informative, the remaining six informants were randomly assigned to two categories. The head of the chamber of commerce, the head of the labor council, and the leading banker constitute set I. The head of the Democratic party, the head of the Republican party, and a leading newspaper publisher or editor constitute set II. Four different estimates of z_{ij} in equation 7.1 can now be computed with each estimate based on a maximum of three informants and two issues, and each based on a different combination of issues and informants:

$z_{ij(a)}$ is based on issues in set I and informants in set I (the head of the chamber of commerce, the head of the labor council, and the leading banker evaluate the control of actors over the school board election and the mayoral election).

$z_{ij(b)}$ is based on issues in set II and informants in set I (the same informants as above evaluate the control of actors over a municipal bond referendum and an urban renewal project).

**TABLE 7.2   Observed and Predicted Moments Among
Four Estimates of z_{ij}**

	$z_{ij(a)}$	$z_{ij(b)}$	$z_{ij(c)}$	$z_{ij(d)}$
$z_{ij(a)}$	1.000	$\delta^2 + \delta_3^2$	$\delta^2 + \delta_1^2$	δ^2
$z_{ij(b)}$	.523	1.000	δ^2	$\delta^2 + \delta_2^2$
$z_{ij(c)}$	.461	.383	1.000	$\delta^2 + \delta_4^2$
$z_{ij(d)}$	.356	.503	.599	1.000
Standard deviations	.181	.216	.185	.238

NOTE: Correlations and standard deviations are computed from 6120 z_{ij} based on different combinations of issues and informants as given in the text. The predicted correlations are implied by Figure 7.2.

$z_{ij(c)}$ is based on issues in set I and informants in set II (the newspaper publisher or editor, the head of the Democratic party, and the head of the Republican party evaluate the control of actors over the school board election and mayoral election).

$z_{ij(d)}$ is based on issues in set II and informants in set II (the same informants as above evaluate the control of actors over the municipal bond referendum and an urban renewal project).

Correlations and standard deviations among these four estimates of each ersatz network element are reported in Table 7.2. In the same manner that estimates of z_{ij} were correlated with the ratio of their standard error to z_{ij} itself in Figure 7.1, r_{ac} in Table 7.2 is the correlation between 6120 estimates of $z_{ij(a)}$ and $z_{ij(c)}$. Also presented in Table 7.2 are the correlations predicted by the restricted covariance structure in Figure 7.2. The model in Figure 7.2 disaggregates each estimate of z_{ij} into four components: a "true" score common to all estimates (z_{ij}), a random error component peculiar to each combination of informants and issues ($w_{ij(a)}$ to $w_{ij(d)}$), a component due to one or the other sets of informants (IN_I or IN_{II}), and a component due to one or the other of the sets of issues (IS_I or IS_{II}). The arrows in Figure 7.2 describe which components combine to make each estimate of z_{ij}. For example, $z_{ij(a)}$ is based on informants in set I evaluating the control of actors over issues in set I. In Figure 7.2, $z_{ij(a)}$ is given as a result of a "true" score effect from z_{ij}, an "issue" effect from issue factor I, an "informant" effect from informant factor I, and an error term unique to estimating z_{ij} from informants in set I evaluating issues in set I:

$$z_{ij(a)} = \delta z_{ij} + \delta_1 IS_1 + \delta_3 IN_1 + \theta_a w_{ij(a)}$$

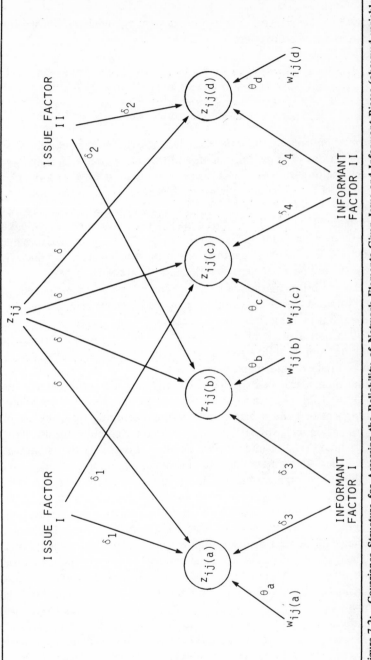

Figure 7.2: Covariance Structure for Assessing the Reliability of Network Elements Given Issue and Informant Biases (observed variables are circled)

Similarly, the structural equations describing the issue, informant, error, and true score effects on the other three estimates of z_{ij} are given as:

$$z_{ij(b)} = \delta z_{ij} + \delta_2 IS_{II} + \delta_3 IN_I + \theta_b w_{ij(b)}$$
$$z_{ij(c)} = \delta z_{ij} + \delta_1 IS_I + \delta_4 IN_{II} + \theta_c w_{ij(c)}$$
$$z_{ij(d)} = \delta z_{ij} + \delta_2 IS_{II} + \delta_4 IN_{II} + \theta_d w_{ij(d)}$$

Correlations among the four estimates of z_{ij} can now be expressed as combinations of issue, informant, and true score effects; δ_1 is an issue effect resulting from the use of issues in set I to estimate z_{ij}, δ_2 is a similar issue effect based on issues in set II, δ_3 is an informant effect resulting from the use of informants in set I to estimate z_{ij}, and δ_4 is a similar informant effect based on informants in set II. Most importantly, δ is a true score effect resulting from the extent to which z_{ij} is stable from one combination of issues and informants to another. To the extent that z_{ij} is high, the estimated ersatz network elements are reliable.

The relative magnitude of issue, informant, and true score effects on the estimated ersatz network elements can be determined from the correlations in Table 7.2. Note that each predicted correlation in Table 7.2 is in part a result of reliability, δ^2. In addition to the correlation resulting from reliability, some correlations are expected to be high as a result of issue or informant biases. For example, $z_{ij(a)}$ and $z_{ij(b)}$ should be higher than would be expected from reliability alone. Specifically, as given in Table 7.2, the correlation r_{ab} is the sum of a reliability component (δ^2) and a bias component (δ_3^2) resulting from the use of informants in set I. Similarly, $z_{ij(a)}$ and $z_{ij(c)}$ have in common the use of the school board election and mayoral elections as issues. To the extent that these issues offer a biased picture of community power, the correlation r_{ac} should be higher than would be expected solely as a result of reliability. Specifically, as given in Table 7.2, the correlation r_{ac} is the sum of a reliability component (δ^2) and a bias component (δ_1^2) resulting from the use of issues in set I. Table 7.3 presents maximum-likelihood estimates of the parameters in Figure 7.2 under different assumptions.

The first column of Table 7.3 assumes that issue, informant, and true score effects exist simultaneously in the estimated ersatz network elements. Under this assumption, the correlations predicted from the estimated parameters are not statistically different from the correlations actually observed. The χ^2 statistic testing the lack of fit is negligible.[12]

The second column of Table 7.3 assumes that issue and informant biases are negligible, so that estimates of z_{ij} are completely stable across different combinations of issues and informants used to estimate z_{ij}. The correlations predicted from the reliability coefficient alone are not

TABLE 7.3 Issue, Informant, and True Score Effects
on Ersatz Network Elements

	Alternative Models		
	All Effects	*No Bias*	*No Reliability*
Reliability			
δ	.608	.688	.000*
Issue bias			
δ_1	.305	.000*	.440
δ_2	.363	.000*	.486
Informant bias			
δ_3	.393	.000*	.623
δ_4	.477	.000*	.681
Residuals			
θ_a	.624	.762	.605
θ_b	.583	.733	.563
θ_c	.553	.710	.535
θ_d	.524	.701	.473
χ^2 testing lack of fit	.031	7.727	12.215
Degrees of freedom	1	5	2
Significance of lack of fit	~.86	~.17	<.01

NOTE: Estimates have been obtained numerically as described in Joreskog. All variables are standardized, and the nine unobserved variables are uncorrelated. Coefficients marked with an asterisk have been forced to equal given value a priori to estimating remaining coefficients. χ^2 statistics have been computed as described in note 12.

statistically different from the correlations actually observed! Although increased from the "all effects" model in column 1, the χ^2 test for lack of fit is still insignificant. Forcing issues and informant biases to have no effect on the estimates of ersatz network elements, the reliability coefficient is estimated to be .688; about half the variance in the z_{ij} is in some sense "true" score variance when the z_{ij} are estimated from three informants evaluating actors in terms of two issues.

The third column of Table 7.3 assumes exactly the opposite relation between reliability and bias. Reliability is assumed to be negligible. Correlations among estimates of z_{ij} based on different issues and informants are assumed to result from issue and informant biases. As occurred in the "all effects" model, the effects of informant bias (δ_3/δ_4) tend to be stronger than the effects of issue bias (δ_1 and δ_2).[13] Taken together, however, informant and issue biases are not capable of predicting the correlations observed in Table 7.2. The χ^2 statistic in Table 7.3 that tests lack of fit between observed and predicted correlations under an assumption of negligible reliability, given high informant and issue bias, is significant beyond the .01 level of confidence.

Together with the results of the previous section, these results demonstrate the statistical adequacy of ersatz power structures, at least for the 51 cities data. I conclude from Table 7.3 that elements of the estimated ersatz power structures are stable over four random combinations of issues and informants such that issue and informant bias per se can be ignored as statistically negligible. Demonstration of adequate efficiency and reliability only shows that the ersatz network data are methodologically plausible as a basis for comparative research. Still to be demonstrated is their substantive validity.

ARE THE DATA SUBSTANTIVELY VALID? TYPES OF STRUCTURES AND THEIR CONCOMITANT COMMUNITY CHARACTERISTICS

In one (not too tortured) sense, the validity of the ersatz power structures has already been discussed. While clearly not describing the relations between actors i and j in a manner corresponding to sociometric data, the ersatz network element connecting i and j has high face validity in the sense that it does capture one manner in which actors i and j are associated with respect to community events. The element is high to the extent that i and j are perceived by informants as exercising control over the same community issues. As I pointed out earlier, there are precedents in case studies for describing such associations between actors as network relations. It is in just such a nonsociometric sense that persons associate with one another to the extent that they are active in the same groups or are perceived as trustworthy by the same groups.

Beyond having face validity, the ersatz network structures have construct validity. They make substantive sense in light of existing research on community power. Construct validity has been demonstrated in two manners. First, the patterns of ersatz network elements in the 51 communities have been classified into types of similar patterns, and those patterns correspond to types of power structures described in case studies of American communities. Second, each type of ersatz network structure was found to occur in cities with characteristics expected from case studies and comparative research. The details of this demonstration are beyond the scope of this chapter; however, they are readily available elsewhere.

The same methodology used to identify structurally equivalent actors was used to identify communities with equivalent power structures (see Burt, 1981b: 164-168, for details and Burt, 1975: 286-293, for an illustration of the same methodology applied to ersatz networks derived from mass media informants). Detailed descriptions of the seven power structure types identified and the typical characteristics of communities in which they were observed are also given in that article (Burt, 1981b: 135-136). In brief, four classes of structures are distinguished. The only significant tendency for power in a MACHINE structure is the dominant power of the Democratic party. This type of structure tended to occur in small communities with low incomes, heterogeneity, centralized decision making, and overstaffing in municipal government (Burt, 1981b; 140-143).

As would be expected in old, URBAN cities that had endured to become major commercial centers, there was a high decentralization of decision making, but the exercise of community power was greatly centralized in community newspapers—not in the sense that newspapers dominated the community so much as the sense that issues were rarely resolved without community newspapers playing a visible role in decision making (Burt, 1981: 143-147). As a variation on the URBAN structure, there was a FACTION type of structure that tended to occur in old, large, densely settled communities characterized by highly decentralized decision making and some councilmen elected at large in partisan elections. This structure contained two factions that became embroiled together in community issues, a faction composed of a variety of actors such as the Republican party and industrial leaders typically representing stabilizing, conservative interests, and a second faction composed of the Democratic party and community newspapers (Burt, 1981b: 147-151).

Finally, four REFORM government structures were distinguished, each containing a highly powerful status occupied by newspapers and economic leaders. In all but one of these structures, political parties had no power independent of other actors. These REFORM structures tended to occur in young communities with high-income homogeneity, reformist governments (city manager and at-large, nonpartisan elections of councilmen), and centralized decision making (Burt, 1981b: 151-156). The general conclusion I draw from the analysis of power structure types is that the ersatz network data are substantively valid in the sense that they imply structures of community power and concomitants of those structures that have been observed in community power studies having the advantage of much more detailed data on individual communities.

CONCLUSION AND COMMENTS
ON SELECTING INFORMANTS

In summary, I conclude that the ersatz network data obtained from informant interviews have considerable potential to narrow the gap between comparative analyses and case studies. Obtained from interviews with a small number of informants in each community to be studied, the ersatz network element connecting actors i and j is the extent to which the actors are perceived by informants as having simultaneous control over the same community issues (equation 7.1). Using data from interviews with informants in 51 American communities, an ersatz power structure for each community has been obtained (e.g., Table 7.1). These structures have been demonstrated to be efficient, reliable, and substantively valid. Not only is it possible to estimate an ersatz structure for each community—a structure visible in spite of variation across issues and informants in the community—but the efficiency of estimation can be adequate to discern network elements of even moderate strength (e.g., Figure 7.1). Moreover, the estimated structures are stable across four random combinations of issues and informants, such that issue and informant biases per se can be ignored as statistically significant (e.g., Table 7.3). Still further, classes of ersatz network structures can be distinguished among the 51 cities where the classes correspond to types of power structures described in available community research in which much more detailed data were available. Beyond their descriptive adequacy, the ersatz network data offer some guidelines for future research.[14]

Specific persons can be recommended as informants. Assuming that informant perceptions are affected by the role-set defining an informant's position in community structure (to the extent that they are affected by anything, Houston and Sudman, 1975), informants should be selected so as to represent the structurally nonequivalent, and significantly powerful, positions in types of structures. So selected, informant perceptions used to generate ersatz network elements in equation 7.1 would span the diversity of significant actor perceptions of power.

The types of structures distinguished here suggest eight significantly powerful positions as statuses. The only powerful status in the MACHINE structure is occupied by the Democratic party. The only such status in the URBAN structure is occupied by community newspapers. The FACTION structure has two powerful statuses, one occupied by relatively conservative actors (actors 2, 3, 7, 10, 12 and 14 as numbered in Table 7.1). The class of REFORM government structures offer five powerful statuses, three occupied by the newspaper and various economic actors (actors 3, 7, 12, 13, 14 and 15), a fourth occupied by local informant groups (actors 4, 9 and 11), and a fifth occupied by labor unions and retailers. Five informants are sufficient to represent all of these powerful statuses. An optimum set of informants would consist of a spokesman for:

(1) the Democratic party,
(2) the Republican party,
(3) the leading community newspaper(s),
(4) the heads of government agencies in the community, and
(5) one of the following: the community chamber of commerce, leading community industrial leaders, or executives of leading financial institutions.

A minimum of two informants per community should be interviewed in regard to at least two issues, so that the bias effects in Figure 7.2 can be assessed. If this minimum is chosen, the two informants should be spokespersons for the leading community newspaper(s) and one of the major economic actors (chamber of commerce, leading industrialist, executive of leading financial institution). Of the five optimum informants indicated above, these two are most often found in separate, powerful positions in the different types of ersatz power structures.

NOTES

1. In fact, Laumann and Pappi (1976: 225) describe the joint structures of elites and community subgroups. Since the relative sizes of the population subgroups and the relative popularity of each elite person was held constant, the fact that there were 27 elites versus nine community subgroups means that the analyzed structure is predominantly a function of the extent to which elites are trusted by the same subgroups. Their methodology for analyzing the community-elite interface could be extended to weigh community subgroups more heavily, of course, simply by distinguishing more than nine subgroups.

2. The mayor's office is conspicuous in its absence from the list of the 15 potentially powerful actors in Table 7.1. Fortunately, other types of data were obtained in the surveys on mayoral power, and these are used elsewhere (Burt, 1981b: Appendix A) to describe the power of mayors in cities with different types of ersatz network power structures. Unfortunately, these data do not correspond to those used to estimate equation 7.1, so the mayor has not been included in the ersatz power structures analyzed.

3. Even among those informants contacted, however, the adequacy of informants varied in the sense that several could not evaluate the control of some actors over some issues. When an informant responds with a "don't know" (DK) rating in place of the above m_{jkq}, either of two conditions can be expected: (1) the informant is familiar with the issue area but is not familiar with the type of actor given a DK rating; (2) the informant is not familiar with the issue area. If more than three of the 15 ratings given by an informant for a particular issue were DK, the informant was assumed to fall into the second category. He or she was treated as a poor informant on that issue and was deleted from the computation

of the z_{ij} for that issue. On the other hand, if 1-3 of an informant's rating on an issue were DK while the remaining ratings were given, then the informant was assumed to be knowledgeable on the issue but unfamiliar with the actors given DK ratings. In this case, the informant's DK rating of an actor's power was interpreted to mean that the actor was unlikely to be an important source of support for the issue. When three or fewer DK ratings were given by an informant for an issue, therefore, the informant was considered to be knowledgeable on the issue, and the three ratings were recoded as zero. The use of three DK ratings to distinguish knowledgeable informants from those who are not is arbitrary but suggested by the data themselves. There were several cases where informants gave one, two, or three DK ratings. See Burt et al. (1980: Table 1) for a tabulation of the frequencies with which each informant tended to give DK ratings on each issue. Also given there is the original wording of the questions soliciting the m_{jkq}.

4. The matrix is the sum of four issue-informant-specific matrices given in the text, each weighted by one-fourth. Each matrix is weighted by one-fourth, since two issues and two informants have been used to obtain Z:

$$p_k = 1/2 \ , \ p_q = 1/2 \ , \ \text{so} \ p_k p_q = 1/4.$$

5. With respect to computer programming, I have operationalized these signed relations by modifying equation 7.1 to be computed from the following expression:

$$z_{ij} = \Sigma_k p_k \ (\Sigma_q p_q \delta_{ij} \ | \ m_{ikq} m_{jkq} \ |^{1/2})$$

where δ_{ij} equals 1 when the two rating are of the same sign (whereupon this expression is identical to equation 7.1), but equals -1 when the product $m_{ijq} m_{jkq}$ is negative.

6. The (15, 15) ersatz power structure, together with each element's standard deviation and the total number of issues/informants from which it is computed, is given for each of the 51 communities in Working Paper 22: "Comparative community power structures in 51 cities representative of American places of residence circa 1967," available from the Reprint Librarian, Survey Research Center, University of California at Berkeley

7. The variability in an element z_{ij} in equation 7.1 is measured by the differences between up to 35 different estimates of the z_{ij}, one estimate for each of the seven informants' perceptions of actor determination of each of the five community issues. Due to missing data (see note 3), the actual number of estimates ranges from 22 up to the complete 35. Given z_{ij} in equation 7.1 as the mean of the quantity $(m_{ikq} m_{jkq})^{1/2}$ across all informants and issues in a community, the variance of z_{ij} across issues and informants is

$$s_{ij}^2 = \sum_{k=1}^{K} \ \sum_{q=1}^{Q} \ [(m_{ikq} m_{jkq})^{1/2} - z_{ij}]^2 / (KQ - 1)$$

where the terms are defined in equation 7.1. While the number of separate estimates of z_{ij} for a community equals KQ, the number of independent estimates is only the number of separate persons interviewed, i.e., K. Routine statistical tests using the standard deviation of z_{ij} therefore (K - 1) rather than (KQ - 1) degrees of freedom.

8. Using the same data model, but applying it to content analyses of the New York *Times* rather than to interviews with informants, the adequacy of estimated z_{ij} decreases as

the number of actors distinguished (N in equation 7.1) increases (see Chapter 8, Table 8.1). In other words, the efficiency and reliability of elements in Z_{NN} decrease as N increases. Unfortunately, data were only gathered from informants in the 51 cities concerning the 15 actors listed in Table 7.1. While it seems likely that the adequacy of the z_{ij} in equation 7.1 will vary with the order of Z in the same manner observed in the content analysis data, i.e., that the elements of a (50,50) structure will be less adequate in general than the elements of a (5,5) structure, this conclusion cannot be reached as definitive without additional data.

9. Details on computing the standard deviation of z_{ij} as s_{ij} are given in note 7.

10. The one exception is z_{ij} estimated to be zero and having a sampling variance of zero—actors whose power is uniformly perceived as negligible. These 47 cases, while used to compute coefficients in equation 7.3, were deleted from Figure 7.1 in order to simplify discussion of the graph. The 47 cases are not counted as being greater than their standard errors.

11. The exponent and constant in equation 7.3 have been estimated by regressing the log of the ratio on the left side of the equation over the log of z_{ij}. The constant is then the antilog of the constant in the regression, and the exponent is the unstandardized slope in the regression. The standardized coefficient corresponding to -1.171 in equation 7.3 is -.817.

12. The χ^2 statistic equals the product of one minus the number of independent observations used to compute correlations and a function of the discrepancy between observed and predicted correlations. While the correlations in Table 7.2 are computed from 6120 different numbers, the ersatz network elements within a community are not independent since they are the average perceptions of up to seven informants. The χ^2 statistics have been computed here using the number of communities as the effective number of independent observation underlying the correlations.

13. This observation can be made more specific by testing the significance of each of the bias effects. Bias effects δ_1, δ_2, and δ_3 can be forced to equal zero without significantly increasing the lack of fit with which Figure 7.2 predicts the correlations given in Table 7.2. When δ_4 is forced to equal zero, however, the χ^2 statistic increases to 4.17 from the .03 value obtained in the "all effects" model in Table 7.3. In other words, ersatz network elements estimated from the perceptions of a community's leading newspaper editor or publisher and the heads of the Democratic and Republican parties tend to be more similar than would be expected as a result of reliability alone. There are no informant and issue biases per se, however, in the estimated z_{ij}. Of course, and as the significance of δ^4 while δ^3 remains insignificant further suggests, it is possible that there are informant and issue biases specific to individual informants and issues. The analysis using Figure 7.2 simply shows that a random partition of issues and informants into four combinations does not result in significant variations on the ersatz power structures estimated from all issues and informants. The tests here are designed to assess informant and issue biases in general versus reliability. It is beyond the scope of this discussion to conduct a thorough analysis of all effects on the informant ratings, the m_{jkq} in equation 7.1. One such analysis is available in an unpublished Ph.D. dissertation in sociology, University of Chicago, by Bruce Phillips.

14. More directly addressing the gap between case and comparative studies, the ersatz network data can be used to sample communities for case study analysis such that research findings can be generalized to other communities. Space limitations prohibit a development of this use here; however, it is described elsewhere in conjunction with computer software available to facilitate generalization (Burt, 1981b; 158-164, 168-174).

Chapter 8

Network Data from Archival Records

RONALD S. BURT

Densities of relations between actors can be inferred from content analyses of archival records. This chapter is a methodological discussion of gathering and assessing the adequacy of the data. Illustrative material is taken from a network analysis of American society from 1877 to 1972 based on events described in the New York Times.

Were it possible to obtain adequate network data from archival records describing a social system, such data could have several advantages over the traditional sociometric data used to define relations. They could avoid at least four drawbacks to traditional sociometric data, drawbacks concerning scope, access, bias, and history. The cost of collecting sociometric data quickly becomes prohibitive as system size increases due to the geometric increase in the number of relations to be recorded. Even network sampling strategies involve a relatively small number of individual actors. There is also the question of access. Actors who do not exist as physical persons cannot be specified in a traditional sociometric design. Examples of such actors would be unorganized collective groups or even formal organizations for which there are many representative spokesmen. Next, there is the question of bias. Sociometric data obtained through personal interviews or informants can be reactive to the interests of the respondents. There are many types of bias, of course, but it would be desirable to have network data robust over the interests of persons involved in the networks. Finally, there is the question of history. Sociometric data are usually confined, temporally, to the time of interviewing. Retrospective sociometric data

Author's Note: *The work reported here was supported by grant SOC73-05504 from the National Science Foundation to J.S. Coleman and a predoctoral fellowship I received from the National Institute of Mental Health. This chapter has been abstracted from material published in* Social Science Research *and* Sociological Methodology *(Burt, 1975; Burt and Lin, 1977). Participants in the Corporate Actor Project at the National Opinion Research Center in 1973 and 1974 provided helpful comments on prepublication draft material.*

could be expected to lose their reliability quickly as relations further and further back in time are discussed in the interview. Panel studies provide a limited corrective to this problem (see Chapter 4, this volume) but cannot provide a complete solution for long periods of time, given the tendencies for actors to die, refuse to continue, ,or otherwise be unobservable over the period of time selected for study.

This chapter outlines some ideas for obtaining network data from archival records so as to avoid the above problems. The ideas involve the content analysis of archival records to describe the relations between classes of actors in terms of their joint involvement in events of consequence in their social system. I will first describe how the data would be obtained, then describe strategies for assessing their adequacy, and close with comments on important assumptions made in obtaining the data.

NETWORK STRUCTURE REFLECTED IN ARCHIVAL RECORDS

I shall define network data in terms of actors, documents, and sections of documents. Let N equal the number of actors to be considered. Each of these actors will be a category in a content analysis so an actor can be any individual or set of individuals referenced in the archival records to be analyzed. The archives of a society are usually recorded within a distinct (not necessarily constant) interval of time. Refer to the archival records produced within a single interval of time as a document. For example, a daily newspaper is produced at the rate of one a day (newspaper = document), textbooks are adopted by educational systems for the interval of one academic year (adopted textbook = document), court records are gathered together for years (years of records = document), minutes of executive meeting are recorded within fiscal years (year of minutes = document), and nonfictional accounts have specific copyright and distribution dates (accounts for a year = document). These documents can be divided into easily distinguishable sections where the relative importance of each section can be measured as the proportion of the total document that is devoted to each section. The metric in terms of which proportions would be measured is dependent on the type of archival records being analyzed. For example, let a newspaper be a document containing articles as sections. The proportion of the total newspaper that is allocated to a particular article can be measured as the ratio of column inches in the article over the total number of column inches in the newspaper. Another example would be a volume of court records constituting a document in which sections are distinguished as separate cases reported. The proportion of the total document that is allocated to a particular case could be measured as the ratio of time spent by the court on the specific case over the total amount of time in which the court was in session.

The network of relations among the N actors can be studied in terms of the occurrence of actors in document sections and the joint occurrence of actors in these sections. The occurrences of actors can then be weighted according to the proportion of a document allocated to describing each occurrence. The more often that an actor (as an individual or class of individuals) is involved in the events described by particular archives, the more often the actor should appear in prominent sections of documents in the archives. Similarly, the more often that pairs of actors have relations with one another in regard to the events described by the archives, the more often the actors should appear together in prominent sections of documents in the archives. Let the network of relations among the N actors be represented by an (N,N) matrix Z, with element z_{ji} representing the relation from actor j to actor i (i.e., the typical relation from class of individuals j to class of individuals i). Symmetric and asymmetric relations could then be generated.

Symmetric relations would be based on the mere joint occurrence of actors in the same sections of description. Let p_k be the proportion of a document that is allocated to section k, and let m_{jk} equal zero unless actor j is mentioned in section k, whereupon it would equal one. An (N,N) symmetric matrix, Z, of relations among the N actors under study could be generated as the sum of joint mentions of pairs of actors, with each mention weighted by the prominence of the section in which it occurred:

$$Z = \left\{ z_{ij} \right\} = \left\{ \sum_{k=1}^{K} p_k m_{ik} m_{jk} \right\} \qquad [8.1]$$

where summation is across all K sections of a document. The diagonal element z_{ii} would be the proportion of the document allocated to describing events in which actor i was involved. It is a measure of the prominence of people being coded as actor i in the content analysis. The off-diagonal element, z_{ij}, would be the proportion of the document allocated to describing events in which actors i and j were involved. It is a measure of the prominence of relations between people being coded as actors i and j in the content analysis.

Let us consider an example. I have elsewhere described an analysis of the relations among types of organizations and people in the United States between 1877 and 1972 as those relations were reflected in the front page of the New York *Times* (Burt, 1975). The front page of an issue of the New York *Times* was treated as a document, and separate articles were treated as sections. The proportion of a document allocated to a single section was measured in terms of column inches, so that p_k was given as the inches of column on the front page that were allocated to article k divided by the total number of inches of column print on the front page containing article k. If one or more people contained in the ith category of actors were mentioned as initiators or objects of action in either the largest headline associated with the kth article or the first paragraph of the kth article, m_{ik} was set equal to one; otherwise it was zero. A central concern in the study was the change in attention to actors as individual people as opposed to actors as corporations. The simplest network considered was a (2,2) Z, with z_{11} being the prominence of people as individuals, z_{22} being the prominence of corporations, and z_{12} being the prominence of events in which people as individuals had relations with corporations.

Consider a hypothetical issue of the New York *Times* containing three articles. The first article discusses both persons and corporate actors and covers a quarter of the front page. The second article discusses only persons and covers the same proportion of the front page. The third article discusses only corporate actors and covers the remaining half of the front page. For this hypothetical issue, Z is the sum of three products:

$$Z = .25 \begin{bmatrix} 1 & 1 \\ 1 & 1 \end{bmatrix} + .25 \begin{bmatrix} 1 & 0 \\ 0 & 0 \end{bmatrix} + .50 \begin{bmatrix} 0 & 0 \\ 0 & 1 \end{bmatrix}$$

$$= \begin{bmatrix} .50 & .25 \\ .25 & .75 \end{bmatrix} \begin{matrix} \text{people} \\ \text{corporations} \end{matrix}$$

The off-diagonal equals the portion of the front page allocated to describing people in interaction with corporations (.25), while the diagonal elements describe the greater attention given to corporate actors (.75) relative to people as individuals (.50). By studying such matrices over time for more narrowly defined actor categories, I was able to identify general trends in the attention being given to types of organizations and patterns of interaction characterizing periods of economic growth versus decline in the United States (Burt, 1975).[1]

Asymmetric relations would extend the symmetric ties in equation 8.1 to distinguish actors initiating action from those who were the object of action in described events. Let a_{ik} equal zero unless actor i is mentioned in section k as initiating action, whereupon it would equal one. An (N,N) matrix, Z, of asymmetric relations among the N actors could now be generated with the following expression (see equation 8.1):

$$Z = \left\{ z_{ij} \right\} = \left\{ \sum_{k=1}^{K} p_k a_{ik} m_{jk} \right\} \qquad [8.2]$$

where summation is still across all K sections in a document, but the substantive meaning of relations is changed. The diagonal element z_{ii} would be the proportion of the document allocated to describing events in which actor i initiated action (i.e., sections k for which the product $a_{ik} m_{ik}$ equals one). The off-diagonal element z_{ij} would be the proportion of the document allocated to describing events in which actors i and j were involved and actor i initiated action. The symmetric relations defined in equation 8.1 are a special case of the asymmetric relations in equation 8.2. If every time that actors i and j were mentioned they were mentioned as initiating action, then equations 8.1 and 8.2 would define identical z_{ij}.

Recalling the hypothetical, three-article front page of the New York *Times*, suppose that people were merely discussed as the objects of action in the first article, while corporations were discussed as initiation action. Where people and corporations were discussed alone, they were both discussed as initiating action. With this additional information on the manner in which actors were involved in decribing events (as opposed to whether or not they were involved), a more subtle network structure can be obtained. The matrix Z in equation 8.2 is again the sum of three products; however, the structure of joint involvement in the first article is changed ($a_{21} = m_{11} = 1$, but $a_{11} = 0$):

$$Z = .25 \begin{bmatrix} 0 & 0 \\ 1 & 1 \end{bmatrix} + .25 \begin{bmatrix} 1 & 0 \\ 0 & 0 \end{bmatrix} + .50 \begin{bmatrix} 0 & 0 \\ 0 & 1 \end{bmatrix}$$

$$= \begin{bmatrix} .25 & .00 \\ .25 & .75 \end{bmatrix}$$

This network shows an even larger discrepancy between the attention given to people versus corporations in terms of their initiation of action (.25 versus .75). It also shows, by z_{12} equal to .00 and z_{21} equal to .25, that when the two categories of actors are discussed with respect to the same events, people were the object of action, while corporations were the source of action.

The network data generated by equations 8.1 and 8.2 capture relations between actors in a very indirect way in comparison to traditional sociometric data. Rather than describing specific connections from one actor to another, actors i and j are being connected here in terms of their tendency to be recorded in archival records as prominent with respect to the same events or issues, the inference being that *actors embroiled in the same events are more likely to have relations with one another than actors involved in different events.* In this sense, the z_{ij} as network elements are clearly inferior to traditional sociometric data and deserve to be discussed as ersatz network elements.[2]

At the same time, these data offer some advantages over more traditional network data. Thinking back to the beginning of this chapter, the archival network data offer four advantages over sociometric data. First, they are inexpensive and easily obtained. Content analyses of a carefully sampled set of documents can generate ersatz network data at a very low cost for a very large system of actors. Second, the data are not restricted to physical respondents. Any conceptualization of an actor can be specified as a category in the content analysis of documents and so enter relations via equations 8.1 and 8.2: individual persons or social categories of persons, individual organizations, of types of organizations. Third, the data are nonreactive to the interests of the actors among whom relations are to be described (see Webb et al., 1966: ch. 3, for a nice review of this issue with respect to archival records). The interests of the actors assembling the content analyzed documents are another matter, of course, and I will return to them at the end of the discussion. Finally, and perhaps most importantly, the archival network data can be used to describe transformations in network structure over enormous periods of time. The only limitation on the time period studied is the availability of archival records.

INFERENCES FROM THE
ERSATZ NETWORK DATA

The ersatz network data generated from archival records can be no more adequate than the content analysis defining the m_{ik} and a_{ik} in equations 8.1 and 8.2. Adequately reliable and efficient network data can be obtained from very few documents, but there are clear trade-offs between number of documents one must content analyze and specificity in the actor categories between which relations can be described. These points can be illustrated with the ersatz network data I generated from the New York *Times*.

Sampling Variability

In contemplating an analysis of the ersatz network data, an individual will have in mind alternative typologies of actor categories and (in the interest of saving time and research funds) will be interested in content analyzing a minimum number of documents while maintaining sufficient efficiency in the estimated z as a network elements to distinguish nonnegligible from negligible relationships. This issue can be addressed by computing several estimates of the the same network elements for multiple typologies.

Suppose that, for a given time interval, a sample of D documents was to be content analyzed to generate ersatz network data on the time interval. Let z be an element of Z in equation 8.1 or equation 8.2 averaged over the D documents: $z = \Sigma_d^D z_{ijd} / D$, where z_{ijd} is the value of z estimated from the dth document. The standard error of z as a mean value of the z_{ijd} is then the standard deviation of the z_{ijd} across the D documents divided by the square root of the number of documents:

$$s_z = s_{ij} / D^{1/2} \qquad [8.3]$$

where s_z is the standard error for z and s_{ij} is the standard deviation of the z_{ijd} around the mean z. A confidence interval around the estimate network element z can be constructed in the usual way from the t-distribution once the standard error for z is defined. One is then able to say that the prominence of the association between actors i and j is z, plus or minus some amount for a given level of confidence.

For a time interval selected as a test interval, suppose several replicate samples of D documents were drawn, each providing an estimate of z as the prominence of the association between actors i and j. The D documents within each replicate sample, multipled by the number of replicate samples drawn, equal K, the total number of documents drawn for the test interval. Let ζ be the value of z computed across all K documents (i.e., $\zeta = \Sigma_k^K z_{ijk} / K$) and let s_ζ be a standard error for this estimated network element across all K documents. Since ζ is based on more documents than z, let ζ be a "true" value of z_{ij} for the test interval. To the extent that the D documents are adequate to generate estimates of z_{ij}, the estimated z for replicate samples should all fall within a reasonable confidence interval around the "true" value ζ. More to the point, the percentage of replicate estimates falling outside the interval indicates how finely network relations can be defined. For increasingly finely defined network relations (shorter time intervals, more narrowly defined actor categories), an increasing number of replicate estimates of z will fall outside a reasonable confidence interval around ζ. The question is: How finely can network relations be defined before too many replicate estimates fall outside a reasonable confidence interval around the true relation ζ? This question was very helpful in legitimating inferences from the New York *Times* network data.

The number of newspapers that could be content analyzed was severely limited by the research budget. Two issues of the New York *Times* were selected per year from 1877 to 1972 using a constrained random sampling procedure. The sampling was constrained, given the small number of newspapers being coded, so as to maximize the representativeness of the eight issues selected for the four years in a four-year inteval. For each year, an issue was selected shortly after the first of April and shortly after the first of October. The issues were randomly assigned to days of the week (Monday through Friday) following April or October 1st so that there would not be large percentages of issues selected from particular days of the week.[3]

The small number of newspaper issues being coded in turn limited the degree to which network relations could be described in fine detail. Four different levels of aggregation were considered in defining actor categories. The m_{ik} in equation 8.3, mentions, were coded for N equal to 2, 4, 11, and 25. The content and rationale for these alternative typologies of actors are given elsewhere.[4] Ersatz network data were obtained among actors in each of the four typologies for each of two time intervals: four-year intervals and one-year, or annual, intervals. The estimated z for a one-year interval was the average of the two z_{ijd} obtained from the two newspapers sampled for that year. The estimated z for a four-year interval was the average of the eight z_{ijd} obtained from the two newspapers sampled for each of the four years in the interval. As described above under equation 8.1, both z expressed the proportion of the front page of the New York *Times* in which relations between actors i and j were discussed.

Three test time intervals were selected for assessing the adequacy of the data collection process—one at the beginning of the time series (1877-1880), one in the middle of the time series (1925-1928), and one at the end of the time series (1968-1972). For each of these test intervals, 16 additional issues of the New York *Times* were randomly selected to be content analyzed in addition to the 8 obtained in the constrained random sample. There were then 24 newspaper issues from which 24 estimates of z_{ijd} were obtained and across which a "true" value was computed: $\zeta = \Sigma_d z_{ijd}/24$, for d equal 1 to 24. A 95 percent confidence interval was constructed around this overall mean for each test interval using the standard error in equation 8.3, but a robust estimate of the standard deviation s_{ij}.[5]

Table 8.1 shows how often annual and four-year estimates of z fell outside the confidence interval around ζ for the different typologies of actors. As an indication of the stability of the four-year estimates, the confidence intervals around ζ ranged from + .00 to +.10, with a mean confidence interval of +.03. The results in Table 8.1 show that estimated four-year interval z were adequate when two, four, or eleven actor categories were distinguished. Only one replicate four-year interval estimate of z fell outside a 95 percent confidence interval around ζ, and that one was only .01 beyond its confidence interval. When 25 actor categories were distiguished, however, 5 of the possible 75 z were outside their confidence intervals. Turning to the annual data, values of ζ were computed for the one year in each test interval, the year in which the greatest number of issues were sampled (for 1878, K = 11, for 1926 and 1970, K = 10). As would be expected, the sampling variability of the annual z was higher than the sampling variability of the four-year interval z. The confidence intervals around the annual ζ ranged from +.00 to +.18, with a mean of +.05.

What is striking about the results in Table 8.1 for annual estimates is the stability they do show. Even though annual z were only based on a content analysis of two issues of the New York *Times*, one in early April and one in early October, the estimates are adequate when two or four actor categories were distinguished. Sampling variance obscures inferences about relations among actors in the 11- and 25-category typologies. Five of the possible 33 estimates were inadequate when 11 actor categories were distinguished, and 8 of 75 estimates were inadequate when 25 actor categories were distinguished.

These results guided the data analysis. Trends in relations among actors in the two- and four-category typologies were described with annual time series estimates of the relations. When 11 or 25 categories of actors were distinguished, however, annual estimates had to be combined into four-year intervals or more in order to provide trustworthy point estimates of network relations.

Reliability

A perennial problem in content analysis is the reliability of the assignment of content to categories in a coding scheme. If the purpose of

TABLE 8.1 Frequency of Inadequate Replicate Estimates of Ersatz Network Elements

Levels of Aggregation	Test Intervals		
Four-Year Estimates			
Levels of aggregation	1877-1880	1925-1928	1968-1972
Two categories of actors	0 (0%)	0 (0%)	0 (0%)
Four categories of actors	0 (0%)	0 (0%)	0 (0%)
Interactions among four categories of actors	0 (0%)	1 (17%)	0 (0%)
Eleven categories of actors	0 (0%)	0 (0%)	0 (0%)
Twenty-five categories of actors	1 (4%)	2 (8%)	2 (8%)
One-Year Estimates			
Levels of aggregation	1878	1926	1970
Two categories of actors	0 (0%)	0 (0%)	0 (0%)
Four categories of actors	0 (0%)	0 (0%)	0 (0%)
Interactions among four categories of actors	0 (0%)	0 (0%)	0 (0%)
Eleven categories of actors	2 (18%)	1 (9%)	2 (18%)
Twenty-five categories of actors	4 (16%)	2 (8%)	2 (8%)

NOTE: Entries in cells are the number of estimates that fall outside a 95 percent confidence interval around the overall mean ζ for the test interval. The percentage of possible estimates which could have been inadequate is given in parentheses.

the content analysis is to generate ersatz network data among specific groups or persons, then each of the N actor categories contains known actor(s). Each actor category is identifiable in terms of a set of concrete symbols, e.g., the government actor "United States" can be referenced with several alternative empirical symbols: "U.S.," "United States," "America," et cetera. The coding process in this situation can most reliably be approached through computer coding of documents that code the presence of an actor whenever one records one or more of the symbols referring to an actor in a discussion (see, for example, Stone et al., 1966; Holsti, 1968: 663-673). It is likely, however, that the specification of exhaustive sets of alternative symbols referencing those actors to be assigned to particular actor categories is inadequate. Actor categories will often be defined in terms of an abstract set of characteristics, which can then be applied to a wide range of empirical symbols describing actors in documents. Examples are actors engaging in similar role behavior or general classes of actors in the social system. In this situation, actors are assigned to categories according to the number of characteristics they share with a specified ideal type that defines each actor category. Willey (1926: ch. 2) remains a succinct discussion of guidelines for constructing a general set of categories for content analyzing varied documents.

Reliability entails different problems to defining actor categories under these two approaches. For networks among actor categories, where each category is composed of known actors, the content analysis will be as reliable as the list of alternative symbols used to reference actors in each category is exhaustive. For the more abstract procedure where actor categories are defined in terms of characteristics of ideal type actors, the reliability of the content analysis of documents will increase as (1) the aggregation of actors into polythetic actor categories increases (see, for example, Janis et al., 1943), and (2) the characteristic of ideal type actors defining each actor category are increasingly stated as a series of binary (yes-no) decisions on whether or not a particular actor shares the given characteristic with the ideal type (e.g., Stempel, 1955; Schutz, 1958).[6]

These two points are illustrated by the reliability results reported in Table 8.2 for the New York *Times* network data. Two people were randomly assigned to code the sample newspaper issues. There were 56 issues that were coded by both people. From these multiple codings, 28 annual estimates of network relations were estimates (28 based on the coding of one person and another 28 based on the coding of the other person), and 11 four-year estimates were obtained. To the extent that the coding was reliable, identical values of z should have been generated from the coding of either person. The intercoder correlations in Table 8.2 show how unreliability began to enter the coding as network relations were increasingly finely defined. These results might not generalize easily to all content analyses generating the network data in equations 8.1 or 8.2; however, they illustrate some general points which confirm common-sense expectations. Three points are illustrated.

First, the four-year estimates of network elements are more reliable than the annual estimates. The correlations in the first column of Table 8.2 are consistently higher than corresponding correlations in the second column. In part, this result is to be expected from the higher sampling variance in the annual estimates, a point demonstrated in Table 8.1.

Second, the prominence of actors is more reliable than the prominence of relations between actors. For each typology of actors (N = 2, 4, 11, and 25) and for annual as well as four-year estimates, the intercoder correlations for the prominence of actors (the z_{ii} in equations 8.1 and 8.2) are higher on average than corresponding correlations for the interaction between actors (the z_{ij} in equations 8.1 and 8.2).

TABLE 8.2 Mean Intercoder Reliabilities

Levels of Aggregation	Mean Intercoder Reliability	
	Four-year intervals $n = 11$	One-year intervals $n = 28$
Two categories of actors	0.93	0.79
Interaction between two categories of actors	0.90	0.75
Four categories of actors	0.67	0.49
Interactions among four categories of actors	0.46	0.43
Eleven categories of actors	0.56	0.43
Interactions among eleven categories of actors	0.34	0.31
Twenty-five categories of actors	0.50	0.44
Interactions among twenty-five categories of actors	0.28	0.25

NOTE: The number of estimates correlated between the two coders is given as n. Correlations between the two coders have been averaged across multiple estimates of a type. For example, two diagonal elements were generated by each coder for the two-category actor typology: z_{11} and z_{22}. The intercoder reliabilities for annual estimates of these two network elements were .765 and .817, respectively. The mean intercoder reliability given in the first row under annual estimates is the average of these two reliabilities $(.79 = (.765 + .817)/2)$.

Finally, the reliability of the network data declines as the number of actors distinguished in a typology increases. For annual as well as four-year estimates, the intercoder correlations at the top of Table 8.2 are high and decline as one reads down the rows of the table.

There are at least two methods of dealing with sharply varying reliabilities. The first and most obvious method is to improve the reliability of the coding used to generate the network data following the guidelines given above. Given the variably reliable network data already collected, this method of dealing with unreliability would involve ignoring the unacceptable data. The results in Tables 8.1 and 8.2, for example, led me to focus on the two- and four-category actor typologies in describing trends in the annual network time series.

A second method for dealing with variably reliable network data already collected is to specify the multiple estimates of the same network elements as multiple indicators of an unobserved variable (the true estimate of the network element) in a structural equation model. In Table 8.2, there is no basis for saying which of the two measures of a network element are more accurate. The two estimates are merely alternatives which should be, in the ideal, identical. Given that they are not identical, a pooled estimate can be obtained by giving the two estimates different weights in determining the pooled estimate. The coder whose estimates had higher construct validity—in the sense of yielding stronger correlations with known concomitants of the estimates—should be given higher weight in determining the pooled estimate. If, for example, I knew that the prominence of the relation between two classes of actors was strongly correlated with the economic conditions of actors, and two coders differed in the estimates of the relation implied by their coding, I would place more confidence in the coding of the person whose estimates were more strongly correlated with the appropriate economic conditions.

This process of weighting alternative indicators of a concept by the manner in which they enter propositions has been discussed as the "substitutability of indices" and the "point of variability" of indices and is an inherent feature of multiple indicator structural equation models (see, e.g., Burt, 1976b, for references and details). As discussed in detail elsewhere, this feature can be exploited to improve inferences from marginally adequate network data obtained from archival records (Burt, 1975: 317-326; Burt and Lin, 1977: 239-247).

TWO KEY ASSUMPTIONS

The ersatz network data discussed here depend on two key assumptions in order to realize their potential advantages over traditional sociometric data: structural equivalence within actor categories and accurate recording of actor activities in the archival records.

All relations between specific actors in two of the N categories of actors defined in an actor typology are represented by a single ersatz network element z_{ij} for actor categories i and j. In order for this one network element to reflect relational patterns in the population of inference accurately, specific actors in each actor category must be structurally equivalent. This assumption says that the set of actors within a category will have similar relations with all actors relevant to the content analysis for all periods of time described in the content analysis (see Chapter 13, this volume, for a detailed discussion of structural equivalence).

When this assumption is violated, actors have been combined into a single category when in fact they constitute multiple categories. The subsequent estimates of z_{ij} will be aggregates of distinct types of relations between actors instead of being estimates of a single relationship. The estimates of z_{ij} will still reflect the relations between actors in categories i and j. However, that relation will be one that does not actually exist among the actors in the social system being described. When the assumption of structural equivalence within content categories is violated, therefore, the erroneously aggregated actor categories should be disaggregated until they are composed solely of actors who are at least equivalent under a weak criterion of equivalence.

At an early stage in the analysis of the New York *Times* network data, for example, it was hypothesized that one of the actor categories of import for relations between people and corporate actors would be that set of corporate actors that made a profit by ensuring the political rights of their investors. Three subsets within this category termed "political corporate actors" were labor unions, political parties, and trade associations. When the data were gathered, however, these subsets of actors had different trends of change in attention over time. The category of labor unions received increasing attention; political parties received decreasing attention. Trade associations received a continuously low amount of attention. These different trends in attention were similarly reflected in the associations involving the three subsets of actors. The general category of political corporate actors was therefore discarded as a violation of the structural equivalence assumption, and the three subsets of actors were analyzed as separate actor categories.

A second, and obvious, assumption for making inferences from the ersatz network data is that the content analyzed records accurately describe the joint involvements of actors relevant to the analysis. Even if the records do not accurately describe the relations between all actors in the social system to be described, they must accurately reflect the connections between the actors specified as one of the N categories in equations 8.1 or 8.2. There are two violations of this assumption that are likely to occur and that can be addressed in the data analysis.

First, bias in estimating the magnitudes of the off-diagonal network elements can be manipulated by judiciously selecting the size of sections in the documents to be coded. By increasing the material to be content analyzed within a section, the observed number of interactions between actors will increase since more actors can be mentioned in a single section (see Osgood's [1959] discussion of contingency analysis of the co-occurrence of content characteristics and Geller et al.'s [1942] analysis of the increase in extent of coding bias with increasing section size). For example, the off-diagonal network elements in the New York *Times* data would have been increased by content analyzing the entire contents of articles instead of first paragraphs. The elements would have been decreased by only content analyzing the first sentence of each article.

The important point here is that the absolute magnitude of the z_{ij} is less important than their relative magnitude. Inasmuch as the absolute magnitude of z_{ij} can be increased or decreased, with increases or decreases in the amount of material content analyzed in document sections, the amount of material coded should be that amount maximizing the variation in the z_{ij} so as to highlight the structure of relations among actors. I decided on the first paragraph of each article on the assumption that the most important actors in an article would be mentioned in the opening paragraph. Still, there were changes over the time period studied in the editorial style of naming actors in the first paragraph of an article. At the beginning of the time series, in the late 1800s, articles mentioned all actors participating or attending a social situation. At the end of the time series, during the post-World War II period, articles focused on actors involved in a specific event or issue associated with a social situation. The raw proportion of network data defined in equation 8.1 were therefore biased downward over time— fewer actors had the opportunity to be mentioned together in later articles than they did in early articles. Consequently, deviation levels of interaction were analyzed, as opposed to raw proportion levels of interaction (Burt, 1975: 283-287, 300-304). In other words, z_{ij} was analyzed as a deviation from the mean tendency for interactions ($z_{ij} = \Sigma_i\Sigma_j z_{ij}$, where $i \neq j$) so that prominent relations were those that were above average, and negligible relations were those that were well below average, for a specific time interval.

A second likely source of bias in the estimation of ersatz network elements stems from the judicious selection of available information by the editors of archival records (see review by Danzer, 1975). With few exceptions, archival records are produced within a social system for consumption by an intended audience. Persons in the intended audience have interests in events, interests they satisfy by consuming the documents in archival records (see Stephanson, 1967, for an elaboration of this point in his play theory of mass communication, and Lin, 1973: 44-86, 182-191, for general review discussion). The editors of archival records retain their positions as long as they can guide the content of the archival records to meet the interests of their intended audience.

In other words, documents should be sampled for content analysis whose intended audience and editors are interested in maximizing the similarity of the content in the documents and the ongoing events in the social system to be inferred from the ersatz network data. It is assumed that a low value of network element z_{ij} does not mean that the editors of the coded documents are ignoring actors in the ith or jth category because they believe that their audience is uninterested in those actors.

Failure to meet this assumption simply invalidates inferences from the ersatz network data to the social system of interest.

Two precautions can be taken to guard against the violation of this second assumption. First, and most obviously, multiple types of archival records can be content analyzed and compared in terms of the inferences they generate. This approach depends on truly different types of records being content analyzed. Merely content analyzing multiple records of the same time can only ensure lower sampling variability in the estimated network elements. Second, exogenous determinants of differences in editorial policy can be specified as confounding influences on the observed estimates of z_{ij} (e.g., Burt, 1975: 322; Burt and Lin, 1977: 246). Controlling for variation in the network elements that is associated with these known disturbances increases the confidence with which inferences can be made from the network data.

NOTES

1. An interesting analysis of the same mass media records was published by Lindenberg (1976), but his analysis went beyond mine to consider asymmetric ties between actor categories. The contrast between our methods for attacking the same problem (How have relations between people and corporate actors changed in terms of their representations in the mass media?) is informative.

2. It should be clear by this point that the network data I am creating from archival records are tendencies for relations to occur between actors. I am not referring to the more obvious data published with the expressed purpose of describing relations in a network (e.g., the input-output tables published by the Department of Commerce to describe transactions between sectors of the American economy [Burt, 1980a, 1982a: ch. 8]), nor am I referring to archival records used to create a tie at one point in time between specific people (e.g., Boyer and Nissenbaum, 1974).

3. The sampling procedure is explained in detail in a National Opinion Report that I completed in 1976: "Corporate Society: A Time Series Analysis of Network Structure," Appendix B, and in Appendix D of my unpublished Ph.D. dissertation from the University of Chicago in 1977.

4. See the references in note 3.

5. Given the small number of newspaper issues being coded, I decided to use a jackknife estimate of the standard deviation (e.g., Mosteller and Tukey, 1968: 128-160). The value of s_{ij} used was computed as an average: $s_{ij} = \Sigma_k s_k / K$, where K equaled the 24 issues in a test interval, and s_k was a pseudo-estimate; $s_k = (K)s_{all} = (K-1)s$ (all but issue k) where s_{all} is the usual estimate of s_{ij} based on the z_{ijd} for the test interval and s (all but issue k) is the same estimate based on 23 z_{ijd} (all but the one issue generating z_{ijk}). Since the jackknife estimate will be robust over extreme differences between the z_{ijd}, it will be a conservative estimate. This will in turn reduce the standard error in equation 8.3 and increase the likelihood that replicate estimates of z fall outside the 95 percent confidence interval around ζ.

6. As pointed out by Markoff et al. (1974: 35-38), additional problems stem from the necessary treatment of humans as consistent measuring instruments over the time spent content analyzing documents. This problem is particularly dangerous in the content

analysis of archival records to generate network time series, since coding over the course of the time period studies can change, thereby confounding coder changes with trends in the network relations. In order to avoid this problem in the New York *Times* analysis, four-year intervals were randomly arranged in terms of the order in which they were coded, th s randomizing the effects of informal changes in coding on the trends inferred from the network data.

Part II

NETWORK STRUCTURE

Chapter 9

Range

RONALD S. BURT

Relations have range to the extent that they connect an actor with an extensive diversity of other actors. Easily obtained and substantively informative, range is a network concept especially useful in empirical research. Substantively distinct measures of range, however, stem from concepts of diversity as volume versus quality of contacts with other actors where actors can be individuals or status groups. These distinctions are easily overlooked when operationalizing the range concept in empirical research. In this brief chapter, I discuss a series of questions highlighting substantive distinctions among range measures and illustrating how erroneous research inferences can be made if alternative range measures are treated as equivalent. In particular, I point out conditions under which measuring range as the number of alters in an ego network could result in erroneous inferences.

Perhaps the least pretentious of network concepts is range, a concept typically defined in terms of ego networks. Given persons, or groups, or corporate bureaucracies as actors, an ego network contains all actors (alters) directly connected with a particular actor (ego). The ego network consists of all relations among ego and his alters. Ego's network has range to the extent that it connects him with a diversity of other actors.

At once simple to compute (as a sum of alters) and substantively informative (as a measure of access to resources such as social support and information on opportunities), range has become a popular network concept in empirical research. At the same time, range can be oversimplified, resulting in erroneous research conclusions.

This chapter is a didactic discussion of range as a variable in empirical research. I discuss answers to a series of questions concerning the operationalization of range. In particular, I point out some problems with equating range to the number of alters contained in an ego

Author's Note: *Work on this chapter was facilitated by secretarial assistance provided by the Survey Research Center, University of California at Berkeley (through the auspices of Percy H. Tannenbaum and James A. Wiley) and a grant from the National Institute on Drug Abuse (to Michael J. Minor at the Pacific Institute for Research and Evaluation, grant DA02566). Dave Knoke and Michael Minor provided helpful comments on a draft of this chapter.*

network. I do not argue that number of alters is at all times an erroneous measure. Rather, I argue that range is a multidimensional concept to such an extent that erroneous inferences can be expected from empirical research ignoring those differences.

WHAT IS RANGE?

I shall make some simplifying assumptions for the purposes here and return to them later as more narrowly defined questions. Assume that one relational content is being considered (e.g., friendship, advice, intimacy), and that the strength of the relation between actors j and i, z_{ji}, is measured on a scale varying from zero to one (i.e., $0 \leq z_{ji}, \leq 1$, and z_{ij} arbitrarily set equal to 1), where relations are symmetric ties between actors (i.e., $z_{ji} = z_{ij}$).

Figure 9.1 contains a hypothetical ego network in which ego has relations with eight alters, where alters are represented by dots, and nonzero relations are represented by solid lines. Note that some alters, too, have relations with one another. Alters who are members of the same status group, groups being undefined for the moment, are enclosed in dashed line boxes. Data such as these can be obtained in standard sociometric interviews with all egos in a system of actors, as well as from mass survey interviews with egos randomly sampled from a large population (although the latter requires a respondent to describe relations among his or her alters). Ego's relations have range to the extent that they involve a diversity of actors. Different range measures emerge from different concepts of diversity.

Volume of Contacts

The simplest concept of diversity equates it to the volume of ego's contacts. Ego's relations have range to the extent that they connect him with many alters: many individual actors and many types of actors. *The number of actors directly connected to an individual is an index of the extent to which the individual is involved in many different relationships.* One measure of the range of an ego network is therefore the number of alters, n, directly connected to ego. In Figure 9.1, ego has contact with eight alters, so n would equal 8. But the diversity of actors indicating network range is often taken to mean more than mere number of actors; it is taken to mean numerous types of actors.

Actors are often classified into types according to the status they occupy in society, statuses associated with occupation, ethnicity, age, sex, and so on. Considering the statuses in the larger society from which ego draws alters for his own network informs the measurement of range

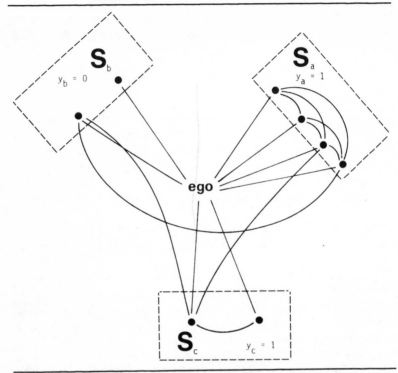

Figure 9.1:   Hypothetical Ego Network Containing Symmetric Relations and Eight Alters Drawn from Three Status Groups

as an index of ego's access to resources in society more generally. Given a social environment stratified into status groups, an ego network has extensive range to the extent that it includes actors from many status groups. Contacting two people from the same status does not increase range across status groups so much as it creates redundancy in contacts because the two people are the same status alter. The greater the number of different status groups to which ego has access, the greater the diversity of information and social support to which he has access.

A second measure of the range of an ego network, therefore, is the number of different status groups, m, represented by the alters directly connected to ego. Although ego has contact with eight alters in Figure 9.1, for example, several come from the same status group, so that the range of ego's relations is less impressive than it might appear from the number of individuals with whom ego has contact. Measured in terms of the status groups with which he is in contact, ego's relations have a range of three statuses (i.e., m = 3).

Despite their crude representation of network structure, measures of range as contact volume can be very informative in empirical research. For example, Berkman and Syme (1979) construct a social network index from counts of ego network alters. A person had a high score on this index to the extent that he or she had frequent contact with many close friends and relatives. This simple count index of network range has a strong association with mortality—the likelihood of death decreasing with increasing range—even after a variety of differences among egos are held constant (e.g., age, socioeconomic status, overall physical health, and health practices). Results such as this have been interpreted as evidence supporting the idea that ego's access to social support increases with the number of relations in which ego is involved (e.g., see Fischer, 1982a: ch. 11, for review and discussion).

Turning from people to corporate actors, there is a research tradition built around analyses of interlocking directorates in terms of range. Two corporations are connected by an interlock tie when at least one person holds a position on the board of directors in both firms. The range of a corporation's network of interlock ties can be measured as the number of other firms directly connected to it by interlock ties (i.e., n) or as the number of economic sectors directly connected to it by interlock ties to organizations in each section (i.e., m). Using either measure to describe the range of interlock ties for large American firms, range is positively associated with corporation size (in terms of assets or sales) and negatively associated with concentration of control over a firm (in terms of dominance by a kinship group or management). With increasing size and decreasing concentration of control in a firm, the firm has an increasing range of interlock ties connecting it to many firms in many sectors of the economy. This finding has been interpreted as evidence for the argument that interlock ties enable firms to coopt environmental threats to their survival given the access that interlock ties provide to information on one another's business activities (see Burt, 1980d, 1982a: ch. 4, forthcoming, for review and discussion).

Quality of Contact

Measuring range as the number of ego's contacts requires the assumption that each of ego's contacts equally increases the range of his contacts. This assumption is obviously false, but eliminating it requires slightly more complex range measures. The range of ego's network is not increased equally by each of his contacts so much as it is increased by the quality of contact. With respect to network range, a contact has quality to the extent that it increases the diversity of alters in ego's network. The quality of ego's relation with a specific alter, in other words, is determined by the more general structural context in which it occurs.

Contact with a status group as an alter, for example, increases the diversity of alters in ego's network to the extent that it represents a small proportion of the interaction in which ego is involved, and the actors within the status group are themselves diverse. More specifically, actor j's relation with status S_i has high quality in the diversity it offers j to the extent that the following expression is close to its minimum value of 0:

$$y_i p_{ji}^2 \qquad [9.1]$$

where p_{ji} is the proportion of j's interaction represented by his relations with alters drawn from the status (i.e., the sum of the z_{ji} for all j's alters drawn from the ith status group divided by the sum of all z_{ji} for the n alters with whom j has relations), and y_i is a measure varying from 0 to 1 of the extent to which the ith status group is highly cohesive, or centralized (indicating that its constituent actors know one another, are aware of the same kinds of opportunities, have access to the same kinds of resources, and share the same kinds of perceptions). (For details on alternative y_i measures, see the discussion by Knoke and Burt in the next chapter, and the discussion of cohesion by Alba and Moore in Chapter 12 and Burt in Chapter 13.)

The product in equation 9.1 will be close to 0 to the extent that a very small proportion of j's relations involve actors from the ith status group, and/or the status group is so diverse that y_i is close to 0 in value. In Figure 9.1, for example, ego's relations are of equal strength, so 4/8s of all interactions are represented by ego's relations with the four alters drawn from status S_a and 2/8s are represented by relations with the two alters drawn from each of statuses S_b and S_c (i.e., $p_{ja} = .5$, $p_{jb} = p_{jc} = .25$). Status S_b is indicated to contain highly diverse actors ($y_b = 0$), while the other two statuses contain minimally diverse actors ($y_a = y_c = 1$). This means that ego's contact with status S_b yields ego access to more diverse actors (equation 9.1 equals 0 times .25 squared, or .0) than does contact with status S_c (for which equation 9.1 equals .06—1 times .25 squared), and ego's contact with status S_a consumes a lot of his interaction, yielding little diversity (equation 9.1 equals 1 times .5 squared, or .25). The sum of equation 9.1 across all status groups i from which ego could draw alters varies from 0 to a maximum of 1. Subtracting that sum from its maximum value of 1 yields the following status group measure of the range of actor j's relations:

$$1 - \sum_{i=1}^{m} (y_i p_{ji}^2) \qquad [9.2]$$

which varies from 0 to 1 as the extent to which a small proportion of ego's interaction involves alters drawn from any one status group (i.e., all p_{ji} are low) and/or each status group from which ego does draw alters contains highly diverse actors (i.e., all y_i are low for nonzero p_{ji}). As an example, the network in Figure 9.1 offers ego a range of .69 (.69 = 1 - .00 - .06 - .25), indicating some diversity of contacts.

I have two reasons for presenting the range measure in equation 9.2. First, the measure is a component in a more general theory of structural autonomy explaining how relations free actors to pursue their interests. Equation 9.2 is the group-affiliation index in the model of structural autonomy explored in detail elsewhere (Burt, 1982a: ch. 7). I value this because it links empirical analyses of network range with more general lines of work in structural theory, thereby increasing opportunity for that theory to inform empirical research. Second, the measure of range in equation 9.2 has been substantively fruitful in explaining differences in market constraints on corporate profits in the American economy and the structure of cooptive interlock ties among large American firms (e.g., Burt, 1980a, 1982a: ch. 8, forthcoming; Burt et al., 1980). A point especially noteworthy here (elaborated in Burt, 1982d, forthcoming: ch. 7) is the fact that the mere volume of relations (i.e., p_{ji} alone) does not predict the strength of cooptive interlock ties nearly as accurately as the quality of those relations (i.e., equation 9.1).

Its conceptual advantages and substantive potential nonwithstanding, the range measure in equation 9.2 can be troublesome in empirical research. It requires that alters be assigned to nonoverlapping status groups, but alters are likely to be members of overlapping status groups where the boundaries of statuses are typically ambiguous—even if network data have been obtained from the alters (see the discussion of structural equivalence in Chapter 13). Moreover, there is the problem of selecting those of the many possible status groups in terms of which alters should be distinguished. Range could be a function of the diversity of ego's contact with occupational groups, kinship groups, ethnic groups, age groups, religious groups, or a host of other possibilities.

Where the status groups pertinent to a substantive problem under study are not clearly defined, therefore, there is merit in defining range purely in terms of the structure of relations in an ego network without worrying about the status groups from which alters have been drawn. *Ego's relationship with an individual increases the diversity of alters in ego's network to the extent that the individual is unconnected with the other alters in the network.* This idea is nicely articulated by Granovetter (1973, 1982) in his discussion of weak ties (compare Laumann, 1973, on radial networks). More specifically, the relation that actor j has with alter i has high quality in the diversity it offers j to the extent that the following expression is close to its minimum value of 0:

$$z_{ji} \left[\sum_{q=1}^{n} (p_{jq} z_{qi}) \right] \qquad j \neq q \qquad [9.3]$$

where z_{ji} is the strength of the relation between actors j and i (ego and alter), and p_{ji} is the proportion of j's interaction represented by j's relation with alter q (i.e., z_{jq} divided by the sum of all z_{ji} for the n alters with whom j has relations).

The bracketed term in equation 9.3 varies from 0 to 1 as the extent to which the greatest proportion of j's interaction is with alters q who in turn have maximum strength relations with alter i (i.e., z_{qi} equals 1 for all nonzero p_{jq}). This means that the entire product in equation 9.3 varies from 0 to 1 as the extent to which ego has a maximum strength relation with alter i, and every other alter in ego's network has a maximum strength relation with alter i. In other words, equation 9.3 varies from 0 to 1 as the extent to which the information and social support that alter i could provide to ego is likely to be redundant with the information and support available from the other n-1 alters in ego's network. In Figure 9.1 for example, ego's relation with the topmost alter in status S_b offers the greatest diversity because S_b is completely unconnected from the other alters (equation 9.3 equals .13; 13 = 1[1/8]), ego's relation with the alter to the right in status S_c offers the next greatest diversity because S_c is connected with only one other alter (equation 9.3 equals .25; .25 = 1[1/8 + 1/8]), and ego's relations with the two alters at the bottom of status S_a offer the least diversity because both of them are connected to four other alters (equation 9.3 equals .63; .63 = 1[1/8 + 1/8 + 1/8 + 1/8 + 1/8]).

The sum of equation 9.3 across all n alters varies from 0 up to a maximum equal to the sum of ego's relations (sum of z_{ji} across all i); the maximum occurring when the bracketed term in equation 9.3 equals 1 for each alter. Subtracting that sum from its maximum value and dividing by the maximum yields the following measure of the range of actor j's relations:

$$\sum_{i=1}^{n} z_{ji} \left[1 - \sum_{q=1}^{n} (p_{jq} z_{qi}) \right] \bigg/ \left[\sum_{i} z_{ji} \right], \qquad i \neq j \neq q \qquad [9.4]$$

which varies from 0 to 1 as the extent to which ego has relations with a large number of alters (i.e., all p_{jq} are low) who have no relations with one another (i.e., all z_{qi} are low). As an example, the network in Figure

9.1 offers ego a range of .56 (.56 = [8 -1/8 -3/8 -4/8 -2/8 -5/8 -5/8 -4/8 - 4/8]/8). The fact that this range score is well below 1 indicates that several of ego's contacts are redundant with one another.

There is a connection here with range measured in terms of ego's contacts with status groups. I have stated equation 9.4 in terms of the connections among alters who are in turn connected to ego, but those alters could be individual actors or status groups. In contrast to the group affiliation index in equation 9.2 focusing on the internal structure of status groups, equation 9.4 computed for status group alters (n being replaced with m) would focus on the structure of connection between status groups, assuming each to be equally cohesive (given z_{ii} equal to 1 for all alters i in equation 9.4). Such an idea has been fruitfully employed by Laumann (1966, 1973) to describe differences between people in their range of social ties.[1]

In summary, I have discussed four range measures based on different features of the diversity of alters in an ego network: (1) The number of actors in contact with ego, n, is a measure of the volume of actors with whom ego is involved. (2) The number of status groups from which ego draws actors for his network, m, is a measure of the volume of types of actors with whom ego is involved. Looking more closely at the quality of ego's relationships, (3) range can be measured in terms of the internal structure of status group alters as the extent to which ego has diversified contacts such that ego does not have strong ties with cohesive groups (equation 9.2), and (4) it can be measured in terms of contacts among alters as the extent to which ego has diversified contacts such that he does not have strong ties with alters who in turn have strong ties with all of ego's other alters (equation 9.4).

HOW DIFFERENT ARE
ALTERNATIVE MEASURES?

Table 9.1 contains range scores for the nine hypothetical ego networks presented in Figures 9.2 and 9.3. Figure 9.2 contains four networks, each containing two alters where one alter is connected to ego by a strong tie (solid line indicating a z_{ji} of 1), and the other has a weak tie to ego (dashed line indicating z_{ji} of .5). These values are arbitrary, of course, but serve to illustrate the point I wish to raise. The first column of Figure 9.2 presents the ego networks when data are available on relations among alters. The second column presents the same ego networks when data are only available on the status groups from which ego has drawn alters. Figure 9.3 contains five hypothetical networks in the same format as Figure 9.2 except that the networks in Figure 9.3

TABLE 9.1   Measures of the Range of Relations in the Hypothetical
Ego Networks Presented in Figures 9.2 and 9.3

			Range Measures	
Network	n	m	Eq. 9.2	Eq. 9.4
Figure 9.2				
1	2	1	1.00	.44
2	2	2	.89	.44
3	2	2	.55	.44
4	2	1	.44	.00
Figure 9.3				
5	3	1	1.00	.63
6	3	2	.94	.63
7	3	2	.88	.50
8	3	2	.69	.38
9	3	1	.63	.00

contain three alters rather than two. I have computed the four range measures by hand for several small ego networks. The volume of contact measures are easily obtained as a coding exercise even for large networks; however, the quality of contact measures are time-consuming to obtain without a computer. Equation 9.4 and number of alters (n) are the range measures output by the network analysis program STRUCTURE (Project, 1981).

The possibilities for differences among the range measures increase with the number of alters in an ego network, but there is obvious variability among the measures even for the simple two- and three-alter networks in Figures 9.2 and 9.3. For example, the first four networks are listed in the first four rows of Table 9.1. All four contain two alters (n = 2); however, they draw those alters from a variable number of statuses (m equals 1 or 2), where those statuses offer variable diversity (equation 9.2 varies from .44 up to 1.00), and the alters are variably connected so as to be variably independent contacts for ego (equation 9.4 varies between .00 and .44). Networks 2, 3, 6, 7 and 8 all draw alters from two statuses (m = 2), as listed in the corresponding rows of Table 9.1. However, the status from which alters are drawn offer variable diversity (equation 9.2 varies from .55 up to .94), the number of alters drawn from the statuses varies (n equals 2 or 3), and the alters are variably connected so as to be variably independent contacts for ego (equation 9.4 varies from .38 up to .63).

More troublesome than the possibility of independent variation among the range measures is the unpredictability of that variation. The

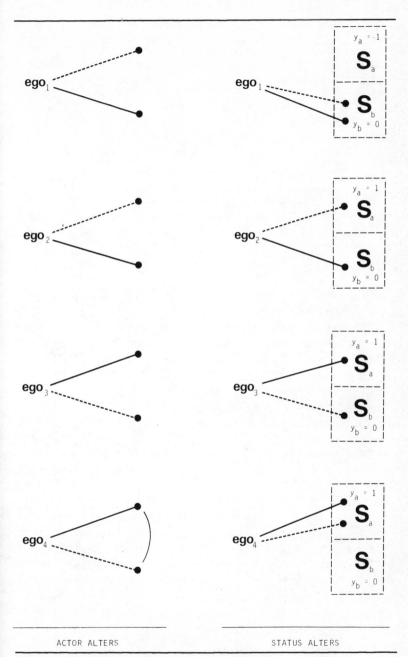

Figure 9.2: Hypothetical Ego Networks Containing Symmetric Relations and Two Alters Drawn from Two Status Groups

ACTOR ALTERS

STATUS ALTERS

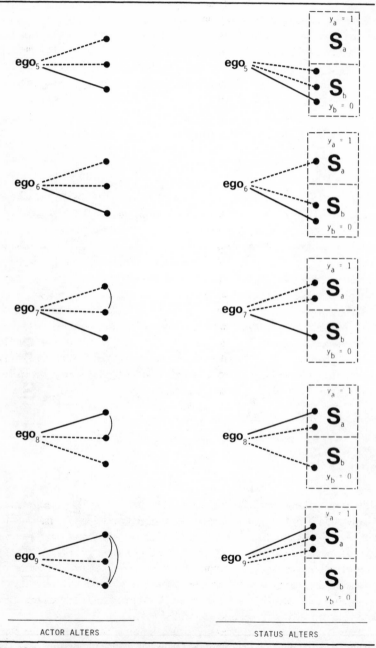

Figure 9.3: Hypothetical Ego Networks Containing Symmetric Relations and Three Alters Drawn from Two Status Groups

extent to which any two of the range measures are correlated can be expected to vary across study populations as a function of the structure of ego networks typical in each population. For example, suppose that some study population consisted solely and equally of actors with ego networks 1, 2, 6 and 7 in Figures 9.2 and 9.3. The following correlations among the four range measures would be expected in sample data representative of the population:[2]

n	1.00	.58	−.37	.81
m		1.00	−.88	.47
Equation 9.2			1.00	−.03
Equation 9.4				1.00

showing that, among other things, the likelihood of a respondent having unconnected alters increases with the number of alters in his network (n has a .8 correlation with equation 9.4), the number of statuses from which alters are drawn increases with the number of alters (n has a .6 correlation with m), and the presence of connections among alters need not mean that they are drawn from cohesive status groups (there is no correlation between the third and fourth measures, equations 9.2 and 9.4). While these results seem to be substantively reasonable, it would be dangerous to generalize them beyond the study population. Suppose that ego networks 1, 2, 8 and 9 were solely and equally found in a study population. The following correlations among the four range measures would then be expected in sample data:

n	1.00	.00	−.95	−.68
m		1.00	−.08	.52
Equation 9.2			1.00	.75
Equation 9.4				1.00

showing that, in contrast to the first study population, the likelihood of a respondent having unconnected alters in his network decreases with the number of alters (n has a −.7 correlation with equation 9.4), the number of statuses from which alters are drawn is uncorrelated with the number of alters (n has no correlation with m), and the presence of connections among alters increases the likelihood that they are drawn from cohesive status groups (there is a .8 correlation between the third and fourth measures, equations 9.2 and 9.4).

This variation in the associations among range measures has implications for testing hypotheses. Consider the proposition that the range of a person's relations indicates the social support available to him, buffering him from stressful events. Suppose that data have been obtained on the stress experienced by sampled respondents and that the question is how to operationalize the range of a respondent's elations so as to predict stress. A negative association between stress and range is hypothesized.

If social support means that ego is involved in many relationships, then n would be the best operationalization of range and would best predict the absence of stress. In the first of the above two study populations, therefore, the hypothesis would be supported if range were measured as: the number of a respondent's alters (n), the number of status groups from which a respondent drew alters (m), or the lack of connections among his or her alters (equation 9.4)—all of which have a strong correlation with the number of relationships in which ego is involved (correlations of 1.0, .6 and .8, respectively). In the second study population, however, the hypothesis would be erroneously rejected if range were not correctly operationalized. The number of relationships in which ego is involved, n, is not associated with the number of status groups from which he draws alters, m, and has a strong negative correlation with the quality of contact measures (correlations of −.95 and −.68).

If social support means that ego is able to draw on alternative, independent relationships so as to avoid social pressure to conform to a particular status group's norms, then the quality of contact measures would be the best operationalizations of range and would best predict the absence of stress. The measure of conflicting group affiliations in ego's network, equation 9.2, would be particularly appropriate for measuring the lack of social pressure on ego. In the second of the above two study populations, range would be negatively associated with stress if range were measured in terms of the lack of cohesion in the status groups from which ego drew alters (equation 9.2), or the lack of connections among his alters (equation 9.4, strongly correlated with equation 9.2 in the second study population). Measuring range as the number of status groups from which ego drew alters would offer no prediction of stress (given the −.08 correlation between n and equation 9.2). The number of alters in ego's network would actually have a strong, positive correlation with stress (given the negative correlation of −.95 between n and equation 9.2 in the second study population). Very different inferences would be made from the data on the first study population. Any measure of range other than the correct measure of conflicting group affiliations would result in the hypothesis being rejected. Both of the volumes of contact measures (n and m) have negative correlations with the group affiliation measure (equation 9.2) and so would have positive correlations with stress. The lack of a correlation between the third and fourth range measures means that range operationalized as the lack of connections among alters (equation 9.4) would be uncorrelated with the criterion variable of stress.

The bottom line here is that the range measures are substantively distinct and can be expected to have different associations with one another in different study populations. Across replicate studies, therefore, erroneous inferences can be expected from empirical research in which the measures are not distinguished, and explicitly considered, as separate dimensions of range.

SOME QUESTIONS OF LESS GENERAL CONCERN

How is Range Associated With Density?

The density of relations in ego's network is typically measured as the mean relation in the network, the sum of all relations divided by the number of relations:

$$[\Sigma_i \ \Sigma_q \ z_{iq}] \ / \ [n(n - 1)], \ i \neq q$$

where i and q are actors in an ego network. The density of the ego network in Figure 9.1, for example, is .5—18 of the 36 pairs of actors are connected by relations.

Density is associated with the redundancy in an ego network that limits range. The higher the density of relations among alters in ego's network, the lower the diversity of alters and so the lower the range of ego's relations. The range measure in equation 9.4 is most clearly connected with density. If every alter has a maximum strength relation with every other alter in an ego network, then density equals 1 ($1 = n[n - 1]/n[n - 1]$) and range equals 0 (equation 9.4 equals 0 when all z_{qi} equal 1). If no alter has a maximum strength relation with any other alter, then density approaches 0 and range approaches 1 as the number of alters increases (density equals the sum of ego's relations divided by $n[n - 1]$, and equation 9.4 equals a constant times 1 minus the sum across all alters i of z_{ji} times p_{ji}).

However, the extremes of completely connected and completely unconnected alters are much less often observed than are networks of incompletely connected alters, and it is in these more often observed networks that density is least strongly associated with range. Density concerns relations among the alters, while range is only concerned with relations among all alters as they affect ego. The two concepts are analytically distinct, one varying while the other is constant. For a given density of relations in an ego network, range will be decreased by ego having his strongest relations with the alters most strongly connected with other alters. The possible difference between range and density increases with the number of alters in an ego network, but differences can be illustrated even with three alters. The density of relations is .5 in ego networks seven and eight in Figure 9.3, but the ranges of the networks are .67 and .55, respectively, according to equation 9.4. Although the same mean strength of relations exists in both networks, ego has weak ties to the connected alters in network seven but a strong tie to one of the connected alters in network eight, so the range of ego's relations is slightly greater in network seven.

How Is Range Associated With Prominence?

Knoke and Burt offer a detailed discussion of prominence in the next chapter, but in a sentence, an actor is prominent within a system of actors to the extent that he is extensively involved in relations with other actors in the system. The close association between range and prominence is clearest when data are available on a complete network. In contrast to the ego network containing actor j and his alters, let the complete network consist of relations among all actors in a system. Of the N actors in a complete network, n + 1 appear in actor j's ego network (ego plus n alters). With data on a complete network, the range of relations in which each of ego's alters is involved can be measured, since each alter's relations are known. The range of ego's relations would be increased by connecting ego to alters who in turn had extensive range. Ego's diverse alters as intermediaries would connect him to even more diverse actors as the alters of his alters. The range of actor j's relations, call it r_j, could be measured as the extent to which ego is connected with actors i, who in turn have an extensive range of relations, r_i:

$$r_j = \sum_{i=1}^{n} r_i z_{ij} \qquad [9.5]$$

which is identical to the general prominence measure Knoke and Burt discuss in the next chapter, except that the summation in equation 9.5 is across the n alters in an ego network, while the summation in equation 10.3 of the next chapter is across the N actors in the complete network from which ego's network has been drawn. What a knowledge of the relations in the complete network enables us to do, in short, is to characterize the range of ego's indirect connections through his alters as immediate contacts.

Range and prominence are thus linked in an intimate way, differing in scale more than substance. What I have discussed here as range in an ego network, in other words, is what Knoke and Burt discuss in the next chapter as prominence in a complete network. In a complete network of symmetric relations, an actor's centrality would be a measure of the range of his relations. In a complete network of asymmetric relations, his prestige could be used as a measure of the range of his relations.

Even where data on complete networks are not available, this close association between range and prominence can be used to advantage in empirical research. Very often, non-network data can be obtained on the prominence of the statuses that alters occupy. Measures of the prestige of occupation statuses are perhaps the best known of such data, but the prominence of statuses based on other attributes could be measured similarly. Equation 9.5 could then be used to measure ego's range of contacts by substituting for r_i a non-network measure of the prominence of alter i's status. This is explicit in some recent work by Lin and his colleagues where the range of ego's job-seeking contacts is measured in terms of the occupation prestige of alter (e.g., Lin, Vaughn, et al., 1981; Lin, Ensel, et al., 1981: see also note 1 regarding Laumann's work on the heterogeneity of ego's contacts).

How Would Asymmetric Relations Affect Range?

I have only discussed symmetric measures of relations (i.e., $z_{ji} = z_{ij}$), although relations are typically asymmetric in the sense that one or more pairs of actors in a network do not have identical relations with one another, with one putting more emotion or time into the interaction than the other. In some circumstances, information on the asymmetry of relations is not available. When ego-network data have been obtained in mass survey interviews, for example, alters are typically not interviewed, so it would be impossible for ego to perceive his relation with alter in a way different from alter's perception (such that z_{ji} is not equal to z_{ij}). We simply take ego's perception of his relations as accurate. The risk run by analyzing range in terms of ego's perceptions alone is the risk of underestimating the range of relations in which prominent actors are involved.

A prominent actor is likely to be the object of many more relations than he acknowledges. This point is discussed by Knoke and Burt in the next chapter. But neglecting to acknowledge relations from followers or subordinates does not mean that a prominent actor could not use these relations as access to resources (e.g., the supervisor confiding in a subordinate, or the indirect communication among professors through graduate students). Although range has not been developed explicitly to consider the asymmetry of relationships, in short, there is a need to do so.[3]

How Can Multiple Contents Be Analyzed?

I have only discussed relations with single content (i.e., the range of ego's friendships, or intimacy ties, or relations with colleagues, and so forth). However, ego's coordination of multiple contents has implications for the range of his relations. Ego has extensive range to the extent that he uses different relations to reach different actors; relations with co-workers, kin, friends, neighbors, and so on. These relations would have less range to the extent that ego reached the same set of actors with each content; friends, kin, co-workers, and intimates all being the same people.

While there are no theoretical models of multiple content range, there are at least two ways to proceed in a data analysis (both of which are illustrated elsewhere: Burt, 1980d, 1982a: ch. 4, forthcoming: ch. 3). The most straightforward way to proceed would be to aggregate corresponding relations of different contents into a single multiplex relation between ego and alter. These multiplex relations could be used to compute range measures as described here with respect to a single content. This is the default method by which multiple network range is computed in STRUCTURE and is the basis for detecting structural equivalence across multiple networks (see Chapter 13).[4] Alternatively, separate range scores could be computed for each of the contents in which ego is involved; ego having some range of friendship relations, another range of colleague relations, another range of intimate relations, and so on. These separate scores could be combined into an aggregate score of multiple content range or used individually as measures of range within separate domains of interaction. In sum, the decision of how to analyze range in terms of multiple contents is still one based on personal tastes, data analysis, and computations—pending the development of theoretical models.[5]

CONCLUSION

Because it is easier to count the number of actors in ego's network than it is to measure their heterogeneity, network range is often reduced to a count measure, a measure of the volume of ego's relations. But a person could have many contacts with actors strongly connected to one another or completely identical in status attributes. Such a person would have a high number of contacts but a low range of contact. The point I have illustrated in this chapter is that range is a multidimensional concept to the extent that erroneous inferences can be made from empirical research in which dimensions of range are not kept distinct. An actor's relations have range to the extent that they involve a diversity of actors. Different range measures emerge from different concepts of diversity. Diversity can be taken to mean a large number of actors connected to ego, or it can mean a large number of *types* of actors connected to ego. Moreover, it can increase linearly with the number of connections to ego, or it can increase as a function of the quality of those connections.

When range is conceptualized as the extent to which ego is involved in many relations, the volume measures would seem to be appropriate operationalizations: (1) The number of actors in contact with ego, n, is a measure of the volume of actors with whom ego is involved. (2) The number of status groups from which ego draws actors for his network, m, is a measure of the volume of types of actors with whom ego is involved.

Looking more closely at the quality of ego's relationships, range can be measured in at least two ways. It can be measured in terms of the internal structure of status group alters as the extent to which ego has diversified contacts such that he does not have strong ties with cohesive groups (equation 9.2). It can also be measured in terms of contacts among alters as the extent to which ego has diversified contacts such that he does not have strong ties with alters in turn strongly connected with all of ego's other alters (equation 9.4). These quality-of-contact measures would seem to be appropriate operationalizations of range as freedom from social presssures to conform to status norms or range as access to diverse items of information and kinds of social support. The quality-of-contact measures look past the volume of relationships in which ego is involved to grasp the diversity of those relationships.

NOTES

1. More specifically, Laumann has measured range as the lack of homogeneity in a person's contacts. Building on the empirical finding that intimate contacts are decreasingly likely between people with increasingly different levels of occupational prestige, Laumann (1966: 114-116) describes the range of actor j's contacts in terms of the aggregate differences between j's occupational prestige, p_j, and the prestige of each of his alters i—the square root of the sum of $(p_j - p_i)^2$ across all alters i—where alters could be named as friends, neighbors, or kin (father or father-in-law). Laumann (1973: 87-92) later presents a slightly more sophisticated measure of the same idea. Actor j's range is measured by the sum of distances between j's occupational status and that of each alter i,

the sum of d_{ij} across alters i, where the distance between occupational statuses reflects the tendency for people in the two statuses not to name one another as friends. A high score on either measure indicates that ego draws alters from occupational statuses very different (i.e., structurally distant) from his own and so has a high range of contacts.

2. A fourth of sampled respondents would have network 1, a fourth would have network 2, a fourth would have network 6, and a fourth would have network 7. For any size sample, the expected correlation between two range measures would be the correlation between scores on the measures for networks 1, 2, 6 and 7 in Table 9.1. The correlation of .58 between n and m, for example, is the correlation between values of n and m in rows 1, 2, 6 and 7 of Table 9.1. Expected correlations for the second hypothetical study population have been similarly obtained by correlating scores in rows 1, 2, 8 and 9 of Table 9.1.

3. In the interim, the following procedure has been written in the program STRUCTURE so that range can be obtained in networks containing asymmetric relations. The number of alters in j's network, n, is defined as the number of actors connected to j as either the source or object of relations with j. Equation 9.4 is then computed as it is written in the text, which means that the range of j's relations is greatly increased by having unreciprocated relations from alters, since p_{jq} and z_{jq} will be zero for any alter q who is not the object of a relation from actor j. This treatment of asymmetric relations is only one of many possible but has the value of registering the range of prominent actors who direct only weak relations to their subordinates, and of being consistent with concepts of prominence as measures of range in complete networks (a point discussed here under the question: "How is range associated with prominence?").

4. More specifically, equation 9.3 is computed for each content of relations separately and then aggregated across contents for equation 9.4. Stated for some content k, equation 9.3 is the following measure of the extent to which alter i is strongly connected by relations of content k with all of ego j's alters:

$$z_{jik}[\Sigma_q (p_{jqk}z_{qik})], \, j \neq q$$

where z_{jik} is the strength of the content k relation from actor j to actor i, and p_{jqk} is the proportion of all content k relations involving actor j that connect him with alter q. That is:

$$p_{jqk} = [z_{jqk} + z_{qjk}]/[\Sigma_i (z_{jik} + z_{ijk})], \, j \neq q$$

so that a multiple content range measure corresponding to equation 9.4 is the following index output by STRUCTURE:

$$\Sigma_i\Sigma_k \, z_{jik}[1 - \Sigma_q(p_{jqk}z_{qik})]/[\Sigma_i\Sigma_k \, z_{jik}], \, i \neq j \neq q$$

5. I have elsewhere described some directions for such work in terms of role strain created for ego by segregated constraints on ego's performance of each role in his role-set (Burt, 1982e).

CHAPTER 10

Prominence

DAVID KNOKE
RONALD S. BURT

An actor is prominent within a social system to the extent that his relations make him particularly visible relative to other actors in the system. Different network concepts of prominence attend to different meanings of actor visibility. Central actors are visible because of their extensive involvement in relations. Prestigious actors are visible because of the extensive relations directed at them. These and other conceptual distinctions underlie a variety of prominence measures easily confused with one another in empirical research but substantively distinct to such an extent that erroneous inferences can be made from empirical research in which the measures are used as interchangeable indicators of prominence. This chapter is a didactic discussion of prominence as a network concept. We highlight conceptual similarities and distinctions among prominence measures so as to provide a guide for operationalizing prominence in empirical research. Illustration is provided with data on the discussion network among physicians in a small community during the mid 1950s.

Within diverse social systems—elementary school classrooms, scientific research communities, political elite communities, municipal bureaucracies, interorganizational commodities markets, international systems of nation states—network analysts have found actors stratified in terms of prominence. Prominent actors are highly visible because of their extensive involvement in substantively important relations. They stand in marked contrast to the anonymity of actors sustaining few relationships. These structural differences between prominent and peripheral, visible and anonymous, have been fruitfully interpreted in empirical research in terms of the greater social integration of prominent actors and the greater control prominent actors have over the flow of commodities, credit, and information as valued resources (e.g., with respect to innovation adopters: Coleman et al., 1966; Walker, 1969; Becker, 1970; Rogers and Shoemaker, 1971; Agnew et al., 1978; Rogers

Authors' Note: *We wish to acknowledge Michael Minor for his helpful comments on drafts of this chapter.*

and Kincaid, 1981; with respect to job seekers: Lin, Ensel, et al., 1981; Lin, Vaughn, et al., 1981; with respect to scientific elites: Crane, 1972; Cole and Cole, 1973; Breiger, 1976; Burt, 1978b, 1982a: ch. 3; with respect to political and organizational elites: Laumann and Pappi, 1976; Galaskiewicz, 1979; Boje and Whetten, 1981; Burt, 1982a: ch. 4; Knoke, forthcoming—to mention but a few applications).

Our purpose in this chapter is to (a) make explicit some of the similarities and distinctions among network concepts of centrality and prestige as measure of prominence, and (b) illustrate the importance of keeping these points in mind when making inferences from empirical research. For many network analysts, the points will be obvious. We will be providing no more than a convenient review bringing together points long known. For a variety of reasons, however, it is all too easy to treat centrality and prestige as interchangeable prominence concepts (e.g., see Burt, 1980e, 1982a: 198-204). We address a series of conceptual and substantive questions that highlight similarities and distinctions among prominence measures so as to offer some guide for selecting a measure well suited to a particular study. Despite the formal similarities among prominence measures, erroneous inferences can be made from research in which they are used as interchangeable indicators of prominence.

To illustrate the discussion, we use data on relations among physicians in Galesburg, Illinois, during the mid 1950s. The physicians were located in a combined saturation and snowball sampling procedure, a saturation sample of 18 general practitioners, pediatricians, and internists, and a snowball sample of 14 Galesburg physicians in other specialities who were cited as advisers and discussion partners by physicians in the saturation sample. Personal interviews were conducted with these 32 Galesburg physicians as part of a more general study of social factors in the physician's decision to begin prescribing a new antiobiotic, tetracycline. We describe physician prominence in terms of the network of discussion relations among interviewed physicians.[1] The sociometric choices from which relations are derived are presented in Figure 10.1.[2] Choices were elicited by the following question: "Who are the three or four physicians with whom you most often find youself discussing cases or therapy in the course of an ordinary week—last week, for instance? An arrow leads from chooser to chosen (e.g., physician 1 cited physician 5 as a discussion partner), and mutual choices are represented with double-headed arrows (e.g., physicians 5 and 6 cited one another as discussion partners). The data are described in the now classic final report, *Medical Innovation,* by James S. Coleman, Elihu Katz, and Herbert Menzel (1966), and in a recent reanalysis (Burt, 1982b) containing a data listing from which we have drawn our numerical illustration.

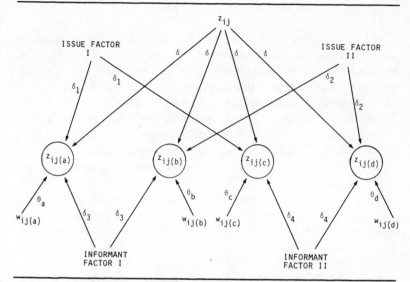

Figure 10.1: Sociogram of Discussion Partner Choices Among Galesburg, Illinois, Physicians in the mid 1950s

We have selected these data to illustrate our discussion for two reasons. First, prominence is a salient feature of the Galesburg medical community. The physicians were clearly stratified in the sense that there were a few prominent physicians involved in many relationships (e.g., physicians 5, 6, 20, 21 and 31 receive more than five citations each in Figure 10.1), and many physicians involved in few relations (e.g., physicians 1, 2, 9, 10, 14, 17, 22 and 30 were mentioned by no one as a discussion partner). The mean number of citations received was 2.5. Second, leaders and followers in the community exhibited very different behaviors toward the new antibiotic, such that the manner in which prominence is measured has clear implications for the often noted empirical finding that prominent actors adopt innovation early in the diffusion process while peripheral actors adopt late. Measuring prominence as a prestige concept, we show that there is a strong association between prominence and early adoption. Measuring prominence as a centrality concept, we show that there is no association. This result has an obvious substantive interpretation in the case of physicians deciding to prescribe a new antibiotic—once the result is known. The importance of correctly operationalizing prominence in a study stems from the fact that such results are typically not known in a study until alternative prominence measures have been tested against one another in the study.

WHAT IS PROMINENCE?

An actor is prominent to the extent that he is involved in relationships that make him an especially visible member of a social system. The emphasis is on visibility in a particular social system. This frame of reference for actor j's prominence goes beyond his ego network—the set of actors directly connected to him or her—to include all other system actors, actors who could have neither direct nor indirect ties to the first actor. The actor's prominence among others in a system is thus a feature of the relational pattern defining his position in the system. Let z_{ji} be a variable measuring the strength of a relation between actor j and actor i with 0 indicating the absence of a relation with z_{ji} increasing up to 1.0 to indicate a maximum strength relation. Relations could be measured directly or derived from sociometric choices, as will be the case here when we derive relations from Figure 10.1. Confining our attention for the moment to a single network (all the relations of one content among system members, such as friendship, advice, or intimacy, and so forth), actor j's position is defined by the pattern of N relations, z_{ji}, directed to each system member i and the N relations, z_{ij}, received from each system member i. With respect to the Galesburg physicians in Figure 10.1, physician j's position in the discussion network is defined by his tendencies to recognize each other physician as a discussion partner (z_{ji}) and their tendencies to recognize him as a discussion partner (z_{ij}). Physician j's prominence within the network is thus defined by this pattern of 2N relations defining his position in the network.

Centrality Versus Prestige

Two classes of prominence concepts—centrality and prestige—can be distinguished by the manner in which the relational pattern defining an actor's network position is assumed to make him visible.

Centrality concepts have been developed from the assumption that prominent actors are those who are extensively involved in relationships. The distinction between being the source versus the object of a relation is less important than the fact of being involved in the relation. Access, control, and brokerage of information is a substantive area particularly well suited to such an assumption in the sense that the difference between source and receiver of information seems less significant in the flow of information among actors than the difference between absent and present relations. This focus on involvement leads to a focus on symmetric relations ($z_{ji} = z_{ij}$). Where the distinction between source and object of relation is deemphasized in favor of involvement in the relation, the order of the subscripts in the variable z_{ji} is less important than its magnitude. With these ideas in mind, it is not surprising that centrality concepts of prominence developed from laboratory experiments on communication networks in which symmetric relations indicated where information could flow between actors (Bavelas, 1948, 1950; Leavitt, 1951).

Prestige concepts have been developed from the assumption that prominent actors are those who are extensively the object of relations. The fact of being involved in a relation is less important than the distinction between being the source versus the object of the relation. Control over valued resources, and the authority and deference produced by inequalities in control, is a substantive area requiring this emphasis on the asymmetry of relations, with the source of a relation being qualitatively distinct from the object of the relation in the sense of the distinction between subordination and superordination.

Prominent leaders are the objects of extensive relations from followers, while the latter are the objects of few relations. Both leaders and followers are involved in relations. The distinction between them, a distinction highlighted in prestige concepts, is that manner in which they are involved in relations. Speaking formally, the order of the subscripts in the relation z_{ji} is significant in determining an actor's prominence, a prominence increasing with the extent to which an actor is the object of relations, but not with the extent to which he or she directs relations to to other system members. Indeed, an individual who is the object of few relations while directing relations to many other actors has a prominent lack of prestige. With these ideas in mind, it is not surprising to find that prestige concepts of prominence developed from studies of deference and popularity in sociometry (Moreno, 1934: 98-103; Katz, 1953; and see Moreno, 1960, for early applications).

Turning to specific prominence measures, consider Table 10.1. Rows of the table distinguish formal operations that measure centrality when applied to the network of symmetric relations (column one) but measure prestige when applied to a network in which the asymmetry of relations is preserved (column two). Five formal operations defining measures are distinguished in Table 10.1: VAR1, VAR2, VAR3, VAR4, and VAR5, so that ten prominence measures are distinguished (five centrality measures when the variables are computed from symmetrized relations, and five prestige measures when they are computed from relations in which asymmetry is preserved). We have relied on the computer

TABLE 10.1 Structural Conditions Captured by Prominence Measures

	Centrality	*Prestige*
	Prominence in a Network of Symmetric Relations	*Prominence in a Network of Asymmetric Relations*
Volume of Relations		
Many Ties (VAR1, VAR2)	many actors directly and/or indirectly connected with ego	many actors directly and/or indirectly connected to ego
Many Close Ties (VAR3)	strong relations with other actors	strong relations from other actors
Quality of Relations		
Kinds of Ties (VAR4)	involvement in all connections between actors	involvement in all asymmetric connections between actors
Kinds of Actors (VAR5)	strong relations with central actors	strong relations from prestigious actors

program STRUCTURE (Project, 1981) to compute prominence scores from the choice data in Figure 10.1.

Volume of Relations

An actor is perhaps most obviously prominent because of the volume of relations in which he or she is involved—this prominence increasing with the extent to which an actor has strong relations with many actors in a system. The first three formal operations in Table 10.1 (VAR1, VAR2, VAR3) measure volume in this sense and can be represented with the following simple equation: Actor j's prominence within a network of N actors is given by the average strength of his relation from each other actor, from actor 1 (z_{1j}), from actor 2 (z_{2j}), and so on:

$$(z_{1j} + z_{2j} + \ldots + z_{Nj})/(N - 1) \qquad [10.1]$$

where j's relation to himself is ignored in the summation (i.e., $z_{jj} = 0$).

The simplest of these volume measures counts the number of actors connected to actor j. For these counts of actors (VAR1 to VAR2, the first row of Table 10.1), relations are treated in a rather primitive way. They are treated as a dichotomy between present and absent (z_{ij} is 1 or 0).

The actors most obviously connected to an individual are those directly connected to him. A person has high *choice status* and *degree* to the extent that many actors are directly connected to him. Let VAR1 be equation 10.1 computed from relations dichotomized between direct connections (z_{ij} = 1) versus (z_{ij} = 0). This is the usual form of raw sociometric choices, with z_{ji} equaling 1 when actor j cites actor i in response to some sociometric question. For example, an arrow from physician i to physician j in Figure 10.1 indicates that i cited j as a discussion partner (the dichotomous z_{ji} equals 1 instead of 0). When computed from such choice data, equation 10.1 is actor j's choice status—the proportion of actors citing j who could have cited j—a measure of prominence first introduced in the formative stage of sociometry (Moreno, 1934: 98-103, 1960: passim). The choice status of physician 6 in Galesburg, for example, is .23: 7 divided by 31 (the number of physicians citing him as a discussion partner; that is, the number of arrows leading to him in Figure 10.1 divided by the number of physicians interviewed who could have cited him, 32 minus 1). In other words, physician 6 was recognized as a discussion partner by 23 percent of the Galesburg physicians who could have recognized him as such. In contrast, physician 1 was peripheral in the discussion network even though this physician had a direct connection to physician 6 as a discussion partner. The choice status of physician 1 is .00; no interviewed physician recognized him as a discussion partner.

Occasionally, in analyses of communication channel networks or particularly sparce networks, sociometric choices are forced to be symmetric so as to focus on the distinction between connected versus unconnected actors (e.g., Laumann and Pappi, 1976: 137; Laumann et al., 1977: 602-603; Alba and Moore, 1978: 179). Any citation between i and j is assumed to create an i, j connection (i.e., z_{ji} is forced to equal 1 when z_{ij} equals 1, which makes choice symmetric, z_{ij} = z_{ji}). When computed from symmetrized choice data, equation 10.1 is the proportion of other actors directly connected to j who could have been connected. In Figure 10.1, for example, physician 6 is connected to 8 of the 31 other interviewed Galesburg physicians (26 percent of the possible), physician 1 is connected to 3 (10 percent of the possible), and physician 30 is connected to none (0 percent of the possible). In his review of centrality measures, Freeman (1979: 221) describes such a measure as an index of degree, the degree of an actor in a graph such as Figure 10.1 indicating his potential communication activity (see Nieminen, 1974).[4] The degree of physician 6's centrality being much greater than physician 30's, for example, we would expect physician 6 to have been much more active in communicating medical information among Galesburg physicians. This degree measure is also a measure of the range of j's ego network (as discussed at length in the preceding chapter) within the context of the more general network among all N actors; however, we have adopted Freeman's "degree" label in order to clearly distinguish this measure from the more general concept of range.

Beyond the actors directly connected to an individual, there are usually many more actors connected to him indirectly by chains of direct connections, with actor A citing actor B, who cites actor C, so that there is a two-step indirect connection from A to C. An individual has high *connectivity* (also discussed as *reachability*) to the extent that he is directly or indirectly connected with (i.e., can reach) every other actor in a network.

Let VAR2 be equation 10.1 computed from relations dichotomized between any connection, direct or indirect, between two actors ($z_{ij} = 1$) versus no connection ($z_{ij} = 0$). As an extension of direct choices, indirect connections are captured in terms of path distances. The path distance from actor j to actor i is the minimum number of direct connections required for j to reach i.[5] In Figure 10.1, for example, the path distance from physician 1 to physician 6 is one (1 cites 6), the path distance from 8 to 18 is two (8 cites 28, who in turn cites 18), the path distance from 8 to 4 is three (8 cites 5, who cites 26, who cites 4), and so on. As a dichotomous relation measured in terms of path distance, z_{ij} in equation 10.1 would be a 1 (rather than a 0) only if actors i and j were connected by a finite number of direct connections (i.e., if either path distance between i and j were finite).[6]

The above examples of 1, 2 and 3 step path distances would all indicate z_{ij} of 1; however, some physicians have no connection with one another in Figure 10.1 (e.g., there is no chain of connections between physicians 4 and 10 or between physicians 1 and 2, so that both pairs of physicians would be connected by a z_{ij} of 0). In measuring prominence by connectivity, we allow prominent actors to maintain a small number of direct contacts through which contact is maintained indirectly with a large number of actors. In Figure 10.1, for example, physician 4 received only one citation as a discussion partner and cited three other physicians as discussion partners. Through those direct connections, however, physician 4 is indirectly connected to an additional 28 actors, for a total of 29. The only physicians to whom physician 4 is not directly or indirectly connected are physicians 30 (the isolate in Figure 10.1) and 32 (no indirect connections lead to 32 in Figure 10.1). In other words, physician 4 can reach 29 of 31, or 94 percent, of the other interviewed Galesburg physicians despite the relatively small range of his direct connections.

Not every physician's connectivity was such a dramatic increase over degree and choice status. For example, physician 32 received a direct citation from one other physician (physician 10), but no one cited the physician citing him (no arrows lead to 10 in Figure 10.1), so his choice status and connectivity are the same (1 of 31, or .03 of the physicians who could have been connected with him). One disadvantage to measuring prominence in terms of connectivity lies in the fact that networks among actors located in part by snowball sampling are often so highly connected indirectly that differences in actor prominence are obscured. For example, connectivity computed from symmetrized choice data does not distinguish levels of prominence among the Galesburg physicians, although it is informative. Every physician is connected to every other physician—excluding the one isolate, physician 30—which means that no one physician was more prominent than another. Each had direct or indirect access to information known to 30 of 31, or 97 percent, of the other physicians.

A second class of prominence measures goes beyond the mere *number* of actors with whom an individual is connected to consider the *strength* of his relations (second row of Table 10.1). Instead of dichotomizing relations as present versus absent, relations are measured on a continuous scale, typically in terms of path distances. An actor is prominent to the extent that he is connected—either directly or by short chains of direct connections—to all actors in a network. Let VAR3 be equation 10.1 computed from continuous relations, where z_{ij} increases from zero to one as the path distance from i to j decreases; or, more generally, as the strength of the relation from i to j increases. A variety of strategies for normalizing path distances as relations are available (for example, see Burt, 1980b, 1982a: 27-29, for review and references). We are using the normalization provided by STRUCTURE (see Burt, 1976a: 118-119, 1982a: 28-29, for measurement details).

As a measure of prestige, actor j's score on VAR3 is the typical strength of the relation directed at him *from* another actor. Katz (1953), Hubbell (1965: 383), Taylor (1969), and Lin (1976: 340-349) propose prestige measures computed as the overall strength of relations an actor receives from others (where strength can be indicated by short path distances). As a measure of centrality, actor j's score on VAR3 computed from symmetrized choice data is the typical strength of his connection *with* another actor. Beauchamp (1965), Sabidussi (1966), Nieminin (1973), Moxley and Moxley (1974), and Freeman (1979) propose centrality measures computed as the overall strength of connections between an individual and other actors (where strength again can be indicated by short path distances). In his review of centrality measures, Freeman (1979: 226) describes this class of measures as closeness measures, with the closeness of an actor to all others indicating the efficiency with which he can communicate information.

VAR3 defines a prestige variable and a centrality variable corresponding respectively to choice status and degree. However, instead of counting actors connected to an individual, the VAR3 measures indicate the strength of the individual's typical relations with other actors. As with choice status and degree, peripheral actors are similarly peripheral on these two prominence measures, while different actors can be prominent—actors who are the object of strong relations from all actors being prominent according to the prestige measure, actors in close contact with all actors being prominent on the centrality measure. In Figure 10.1, for example, physician 30 has a prominence score of zero on both of these measures. He was completely isolated from all other interviewed physicians, so all z_{ij} linking him with other physicians was zero. In contrast, physician 2 has a prominence score of .0 on the prestige measure and a .4 on the centrality measure. The prestige score indicates that he was the object of neither direct nor indirect discussion relations from other physicians. The centrality score indicates that he was nevertheless in close contact with most other physicians in the sense that he could reach each other physician in a small number of (symmetrized) direct connections. Put another way, he was well plugged into a flow of information because the few people with whom he discussed medical matters in turn discussed medical matters with many other physicians. Put in still another way, his few relationships were of high quality.

Quality of Relations

By the quality of relations we refer to the structural context in which a relationship occurs. The first two rows of Table 10.1 (i.e., VAR1, VAR2, VAR3) concern the volume of an actor's relations: number of ties and typical strength of ties. The second two rows (i.e., VAR4 and VAR5) take into account the structural context in which the volume of an actor's relations occur.

The simplest prominence measure in which relations are considered with respect to a more general structural context is the proportion of relations in a network that involve actor j. An actor is prominent to the extent that the volume of his relations is a large proportion of the total volume of network relations. Let VAR4 be the sum of all the relations involving actor j divided by the sum of all relations in a network:

$$(\Sigma_i [z_{ij} + z_{ji}]) \, / \, (\Sigma_i \Sigma_j z_{ij}), \, i \neq j \qquad [10.2]$$

so that actor j's score on this variable is the proportion of network relations that involve him personally. The more that all interaction in a network involves actor j, the higher this proportion will be, indicating actor j's high prominence within the network. This measure has its clearest antecedent in the widely cited centrality measure proposed by Bavelas (1950) for small networks of symmetric relations: the ratio of the sum of all path distances separating each actor among actors in a network divided by the sum of path distances from one individual.[7]

There is no history of VAR4 being computed from asymmetric relations to measure prestige.[8] The principal advantage that VAR4 offers as a prominence measure over the initial three is the distinction between prominence and extensive involvement in relations within a pluralist system.[9] In a network of completely interconnected actors, each actor will have scores on VAR1, VAR2, and VAR3 of 1.0, but each will have a low score on VAR4 (equal to $1/N$) because no one actor is involved in all relations. VAR4 only registers an actor as highly prominent when he is involved in all interaction within a network.

There are prominence measures which take into account more explicitly than equation 10.2 the manner in which an individual is involved in all connections between other actors. We shall briefly discuss two as illustration.

Focusing explicitly on prominence within a network of asymmetric relations, Burt (1976a, 1982a: 49-55) proposes that actor prestige be measured in terms of the *primary* form in an actor's relation and has used the measure to describe prominence within an invisible college of social scientists (Burt, 1978b, 1982a: 107-111). An actor's relations have primary form to the extent that he is the object of strong relations from all other actors in a system, while the actor himself only reciprocates relations from his structural peers, that is, other actors jointly occupying his network position in the system.[10] Thus, prestige is measured in terms of the volume of unreciprocated relations in which an actor is involved. An actor so involved in relations is an actor controlling valued resources in the sense that he need not maintain relations with actors beyond his structural peers while actors more generally maintain unreciprocated relations to him. Leaders as prestigious actors are involved in the connection among actors more generally in the sense that they have strong relations with one another and the unreciprocated relations they receive from followers define indirect connections among the followers. A high volume of relations is not sufficient to ensure prominence. An actor who is the object of strong relations from many other actors but who reciprocates those relations can be as peripheral under this measure as one who is the object of no relations.[11] High prominence only results from receipt of unreciprocated relations. When symmetry is imposed on relations, of course, prominence cannot be measured as a volume of unreciprocated relations.

Focusing explicitly on prominence within a network of symmetric relations, Freeman (1977, 1979, 1980) proposes to measure actor centrality in terms of the extent to which the actor could broker communication *between* any pair of other actors and has used the measure to describe centrality within small, experimental task groups (Freeman, 1977; Freeman et al., 1980). An actor j lies between a pair of actors to the extent that the path distance between the actors involves indirect connections through j as an intermediary. An actor is prominent as a central actor to the extent that he lies between every pair of connected actors.[12] An actor j, so involved in relations, is an actor controlling valued resources in the sense that actors can only communicate with one another if they communicate through actor j. Here again, an actor can be extensively involved in relations but remain peripheral. An actor who is strongly connected to all other actors in a network of completely connected actors would be as peripheral under this measure as a completely isolated actor.[13] Neither actor stands between any pair of other actors.

Another approach to capturing the quality of relations is to take into account the prominence of actors involved in them. Suppose that two actors, A and B, each is involved in the same volume of relations, but the actors connected to A are themselves the objects of strong relations from many other actors, while the actors connected to B are only connected to B. These two actors would be similarly prominent in terms of their volume of relations but quite different with respect to the quality of the relations in which they are involved. The relations in which A is involved connect her within a group of prominent actors, while the relations in which B is involved connect her to peripheral actors. In other words, A's relations are of higher quality because of the higher prominence of A's partners in those relations.

Rather than summing the z_{ij} leading to actor j as if each other actor were equally significant in determining j's prominence—an assumption implicit in all other measures we have discussed—this understanding of prominence suggests that the prominence of a source of relations determines, in part, the prominence of the actor who is the object of the relations. The relation actor j receives from actor i, z_{ij}, contributes to his prominence, p_j, to the extent that i is prominent, p_i. Let VAR5 measure actor j's prominence as a weighted sum of j's relations; the strength of the first actor's relation to him weighted by actor l's prominence, p_1z_{1j}, plus the second actor's relation to him weighted by actor 2's prominence, p_2z_{2j}, and so on across all N actors in the system:

$$p_j = p_1z_{1j} + p_2z_{2j} + \ldots + p_Nz_{Nj} \qquad 10.3$$

which is the same as equation 10.1, except that the variable p_i in this equation is assumed in equation 10.1 to be identical and equal to $1/(N-1)$, so that the sum of weights across all other N-1 actors equals one.

Prominence scores can be computed here as a routine eigenvector problem, which means that each actor's prominence will be determined jointly with each other actor's prominence. The prominence scores in Equation 10.3 are scaled in the STRUCTURE output so that they are fractions and—like the weights given to actors as sources of relations in Equation 10.1—they sum to one across all actors.[14] The highest level of prominence will be the prominence of the actor with the strongest relations from the most prominent actors. Bonacich (1972) provides a marvelously succinct discussion of the p_j in equation 10.3 as centrality scores when the equation is computed from symmetric relations. This measure of centrality has been informatively applied and modified in descriptions of interorganizational connections through boards of directors (e.g., Mizruchi, 1982: 55ff; Mizruchi and Bunting, 1981).

With respect to prestige, there is a rich theoretical literature on equation 10.3 when the equation is computed from relations in which asymmetry is preserved (see Burt, 1982a: 36, for a more detailed review). Hubbell (1965) draws on input-output analysis to articulate its use with respect to choice data. Coleman's (1966, 1972, 1973) model of power is formally equivalent to equation 10.3 where prestige is power and z_{ij} is the extent to which events of interest to actor i are controlled by actor j (for more direct applications of this model to network data, see Burt, 1979; Taylor and Coleman, 1979; Marsden, 1981b, 1982a, forthcoming a, forthcoming b). Although equation 10.3 can involve some computational inconvenience (discussed below), it provides the single most general prominence measure in the sense that it combines, with stark simplicity, the most important features of prominence: strong ties from many actors who are themselves the object of strong ties from many actors. In other words, equation 10.3 offers a measure of prominence in which an individual's prominence is determined both by the volume of his relations as well as their quality.

HOW DIFFERENT ARE
ALTERNATIVE MEASURES?

We have distinguished a variety of alternative prominence measures as they reflect centrality versus prestige in terms of the volume and quality of an actor's relations. These distinctions are easily overlooked in empirical research, an oversight that can result in erroneous conclusions being drawn from research. The discussion network among Galesburg physicians provides illustration.

Table 10.2 presents prominence scores output by STRUCTURE, with the five centrality scores (C1 to C5) being VAR1 to VAR5 computed from choices forced to be symmetric, and the five prestige scores (P1 to P5) being VAR1 to VAR5 computed from the choices with their observed asymmetry preserved.[15] Scores are presented for 17 general practitioners, internists, and pediatricians—the saturation sample of Galesburg physicians likely to have a use for the new antibiotic studied in *Medical Innovation*. For these 17 physicians we have data on the time at which they began prescribing the new antibiotic. Each physician's adoption date is given in Table 10.2 as a number from 1 to 18—roughly the number of months that elapsed before the physician began prescribing the new antibiotic once the antibiotic was available. Based on the results reported in *Medical Innovation* and many other diffusion studies, we expect prominence to have a strong, negative correlation with adoption date, with early adoption being increasingly likely with increasing prominence.

There appears to have been a single dimension of prominence stratifying Galesburg physicians—the alternative prominence measures in Table 10.2 are strongly correlated with one another. There are differences in the prominence of individual physicians under the different measures, some of which we have pointed out in discussing the measures. These differences can be detected by looking across the rows of Table 10.2. However, the physicians with low prominence on one measure tend to have low prominence on other measures (e.g., physicians 3, 12 and 16 have scores consistently close to zero in Table 10.2). Moreover, centrality and prestige are highly correlated, as evidenced by the tendency for physicians prominent on one measure to be prominent on others (e.g., physicians 5 and 6 have consistently high scores in Table 10.2). In fact, correlations between centrality and prestige measures are often as high as correlations among measures in either group. The average correlation between a pair of prestige measures is .87, between a pair of centrality measures it is .74, while the average correlation is .65 between centrality and prestige measures. The same pattern is observed across other physicians in Galesburg.[16]

Similarities among the prominence measures are clearly evident in Figure 10.2. This figure presents the results of an exploratory factor analysis of correlations among 14 variables: the 5 prestige measures in Table 10.1 (indicated in Figure 10.2 as P1 through P5), the corresponding 5 centrality measures (indicated in Figure 10.2 as C1 through C5), the measures of primary form (P6 and C6 in Figure 10.2), and isolation computed for both symmetric and asymmetric relations (see note 10 for calculations). Correlations are based on prominence

TABLE 10.2 Prominence Scores for 17 General Practitioners, Internists, and Pediatricians in Galesburg

Physician	Adoption Date	VAR1		VAR2		VAR3		VAR4		VAR5	
		C1	P1	C2	P2	C3	P3	C4	P4	C5	P5
1	18	.097	.000	.968	.419	.318	.000	.031	.015	.032	.004
2	18	.097	.000	.968	.419	.398	.000	.033	.014	.037	.004
3	4	.032	.032	.968	.452	.108	.026	.021	.091	.041	.004
4	5	.129	.032	.968	.935	.441	.175	.035	.029	.041	.041
5	8	.323	.323	.968	.935	.520	.515	.041	.060	.049	.104
6	4	.258	.226	.968	.935	.529	.501	.040	.058	.048	.094
7	3	.161	.129	.968	.613	.432	.407	.035	.052	.041	.092
8	8	.097	.032	.968	.581	.332	.029	.031	.025	.032	.004
9	13	.097	.000	.968	.452	.328	.000	.032	.021	.029	.004
10	6	.097	.000	.968	.677	.373	.000	.032	.016	.034	.004
11	3	.129	.097	.968	.677	.354	.162	.033	.035	.029	.004
12	6	.097	.064	.968	.452	.250	.154	.028	.035	.021	.004
13	14	.032	.032	.968	.419	.341	.030	.032	.019	.032	.004
14	7	.097	.000	.968	.452	.293	.000	.030	.016	.031	.004
15	4	.129	.032	.968	.452	.333	.026	.032	.016	.034	.004
16	14	.064	.032	.968	.677	.204	.137	.026	.034	.018	.004
18	7	.194	.161	.968	.677	.310	.203	.031	.039	.025	.004

NOTE: Physicians are identified by number in Figure 10.1, adoption date is roughly equal to the number of months elapsing before a physician began prescribing the new antibiotic once it became available, and prominence measures generated by VAR1 to VAR5 have been described with respect to Table 10.1 (see note 15 for specific connection with STRUCTURE output).

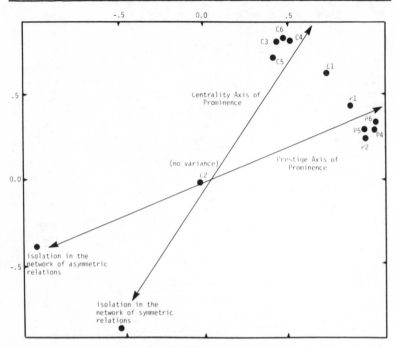

PROMINENCE MEASURES IN GRAPH
C1 and P1 Measure Volume of Direct Contact
(Var1 in Table 10.1)
C2 and P2 Measure Volume of Direct and Indirect Contact
(Var2 in Table 10.1)
C3 and P3 Measure Typical Strength of Relations
(Var3 in Table 10.1)
C4 and P4 Measure Involvement in All Relations
(Var4 in Table 10.1)
C5 and P5 Measure Strength of Relations with Prominent Actors
(Var5 in Table 10.1)
C6 and P6 Measure Primary Form
(Note 10)

Figure 10.2: Graph of Factor Loadings Illustrating the Close Association Between
Centrality and Prestige Measures in the Galesburg Discussion Network

scores for 31 Galesburg physicians. The first principal component
describes 81 percent of observed variance in prominence scores, the
second 11 percent, and the third 3 percent. Figure 10.2 presents each
variable's loading on the first two principal components after
orthogonal rotation.

There are two minor points to note in the graph: (1) the centrality
measure VAR2 computed from symmetric relations (C2 in Figure 10.2)

has a zero loading on both factors. The lack of variance in C2 created by the complete connectivity among physicians means that it cannot have nonzero correlations with other variables. (2) Prominence in terms of direct ties is most distinct from the other prominence measures in the sense that C1 and P1 are closer to one another than any other pair of centrality and prestige measures, and both stand apart from a tight cluster of centrality measures (C3, C4, C5, C6) and a tight cluster of prestige measures (P2, P3, P4, P5, P6).

The most striking feature of Figure 10.2, however is the high association between centrality and prestige. Centrality contrasts isolation with extensive involvement in relations within a network of symmetric ties (note the centrality axis in Figure 10.2). Prestige contrasts isolation with extensive receipt of relations within a network of asymmetric ties. Both centrality and prestige are almost perfectly associated with a single dimension of prominence on which isolated, peripheral physicians (low left-hand corner of Figure 10.2) are contrasted with prominent (central and prestigious) physicians (upper right-hand corner of Figure 10.2).

The high association among centrality and prestige measures notwithstanding, it would be wrong to conclude that the measures can be used as interchangeable indicators of prominence in predicting non-network variables. Figure 10.3 presents a graph of adoption data for each of the 17 Galesburg physicians in Table 10.2 against their prominence as centrality (top graph) and prestige (bottom graph). Prominence is measured by the typical strength of a physician's relation from any other physician (VAR3 in Tables 10.1 and 10.2). There is no systematic association between a physician's centrality and the date by which he or she began prescribing the new antibiotic. The data in the top graph of Figure 10.3 appear random. But the expected negative association is evident in the lower graph. There is an exponential increase in a physician's tendency to adopt early, with increasing physician prestige in the discussion network. Table 10.3 presents correlations between log scores of adoption date and the other prominence measures, generalizing the distinction between centrality and prestige evident in Figure 10.3.

There is a ready explanation for this result. The distinction between leader and follower among physicians considering the new antibiotic was important for actual adoptions. As described in detail elsewhere (Burt, 1982b: ch. 5), leaders tended to begin prescribing the new antibiotic soon after it was released, while followers held back until well after the adoptions by leading physicians. The three early adopters in the lower right-hand corner of the prestige graph in Figure 10.3 are the highly prominent physicians 5, 6 and 7 in Figure 10.1 and Table 10.2.

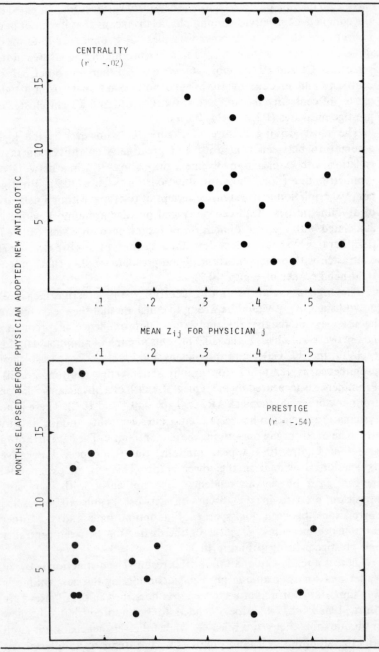

Figure 10.3: Graphs Illustrating the Different Associations Between Adoption Date and Physician Prominence as Centrality Versus Prestige

TABLE 10.3 Correlations Between Adoption Date and Prominence

	Centrality	*Prestige*
	Prominence in a Network of Symmetric Relations	*Prominence in a Network of Asymmetric Relations*
Volume of Relations		
Volume of Direct Contact (C1 and P1)	−.23	−.56*
Volume of Direct/Indirect Contact (C2 and P2)	undefined	−.45*
Typical Strength of Relations (C3 and P3)	−.02	−.54*
Quality of Relations		
Involvement in All Relations (C4 and P4)	−.07	−.45*
Primary Form of Relations (C6 and P6)	−.02	−.54*
Strength of Relations with Prominent Actors (C5 and P5)	−.28	−.37

NOTE: Correlations are based on the natural logarithms of the data in Table 10.2 where prominence scores have been increased by .001 to eliminate zeros (primary form measure is not reported in Table 10.2; see note 10). Correlations significantly negative at a .05 level of confidence are marked with an asterisk. The correlation with C2 is undefined, because all 17 physicians in Table 10.2 were equally well connected within the symmetrized discussion network.

These three enjoyed high prestige among Galesburg physicians; however, they had many followers who were as central as they were but who did not adopt the new antibiotic until long after its release.

The distinction between leaders and followers, between object and source of relations, is obliterated in symmetrized relations in order to focus on extent of involvement in relations. Both leaders and followers were extensively involved in discussion relations, as Figure 10.3 illustrates. The spread of mean relation strengths as prestige scores in the lower graph of Figure 10.3 shifts to the right of the upper graph, indicating the higher and more equal centrality of physicians. While leaders and followers were extensively involved in discussion relations, it was the physician who was extensively sought out as a discussion partner who was most likely to begin prescribing the new antibiotic early—not the physician who sought him or her out. Had the adoption decision been based on access to information, this distinction between leader and follower might not have been so significant. However, marketing by drug companies ensured that physicians were aware of the new antibiotic.

In sum, alternative prominence measures present a contradiction. They could be argued to be interchangeable. Such an argument could proceed on the logical grounds that a single formal operation (VAR1, VAR2, VAR3, and so on) generates a centrality measure when applied to symmetrized relations and a prestige measure when applied to asymmetric relations. This is the point emphasized in Table 10.1. The same conclusion could be reached empirically because centrality and prestige measures are highly correlated in stratified systems such as the Galesburg medical community. This point is illustrated in Table 10.2 and Figure 10.2. On the other hand, distinctions among alternative prominence measures must be maintained. The measures reflect substantively distinct features of an actor's position in social structure. The centrality measures reflect an actor's aggregate involvement in relations and so index his access to and control of information. The prestige measure reflects the extent to which an actor is the object of relations and so index the deference accorded him by other actors and his probable control of valued resources. These distinctions, and the more subtle distinctions between measures of relation volume versus quality, are the basis for Table 10.1. Failing to maintain these substantive distinctions in empirical research can result in substantively erroneous inferences from the research. Table 10.3 and Figure 10.3 show that prominence operationalized as centrality among Galesburg physicians has no association with innovation, but that prominence operationalized as prestige has the strong association expected from previous diffusion studies. This clear difference between centrality and prestige measures occurs despite the equally clear unidimensionality of prominence measures in Figure 10.2. The answer to the question of how different alternative prominence measures are is no more than the statement that they can be completely different in their correlations with non-network variables, even when they are highly correlated with one another.

Obviously, different results can be obtained in other networks with respect to non-network variables other than adoption data. However, these results illustrate a general methodological point. *Two prominence measures can only be treated as interchangeable when they have similar associations with a third variable—and then only with respect to that variable and the system in which it was observed.* A high association between two prominence measures is insufficient reason for treating them as interchangeable indicators of prominence. Their high correlation with one another does not prevent them from having quite different associations with a third variable.[17] An argument concluding that two or more measures are interchangeable prominence indicators because they are highly correlated is an argument ill founded. The risk of accepting such an argument is less the problem it involves of incorrectly distinguishing dimensions of prominence than it is the risk it creates of erroneously rejecting a proposition correctly explaining actor attitudes or behaviors by actor prominence. Had prominence been operationalized as centrality in Galesburg, for example, the analytically correct inference from graphs such as the one at the top of Figure 10.3 would be the substantively erroneous inference that there is no association between a physician's prominence and the date at which he began prescribing the new antibiotic under study.

SOME QUESTIONS OF LESS GENERAL CONCERN

Beyond identifying types of prominence measures and the extent of their differences in empirical research, there are three less general questions we wish to address before concluding the discussion.

How Easily Available are the Alternative Measures?

We have obtained alternative prominence scores from the output of STRUCTURE, but the measures can be grouped into three classes in terms of their more general availability. Measuring prominence in terms of direct ties, VAR1 in Table 10.1, is most easily available because it can be obtained without computer software; one simply counts the number of actors connected to an individual. This might seem simplistic, but note that these simple counts of direct contacts yield correlations in Table 10.3 as strong as any obtained with more sophisticated measures. The measures based on path distances (VAR2, VAR3, VAR4, primary form and betweenness) require computer software written specifically for network analyses. However, path distances are typically available in general purpose programs. Computation of prominence measures in terms of path distance poses no special problem except that it can be expensive to analyze large networks. The eigenvector measures (VAR5) have the advantage of not requiring computer software written especially for network analyses. Computer routines for extracting eigenvalues and eigenvectors are standard fare in large computers. Unfortunately, the eigenvector measures can be affected adversely by the presence of unconnected subgroups within a network.[18]

How Can Network Structure Be Summarized?

It is sometimes valuable to summarize the distribution of prominence scores among actors in a single score measuring the extent to which actors in a network are stratified. This can be accomplished with models of network hierarchy and centralization. A network is centralized to the extent that all relations in it involve a single actor. A network is hierarchical to the extent that a single actor is the object of all relations in it. Hierarchy refers to the prestige of positions in a network. A system is hierarchical to the extent that a single actor has high prestige. Although both models describe the extent to which a dominant elite is defined by a network, they are not identical. A centralized structure of symmetric relations is not a hierarchy.

Nevertheless, centrality and hierarchy both describe inequality in the extent to which actors are involved in relations. Concluding a review of centrality models, Freeman (1979) proposes a general form for such models as the ratio of summed differences between all actors and the most central actor over the maximum sum possible.[19] Similarly, a network has a hierarchical structure to the extent that there are differences in the prestige of actors in it. For example, Coleman (1964: 434-444) proposes two models of network hierarchy (see Rapoport and Hovarth, 1961). A network is hierarchical to the extent that the distribution of p_j across all actors j is nonrandom or unequal, where p_j is the proportion of all relations (sociometric choices) in the network that are directed at actor j. A diversity of models have been used to describe centralization and hierarchy, but there are good reasons for treating such models as applications of more general inequality models. Such a treatment would bring these network models directly into the mainstream of macrolevel descriptions of social structure (e.g., Blau, 1977b) and would allow centralization and hierarchy to be stated in terms of models with well-known properties (e.g., Allison, 1978).

As a fortunate coincidence, Coleman's (1964: 441-444) hierarchy model based on the information-theoretic concept of disorder is equivalent to Theil's (1967: 91-95) well-studied inequality model when the latter is normalized by its maximum value (see Burt, 1982: 62, for details). In terms of this model, a network is stratified to the extent that there is no disorder in its relations. Relations are disordered to the extent that all actors are equally involved in them. Where p_j is the extent to which actor j is involved in relations (ignoring for the moment how he is involved), a network is stratified to the extent that there is maximum inequality in the p_j, a condition measured by the following equation:

$$(\Sigma_j \; [p_j/p] \; \ln \; [p_j/p] \; / \; (N \; \ln[N]) \qquad [10.4]$$

where ln refers to the natural logarithm for which ln (0) is assumed to be 0 and $\bar{p}$ is the mean of all p_j. Equation 10.4 varies from 0 to a maximum of 1 describing the extent to which a system is stratified. If p_j is a measure of j's centrality in a network, then equation 10.4 would describe the extent to which all relations in the network involve a single actor. If p_j is actor j's prestige, equation 10.4 would describe the extent to which a single actor is the object of all relations. The p_j summarized in equation 10.4 could be defined by any of the prominence measures we have discussed.[20]

Drawing from Allison (1978), equation 10.4 has several desirable properties (not the least of which is that the properties are known); (a) It is scale invariant in the sense that multiplying all relations by a constant—either as a result of arbitrary relation measurement scales or summation across an arbitrary number of separate networks as mentioned below—will not alter the extent of stratification. (b) It implies marginally decreasing effects of changes in prominence in the sense that a unit change in prominence within a highly stratified network will have less effect on equation 10.4 than the same change in an unstratified system. (c) It can be disaggregated across nonoverlapping subgroups in a network so that the extent to which individual subgroups contribute to overall network structure can be described. Subgroups are discussed in Chapters 12, 13, and 14 of this volume. (d) It is similar in interpretation to the well-known Gini index, but is more easily computed and is theoretically grounded in information theory.

How Can Multiple Networks Be Analyzed?

Coordination of prominence across multiple networks has implications for the level and stability of an actor's prominence. An actor who is prominent among others in terms of friendship relations, work relations, and kinship relations is more prominent in some sense than an actor who is prominent in only one of these networks. However, explicit treatment of structure across multiple networks is a relatively recent concern in network analysis. Prominence measures are typically not discussed in terms of multiple networks.

The most straightforward way to proceed in an analysis of multiple network prominence would be to aggregate corresponding relations in separate networks into a multiplex relation within a single, aggregate network. These multiplex relations could then be used to compute prominence as described here with respect to a single network. This is the default method by which multiple network prominence is computed in STRUCTURE and is the basis for detecting structural equivalence across multiple networks (see Chapter 13). However, this aggregation of multiple network data into a single network has an expedient character that could make some analysts uneasy. At times, then, some might prefer to compute prominence scores for actors in each network separately, and subsequently either combine them into an aggregate score of multiple network prominence or use them individually as measures of prominence within separate domains of interaction. Our point is that the decision of how to analyze prominence across multiple networks is one based on personal tastes, data analysis, and computations. Measures have not been developed in theory to address the issue of multiple network prominence specifically.

CONCLUSION

Our general conclusion is that it is important and fruitful to maintain distinctions among prominence measures in empirical research but all too easy to overlook them. Distinctions are easily overlooked both because very similar formal operations are used to define alternative prominence measures (Table 10.1) and because alternative measures are highly correlated in stratified systems of actors (as illustrated by Figure 10.2).

Nevertheless, it is important to maintain substantive distinctions between measures in the interest of making correct inferences from empirical research. We have illustrated the very different inferences possible even with highly correlated prominence measures. Strong correlations among prominence measures are an insufficient criterion for concluding that the measures will yield similar association with non-network variables on the same actors, let alone actors in other systems.

In order to correctly operationalize prominence for a specific research project, alternative measures could be compared in either of two ways: (1) Measures could be compared algebraically in terms of the structural properties they reflect so that a measure could be selected that reflects the properties assumed to be pertinent for the substantive problem under study. For example, the distinction between leaders and followers is pertinent to the adoption decision by Galesburg physicians, so that prestige measures would be most appropriate in an explanation of their adoption behavior. (2) Alternative measures could be computed and each correlated with the class of substantive variables of interest in order to identify those measures more clearly associated with the substantive variables. The structural properties those measures capture could then be identified as most pertinent to the substantive problem under study. If a criterion variable is more strongly correlated with centrality measures than with prestige measures, for example, then it is access to the control of information that is most pertinent to predicting the criterion variable. If the variable is more strongly correlated with prestige measures than with centrality measures (as is the case in

Galesburg), then it is the distinction between leader and follower that is most pertinent to predicting the criterion variable. In this sense of using alternative prominence variables to identify structural properties especially pertinent to a substantive problem under study; it is fruitful to maintain distinctions among the measures in empirical research.

NOTES

1. Discussion relations in Galesburg actually involved 35 physicians; however, three of them were cited as discussion partners by interviewed physicians without being interviewed themselves. They could not be a source of citations so we have deleted them here as an unproductive complication. The social structure of professional relations among the Galesburg physicians is described in detail elsewhere (Burt, 1982b: ch. 3, esp. pp. 63-67). Only one of these physicians was cited as a discussion partner by more than a single interviewed physician. The snowball phase of sampling physicians in Galesburg was apparently quite successful.

2. The sociogram in Figure 10.1 differs from the sociogram of the same data presented in the original report (Coleman et al., 1966: 76): physician 29 cites physicians 12, 18, and 21 in Figure 10.1, but cites 12, 18, 11, and 26 in the original report. The citations reported here were taken from the original card decks for the *Medical Innovation* study as described elsewhere (Burt, 1982b: Data Appendix). The card deck sociometric citations for Galesburg corresponded for all other physicians to the discussion sociogram reported in the final report and corresponded for all physicians, including 29, in the advice and friendship networks.

3. The connection between the range of an actor's ego network and his or her prominence within a network has been discussed more generally in the preceding chapter under the question: "How is range associated with prominence?"

4. For the purposes of this discussion, we are ignoring the graph theoretic distinction between in-degree (choices received) and out-degree measure—because the labels— "choice status" and "degree" are more clearly identified with substantive network analyses or prominence.

5. Illustrative computations of path distances are readily available elsewhere (e.g., Mitchell, 1969; Barnes, 1969; Doreian, 1974; Burt, 1980b, 1982a: 26-29). Coleman (1964: 444-455) discusses connectivity in terms of path distances (an operational definition of earlier work in the probability of a given actor being conneced to a randomly selected other actor), and Harary et al. (1965: 117-123) discuss reachability in terms of path distances (but define actor j's reachability only in terms of the actors to whom he or she is connected).

6. Connectivity typically does not distinguish relations received from those sent, even when the asymmetry of choice is preserved. It is obviously possible to focus only on direct and indirect connections leading to an actor (e.g., Lin's [1976: 340-349] measure of "influence domain"); however, such a focus is not often seen in empirical research.

7. It also corresponds to two less well-known indices. Extending the numerator to include relations between the actors connected to j, anthropologists have discussed this concept as "network span" (see Kapferer 1969: 222)—the proportion of all network relations contained in an ego network. Also describing symmetric path distances in a network, Laumann and Pappi (1976: 139ff) analyze an actor's "integrative centrality" as the extent to which he occupies the centroid in a smallest space analysis of the path distances (see Galaskiewicz, 1979: 61ff; Boje and Whetten, 1981, for applications in

interorganizational networks). The centroid is the geometric center of the space and is occupied by an actor whose path distances to others in a network are, on average, lower than any other actor's. In this sense of comparing one actor's path distances with path distance generally, the Laumann and Pappi integrative centrality measure is quite similar to the classic Bavelas centrality measure.

8. However, such an index is the default measure of prestige in the STRUCTURE program when computation of the eigenvector measure described in equation 10.3 fails to converge on a final solution. More specifically, the default measure is the sum of normalized relations received by actor j divided by the sum of relations among all actors, that is, the proportion of all relations received by actor j.

9. This point is raised by Flament (1963: 51) as a criticism of the original Bavelas centrality model (see Burt, 1982a: 35n, for illustrative discussion).

10. More specifically, the measure is a product of two sums. Let d_{ij} be the distance between actors i and j as defined for equations 13.1 and 13.2 in Chapter 13. Actors i and j are structurally equivalent (i.e., structural peers jointly occupying the same network position) to the extent that d_{ij} equals zero. The following index varies from 0 to 1 as the extent to which actor j only directs relations to actors with whom he is structurally equivalent:

$$\text{SELF} = (\Sigma_i \ [1 - z_{ji}]d_{ij})/(\Sigma_i \ d_{ij})$$

Actor j's relations have primary form to the extent that this index equals 1 (indicating that he only directs relations toward his structural peers) at the same time that VAR3 for actor j equals 1 (indicating that he is the object of a maximum strength relation from each other actor). Thus, the product of the above index and actor j's score on VAR3 is a measure, varying from 0 to 1, of the primary form in j's relations:

$$\text{(SELF) (VAR3)}$$

Moreover, the following product measures the extent to which actor j is a follower: the object of no relations from other actors (1 - VAR3 being close to one) and directing relations to actors distant from his own position (1 - SELF being close to one);

$$\text{(1 - SELF) (1 - VAR3)}$$

and the following product measures the extent to which actor j is an isolate: the object of no relations from other actors (1 - VAR3 being close to one) and restricting his relations to others jointly occupying his position (SELF being close to one):

$$\text{(SELF) (1 - VAR3)}$$

These computations could be applied to symmetric or asymmetric, discrete or continuous measures of relation. For methods of characterizing the form of the aggregate relational pattern defining the position actor j jointly occupies with his or her peers, see Burt (1982a: 51-55) and Marsden (1982b).

11. Using the terms in note 10, the first actor would have a low value of SELF and a high value of VAR3, combining in a low product (SELF) (VAR3) measuring prominence, and VAR 3 would equal zero for the second actor so his prominence too would equal zero as the product (SELF) (VAR3).

12. More specifically, betweenness is captured in terms of geodesics, where a geodesic from actor j to actor i is any chain of direct connections equal to the path distance from j to i. Although there is only one path distance from j to i, there can be multiple geodesics as indirect connections of length equal to the path distance. An actor j is between two others i and t to the extent that all geodesics between i and t involve j. The proportion of geodesics between i and t involving j is the ratio g_{itj}/g_{it}, where g_{it} is the number of geodesics between i and t and g_{itj} is the number of those geodesics in which j is an intermediary. The extent to which j stands between all other actors is given by the sum of this proportion for each pair of actors i and it:

$$SUM = \Sigma_i \Sigma_t \ (g_{itj}/g_{it}), \ i \neq j \neq t$$

and dividing this observed value by its maximum possible value defines a measure varying from 0 to 1 of the extent to which actor j brokers relations between all actors;

$$SUM/(N^2 - 3N + 2)$$

The computations in SUM could be applied easily to asymmetric choice data or continuous relations from which indirect connections could be computed. However, the normalization of SUM by its maximum value is unknown for such data.

13. Using the terms in note 12, both actors would have values of g_{itj} equal to zero; the first actor because each pair of actors i and t are directly connected, which excludes any third actor j as an intermediary, and the second actor because he is involved in no geodesics between other actors.

14. In other words: $0 \leq p_j \leq 1$, and the sum of the p_j across all actors j equals 1. The connection between equation 10.3 and a routine eigenvector problem is informative. Equation 10.3 can be rewritten as the following matrix equation; $P = PZ$, where Z is the (N,N) matrix of relations z_{ij}, column j of which is given in equation 10.3, and P is a (1,N) vector of prominence scores, the jth element of which is p_j. Subtracting P from both sides of this equation yields the following expression: $0 = PZ - P$, which is equivalent to the following: $0 = P(Z - I)$, where I is an (N,N) identity matrix. If Z is row stochastic (i.e., if the sum of the z_{ij} in each row i equals one), then the vector of prominence scores in this final expression corresponds to the left-hand eigenvector of the matrix Z (because the largest eigenvalue of the matrix will be 1.0) and can be computed from the Z matrix with a routine eigenvalue computer routine. If it is impossible to normalize relations to sum to one across elements in each row, then a variable eigenvalue must be specified in the expression (resulting in : $0 = P(Z - \lambda I)$, where λ is the largest eigenvalue for the matrix Z), and the largest eigenvalue of Z must be computed before prominence scores can be computed. Discussion of these issues is readily available (e.g., Searle, 1966: 165-193; Van de Geer, 1971: 62-74). The computation of these prominence scores in STRUCTURE forces Z to be row stochastic by setting z_{ij} equal to 1 and dividing row elements by row sums. This means that the prominence scores computed below for symmetrized relations are in fact computed from such relations after they have been normalized to be row stochastic.

15. More specifically, connecting these measures with STRUCTURE output, VAR1 has been computed from the number of choices j receives by dividing it by 31 (i.e., N-1), VAR2 has been computed from the number of actors connected to j by subtracting j from the total and dividing by 31 (i.e., [NUMBER CONNECTED - 1]/[N-1]), and VAR3, VAR4, VAR5, and the measure of primary form and isolation are output directly by the program (see note 14 regarding C5).

16. The average correlation between a pair of prestige measures is .85, the average correlation between a pair of centrality measures is .86, while the average correlation is .70 between a centrality and a prestige measure. The correlations averaged in these means have been computed from the prominence scores for 31 of the physicians in Figure 10.1. Physician 30 has been deleted here and in the text because this person is a perfect isolate and so constitutes an outlier in the distribution of prominence scores. Deleting physician 30 means that the high correlations reported in the text cannot be attributed to the tendency for perfect isolates to have prominence scores of zero on all of the measures. The means reported here are averages of all 10 correlations among the five prestige measures $(5(5-1)/2 = 10)$, 6 correlations among four of the five centrality measures $(4(4-3)/2 = 6)$, and 20 correlations between prestige and centrality measures $(5 \times 4 = 20)$. The centrality measure created by VAR2 computed from symmetric relations is excluded because there is no variance in the measure (all 31 physicians are connected by symmetrized path distances) so it has no correlation with any other variable.

17. This point refers to Lazarsfeld's (1959: 63-64) criterion for the "interchangeability of indices"—two indices being interchangeable indicators of a concept in a specific proposition when they have similar associations with the second concept in the proposition. Centrality and prestige measures are clearly not interchangeable indicators of prominence in the proposition predicting adoption date from adopter prominence. The methodological problem of locating interchangeable indicators is discussed in terms of confirmatory covariance structures in Burt (1976b). The comparative analysis of centrality measure by Freeman et al. (1980) is an exemplary methodological study in the sense that alternative measures are compared in terms of their association with a substantive variable, presumably predicted by centrality correctly measured (compare Lankford, 1974).

18. In particular, negative prominence scores are likely to occur in applied work. For example, physician 30 in Figure 10.1 is an isolate and so constitutes a subgroup unconnected to the group composed of the other 31 physicians. Physician 30 has a negative prominence score in equation 10.3. Since the scores generated by equation 10.3 are only fixed in proportion to one another, this problem can be handled by adding a constant to each score so as to raise the minimum score to zero, and then dividing each by the sum of the increased scores. This elimination is carried out automatically in STRUCTURE, and a message is printed indicating that it was necessary to eliminate one or more negative prominence scores.

19. Bavelas (1950) proposed the well-known idea of summing centrality scores across actors to describe network centrality. Problems with this index (Flament, 1963: 50-52; Freeman, 1979) suggest that measures of network centralization are better stated in terms of differences in actor centrality.

20. However, equation 10.4 need not have an upper limit of 1 for all prominence measures. Its upper limit is reached when one and only one actor in a network has nonzero prominence. If such a condition is impossible (e.g., it would be impossible to obtain a single nonzero value of equation 10.2), then the upper limit equation 10.4 will be a determinable amount less than 1.

Chapter 11

New Directions in Multiplexity Analysis

MICHAEL J. MINOR

Multiplexity analysis entails examining the patterns, causes, and consequences of overlap in relations. This chapter shows how attention to three relatively neglected dimensions of multiplexity analysis, specificity, aggregation level, and temporal variability, can contribute to the understanding of exchange overlap. I use a three-wave panel data set based on interviews with a sample of 181 former heroin addicts to first create multiplexity indicators at both dyadic and ego network levels; next, to examine the distributions of these indicators within networks and across time; and finally, to see how these indicators are associated with some variables of importance to network analysis: social foci, intimacy durability, acquaintance volume, and social constraint. These analyses illustrate key methodological issues in formulating and carrying out investigations of exchange overlap.

Multiplexity has no consensual definition, though it typically denotes the overlap or redundancy in relations (Gluckman, 1962; Barnes, 1972). Numerous analyses have been conducted on multiplexity in roles and affiliations (e.g., Laumann, 1973; Fischer et al., 1977; and Verbrugge, 1979). However, there are only a few published accounts on exchange overlap. Kapferer's (1969) investigation of a dispute among 23 workers in an African factory is perhaps the most widely cited analysis of exchange multiplexity. In that study multiplexity was defined as relations that contained two or more channels of behavioral interaction (such as joking and conversation). The analytic context was essentially a closed system (the workers within the production group), and the units of measurement were coded observations (by the investigator) of microsocial behavior over an unspecified period of months.

This chapter examines three dimensions of multiplexity in personal networks that have received minimal attention to date: specificity in

Author's Note: *Portions of this chapter were presented at the Second Annual Sun Belt Social Networks Conference, Tampa, Florida, February 1982. This research is supported by grant DA02566-03 from the National Institute on Drug Abuse. I thank Bob Saltz and Chris Beard for their assistance in carrying out the computational work and also for their valuable comments. Ron Burt also provided helpful comments on drafts of this chapter.*

type of exchange overlap, aggregation level, and temporal variability. I illustrate the utility of these dimensions by analyzing the overlap in exchange relations for a sample of former heroin addicts who were interviewed three times at approximately six-month intervals during October 1978 to December 1980. A survey methodology initially developed by Laumann (1966, 1973) and subsequently expanded by Fischer and his associates (1982a) is used to show how a pool of exchange items can supply multiplexity indicators that reflect overlap both across and within types of exchange at two levels of aggregation: dyadic (ego-alter relations) and complete (measured) ego network. The panel component of the data set is used to illustrate four ways in which time can enter into multiplexity analysis: to assess the temporal stability of multiplexity at different levels of aggregation, as a specification variable in estimating the effects of multiplexity, in the operationalization of variables that covary with multiplexity, and as a vehicle for providing replicates to examine the reliability of findings. Together these illustrations underscore the central role that time should play in future investigations of multiplexity.

The following pages first describe the former heroin addict sample, data collection procedures, questionnaire items, and multiplexity indicators. Next is multiplexity's distribution within networks and across time. The within-network findings show consistent evidence of no clustering effects and thus legitimate the use of dyads as primary analytic units. Third is multiplexity's association with five variables used frequently in network analysis: social foci, relational intimacy, relational durability, acquaintance volume, and social constraint. The concluding section reviews how the dimensions of specificity, aggregation level, and time contribute to the understanding of multiplexity; speculates on what the findings suggest about multiplexity in former heroin addicts' relations and networks; and describes current research we are carrying out on multiplexity.

METHODOLOGY

Sample

The sample is drawn from a pool of clients and a comparison group who participated in an experimental aftercare study designed to facilitate disengagement from a lifestyle based on heroin addiction (Minor et al., 1982). Eligibility criteria for involvement in the social experiment were : (a) a history of addiction to heroin; (b) enrollment in a drug treatment program or similar drug monitoring program (such as probation with urine surveillance) for at least three months during the nine-month period prior to intake; (c) residence in the catchment area (Northern Alameda and Western Contra Costa Counties); and (d) voluntary participation in the aftercare project. The 181 persons reported on here are the subgroup who were interviewed three times during the experiment: at intake or baseline (T1), at a six-month followup point (T2), and at a twelve-month followup point (T3). Respondents were paid $20 for each completed interview.

Referrals to the aftercare experiment came from 14 different sources. Eligible referrals (97 percent of those referred to the experiment) were assigned randomly to one of three aftercare programs. The aftercare programs varied in their availability of three general service delivery strategies: referral to community agencies, advocacy assistance, and the provision of in-house services. About one-fourth of those persons eligible for aftercare services did not show up for an intake interview and thus comprise a no-services comparison group. Client activity in an aftercare program ranged from 2 to 46 weeks.

Aside from common drug treatment programs, the vast majority of respondents were not interconnected by kinship or other ties. The sex ratio was almost 1 to 3, females to males. The largest single group was Black males, comprising almost 47 percent of the sample. Respondents were relatively young; only 14 percent were 40 or older at T1. Of the sample, 63 percent reported having a spouse or a spouse-like relation at T1. This proportion increased to 74 percent and 76 percent at T2 and T3, respectively. Two-thirds of the repondents had children. Of the sample, 91 percent were enrolled in a drug treatment program (either methadone or therapeutic community) at T1, 89 percent at T2, and 81 percent at T3. The proportion on parole or probation decreased from 63 percent at T1 to 52 percent at T2 and T3. About 50 percent of the sample were employed sometime during the six-month periods prior to each interview point. Reported opiate use during the same periods ranged from 23 percent of the sample at T1 to 45 percent at the two followup points. About 60 percent of the sample reported legal problems during the six-month periods preceding each interview point.

Data

The data were collected in face-to-face interviews. The questionnaire consisted of items asking about current status in 12 life domains (such as employment, finances, and family) and about personal networks.[1] The format of the network items was to ask for the names (first name and last initial) of alters via specific questions, such as: "Who have you borrowed money from during the past six months?" These items were "open" in two regards: responses (reported alters) were not constrained by responses given to other network items; and, except for the question about best friend, the number of responses per item was not limited. The network items were placed throughout the questionnaire to minimize the likelihood of response effects (Sudman and Bradburn, 1974) in reporting same alters across questions.

The objectives in constructing the pool of network items were fourfold: (1) to include exchange items that Fischer (1982a) had used in the Northern California Community Survey;[2] (2) to ask about key roles and statuses in personal networks, such as best friend and spouse; (3) to measure linkages that might be affected by participation in the aftercare experiment, namely, referrals to community services; and (4) to measure aspects of personal networks that pertain specifically to the reentry of ex-addicts, such as friends at drug treatment programs. Like Fischer's exchange questions, these exchange items asked about theoretically positive exchanges with the respondent as the recipient.[3] In contrast to Fischer's questions, this item pool contained a mix of hypothetical and specific event questions, and most of the questions were timebound, that is, they asked about current relations or relations during the six-month period prior to the interview.

The network data analyzed here are responses to the exchange items shown in Table 11.1 and responses to six other questions: friend(s) at job, friend(s) at treatment program, household members(s), spouse, best friend, and someone special to spend time with. These questions generated 3502 alters across the three waves of interviews: 1455 at T1, 1975 at T2, and 1952 at T3. The first column within each time point in Table 11.1 contains the number of respondents who cited at least one alter in response to a query about the exchange. The second column contains the number of alters cited on each exchange. For example, at T1, 143 respondents cited 203 alters whom they talked to about personal problems. The item pools for T2 and T3 were the same, except that one item—"how found out about job didn't get"—was not asked at T2. The item pool at T1, however, was much smaller and contained two items that were dropped at T2 and T3—"who gave transportation information" and "referral to the aftercare experiment." T1 served essentially as a pilot study for the network questions, and the relatively smaller item pool reflected our uncertainty about respondents' willingness to disclose alters' names. There was considerable variability at the item level in the number of respondents who reported an exchange, ranging from one respondent who cited an alter at T2 as a referral to a child care program which refused services, to 171 respondents who gave the name of someone they could depend on in an emergency at T2. The total number of alters cited per item ranged from one to 348.

Multiplexity Indicators

Multiplexity analysis requires rules for classifying questionnaire items (or their analogs) into types of exchange. Here I delineate three types of exchanges: affect/advice, direct help, and bridges. The basic idea is that most of the person's daily social encounters can be classified into two broad contents: verbal exchanges of sentiment (affect) or information (advice), and physical exchanges of goods and services (direct help). In addition to these common social encounters, there are also significant exchanges (usually less frequent than daily) that provide links to the social system, or community, at large. Illustrations of such exchanges are referrals to jobs (e.g., Granovetter, 1973) and referrals to institutional help, such as psychiatric services (e.g., Kadushin, 1966; and Horowitz, 1977). The term "bridge" is used to denote this type of exchange. Bridges are thus a form of exchange, whereas affect/advice and direct help are contents of exchange. The assignment of specific items to types of exchange is shown in Table 11.1. Almost all of the 181 respondents have each type of exchange at the three time points.

Exchange overlap can obviously occur both within and across the three types of exchange distinguished here. For example, a friend may refer you to a new job and a new place to live (bridge exchanges), and may also be someone to whom you go for advice about your children (an affect/advice exchange). Multiplexity indicators have typically reflected only the overlap across contents of exchanges, in part because studies do not usually include multiple measures within and across forms and contents of exchange. Consequently, the primary focus of most prior investigations of exchange multiplexity has been diversity in exchange instead of overlap. Indicators of both overlap within and across types of exchange are used in this analysis. The three indicators of multiplexity within type of exchange are affect/advice, direct help, and bridges; overlap across types of exchange is referred to as diverse multiplexity.

Table 11.2 summarizes the 12 multiplexity indicators constructed for this analysis. Each ego-alter relation receives a wave-specific vector of four scores denoting dyad multiplex status (alter cited on more than one item) on the within and across types of exchange. Each of the 181 ego networks receives a wave-specific vector of eight scores denoting marginal and conditional proportion multiplex on the within and across types of exchange. The former shows how exchange overlaps are

TABLE 11.1 Exchange Items

	T_1 (Intake/Baseline)		T_2 (Six Month Followup)		T_3 (Twelve Month Followup)	
	Number of Egos Who Cited an Alter	Number of Alters Cited	Number of Egos Who Cited an Alter	Number of Alters Cited	Number of Egos Who Cited an Alter	Number of Alters Cited
Affect/Advice						
Talk to about personal problems	143	203	169	286	163	332
Helps with decisions	118	162	151	281	146	308
Talk to about legal hassles	81	108	131	217	129	226
Gives transportation information	70	89	NA	–	NA	–
Gives advice about children	42	50	62	80	49	68
Talk to about housing problems	NA*	–	150	203	146	224
Totals	171	384	180	623	177	678
Direct Help						
Depend on in an emergency	153	262	171	343	163	348
Can borrow $100 from	68	94	123	210	125	230
Help when get sick	133	154	142	198	142	196
Drives you in car	85	109	103	142	82	135
Who children live with	82	109	80	101	74	110
Babysits children	63	77	85	142	82	134
Helps support children	24	29	23	29	22	24
Takes phone messages	39	45	44	44	38	43
Bail out of jail	NA	–	151	237	142	257
Stay with for a short time	NA	–	146	212	151	232
Helps around the house	NA	–	115	189	114	199

Got money from	NA	—	124	67	64	159
Provided legal services	NA	—	65	35	15	39
Totals	174	566	910	181	181	971

Bridges

How found place to live	101	109	125	113	114	125
How found out about job	89	89	48	47	44	46
Referral to drug treatment program	53	53	101	93	76	83
How found regular M.D./clinic	49	54	87	80	73	74
Referral to help with emotional problems	11	11	144	109	76	104
Referral to educational program	8	8	34	32	23	26
Referral to vocational counseling	8	9	134	89	35	53
Referral to child care services	6	6	18	16	16	19
Referral to aftercare experiment	140	148	—	NA	NA	—
Referral to family counseling	NA	—	33	30	27	31
Referral to housing services	NA	—	28	22	13	15
Referral to voc. counseling (refused)**	NA	—	18	16	4	4
How found M.D./clinic (refused)	NA	—	12	12	7	7
Referral to drug treatment program (refused)	NA	—	12	12	5	5
Referral to housing services (refused)	NA	—	11	10	8	8
Referral to ed. program (refused)	NA	—	9	9	4	5
Referral to legal services (refused)	NA	—	9	9	3	3
Referral to help with emotional problems (refused)	NA	—	10	8	4	4
Referral to family counseling (refused)	NA	—	4	4	3	3
Referral to child care services (refused)	NA	—	2	2	2	2
How found out about job didn't get	NA	—	1	1	20	27
Totals	176	454	619	176	161	523

*NA = Not Asked.

**(Refused) indicates that the ego (respondent) was refused services typically offered by the program he or she was referred to.

229

TABLE 11.2 Multiplexity Indicators (constructed at each interview point)

		Within Type of Exchange	Across Type of Exchange
I. *Dyadic* (ego-alter relation)	*Affect/Advice* *Direct Help* *Bridge*	alter cited on more than one item within type of exchange	*Diverse:* alter cited in two or three areas of exchange
II. *Ego Network* A. Marginal Proportion	*Affect/Advice* *Direct Help* *Bridge*	the number of multiplex alters ÷ the number of alters in ego's network	*Diverse:* the number of diverse multiplex alters ÷ the number of alters in network
B. Conditional Proportion	*Affect/Advice* *Direct Help* *Bridge*	the number of multiplex alters ÷ the number of alters with an exchange	*Diverse:* the number of diverse multiplex alters ÷ the number of alters with any type of exchange

patterned within the total set of opportunities for exchanges, ego's entire (measured) personal network. The latter shows how likely overlaps are once exchanges have been established.

BASIC DISTRIBUTIONAL PROPERTIES

The proportions of dyadic multiplexity at T2 and T3 are very similar and higher than those at T1. About 35 percent of the dyads are multiplex, and the probability of an exchange being multiplex is .45. The distribution of diverse multiplexity is relatively consistent across the three time points: About one-fourth of the alters were cited on more than one type of exchange. The ranking of proportion multiplex within type of exchange is identical at each time point: Direct help exchanges are the most multiplex (14 percent at T1, 23 percent at T2, and 24 percent at T3), and bridge exchanges are the least multiplex (2 percent at T1, and 8 percent at T2, and 5 percent at T3).

All of the the network-level indicators show considerable variability except for bridges, which show a large number of networks without multiplexity (153 at T1, 71 at T2, and 111 at T3). Network multiplexity at T2 and T3 is very similar and greater than network multiplexity at T1. Fully 80 percent of the networks at T2 and T3 have at least one multiplex exchange on all the indicators, except for bridge multiplexity, which occurs in only 61 percent of the networks at T2 and 39 percent of the networks at T3.

Network Homogeneity

Role multiplexity (the co-occurrence of kin, neighbor, and co-worker roles) among best friends has been reported by Verbrugge (1979) in her analysis of two well-known data sets on personal networks: the 1966 Detroit Survey and the 1971 Altneustadt Study. Verbrugge (1979: 1296) found that respondents had "a pervasive tendency to accumulate multiplex friendships. Having one such friend, an adult is likely to have others. The converse is: when a friendship is uniplex, the others are probably uniplex too." She uses the concepts of contact opportunities and preferences to explain this tendency toward homogeneously multiplex personal networks. Besides its substantive import, this homogeneity has implications for statistical analysis of personal network data.

Typical personal network studies use a sample of egos to generate data on ego-alter (and sometimes alter-alter) relations, for example, respondents' three best friends in the Detroit and Altneustadt studies. In brief, this methodology is a cluster sampling procedure with egos equivalent to clusters and ego-alter or alter-alter relations equivalent to sample elements. Hence, appropriate analysis of data at the dyadic level should take into account cluster effects, that is, the fact that attributes of relations (such as multiplexity) may be correlated within ego networks.

I examined the intranetwork homogeneity of exchange multiplexity for three reasons: (1) to test the generalizability of Verbrugge's findings to a wider scope of personal networks (beyond best friends) and to multiplexity indices derived from exchanges instead of roles; (2) to see whether statements about within network homogeneity must be qualified with regard to type of exchange multiplexity; and (3) to determine what adjustments are required for cluster effects in the analysis of dyadic level data. Within-network homogeneity is estimated by an intraclass correlation coefficient for each of the dyadic multiplexity indicators at each time point. The intraclass correlation "measures the homogeneity in terms of the portion of the total element (indicator) variance that is due to group (ego-network) membership" (Kish, 1965: 163). The intraclass correlation coefficient has an upper bound of 1 when networks are completely homogeneous and a lower bound of -.14 at T1, and of -.10 at T2 and T3 when networks are perfectly heterogeneous.[5]

The intraclass correlations for all of the dyadic multiplexity indicators at each time point are close to their minimum values: diverse = -.12, -.09, and -.08; affect/advice = -.10, -.09, and -.09; direct help = -.11, -.09, and -.08; and bridge = -.14, -.08, and -.10. In sum, dyadic multiplexity does not appear to cluster within these personal networks. Thus, Verbrugge's findings on the repetitiveness of multiplexity are not supported in this data set. On the other hand, statements about the heterogeneity of dyadic exchange overlap within networks do not have to be qualified in terms of the types of multiplexity; the results are consistent across all of the indicators. Finally, these findings inform us that cluster effects are not important in the analysis of dyadic multiplexity here.

Temporal Stability

The question of how multiplexity is distributed across time can be subdivided into at least three more tractable questions: Do multiplex relations at one point tend to be multiplex at other points? How stable is the level of multiplexity within ego networks? Does the stability of multiplexity vary by indicator? Note that stability at the dyadic level is a sufficient but not necessary condition for stability at the ego-network level. Conversely, stability at the ego level is neither a necessary nor sufficient condition for stability at the dyadic level.

The two-wave and three-wave serial conditional probabilities present one perspective on the temporal stability in exchange multiplexity at the dyadic level (Table 11.3a).[6] All of the multiplexity indicators demonstrate positive temporal associations. This is most evident by comparing the two-wave conditional probabilities with the respective marginal probabilities of multiplexity. The ratio of conditional to marginal proportion varies from 1.8 for the diverse and bridge indicators to 3.0 for the affect/advice indicator. In other words, an affect/advice multiplex relation was three times more likely if the relation was affect/advice multiplex at another time point (either before or after). Not all of the two-wave conditional probabilites of multiplexity, however, are greater than the within-wave conditional probability of multiplexity probabilities, the $P(T1|T2)$s and the $P(T1|T3)$s for affect/advice, and direct help multiplexity are less than the respective within-wave conditional probabilities for multiplexity.

Dyadic exchange multiplexity at any two points increases the chances of multiplexity at the third point by three (direct help) to almost fivefold (affect advice). Similar to most behavioral data, the time-adjacent conditional probabilities of multiplexity (those involving T1T2 and T2T3) are greater than the nonadjacent conditional probabilities (those involving T1T3), except for $P(T3|T1)$, which is greater than $P(T3|T2)$ in three of the four indicators. Temporal stability varies among the multiplexity indicators: The most stable is direct help, the least stable is bridges. The mean ratios of the conditional probabilities show that direct help multiplexity is about 6 percent more stable than diversity, 19 percent more stable than affect/advice, and 29 times more stable than bridges. Multiplex temporal stability appears to be isomorphic with exchange temporal stability, except for bridges, where exchanges are on the average 2.3 times more stable than multiplexity (Table 11.3b). In comparison with alter citation (Table 11.3c), the direct help multiplexity indicator shows slightly greater temporal stability, diverse multiplexity has about the same stability, affect/advice multiplexity has slightly less stability, and bridge multiplexity has considerably less stability.

Turning to temporal stability at the network level, the indicators overall show low positive correlations across waves (range = -.07 to .34, median = .12). The T2T3 serial correlations are in most instances larger (median = .20) than the T1T2 (median = .10) and T1T3 (median = .09) serial correlations. Affect/advice tends to be the most stable network exchange multiplexity indicator (median = .20). Temporal stability does not differ systematically between the marginal and conditional

TABLE 11.3 Stability of Dyadic Multiplexity: Conditional Probabilities of Relational Exchange Across Time

Conditional Probability	a. Dyadic Multiplexity				b. Dyadic Exchange			c. Dyadic Stability (Alter Citation)
	Diversity	Affect/Advice	Direct Help	Bridge	Affect/Advice	Direct Help	Bridge	
Two-Wave:								
$P_{T2|T1}$	.54	.55	.68	.23	.52	.62	.35	.53
$P_{T3|T1}$	.52	.48	.63	.07	.48	.62	.23	.47
$P_{T3|T2}$	.49	.44	.56	.11	.45	.57	.30	.50
$P_{T2|T3}$	.45	.42	.55	.19	.42	.53	.35	.50
$P_{T1|T2}$	.33	.32	.30	.04	.32	.38	.35	.39
$P_{T1|T3}$	.29	.26	.27	.02	.27	.36	.20	.35
Three-Wave:								
$P_{T2|T1T3}$	.87	.79	.88	1.00	.76	.82	.68	.82
$P_{T3|T1T2}$	.83	.68	.83	.29	.70	.82	.45	.72
$P_{T1|T2T3}$	.56	.49	.44	.11	.49	.56	.39	.57
$P_{T2T3|T1}$	.45	.37	.56	.07	.36	.51	.16	.38
$P_{T1T3|T2}$	.28	.21	.25	.01	.22	.32	.12	.28
$P_{T1T2|T3}$	.25	.20	.24	.02	.21	.30	.14	.28
Summary:								
$P_{T_i|T_j}$	.42	.39	.46	.09	.40	.50	.28	.45
$P_{T_i|T_jT_k}$	.73	.63	.65	.22	.63	.71	.48	.68
$P_{T_iT_j|T_k}$	.30	.25	.30	.02	.25	.35	.14	.31

proportion multiplexity indicators, nor does level of network multiplexity appear to be systematically more or less stable than level of network exchange.

ASSOCIATION WITH OTHER VARIABLES

Social Foci

The notion that exchanges are organized by social and physical environments is a pervasive theme in relational analysis (Homans, 1950; Laumann, 1973; Boissevain, 1974; and Feld, 1981). Social foci can facilitate overlap in exchanges or suppress it. They can also emerge and disappear, and their structuring of exchange multiplexity can change across time. For example, job settings can vary in their organization of exchanges depending on whether a person is a new, long-term, or ex-employee. A flat distribution in multiplexity across potential social foci would suggest that overlap in exchanges are diffuse and not contingent on social foci.

Figure 11.1 shows the likelihood of exchange multiplexity in five social foci: spouse or spouselike relation, kinship, household membership, friend(s) at drug treatment program, and friend(s) at job.[7] The odds ratio of multiplexity for alters in a particular social focus are calculated as follows:

$$\text{Odds} = [P(m)_{sf}]/[P(m)_{\overline{sf}}]$$

where

> $P(m)_{sf}$ = proportion of multiplex alters in social focus
> $P(m)_{\overline{sf}}$ = proportion of multiplex alters not in social focus.

Odds ratios close to 1 indicate that the focus does not affect the likelihood of exchange multiplexity; values greater than 1 indicate a facilitation effect; values less than 1 indicate a suppression effect.

The findings point to spouse relations and their surrogates, kinship and household membership, as facilitators of exchange multiplexity, except for bridge multiplexity, which appears to be randomly distributed across the five social foci. The spouse or spouselike relation consistently has the strongest facilitating effect on two of the multiplexity indicators: affect/advice and diversity. The kin focus has the strongest facilitating effect on direct help at each of the three interview points (7.8, 5.7, and 4.4). Turning to the other two social foci, drug treatment programs and jobs, we find that all of the odds ratios are less than 1, except for the affect/advice indicator at T1 for friends at

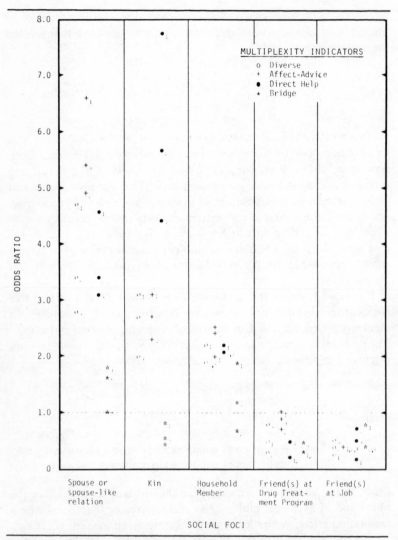

Figure 11.1: Dyadic Exchange Multiplexity as an Odds Ratio Across Social Foci (subscript indicates interview wave)

drug treatment programs. Such results are consistent evidence of foci supressor effects. In other words, the likelihood of exchange multiplexity is reduced substantially in the settings of drug treatment programs and jobs.

Looking at the cumulative effect of these five social foci, we find that there is a general pattern of increases in the likelihood of exchange multiplexity, except for bridge multiplexity, as the number of shared social foci increases. This pattern holds across the three time points. The largest increases in exchange multiplexity are demonstrated in the jump from two to three foci.

Intimacy

One common assumption about multiplexity is that it covaries positively with intimacy—the more intimate a relation, the greater liklihood of multiplexity. Intimacy is a qualitative judgment about a relationship that is grounded in the mental calculus of the respondent (Lowenthal and Haven, 1968; Litwak and Szelenyi, 1969; Rubin, 1973; Levinger and Rausch, 1977; and Wellman, 1979). The bases for such judgments may entail affective attachments (e.g., liking, loving), or behavioral interactions (e.g., sexual activity), or traditional roles (e.g., mother and daughter). Instead of requesting respondents to rate alters in terms of "closeness," a common procedure for measuring intimacy (e.g., Wellman, 1979; and Fischer, 1982a), we asked about intimate alters in two questions: "Is there someone special you like to spend time with?" and "Who is your best friend?" Only a few respondents had neither a best friend nor someone special to spend time with (17 at T1, 9 at T2, and 11 at T3).

Figure 11.2 contains distributions of the proportion multiplex across three groups of alters: those cited on both intimacy questions, those cited on only one intimacy question, and those not cited on either intimacy question. The cross-sectional findings are stable across the three interview points; the likelihood of exchange multiplexity on all measures, except bridges, increases with increased intimacy. Alters cited on both intimacy questions were about 1.8 times more likely to be exchange multiplex than alters cited on only one intimacy question and about 3.4 times more likely to be exchange multiplex than alters not cited on either intimacy question. The affect/advice indicator shows the strongest relationship with intimacy: An alter who was both someone special and a best friend was nine to ten times more likely to be affect/advice multiplex than an alter who was neither someone special nor a best friend.

Durability

The stability of relations over time, their durability, is a component of the structural continuity in a person's social environment. It is assumed generally that exchange multiplexity covaries positively with relational durability. I examined this assumption by looking at the distributions of proportion multiplex across alter groups defined by the number of interview points cited: three times (the T1T2T3 group—16 percent of the alters), twice (the T1T2 only, T2T3 only, and T1T3 only groups—22

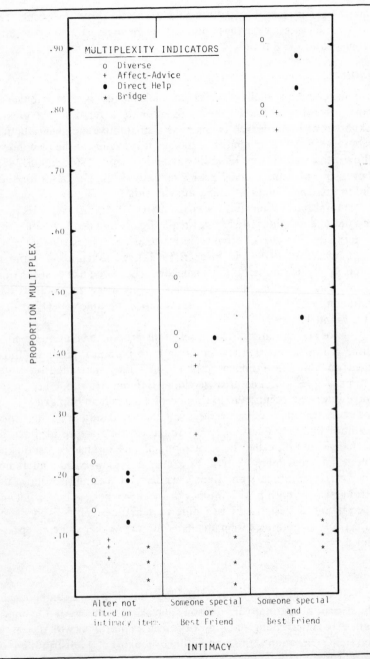

Figure 11.2: Relational Intimacy and Exchange Multiplexity (proportion multiplex)

percent of the alters), and once (the T1 only, T2 only, and T3 only groups—62 percent of the alters).

The results, presented in Figure 11.3, show that durability is positively associated with exchange multiplexity. In every instance, except for bridge multiplexity, those alters cited at all three interview points were more likely to be multiplex than alters cited at only two interview points, who in turn were more likely to be multiplex than those alters cited at only one point. Although three time points do not allow exact specification of a functional form, the overall pattern of results suggests that the likelihood of exchange multiplexity increases exponentially with increments in six-month periods of relational durability—at least in the short run.

Acquaintance Volume

Acquaintance volume, often used interchangeably with network size and range, usually refers to the number of alters an ego either "knows" or has (had) "contact with" (see Chapter 9 of this volume). As a variable of interest to network analysts, acquaintance volume provides a measure of the extensiveness of potential social resources. With regard to the association between acquaintance volume and exchange multiplexity, I expect that larger personal networks would contain proportionally fewer multiplex ties. With more social demands (relations to maintain) and more alternative sources of supply (alters from whom to obtain direct help, bridges, and affect/advice), I expect there to be less chance for exchange overlap.

In this analysis, a respondent's acquaintance volume is defined as the number of alters cited within a time point on the exchange items (Table 11.1) and the six other network items used above (friends at job, friends at treatment program, household members, spouse, best friend, and someone special to spend time with). Acquaintance volume ranged from 1 to 18 alters at T1, 2 to 20 at T2, and 1 to 27 at T3; had medians of 8 (T1), 11 (T2), and 10 (T3); and was relatively unstable at the respondent level across time (the serial correlations are T1T2 = .33, T2T3 = .45, and T1T3 = .28). Except for bridges, all of the network multiplexity indicators show small negative correlations with acquaintance volume at each time point (median = −.16). Again excluding bridge multiplexity, in each case the marginal proportion correlations are more negative than the conditional proportion correlations. Although the differences are small (a median difference of .07), such findings suggest that marginal rates of network exchange multiplexity may be more sensitive to acquaintance volume than are conditional rates of multiplexity. In other words, the overall proportion of multiplex ties in a personal network decreases as the network size increases, but given a set of exchange ties, the

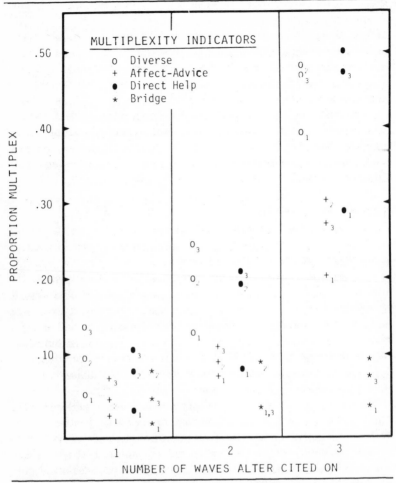

Figure 11.3: Relational Durability and Exchange Multiplexity (proportion multiplex)

probability that these ties will become multiplex is less affected by network size.

Social Constraint

The ideal that personal networks place constraints on social action is a common theme in theorizing about social structure (see Blau, 1977b, and Van Poucke, 1980). In brief, whom one knows and has contact with sets up boundaries for psychosocial functioning. These boundaries not only help delineate personal and collective goals, but they also specify acceptable means for achieving such goals. Network-defined boundaries can vary across individuals, across areas of psychosocial functioning, and across time.

One hypothesis about network constraint is that it increases with network multiplexity. I examined this hypothesis by looking at the permeability of personal networks to new relations, new exchanges, and new multiplex ties. If multiplexity does decrease the permeability of a network, I would expect new relations, new exchanges, and new multiplex ties to decrease as network multiplexity increases. Thus, the predominance of negative correlations between network multiplexity at one time point and new relations, exchanges, and multiplex ties at the following time point would be supportive evidence for the multiplexity-constraint hypothesis.

I first looked at the number and proportion of new alters. An alter was defined as "new" if he/she was not cited by the respondent during any previous interview. The proportion of new alters was calculated by dividing the number of new alters by acquaintance volume (total number of alters mentioned) at the same interview point. Two-thirds of the correlations between ego-network multiplexity and new relations are negative; however, the median negative correlation is only −.08. There appears to be no systematic departures from this pattern of predominantly low negative correlations, except for T1 affect/advice multiplexity, which had five positive correlations. Thus affect/advice multiplex ties at T1 appear to facilitate, nor inhibit, the development of new relations, at least in the short run (three of the four T3 correlations involving this indicator, however, were negative).

Turning to new exchanges, there is similar evidence of multiplexity contrast effects. In all, 69 percent of the correlations between network multiplexity and new exchange indicators are negative. The median correlation was again −.08. A slightly larger proportion (.76) of the marginal proportion indicators were negative. The correlations within type of exchange are not systematically larger than the correlations across type of exchange. Diverse multiplexity appears to be the most extensive constraint, with 90 percent of its correlations negative. Affect/advice and direct help multiplexity are the least constraining, with slightly more than half of their correlations negative. On the other hand, the development of new affect/advice exchanges is most constrained by network multiplexity at the prior time point. In all, 76 percent of its correlations are negative, and new bridge exchanges are the least constrained, with only 60 percent of its correlations negative.

Network multiplexity has a more extensive and stronger constraining effect on the establishment of new multiplex ties. Of the lag correlations, 81 percent are negative. The median negative correlation is −.13. Similar to the exchange constraint findings, a slightly higher proportion of the marginal proportion indicators are negative (.87), and diverse multiplexity is the most extensive constraint, with 93 percent of its correlations negative. Contrary to the exchange results, though, the establishment of new multiplex ties is usually most constrained by the degree of the same type of multiplex ties in the prior period. Overall, the formation of new direct help multiplex ties is the most constrained by network multiplexity at a prior point, with 92 percent of its correlations negative. Bridges are the least constraining of the multiplexity indicators, with 67 percent negative correlations, and also the least affected by prior network multiplexity, with 65 percent negative correlations.

CONCLUSION

In this chapter I have illustrated how three relatively neglected dimensions of multiplexity (temporal dynamics, aggregation level, and specificity) can be used to describe exchange overlap and its association with other variables of substantive significance. The temporal dimension in this analysis enabled the estimation of (a) the degree of stability in multiplexity at both dyadic and network levels; (b) the constraining effect of multiplexity on the development of new relations, new exchanges, and new multiplex exchanges; (c) whether durable relations tend to be more multiplex; and (d) the over-time consistencey of selective findings (network homogeneity, social foci, intimacy, and acquaintance volume). Similarly, the distinction between dyadic and network multiplexity enabled the examination of statistical associations at both the individual and relational level (intimacy and durability) and the collective relational level (acquaintance volume and social constraint).

Differences in the empirical profiles of the four types of exchange overlap described here (diverse, affect/advice, direct help, and bridge) point to the importance of specificity in multiplexity analysis. Bridge multiplexity and overlap in links to the broader social system had an empirical pattern that was particularly distinct from the other indicators, except in two instances: the constraint of new relations and the lack of within-network homogeneity. Bridge multiplexity was relatively infrequent and temporally unstable, and was not systematically facilitated or suppressed by the five social foci examined here. Furthermore, bridge multiplexity did not covary with either relational intimacy or durability and was correlated positively with acquaintance volume in four out of six instances. Finally, bridge multiplexity was the least constraining in the formation of new exchanges and multiplex ties, and also the least constrained by network multiplexity at a prior time period.

Investigations of ego networks, particularly those entailing multiplexity, should obviously separate bridges from other ties. The significance of these personal relations has recently received some recognition in the job attainment area (see Lin, Ensel, et al., 1981; Lin et al., 1978), but bridges have usually played a secondary role in the ego-network analysis. Their distinctive empirical behavior and obvious theoretical importance, though, should make bridges a high priority topic for future network studies.

With regard to substantive issues about the networks of former heroin addicts, we find that the vast majority of respondents reported having intimate and durable relations and also were engaged in social foci that organized exchange overlap. The two somewhat surprising findings, the paucity of exchange multiplexity at jobs and the heterogeneity of multiplexity within network, however, may reflect the sample's special status vis-à-vis heroin use. Although comparative data are unavailable, I also suspect that the temporal stability of relational and network multiplexity may be less than that for persons not associated with heroin addiction. The mapping of common and unique features of former heroin addicts' personal networks is a component of a long-term panel study we are conducting in the San Francisco Bay Area. In sharp contrast to preconceptions about such networks, we are finding several "normal" structural and functional properties, as well as considerable within-sample variability in network properties.

In closing, our current research program on personal networks involves pursuing the analysis of multiplexity in four directions. One is developing a more complete picture of the internal dynamics of multiplexity. This entails use of longer time periods (up to five years); higher-order relational systems, for example, couples; and more social foci, such as leisure activities. A second line of investigation is the consequences of multiplexity for psychosocial functioning, particularly with regard to traditional measures of disengagement from the addiction lifestyle (abstinence of drug use, lack of criminality, and gainful employment) and global indicators of psychological well-being (such as affect balance and satisfaction). A third analysis consists of identifying those sociodemographic factors that discriminate alters who tend to have multiplex relations with respondents. These factors will help illuminate the social stratification of the transition process for changes in addiction status. Fourth, we are examining methodological issues in the measurement of exchange multiplexity, specifically, the consistency in reports of exchanges between egos and alters, and the sensitivity of multiplexity findings to the composition of exchange item pools. These substantive and methodological investigations will yield more precise and comprehensive ideas about how the overlaps in relational exchanges are patterned and about their influence on social roles and status.

NOTES

1. Field materials are available from the author.

2. "Exchange" is used here in a special sense, referring only to ego's receipt of affect, advice, goods, services, and so forth. The concept of exchange has traditionally emcompassed both receipt and supply facets of a transaction (e.g., Thibaut and Kelley, 1959). Assumption of symmetry in these ego-alter relations, though, is unwarranted.

3. We are currently conducting a long-term panel study on personal networks that entails the use of questions about both negative and positive exchanges. Field materials for this study are also available from the author.

4. There is considerable intra-item variability in alter citations across the three interview waves. The very high across-wave correlations, though, at the item level in the number of respondents who cited an alter (T1T2 = .79, T2T3 = .98, and T1T3 = .87), in the number of alters cited (T1T2 = .84, T2T3 = .98, T1T3 = .89), and in the ratio of alters cited to respondents who cited an alter (T1T2 = .83, T2T3 = .94, and T1T3 = .83) suggest that the aggregate temporal changes in the exchange citations were structurally consistent.

5. The intraclass correlation is computed as:

$$r = [V_b - V_w]/[V_b + V_w (\bar{n}-1)]$$

V_b = variance between networks

$$= \sum_{j=1}^{181} (\bar{Y} \cdot_j - \bar{Y} ..)^2 / 180$$

V_w = variance within networks

$$= \sum_{j=1}^{181} \sum_{i=1}^{n} (Y_{ij} - \bar{Y}_j)^2/(N-1)$$

n = number of alters in network
N = total number of alters
$\bar{n}$ = average number of alters per network
The lower bound of r = $-1/(\bar{n} - 1)$, i.e., $V_b = 0$

6. The two-wave serial conditional probabilities are computed as:

$$P_{(T_i \mid T_j)} = {}^{N}T_iT_j / {}^{N}T_j$$

$^{N}T_iT_j$ = number of alters cited at both T_i and T_j

$^{N}T_j$ = number of alters cited at T_j

The three-wave serial conditional probabilities are computed as:

$$P_{(T_k \mid T_iT_j)} = {}^{N}T_kT_iT_j / {}^{N}T_iT_j$$

$$P_{(T_iT_jT_k)} = {}^{N}T_kT_iT_j / {}^{N}T_k$$

$^{N}T_kT_iT_j$ = number of alters cited at all three interview points.

7. These social foci are, of course, not mutually exclusive, and the foci of relations may change over time. For example, a spouse may also be a household member and a friend on the job at T1, only a spouse at T2, and not be mentioned at T3. The cross-sectional marginal overlap in social foci show that very few relations span more than these three social foci.

Chapter 12

Elite Social Circles

RICHARD D. ALBA and GWEN MOORE

We describe a method for locating the denser, or more cohesive parts of networks. The method starts from the identification of cliques, or maximal complete subgraphs. Since there are numerous such subgraphs in most networks, they are then aggregated when they overlap sufficiently. The resulting aggregated subgraphs are frequently large, not necessarily disjoint, and comparatively denser regions of the full network; frequently, they have the characteristics of social circles. Applied to an interaction network containing nearly 900 individuals from the American Leadership Study, we identify a number of these denser regions, most of which are small cliques, based on the shared interests and institutional locations of their members. One large central circle also results, and we discuss its interpretation in terms of integration of the overall network.

The degree of a network's integration is one of the most important structural variables which arises in the study of social networks. Perhaps the most compelling aspect of such study lies in its frequent emphasis on informal structure, and especially on the analytic tension between informal networks, the degree to which all or most individuals are sufficiently integrated into chains of interaction so that they are affected by currents moving through it—or, by contrast, the degree to which the network is but a series of loosely linked and largely encapsulated small groups—appears as a crucial structural feature, likely to be related to other of its structural aspects or the processes taking place within it.

A striking illustration of the importance of network integration as a structural feature lies in the debate over the structure of power in the United States, where the cohesion and unity of national elites constitute the turning point of debate. Ruling class and power elite theorists such as Floyd Hunter, C. Wright Mills, and G. William Domhoff argue that

Authors' Note: *The research reported here was supported by a National Science Foundation grant to Charles Kadushin and by additional computer funds extended by the Columbia University and City University of New York Computer Centers. We are grateful for the comments of Howard Aldrich, Ronald Burt, and David Phillips to a previous draft of this chapter. Our debt to Charles Kadushin, who introduced us to network research and to each other, is greater than can be expressed adequately here. An earlier version of this chapter appeared in* Sociological Methods & Research, *November 1978.*

American elites are integrated through such institutions as elite social clubs and policy-planning groups, and thus constitute a united ruling group with a consciousness of its interests. In opposition, pluralists such a Robert A. Dahl and Arnold M. Rose contend that American elites are fragmented by divergent interests and constituencies, with the result that power is widely diffused throughout American society. In essence, those who believe in a "power elite" or "ruling class" see one elite where others see many.

Despite their intuitive familiarity, the concepts of network integration and group cohesion are difficult to apply in practice. As an example, although these concepts inform some of the fundamental structural conceptions in the literature on power—such as that of "the higher circles," composed of "overlapping 'crowds' and intricately connected 'cliques' " (Mills, 1956: 11; Domhoff, 1970)—the basic issues of that literature, including the existence and nature of those higher circles, are still widely debated.

As the "higher circles" conception suggests, one important approach to the study of network integration rests on an attempt to identify collectivities or groups with certain characteristics, chiefly a definable degree of cohesion among their members. In this approach, the existence of such a collectivity or group, particularly one centrally situated in relation to the whole network and possessing a broad membership, is evidence that a network is integrated. By contrast, the absence of such an entity or the existence of many small ones, widely dispersed and with narrowly defined memberships, shows a network to be fragmented. In essence, this approach highlights the existence and number of cohesive collectivities, their relationships to each other and the rest of the network, and the nature of their memberships as crucial for the assessment of integration.

The defining structural characteristics of such a collectivity must be chosen with care. At first sight, the traditional concept of a *clique* might seem the appropriate aggregate unit for the analysis of integration. But, on close inspection, the clique concept—with its emphasis on direct interaction among all or most of a clique's members—appears too restrictive. It is capable of defining only relatively small groups of individuals, who are unlikely to be representative of the social diversity of the network within which cliques appear. To put it somewhat differently, if the world is viewed in terms of cliques, it must appear as fragmented.

The concept of a *social circle* (Kadushin, 1966, 1968, 1978) offers a more appropriate base for the empirical analysis of integration. The characteristics of a circle—especially, the integration of its membership through short chains of interaction, rather than face-to-face contact—

are compatible with the cohesion necessary for circles to be seen as the units in which subcultures are maintained or through which influence flows. Yet these characteristics allow for a realistic possibility that circles of broad and representative membership can be identified even in large networks, involving hundreds of individuals. In addition, the absence of institutionalization and formal leadership which is characteristic of circles makes the circle concept suitable for the study of interstitial networks, linking different institutional areas of society, like those typically found in the study of elites. In short, the concept of social circle suggests powerful ways of joining the microlevel of interactions and relationships to the macrolevel concerns of elite integration.

In this chapter we outline a procedure for locating the denser, or more cohesive parts of networks. The procedure starts from the identification of cliques, or maximal complete subgraphs in the language of graph theory (Harary, 1969; Alba, 1973). Since there are numerous cliques in most networks, we aggregate them when they overlap sufficiently. The resulting aggregated subgraphs are frequently large, not necessarily disjoint, and comparatively denser regions of the full network; often, they have the characteristics of social circles. We illustrate this procedure by analyzing an interaction network drawn from a study of American leaders. Our analysis shows these leaders to be integrated through a circle which spans different institutional areas and issue concerns. In this sense, we find that American elites are integrated, not fragmented.

PRELUDE: FINDING CLIQUES

The search for a viable clique identification procedure has a fairly long history in quantitative sociology and psychology (e.g., Luce and Perry, 1949; Coleman and MacRae, 1960; Hubbell, 1965). Although a definition of the object sought (by Luce and Perry, 1949) emerged early in the search, attempts to identify cliques by procedures based on formal definition stumbled over computational difficulties and were quickly abandoned in favor of more readily imagined, ad hoc methods which seemed to offer the promise of locating the denser portions of a network. A number of these methods were proposed, ranging in character from Coleman and MacRae's (1960) procedure for permuting the rows and columns of an adjacency matrix in order to cluster 1s along the diagonal, to Hubbell's (1965) proposal to cluster a proximity matrix created by raising the adjacency matrix to successive powers.

None of these ad hoc procedures found general acceptance. They too had computational difficulties and thus could not be applied with certainty of results to all data sets, especially large ones. And, since the mathematics on which they were based was often obscure and not rooted in a firm conception of the object sought, the properties of the objects they identified as cliques were usually unclear. It was only in the early 1970s that graph-theoretic concepts came together with developments in computational procedures to make feasible an identification procedure based on a formal definition.

Many have looked to graph theory for a natural language with which to describe structural features of networks (e.g., Harary et al., 1965; Granovetter, 1973). One of its more appealing concepts is that of a *clique*: a maximal complete subgraph in graph-theoretic terminology.[1] Stated in other words, a clique is a part of a graph which has the property that every pair of its points is joined by a line (and hence by the relationship a line represents) but is not properly enclosed within any other subgraph having the same property. Since a pair of individuals linked by a relationship but not part of a larger clique may trivially satisfy this definition, it is necessary to specify the additional restriction that a maximal complete subgraph must contain at least three points to be considered a clique. An example is a clique of three or more friends which is a group such that every two of its members are friends and which is not a part of a larger group with the same property.

Computational algorithms for locating cliques in this sense began to appear in the 1960s, starting with that of Bonner (1964). The Bierstone algorithm, described by Augustson and Minker (1970), represented a major advance in computational efficiency, and even more efficient algorithms have been proposed recently (e.g., Bron and Kerbosch, 1973). The advent of these algorithms has fundamentally altered the practical limits on the size of a network which a researcher can expect to be able to analyze. These algorithms not only make the identification of cliques in large networks possible in principle but feasible in practice. Consequently, it is appropriate to explore how that possibility may be used in the analysis of social networks.

FINDING SOCIAL CIRCLES FROM CLIQUES

One potential application of the social circle concept is to social networks which have central and peripheral regions. The central region is one in which relationships are relatively dense among individuals who are "influentials" or "cosmopolitans." In the peripheral regions, relationships are often sparse among the "locals," whose important links are usually those which lead to the center. The center-periphery pattern seems especially characteristic of elite networks. The central region is occupied by the elite's most influential members and is tied by outward lines of influence and inward lines of communication to numerous disconnected peripheral elite cliques, some of whose members are usually directly tied to members of the central region by client-patron relationships.

The social circle concept seems particularly appropriate for a central region and draws attention to some of the most important features of such a region's social organization. Like the social circle, the central region is usually poorly instituted, interstitial, and relatively invisible (Kadushin, 1978). That is, the central region is not a recognized social group whose members share a "consciousness of kind" and which possesses identifiable norms defining the behavior appropiate for members. Also, the central region typically crosses recognized boundaries of groups or institutions. Finally, a central region is generally only dimly visible. It does not have clear boundaries, and even its members may not see beyond their direct relationships to the larger entity of which they are a part. (Characteristically, for example, the members of "establishments" deny their existence.) Thus, circles and central regions have an "emergent" character; usually arising from the relationships individuals enter out of a variety of immediate concerns, they are largely invisible to the "natives" of any network and are best seen by the observer with a "bird's-eye" view of the social terrain.

Assuming the existence of data about who is linked to whom within a network, how does the clique definition given earlier behave in the presence of a central region, or social circle? Figure 12.1 depicts a central region of a larger, hypothetical network. The central region is indicated by a boundary line, and the relationships linking it to peripheral regions are indicated by dotted lines. (In practice, the distinction between central and peripheral regions is often harder to draw than in this simplified example.)

The greater density of such a central region usually results in a proliferation of objects identified as cliques. Thus, the bounded portion of Figure 12.1 encloses eight cliques, none containing more than four individuals. These cliques are highly overlapping. Each clique shares at least two members with some other, and every individual appears in at least two of them. In other words, this central region appears woven with a tight mesh out of a number of small "grouplets." What this example (and our experience with elite networks) suggests is that central regions and social circles more broadly can generally be identified— admittedly, with some arbitrariness concerning their precise boundaries—by aggregating cliques, identified as maximal complete subgraphs.

In practice, we have found there to be two distinct stages of aggregation. Usually, there are numerous pairs of cliques in a large

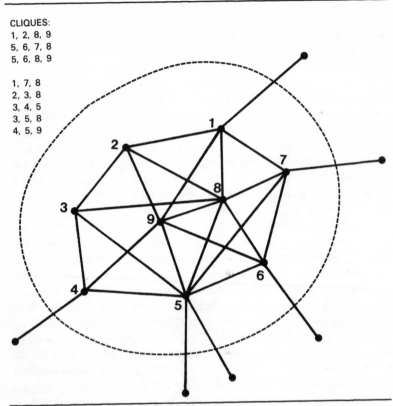

CLIQUES:
1, 2, 8, 9
5, 6, 7, 8
5, 6, 8, 9

1, 7, 8
2, 3, 8
3, 4, 5
3, 5, 8
4, 5, 9

Figure 12.1: A Hypothetical Social Circle and Its Cliques

graph which differ from each other by only one point, or individual; that is, the deletion of one point from one of the cliques would make it wholly enclosed within the other. One example in Figure 12.1 is provided by the overlap of the clique containing the individuals 5, 6, 7 and 8 with the clique containing 5, 6, 8 and 9. Since the minimal size of cliques is three members, a clique must share at least two-thirds of its members with another for the two to differ by only one individual. Once such closely related cliques are merged, the resulting aggregated subgraphs may still overlap highly, with a large percentage of the members of any one also members of some other. It is desirable to merge subgraphs which are scarcely distinguishable from each other, although the choice of precise percentage of overlap for such further merging is arbitrary to a degree. Consistent with our first stage of merger, we generally have merged subgraphs when two thirds or more of one were also members of the other.

Despite our focus on central circles or regions to introduce the use of cliques to identify social circles, a wide variety of different structures may emerge from this procedure; the emergence of a central social circle is not inevitable. As one possibility, the network may be composed of a number of dispersed (i.e., largely disjoint) small cliques; in other words, the network may be largely fragmented. Even when a circle is found, it may not constitute a central region. The procedure by which a circle, assuming one exists, is constructed guarantees that it will be denser than the remaining parts of the network but indicates nothing concerning its relationship to the rest of the network. It is possible that the circle will be relatively isolated, with few links connecting it to the remainder of the network (although we have yet to encounter this possibility in practice). More often, numerous links will tie members of the circle to the remainder of the network.

Finally, this procedure may result in the identification of several social circles. The existence of several circles is not necessarily an indication that the network containing them is fragmented, but it does throw attention to the overlap of the circles and to the possibility that the different circles, which are likely to differentiated in terms of a number of social attributes, are integrated by individuals who belong to two or more of them and thus serve to link them.

One important feature of the boundary of circles, as it is identified by our procedure, needs discussion. Since the circles will usually not be isolated from the rest of the network, there will often be individuals outside of the circles who have several or more links to their members, raising the possibility that these outsiders ought to be included in their membership. What distinguishes an individual outside of the circles from those within them is the absence of links joining the outsider to insiders *who are directly linked themselves.* The reader can easily verify that an individual who is tied to two circle members who are directly tied to each other must be a member of a clique (as defined earlier) containing these two. Under most circumstances, this clique will be aggregated with others to form the circle in question.[2] Cohesion, then, as an aspect of the circles identified by our procedure, is not simply equatable with a greater density of links among circle members, but rather with the integration of each member into tightly knit groups with other circle members.

The identification of circles opens up a series of questions whose answers provide considerable insight into the structure of a network. We have already discussed the important questions concerning the relations among multiple circles, should they exist, and the relations between circles and the rest of the network. Other questions concern the nature of their membership. It must not be assumed that all major variables in any situation will differentiate between circle members and nonmembers. In the case of elite networks, for example, variables that measure influence ought to distinguish between the members and non-members of a central circle—otherwise we would have to question whether the procedure has captured anything essential—but social background variables may not or may do so only poorly. Indeed, one important difference between "pluralists" and "elitists" concerns the advantages or disadvantages adhering to particular class origins in the process of mobility into the highest circles of power and influence (e.g., Domhoff, 1970; Polsby, 1963). Thus, in the analysis of an elite network the relationship between an individual's parental social class and his or her circle membership is a theoretical strategic question on which analysis focuses once circles have been identified. Analogous questions will arise in most other situations.

SOME PRACTICAL CONSIDERATIONS

The procedure we have described for identifing social circles has been incorporated into a computer program, COMPLT (Alba, 1972), designed for IBM 360 and 370 computers.[3] We have used this program to analyze several large networks arising from national elite studies (in Australia, Norway, the United States, and Yugoslavia) and a number of smaller networks from a variety of sources. Three of the elite networks contain more than 500 individuals each, and one contains nearly 900. In addition, Sonquist and Koenig (1975) have used this program to analyze corporate interlocks among the 797 largest American corporations and financial institutions.

Our experience and that of others demonstrates the feasibility of analyzing large networks containing as many as 1000 individuals. Nonetheless, the decision to analyze a large network cannot be made lightly, since the cost of such an analysis by any network procedure is vastly greater than the cost of a statistical analysis (with SPSS, for example) of sample data of comparable size. As an extreme example, our recent analysis of Australian elite data collected by Higley and his colleagues (1978) required over 100 minutes of computer time on an IBM/370, model 168, and 600K of memory. The cost of this single run to analyze a network containing 750 individuals was $1200 at our computer installation. Clearly, a computer run of this magnitude is enough to challenge the intestinal fortitude of even the most self-confident programmer.

Our experience provides some loose guidelines that are useful in estimating the ease or difficulty of any analysis. The time and memory required by any analysis rise steeply and nonlinearly with the number of nodes in a network and, somewhat inexactly, with its density. (More precisely, the computer resources which are required depend on the structure of the network, especially the number of cliques it contains, but the structure cannot be known until after the analysis is done.) In our experience, any network with fewer than 100 nodes—and thus most of the networks in the published literature—can be analyzed by COMPLT in a brief time, often less than a minute, and in a small amount of memory. And, except in cases of unusual density, networks with fewer than 250 nodes require only modest amounts of time and memory. For networks containing between 250 and 500 nodes, density becomes a crucial factor. We have found networks arising from free-choice sociometric questions on surveys, where the respondent is asked to name individuals related to him in specific ways, to be generally less dense than networks arising from many other kinds of data, such as networks of scientists in which a link is established through co-citation. With this number of nodes, then, the former will usually be readily analyzable, whereas the latter may require more care, especially when their density rises above 10 percent. It is not possible for us to give any rules of thumb for networks with more than 500 nodes. They are usually costly to analyze, and their exact cost depends on their structure in ways that cannot be identified prior to their analysis.

Our experience has also led to one important modification of the strategy for network analysis advanced in an earlier study (Alba, 1973), where graph-theoretic concepts were advocated as important tools for analyzing networks. There, a relaxation of the present clique definition was proposed on the grounds that it was too stringent and was likely to exclude from consideration groups which were very dense but failed to satisfy the completeness criterion for want of a few relationships. The concept of an n-clique (Luce, 1950) was proposed in its place. In an n-clique, every pair of individuals is connected by a path containing n or fewer links, which may lie partly outside the n-clique.

We have abandoned the n-clique because our experience has brought the realization that the clique concept is not as severe a standard as it first appears and also because the use of n-cliques is fraught with difficulties. Although it is possible to identify n-cliques (assuming "n" to be fixed) by using the same algorithms used to identify maximal complete subgraphs (Alba, 1973), their identification is far more time-consuming than the identification of simple cliques in the same network. Moreover, many of the n-cliques will have undesirable properties: for example, some of them will not be fully connected by paths internal to them. Further sifting of the n-cliques not only makes the computation task more tedious but may not lead easily to subgraphs with desirable properties (Mokken, 1979.) But more importantly, the clique concept is not as restrictive as it seems. Since dense regions of a network which do not satisfy the definition of a clique are generally composed of numerous small cliques, they are not lost to our strict definition of a clique and are discovered when cliques are aggregated.

ELITE SOCIAL CIRCLES IN THE UNITED STATES

The usefulness of our procedure for identifying social circles can be illustrated through application to the study of elite integration in the United States. Our analysis is based on data from the American Leadership Study, a survey of 545 top position holders in key American institutions conducted in 1971-1972 by the Bureau of Applied Social Research.

The positional universe from which the sample for this study was drawn consists of occupants of the highest positions in ten powerful institutional sectors: industrial corporations, nonindustrial corporations, holders of large wealth, labor unions, political parties, voluntary organizations, the media, Congress, federal administration, and the civil service. To guard against important omissions from the positional sample, it was supplemented by a snowball sample, which contains persons not included in the original sample but mentioned frequently by respondents as influential. Most such persons were in one of the original ten sectors, but a few were not; these include White House staff, academics, governors, and mayors. In all, 50 to 60 interviews were completed in most positional sectors, for an overall completion rate of 70.4 percent (see Barton, 1972, for a full description of the sampling procedure).

Each respondent was personally interviewed about a wide variety of matters such as his or her social background and opinions on important political issues, but the bulk of the interview concerned the respondent's policy-influencing and policy-making activities. As part of the examination of policy-relevant activities, the respondent was asked a series of sociometric questions about one national issue in which he or she had been deeply involved. These questions dealt with both reputational influence (e.g., Who currently has the most influence on opinions of leading Americans on this topic?) and interpersonal contact (e.g., Of the various people you have talked with on this issue, who had the most useful and interesting things to say?). Each respondent was allowed an unlimited number of nominations in response to any of the sociometric questions.

The network analyzed here is constructed from all responses by sample members to questions about their direct contacts.[4] Relations in this network are treated as symmetric under the assumption that they represent direct communication (see Laumann et al., 1977, for a similar assumption). In addition, our concern to place individuals within their social milieus in a large network, and thereby to identify social circles, makes the reciprocity of an individual's connections less important than the identities of those to whom he or she is linked. Consequently, a link between a pair of persons is defined as present if at least one of the two reported talking to the other and absent if neither named the other as an interaction partner. The network formed in this way does not contain only 545 nodes, one for each sample member. As might be expected in the case of a relatively small sample, many individuals not included in it were named as interaction partners, and at least some of these must be included in the network. Precisely, those named by only a single respondent cannot contribute to the clique structure and hence can be excluded. But 396 persons outside of the sample were named by two or more sample members and hence contribute to the linkages among sample members. They must be included in the network as analyzed.

Not all of this network containing 941 individuals is connected. In all, 65 sample members are isolates; neither naming other sample members nor named by them as interaction partners, they also did not name individuals who were named by others. The remaining 876 individuals form a single connected component; a path can be found to link any pair of them. This connected part of the network, the part actually analyzed by the program, is not very dense. Less than 1 percent (more exactly, .7 percent) of all possible links are present.

Despite its low density, this network yields a large number—442—of highly overlapping cliques. These cliques are uniformly small; the vast majority contain the minimal three members and only a few contain as many as five members. However, all but two of these cliques share at least one member with some other, and many share two or more members. When cliques which differ by only one individual are joined—remember that such cliques must share at least two members—46 aggregated subgraphs result.

These aggregated subgraphs range considerably in size and overlap with each other. Nearly half of them are cliques with three members whose overlap with other cliques is not sufficient for merger. At the other extreme are six aggregated subgraphs with over 150 members each. These six and some others overlap highly, with more than 90 percent of the members of some also members of another. When such highly overlapping subgraphs are merged—as we noted earlier, we have merged two subgraphs whenever two-thirds of the members of one are members of the other—32 aggregated subgraphs result.

TABLE 12.1 Characteristics of Elite Cliques and Circles

Group Number	No. of Members	Density*	Common Issue/Sector†	Other Unifying Feature	Overlapping Groups
1	227	3.8	-/-	—	‡
2	3	100.0	-/media	—	1
3	3	100.0	-/-	—	19, 20
4	3	100.0	-/media	—	1
5	3	100.0	defense/media	Vietnam	1, 6
6	3	100.0	defense/media	Vietnam	1, 5
7	5	70.0	defense/-	—	1, 13, 15, 24
8	3	100.0	press/media	freedom of press	1
9	3	100.0	press/media	freedom of press	None
10	3	100.0	social/vol. org.	race relations	1
11	3	100.0	economy/vol. org.	agriculture	29
12	5	70.0	ecology/-	geographic location	1
13	6		-/-	geographic location	7, 15, 24
14	4	83.3	defense/-	Vietnam and geographic location	1
15	7	52.4	defense/-	—	1, 7, 13, 24

16	3	100.0	–/civil ser.	veterans' affairs	None
17	3	100.0	social/–	urban affairs	1
18	3	100.0	economy/–	Commerce Dept.	1, 28, 32
19	13	32.1	ecology/–	–	1, 3, 20
20	4	83.3	ecology/appt. offic.	–	1, 3, 19
21	3	100.0	social/appt. offic.	health care	22
22	6	60.0	social/appt. offic.	HEW	1, 21
23	3	100.0	–/appt. offic.	transportation policy	1, 30
24	5	80.0	defense/Congress	–	7, 15
25	3	100.0	–/Congress	–	1, 29
26	3	100.0	economy/appt. offic.	agriculture	29
27	3	100.0	economy/Congress	–	1, 32
28	3	100.0	economy/–	unions	1, 18, 32
29	19	26.9	economy/–	agriculture	1, 11, 25, 26
30	3	100.0	–/–	transportation policy	1, 23
31	3	100.0	economy/labor	unions	1
32	5	70.0	economy/–	–	1, 18, 27, 28

* Density is given as percentage of possible ties which are present.

† Issue or section is defined as common to group when two-thirds of its sample members share it.

‡ The first group, the central circle, overlaps with so many other groups that they are not reported on its line.

These last aggregated subgraphs are the endproduct of our procedure. To aid our discussion of them, some of their important characteristics are shown in Table 12.1. Leaving aside for the moment the large, first group, most of the remaining groups are small cliques, rather than social circles. The most frequent size is, in fact, three members. In addition, most of these groups are very dense. Only the two largest have densities which dip below .5, or, in other words, only two have fewer than 50 percent of possible relationships actually present.

Virtually all of the small groups rest on identifiable social bases. They are, in other words, groups arising out of numerous social propinquities and thus do not serve to bridge diverse institutional areas. As examples, the group numbered 12 in the table consists of five Republican politicians from a Western state, all of whom are concerned with the issue of ecology, while the next group is formed from the Republican establishment of a Southwestern state. Most of these groups have members who share a concern with a common issue or come from the same institutional sector (or both). We have identified these common issues and sectors in Table 12.1 when at least two-thirds of sample members in a group discussed the same issue or belong to the same sector, and it is obvious that only a very few do not share one of these unifying features. There are, of course, other unifying features, and we have identified some of these in the table. Undoubtedly, some of these have escaped us, since they are sometimes rather subtle features, best known to those who are familiar with the locales of the group (as in the case of one group composed of Catholic Democrats with roots in one part of a large Northeastern city).

There is one striking exception to the propinquity principle of clique or circle formation. The first group in the table consists of 227 persons drawn from all sectors and regions and concerned with a wide variety of issues. This group appears to constitute the dense core of the entire network. Although its density at first appears low by comparison with the densities of the small groups, it members have an average of 8.7 relations with other members, far above the average number of relations tying individual members into other groups. In other ways, too, this large group appears woven with a tight mesh. It contains more than 350 of the original cliques. Nearly 70 percent of its members belong to at least two of the cliques that have been aggregated to form it, and over half belong to three or more of these cliques. In light of its size, weblike structure, and—as we will discuss below—place in the network, we refer to this group as the "central circle."

The central circle appears to integrate this elite network in part by its relationships with other groups and the rest of the network generally. This social circle has numerous bridges to the smaller, outlying groups.

While these small groups rarely overlap with each other, most have at least one member in common with the central circle, and most of those which lack such an overlap with the circle itself share some members with those groups which do. (The overlaps among groups are reported in Table 12.1). In addition, nearly all of the groups are linked to the central circle by relations between some of their members and others in the circle (in addition to any relations involving individuals in overlapping portions). In fact, each group in the table is linked to the central circle in one of these ways.

The central circle is also closely tied to most of the individuals who lie outside of any group. About one-third of the whole network (including the 65 isolates) belongs to one of the groups in Table 12.1, but many more are socially adjacent to them. If we designate a nonmember of a group as peripheral to it when he has a direct relation with one of its members, then over two-thirds of those outside of any group are peripheral to the central circle (as well as, in most cases, to other groups). Additionally, 7 percent of nonmembers are peripheral to other groups but not to the central circle. Aside from the isolates, the remaining nonmembers require at least one intermediary to "reach" a member of a group.

Who belongs to this central circle? Individuals from all ten sample sectors are represented in the circle, with some overrepresentation of members of Congress and politically appointed federal administrators by a comparison with the rest of the network. And, as would be expected of a leadership circle, those who are among its membership are more influential on several measures than their colleagues in similar high-level positions who are not its members. Central circle members are generally more active in policy influence activities, more visible beyond their primary organization, and have a greater reputation for influence among other leaders (Moore, 1979).

We believe that our analysis of this elite network provides important evidence of the integration of political elites in the United States. The existence of a central circle facilitates communication and interaction both within a large, diverse leadership group and between the members of that circle and more specialized elite groups. Despite the presence of numerous cliques arising from narrow social bases, the pluralist expectation of fragmentation of elites in different sectors resulting from divergent interests and constituencies is not supported by these data. Rather, these cliques are seen to be articulated within a larger structure that makes for integration.

Clearly, further analysis of this central circle—particularly its social composition—is of considerable interest for understanding the structure of power in the United States. This analysis is provided in a separate paper (Moore, 1979).

SOME CLOSING COMPARISONS

Like other recently developed strategies for analyzing social networks, the identification of social circles sheds light on important aspects of network structure. But how does it compare to them? The strategy which has probably attracted the most attention in the last few years is the blockmodeling approach developed by White and his colleagues (1976; Breiger, 1976; Burt, 1976a). The blockmodeling approach leads to a partitioning of the population of a network into disjoint blocks, or sets of structurally equivalent individuals. This approach has some important advantages over other approaches originating in graph theory—chiefly in the ease with which it handles asymmetric and multiple relationships—but it is not directed toward the study of social integration. Its focus lies on the structural equivalence of individuals, i.e., similarity between them in their relationships *to others*, and not on the direct and indirect relationships which link them to each other. As a result, the relationship of blockmodels to the integration of a network is problematic. Thus, although relations are frequently dense among the members of a block (in the case of a "1-block"), this density guarantees little about the integration of the block's membership. The block may still be disconnected overall, or composed of distinct circles and cliques. Thus, to address the issue of integration, it appears to us that blockmodels must be supplemented by graph-theoretic analyses.

Our approach to the analysis of networks has considerably more in common with attempts to represent the social distances among the members of a network, as in Laumann and Pappi's (1973) spatial representation of relations among the members of a German community elite (see also Laumann et al., 1977). Laumann and Pappi's strategy leads to analytic considerations that are similar to our own in some ways—for example, in their focus on centrality (in their case, centrality in a social space) and its relationship to the social attributes of individuals. Their approach may even seem to offer some advantages by comparison with our own, since it does not force a definition of the boundary between center and periphery. But the difficulty with their approach lies in its reliance on smallest space analysis or some similar numerical procedure to achieve estimates of the social distances, or a spatial representation. Practically, smallest space analysis is useful only in the cases of small networks. For large networks, some other procedure to cluster matrices of social proximities (Alba and Kadushin, 1976) will have to be used, and the identification of the boundaries of groups will be necessary. In other words, the Laumann-Pappi strategy does not solve the problems our procedure is intended to address, especially when large networks are analyzed.

In conclusion, we have shown that a procedure based on the identification of cliques can be used to delineate the more cohesive parts of a large network and to identify social circles. Applying our procedure to an elite network drawn from the United States, we found a single central circle that appears to integrate the network through its relationships to more specialized groups and to individuals situated on its periphery. The existence of this circle constitutes important evidence against the pluralist image of multiple and fragmented political elites.

NOTES

1. Although mathematicians define a clique as a maximal complete subgraph, that definition is not the only formalization of the clique as a social science concept which can be drawn from graph theory. Seidman and Foster (1978), for example, recently have proposed a novel approach based on the concept of a k-plex. Also, Burt has reminded us that in the analysis of directed graphs, other formalizations—such as that of a maximal strong component (Harary et al., 1965: 54-56)—are very appealing (e.g., Laumann and Pappi, 1976).

2. One circumstance in which this merger will *not* happen is when the clique contains more than these three individuals but only two of its members belong to the circle.

3. The COMPLT program has been written in FORTRAN, supplemented by some assembly language subroutines. Although the use of assembly language limits the program (without substantial conversion work) to IBM computers, this disadvantage is more than counterbalanced by the considerable efficiency introduced to the analysis of large networks. Thus, the assembly language routines permit operations at the bit level (consequently, no wastage in memory used) and the use of single machine instructions to carry out logical operation on entire binary vectors. In addition, the assembly language routines permit the program to allocate memory dynamically, so that COMPLT adjusts the memory it requires to the size of the problem. A companion program, SOCK (Alba and Gutmann, 1972), can be used for preliminary analysis and data handling.

4. In addition to that previously listed, interaction questions are: Have you drafted proposals or written memoranda recommending policies to follow on this issue? to whom? Have you talked with individual legislators about your policy position on this issue? with whom? Have you talked with federal officials about your policy position on this issue? which people? Have you tried to get people that you know to support or oppose legislation on this issue? who? An additional six questions were asked of snowball respondents: Have you talked with (substitute the phrases—people in business and finance, labor leaders, other interest group leaders, mass media people, people in the political party organizations, people in the White House) about your policy position on this issue? Finally, the following questions about contact with organizations were asked of all, and nominations of individuals offered in response to them were included among the interaction nomination: Have you testified before legislative committees about this issue? Have you worked with an interest group or organization trying to influence public policy on this issue? Have you worked within your own organization on this issue?

Chapter 13

Cohesion Versus Structural Equivalence as a Basis for Network Subgroups

RONALD S. BURT

Two approaches to network analysis are compared in terms of the network subgroups each produces. A relational approach, developing from traditional sociometry, focuses on relations between actors (people, groups, or formal organizations) and aggregates actors connected by cohesive bonds into cliques. A positional approach, on the other hand, focuses on the pattern of relations in which an actor is involved and aggregates actors with similar patterns (i.e., structurally equivalent actors) into jointly occupied positions. There are several questions that can be posed for a specific research project that would help in selecting between cliques and jointly occupied positions as the subgroups best suited to project goals. Some of these questions are conceptual, others technical. I consider a series of such questions here and conclude that subgroups based on structural equivalence are to be preferred to those based on cohesion in most circumstances. Cliques can be analyzed as a special type of jointly occupied network position. Illustration is provided with data on elite experts in sociological methodology as of 1975.

The social environments of actors are often analyzed by first classifying them into types—two actors being in the same environment to the extent that they are members of a single subgroup within a larger system of actors. Two general themes can be discerned in the myriad criteria used to justify aggregated actors into subgroups. A clique is composed of actors among whom there are intense, mutual relations. Actors are aggregating into a clique to the extent that they are connected by cohesive bonds. A second type of subgroup, the jointly occupied network position or status, is composed of actors who stand in a common orientation to a larger system in the sense of having similar relations with actors in the system. Actors are aggregated into a jointly

Author's Note: *Work on this chapter was supported by a grant from the Director's Fund, National Opinion Research Center, University of Chicago, and by a grant from the National Science Foundation (SOC77-22938). This chapter is based on an article published in a special issue of* Sociological Methods & Research *on applied network analysis (Burt, 1978a). For their comments on a prepublication draft of the article, I wish to thank R. D. Alba, R. L. Breiger, K. Christman, C. S. Fischer, and J. A. Wiley, none of whom is responsible for my interpretations.*

occupied position to the extent that they are structurally equivalent to one another.

My purpose in this chapter is to make explicit some of the implications of deciding to analyze network subgroups in terms of cohesion versus structural equivalence. There are two parts to the discussion. In the first part, I consider some conceptual questions regarding the formal meaning of network subgroups and the social homogeneity one can expect to observe in the alternative types of subgroups. In the second part, I consider a series of more technical questions regarding available subgroup operationalizations, robustness over measurement error, goodness-of-fit tests, and the like.

My conclusion from the review is that subgroups based on structural equivalence are to be preferred to those based on cohesion. The concept of clique is substantively useful and, in some circumstances, methodologically useful. A comparison of the overall merits and faults of subgroups based on cohesion versus structural equivalence, however, suggests that cliques could be analyzed most usefully as a special type of jointly occupied position.

As illustration of the points to be made, I have drawn on the relations among elite experts in sociological methodology as of 1975. These elites were located using a combined positional and snowball sampling procedure, and the invisible collage they formed in 1975 is described in detail elsewhere (Burt, 1978b, 1982a: chs. 3, 6). Complete information was obtained on 52 of the 59 identified elite experts. Network data were obtained in the substantive exchange and influence relations between elite experts. Only influence relations are considered here. Each expert was asked to name individuals with whom he or she had direct personal communication and whose comments had significant impact on the respondent's own methodological or mathematical work. The influence relation from expert j to expert i, z_{ji}, derived from these sociometric citations measures the tendency for j's methodological and mathematical work to be influenced by personal comments from expert i. The relation is zero if there is no direct or indirect chain of citations through which expert j could have been influenced by (i.e., reached) expert i. The more direct the influence on expert j from i (that is, the shorter the chain of citations from i to j—see Burt, 1976a: 118-119, 1982a: 29-29), the closer to 1 is z_{ji}.

WHAT IS A SUBGROUP BASED ON COHESION VERSUS STRUCTURAL EQUIVALENCE?

For the sake of simplicity, we will temporarily assume that there is a single network of relations to be analyzed among N actors, where z_{ji} is the relation from actor j to actor i. In order to aggregate actors into subgroups, the (N,N) matrix of these relations is converted into an (N, N) symmetric matrix of criterion linkages between actors.

From a positional perspective, the criterion linkages between actors are the distances between actor positions in the network. To the extent that actors i and j have different relations *to* each actor q in the network the following sum of squared differences between their relations will be a large, positive number; $\sum_{q=1}^{N} (z_{jq} - z_{iq})^2$. To the extent that they are the object of very different relations *from* each actor q, the following sum will be a large, positive number; $\sum_{q=1}^{N} (z_{qj} - z_{qi})^2$. The relations from actor j and the relations to actor j, a pattern of 2N relations in total, define j's position in the network. Combining the above sums of differences in relational patterns for the two actors i and j defines the Euclidean distance, d_{ij}, between their respective positions within the network:

$$d_{ij} = d_{ji} = \left[\sum_{q=1}^{N} (z_{jq} - z_{iq})^2 + \sum_{q=1}^{N} (z_{qj} - z_{qi})^2 \right]^{\frac{1}{2}}$$

When two actors have identical patterns of relations within some network, they jointly occupy the same position in the network. In other words, the relational pattern in which one is involved is equivalent to the relational pattern in which the other is involved, and either pattern defines their joint position in the network. Such actors are structurally equivalent within the network. Actors i and j are structurally equivalent under a strong criterion when there is zero distance between them:

$$d_{ij} = 0 \qquad\qquad [13.1]$$

and are structurally equivalent under a weak criterion when there is only negligible distance between them:

$$d_{ij} \simeq 0 \qquad\qquad [13.2]$$

A jointly occupied position is now a set of actors structurally equivalent to one another and nonequivalent to other actors in the network. Building from this simple concept of equivalence, more abstract concepts can be generated by focusing criterion distances on specific features of relational patterns assumed to define network positions (see Burt, 1980b, 1982a: 42-49, 63-69; White and Reitz, 1982, for review).

TABLE 13.1   A Density Table of the Influence Network Among the Elite Experts

	I_1	I_2	I_3	I_4	I_5	I_6	I_7	Residual
I_1 (SSE)	.75	N	N	N	N	N	N	N
I_2	.10	.05	N	N	N	N	N	.05
I_3	.06	N	N	.29	N	N	N	.04
I_4 (SPL)	.17	N	N	.37	N	N	.02	.06
I_5	N	.03	N	N	.50	N	.04	N
I_6	.14	.01	N	N	N	N	.14	N
I_7 (MSE)	.08	N	N	.02	N	N	.24	.02
Residual	.13	.03	N	.06	N	N	.02	.07

NOTE: The density in cell (a, b) is the number of choices made by experts in position I_a to those occupying position I_b divided by the number of choices possible. An "N" in a cell indicates that there were no citations between position occupants. Reading from left to right, the number of experts in each social category is 4, 13, 4, 6, 3, 7, 9 and 6.

A general purpose network analysis program, STRUCTURE, was used to locate structurally equivalent experts in the network of influence relations (Project, 1981). As presented elsewhere (Burt, 1978b: 123, 1982a: 116), a cluster analysis of interexpert distances revealed seven positions jointly occupied under a weak criterion of structural equivalence. No experts were equivalent under a strong criterion. Those experts who did not jointly occupy a position with two or more other experts were placed in a residual category.

Table 13.1 summarizes the patterns of relations distinguished within the influence network. Choice densities are presented. For example, cell (7,1) of the table equals .08 because the number of observed choices from occupants of position I_7 to occupants of positions I_1 was 8 percent of the number of choices possible (3 out of 36, where the 36 is the number of occupants of position I_1 who could have received citations, $36 = 9 \times 4$). To the extent that all possible choices between two positions occurred in fact, the density of choices equals one. An "N" indicates the complete absence of choices; for example, no occupant of position I_1 acknowledged influence from any occupant of position I_2, as indicated by the N in cell (1, 2) of Table 13.1. The density table can be transformed into a blockmodel of the network by recoding the densities as zeros and ones.[1] The following image matrix is obtained when all Ns in Table 13.1 are coded as zeros, and any nonzero density is coded as a one:

$$
\begin{array}{ccccccc}
1 & 0 & 0 & 0 & 0 & 0 & 0 \\
1 & 1 & 0 & 0 & 0 & 0 & 0 \\
1 & 0 & 0 & 1 & 0 & 0 & 0 \\
1 & 0 & 0 & 1 & 0 & 0 & 1 \\
0 & 1 & 0 & 0 & 1 & 0 & 1 \\
1 & 1 & 0 & 0 & 0 & 0 & 1 \\
1 & 0 & 0 & 1 & 0 & 0 & 1 \\
\end{array}
$$

The density table, and this blockmodel ideograph of the density table, are a summary of the structurally nonequivalent, the nonredundant, relational patterns in the influence network. The structure of influence is more easily observed in the relations among the seven network positions in Table 13.1 than it would be in the welter of relations among all 52 experts. In particular, three groups of prestigious leaders are apparent. One group, indicated by Robert Hauser and Leo Goodman, specialized in social statistics. The four "social statistics elite" (SSE) occupy position I_1 in the influence network. Note in Table 13.1 and the above blockmodel that the occupants of position I_1 influence one another (the density in cell 1,1 of Table 13.1 is .75), do not acknowledge influence from the occupants of other positions (all other densities in row one of Table 13.1 are null), but are acknowledged as sources of influence by the occupants of other positions (most densities in column one of Table 13.1 are nonzero). A second group, indicted by James Davis, Sam Leinhardt, David Heise, and George Bohrnstedt, specialized in methods applied to problems in social psychology. The six "social psychology leaders" (SPL) occupy position I_4 in the influence network. A third group, indicated by James Coleman and Seymour Spilerman, specialized in mathematical models. The nine "mathematical sociology elite" (MSE) occupy position I_7 in the influence network.

Where structural equivalence concerns relational patterns, cohesion concerns the intensity of specific relations in those patterns. *A clique is a set of actors with cohesive bonds to one another and without cohesive bonds to other actors in the network.* A relationship between two actors is cohesive to the extent that relations between the actors are strong, intense relations.There is no single-criterion intensity of relationship after which two actors are co-members of a clique; however, there are some well-known alternative criteria taken from graph theory (see Burt,

1980b, 1982a: 37-40, for review). As illustration, I used STRUCTURE to locate cliques of elite experts based on their influence relations with one another. The cliques were composed of the leaders mentioned above. Figure 13.1 is a sociogram of influence citations among these scholars: the social statistics elite (SSE, occupants of position I_1 in Table 13.1), the social psychology leaders (SPL, occupants of position I_4), and the mathematical sociology elite (MSE, occupants of position I_7). A sociometric choice is represented with an arrow leading from chooser to chosen. Mutual choices are represented with double-headed arrows.

As defined in graph theory, a clique is a "maximal complete subgraph," or component. Experts A, B and C define a clique if they are connected by mutual, maximum strength relations, and no further expert can be added to the clique without losing this property of mutuality. In other words, experts i and j can be aggregated together as co-members of a clique if z_{ij} and z_{ji} are both equal to their maximum value:

$$z_{ij} = \text{maximum}, \; z_{ji} = \text{maximum} \qquad [13.3]$$

With respect to the elite experts, equation 13.3 requires that all members of a clique of experts cite one another as sources of influential comments on their work. While there are several pairs of experts with mutual citations, there is only one subgroup larger than a dyad that meets the criterion of equation 13.3: a triad composed of leaders in social statistics and given in Figure 13.1. Following the experience of others (see, for example, the preceding chapter by Alba and Moore), limiting cliques to maximal complete components is substantively uninformative here.

A less severe definition of cohesion defines cliques as "maximal strong components" in graph theory. Experts A, B and C define a clique as a maximal strong component if they can at least reach one another directly or indirectly and if no further experts can be added to the clique without losing this mutual reachability between clique members. In other words, experts i and j can be aggregated together as co-members of a clique if the smaller of z_{ij} and z_{ji} is at least greater than zero:

$$\text{minimum} \; (z_{ij}, z_{ji}) > 0 \qquad [13.4]$$

Figure 13.1 presents the strong components located among the elite experts. The social statistics elite form one clique. Each expert in this group is capable of reaching each other expert directly or through indirect choices. Also, there is no additional expert who could be added to the clique, since the SSE can reach no experts labeled MSE or SPS in

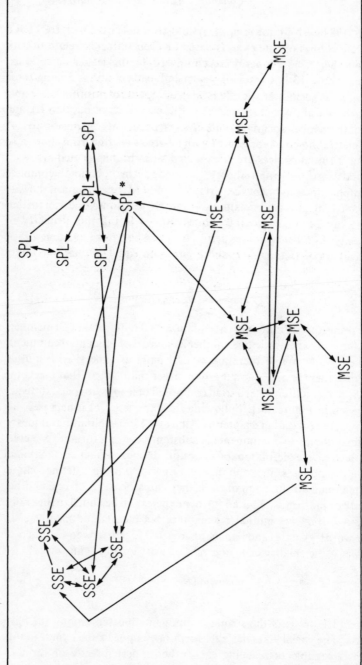

Figure 13.1: Sociogram of Influence Citations Among the Social Statistics Elite (SSE), the Methodology Leaders in Social Psychology (SPL), and the Mathematical Sociology Elite (MSE)

Figure 13.1. The second clique combines the social psychology leaders with the mathematical sociology elite. Were it not for one leader in social psychology, marked in Figure 13.1 as SPL*, the social psychology leaders would constitute a clique separate from the mathematical sociology elite. Although the SPL and MSE are combined into a single clique using equation 13.4, the tenuousness of the linkages between the two groups suggests internal differentiation within the clique (see Laumann and Pappi, 1976: 108-116, for a treatment of social differentiation within a strong component clique, and Alba's, 1973, use of the concept of an n-clique).

Still less severe a treatment of cohesion defines cliques as "maximal weak components" in graph theory. Experts A, B and C define a clique as a maximal weak component if each pair is connected directly or indirectly and if no further experts can be added to the clique without losing this asymmetric reachability between clique members. In other words, experts i and j can be aggregated together as co-members of a clique if the larger of z_{ij} and z_{ji} is at least greater than zero:

$$\text{maximum } (z_{ij}, z_{ji}) > 0 \qquad [13.5]$$

While equation 13.5 can be useful in analyzing sparse networks, networks with very few nonzero relations, it is too lax as a general criterion. For example. the elite experts were located by the common procedure of snowball sampling, which means that every expert is cited by or cites at least one other expert. In other words, every expert is able to reach or is reachable by every other expert (for example, all of Figure 13.1). According to equation 13.5, the entire system of experts would be a single clique. While maximal complete subgraphs are uninformative here because they require too severe a condition of cohesion among clique members, maximal weak components are uninformative because they require too minimal a condition of cohesion among clique members.[2]

HOW DIFFERENT ARE THE ALTERNATIVE SUBGROUPS?

Obviously, subgroups based on cohesion versus structural equivalence are extracted from observed networks under different criteria. How do these different criteria yield different types of subgroups?

Some types of subgroups obtained under structural equivalence are illustrated in Table 13.1. The cliques of Figure 13.1 as strong components have been detected as primary positions in Table 13.1; position I_1 is occupied by the prestigious social statistics elite, position I_4 is occupied by the prestigious social psychology leaders, position I_7 is occupied by the prestigious mathematical sociology elite. Of the remaining four jointly occupied positions, positions I_3 and I_6 are particularly relevant here, since occupants of these positions make no citations at all to others occupying their positions. Rather, occupants of each position have in common their similar relations to prestigious others. The occupants of I_3 direct the bulk of their citations to the social psychology leaders occupying positions I_4 but have none of their citations reciprocated. The occupants of positions I_6 direct almost all of their citations to the social statistics elite (position I_1) and the mathematical sociology elite (position I_7) but receive citations from no one at all. Positions I_3 and I_6 illustrate the form of secondary positions; occupants of each position are not the objects of relations from any actors in the system and themselves claim personal relations with actors occupying other, high-prestige positions. Related to the secondary form is the broker pattern of relations, in which occupants of a position are the objects of relations from other actors but themselves claim personal relations with actors occupying other positions. A variety of interesting substantive processes concern the activities of actors occupying secondary and broker positions within a system (e.g., see Coser, 1974; Schmidt et al., 1977).

In general, subgroups based on structural equivalence include a broader range of subgroup types. In particular, they include subgroups whose members have no relations with one another, such as secondary and broker positions. These types of subgroups are ignored if cohesion is the criterion for aggregating actors into subgroups. Further, cliques as cohesive subgroups will correspond to subgroups based on structural equivalence if members of a clique have similar relations with actors not in the clique. To the extent that members of a clique have strong relations wih one another, it seems reasonable to assume that they have the same persons as friends and enemies outside the clique. Indeed, this assumption is quite explicit in some factor analytic "clique" detection methods, as discussed below with respect to alternative computer algorithms. Therefore, subgroups based on cohesion can be discussed as a special case of the network subgroups based on structural equivalence—cliques are positions jointly occupied by actors connected by cohesive bonds.

HOW DOES STRUCTURAL EQUIVALENCE
VERSUS COHESION PROVIDE A BASIS
FOR SOCIAL HOMOGENEITY?

The above questions concern the relational forms that define network subgroups. Cliques are different from jointly occupied positions in the sense that cliques can be seen as a particular type of jointly occupied network position. There remains the question of how the two types of subgroups could be used in substantive analyses. Why bother with either type of subgroup?

Perhaps the most common use to which subgroups are put is to explain social homogeneity among actors. Actors within a subgroup are expected to have similar attitudes and behaviors. It is useful to know the distribution of actors across subgroups in order to understand the pattern of attitudinal and behavioral similarities between actors in a system. To no small extent attributable to the Festinger et al. (1950) study of social pressures in informal groups, homogeneity is to be expected within a cohesive clique because clique members interact frequently with one another and through this interaction they constantly socialize one another, so that a clique norm is created. Clique members reinforce their like-minded opinions and change deviant opinions to conform to the clique norm.

As pointed out in the preceding section, a set of structurally equivalent actors need not be a cohesive group. If the actors are connected by intense relations, then one can expect within-group homogeneity, as argued above. For example, one could expect the elites occupying positions I_1, I_4 and I_7 to have higher than average attitudinal homogeneity within positions, since each position is also a clique. But secondary and broker positions are jointly occupied by actors having no relations with one another. These positions are quite the opposite of cohesive, integrated groups. The elites occupying positions I_3 and I_6 in Table 13.1 illustrate secondary positions. Does this mean that structural equivalence fails to produce subgroups within which one could expect homogeneous attitudes and behaviors and subgroups norms?

No, it does not. There are two theoretical arguments for expecting homogeneity among structurally equivalent actors. Using the socialization argument predicting within-clique homogeneity, structurally equivalent actors should have similar attitudes and behaviors because they tend to interact with the same types of other actors in the same manner. In other words, structurally equivalent actors are similarly socialized by others. As a result, they should have similar attitudes and behaviors. Using a more general symbolic interaction argument in which socialization occurs between actors both as a result of direct communication and as a result of symbolic communication, structurally equivalent actors should have similar attitudes and behaviors because they put themselves in one another's roles as they form an opinion. Each would be expected to ask himself the question: "How would this object or action appear to each of my structural peers, the typical person occupying my position in the system?" The process of each position occupant answering this question with respect to co-occupants of his position creates a homogeneity of perceptions among the position occupants. I have elsewhere discussed conditions under which homophily is to be expected among structurally equivalent actors (Burt, 1980c, 1982a: ch. 5).

The crucial empirical test of this assertion is to see if structurally equivalent actors unconnected by relations tend to have higher attitudinal and behavioral homogeneity within positions than could be expected by random chance. Under socialization through cohesive relations, such positions should be heterogeneous. Under the positional role argument, such positions should exhibit homogeneity. In studies of innovation adoption by physicians (Burt, 1982b) and academic perceptions of journal significance (Burt, 1982a: ch. 6; Burt and Doreian, 1982), structural equivalence has been much more accurate than cohesion in predicting social homophily.

While in no sense a crucial test, Table 13.2 presents data on the elite experts that illustrate the above point. Experts were asked to indicate their relative interest in alternative journals publishing significant work in methodological and mathematical sociology. Only eight journals were of greater than zero interest to the experts as a whole and so constitute core journals for the system of elite experts. Dichotomizing at the median value of interest in each journal creates eight variables, with approximately 50 percent of the experts falling into the "high interest" category.

Each of the seven jointly occupied positions can now be characterized by a norm of interest in the core journals. The modal level of interest in each journal is given in Table 13.2 as the norm for each position. For example, the social statistics elite occupying position I_1 have a norm of high interest in the *Journal of the American Statistical Association* (JASA) and low interest in the other seven core journals. Also presented in Table 13.2 is the average level of agreement that exists between experts occupying each position and the position norm. For example, the .84 in row one of the table means that an average of 84 percent of the social statistics elite had the same level of interest in each of the core journals. In contrast, the average level of agreement in the whole system

TABLE 13.2 Journal Norms, Homogeneity, and Density for the Seven Jointly Occupied Positions Among Elite Experts

Position	Position Norm*								Average Proportion of Agreement with Position Norm†	Density of Binary Relations Among Occupants‡
	ASR	AJS	SM	JASA	SMR	SF	JMS	SSR		
I_1	L	L	L	H	L	L	L	L	.84	.75
I_2	L	H	L	H	L	L	L	L	.60	.05
I_3	H	H	H	L	H	L	L	L	.75	.00
I_4	H	L	H	L	H	L	H	L	.70	.37
I_5	H	H	L	L	L	H	L	L	.83	.50
I_6	L	H	H	L	H	L	L	L	.70	.00
I_7	H	L	H	H	L	L	H	L	.75	.24
Whole System	H	H	H	H	L	L	L	L	.60	.04

*Presented are the modal levels of interest in each core journal for each position. Interest has been dichotomized at the median level expressed by the whole system (H-above median, L-below median). The journals are: ASR—*American Sociological Review*, AJS—*American Journal of Sociology*, SM—*Sociological Methodology*, JASA—*Journal of the American Statistical Association*, SMR—*Sociological Methods & Research*, SF—*Social Forces*, JMS—*Journal of Mathematical Sociology*, and SSR—*Social Science Research*.

† This is the average proportion of the experts occupying a position who agreed with the position norm level of interest in each of the core journals.

‡ These are the densities taken from the diagonal of Table 13.1 based on binary sociometric citations.

of experts is 60 percent (.60 at the bottom of Table 13.2). Finally, Table 13.2 presents the density of influence relations among experts occupying each position. These densities are the diagonal entries in Table 13.1. The .75 in cell (1,1) of Table 13.1 appears in row one of Table 13.2 and means that 75 percent of the possible influence citations among the social statistics elite were actually observed.

The experts occupying positions I_1, I_4, and I_7 also define cliques as strong components (see Figure 13.1). As expected, the level of agreement with a position norm is high for these three positions as cliques. In addition, however, the level of agreement with position norm is equally high for the experts occuping secondary positions I_3 and I_6 despite the lack of direct relations between co-occupants of these positions (note that the densities in rows three and six of Table 13.2 are zero). In keeping with the cohesion argument, it should be noted that experts occupying position I_2 have weak relations with one another and, despite their structural equivalence, have no more than average homophily. Of the seven jointly occupied positions expected to exhibit homogeneity, in other words, all but one exhibit high agreement on the positional norm—despite the fact that two of the high-agreement positions are occupied by experts having no direct influence relations with one another.

In summary, the substantive justification for expecting social homogeneity within cohesive groups similarly leads one to expect such homogeneity among structurally equivalent actors. Since there are more types of subgroups identified under structural equivalence than under cohesion, structural equivalence provides a substantively more powerful basis for understanding the pattern of attitudinal and behavior similarities between actors in a system.

SOME QUESTIONS OF LESS GENERAL CONCERN

The conceptual advantages of analyzing subgroups in terms of structural equivalence versus cohesion are for naught if several technical questions cannot be answered.

How Do Available Subgroup Detection Algorithms Differ?

At the outset, the complexity of analyzing a network of even moderate size requires the use of a computer algorithm for detecting subgroups. There are a host of computer programs available, with more appearing every year. Rather than attempt to discuss every algorithm in particular, it seems more useful to identify generic algorithms. One of the first questions to address in a network analysis of subgroups concerns the selection of a convenient and substantively appropriate algorithm. The more diverse the output of different algorithms purporting to detect the same subgroups, the less adequately results from separate studies can be compared.

There are two algorithms generally employed to detect jointly occupied positions within and across networks. One strategy is to begin with the whole system of actors and decompose it into subgroups composed of structurally equivalent actors (CONCOR, Breiger et al., 1975). Another strategy is to begin with actors as individuals and aggregate them into subgroups composed of structurally equivalent actors (STRUCTURE, Project, 1981). Similar results are obtained from either strategy; however, there are some differences worth noting. The CONCOR algorithm computes correlations between the relations directed at actors (i.e., columns of a network matrix) and then decomposes the system of actors into pairs of structurally nonequivalent actors: first into two sets, then each set is subdivided into two sets, and so on (see White et al., 1976, Brieger, 1976).

The algorithm in STRUCTURE computes Euclidean distances between actor positions and then submits the distances to Johnson's (1967) hierarchical cluster analysis in which subgroups of structurally equivalent actors are found by aggregating actors one at a time into jointly occupied positions (see Burt, 1976a, 1977c, 1978b, 1982a: ch. 3, and Figure 14.1 in the next chapter of this volume). When these two algorithms differ, the CONCOR algorithm will be overstating structural equivalence for any of three reasons: (1) actors are being treated as structurally equivalent when they are similarly the object of relations (similar column entries in network matrix) without a consideration of the extent to which they are similarly the source of relations (similar row entries in the network matrix); (2) the use of correlations ignores "level" and "dispersion" in relational patterns, so that structurally nonequivalent actors can appear to be equivalent (see Cronbach and Gleser, 1953; Burt, 1980b, 1982a: 43); and/or (3) there is no allowance for the possibility of residual actors, since every observed actor must be structurally equivalent to one of the available subgroups. Invoking the algorithm in STRUCTURE is a more conservative procedure in sense that jointly occupied positions will be occupied by structurally equivalent under a stronger criterion. As is usual, this greater accuracy means that a larger number of joint positions are distinguished in the STRUCTURE any Fortunately, the ability to assess statistically the structors. of actors (discussed below) provides a check on 4) offer algorithm purporting to detect sets of structurally detection

Lankford (1974) and Rogers and Kincai illustrative, if nongeneralizable, comparisons algorithms. Available algorithms can be segregated into three classes: direct factor analysis, or eigenvector, algorithms such as those proposed by MacRae (1960) or Wright and Evitts (1961); graph theoretic algorithms, as contained in COMPLT (Alba, 1972), SONET (Seidman and Foster, 1979), NEGOPY (Richards and Rice, 1981) or STRUCTURE (Project, 1981); and spatial algorithms, such as Smallest Space Analysis (see Lingoes, 1972). The eigenvector algorithms extract linear composites, "factors," from the matrix of relations among actors. These linear composities are then termed cliques, and members of a clique have positive loadings on the linear composite defining the clique. The cliques identified in this manner are not concerned with relations among clique members, however, so much as with capturing the similarity of relations involving clique members with other actors in a network (see Burt, 1980b, 1982a: 47-49, for a more detailed review). The eigenvector algorithms are accordingly to be viewed as position-detecting algorithms similar to the CONCOR algorithm (e.g., see Schwartz, 1977) rather than as clique-detection algorithms.

The graph theoretic algorithms seek to locate maximal complete, strong, or weak components in a network, as discussed above (equations 13.3, 13.4, and 13.5). The clarity of a graph theoretic basis for cliques suggests that these algorithms are likely to produce the most reliable subgroups as cliques (or social circles, as discussed in the preceding chapter). Further, the fact that the graph theoretic algorithms ignore whole patterns of relations in favor of dyadic bonds means that they can search for subgroups in very large systems. The algorithms in COMPLT and NEGOPY are capable of searching for cliques in systems composed of several thousand actors, while eigenvector, spatial, and structural equivalence algorithms are typically limited to systems composed of less than a couple of hundred actors.

The spatial algorithms seek to represent observed relations among actors in a relational space where actors connected by the most intense relations are closest together in the space and those connected by weak or antagonistic relations are far apart in the space (see Laumann and appi, 1976; Burt, 1976a: 119-120). These algorithms have an advantage r the graph theoretic algorithms in that they require no absolute rion for identifying cohesive bonds. Cohesive relations among members are those relations which are more intense than other s in the network. This is also a drawback, however, since anyone a matrix of relations into a smallest-space analysis or cluster nd produce "cliques" no matter how intense the relations rel members. The intensity of relations among clique ne network need not be the same as the intensity of clique members in another network. This variable criterion for cohesive bonds can have substantive merit, however, it makes the comparability of cliques detected by spatial algorithms in separate networks problematic.

Can the Goodness-of-Fit of a Proposed Subgroup Be Tested?

If proposed subgroups cannot be tested for their goodness-of-fit to observed data, then the analysis of subgroups is seriously weakened, since anyone observing networks can propose some set of subgroups as implied by the observed data. There is no statistical test for the extent to which a set of actors is a clique. Either the actors are interconnected by relations that meet the criteria of equations 13.3, 13,4, or 13.5 or the set does not define a clique. In contrast, the hypothesis that a set of actors jointly occupies a single position can be tested. As defined and illustrated in detail elsewhere (e.g., Burt, 1976a, 1980b, 1982a: 73-89), structurally equivalent actors have similar distances to every other actor in a system so that distances to structurally equivalent actors are almost perfectly correlated. In other words, a factor analysis of the covariance matrix among distances to structurally equivalent actors should yield a single factor if the actors are equivalent under a strong criterion (equation 13.1). The closer to the center of the jointly occupied position that an actor is, the higher the actor's loading on the factor and the better the actor's position indicates the jointly occupied position. Testing the hypothesis that several actors are structurally equivalent thus yields two kinds of information: the extent to which the hypothesis is true, and the extent to which each of the actors is involved in a relational pattern typical of the set of structurally equivalent actors.

As illustration, Table 13.3 presents test information on the structural equivalence of experts jointly occupying the seven positions in Table 13.1. The results in column one of Table 13.3, for example, concern the four social statistics elite occupying position I_1. The (4,4) matrix of covariances among distances to the occupants of I_1 was obtained from the STRUCTURE output and subjected to a principal components analysis. The principal component accounted for 97 percent of the observed variance (note the .97 in the second row of the table), which means that the occupants of I_1 are structurally equivalent under a rather strong criterion of equivalence. If they were perfectly equivalent, the principal component would account for 100 percent of the observed variance.

Turning to the individual experts occupying position I_1, the remaining entries in the first column of Table 13.3 are standardized loadings on the principal component. They can be interpreted as correlations between distance to an individual expert and distance to the

TABLE 13.3   Assessing the Structural Equivalence of Experts in the Influence Network

	Position						
	I_1	I_2	I_3	I_4	I_5	I_6	I_7
Number of Experts in Position	4	13	4	6	3	7	9
Ratio of Variance Predicted by First Principal Component Over Total Observed Variance	.97	.87	.94	.88	.97	.92	.84
Standardized Loadings on the First Principal Component in Descending Order	†.98	†.96	†.97	†.98	†.96	†.98	†.96
	.97	†.95	.97	.98	†.96	.98	.96
	.97	.95	†.96	†.97	.87	†.97	†.94
	†.96	.95	.96	.92		.97	.94
		.94		.90		.95	.94
		.92		.85		.92	.94
		.92				.74	.88
		.92					.74
		.91					.68
		.91					
		.91					
		.90					
		.85					

NOTE: Indicator experts occupying each position are marked with daggers as discussed in the text.

jointly occupied position I_1. The loadings are all quite high, .96 to .98, showing that each member of the social statistics elite is involved in a pattern of influence relations typical of their collective relational pattern. The two experts having the highest unstandardized loading on the principal component are marked with daggers in Table 13.3 as optimal indicators of position I_1. Their relational patterns most closely resembled the pattern typical of the social statistics elite jointly occupying position I_1: Leo Goodman is the first indicator occupant and Robert Hauser is the second.

Across the seven jointly occupied positions in the influence network, the mean ratio of variance predicted by the principal component over observed variance is .91, and the standardized loadings of occupants on each principal component are high, indicating that each of the seven positions is jointly occupied by experts structurally equivalent under a relatively strong criterion of equivalence. In fact, experts were only proposed as jointly occupying a position when they were structurally equivalent at an acceptable level (see Burt, 1978b, 1982a: ch. 3). James Davis and David Heise indicate the position occupied by the social psychology leaders (position I_4). James Coleman and Seymour Spilerman indicate the position jointly occupied by the mathematical sociology elite (position I_7). Position I_7 is the most problematic of the positions, inasmuch as the principal component accounts for the least variance in observed distances (84 percent), and one occupant had a standardized loading of only .68, as reported in Table 13.3. Nevertheless, this evidence of internal differentiation within the position is far weaker than the evidence of structural equivalence (see Burt, 1982a: 115, for details).

The bottom line here is that easily available computer programs for extracting principal components from covariance matrices provide one method for assessing the adequacy of subgroups proposed as structurally equivalent actors. The next chapter in this volume provides an example of an analysis of subgroups in which this precaution was not taken and the proposed subgroups turned out to be little more than random aggregations of actors.

How Robust Are Subgroups Over Changes in System Boundaries ?

Neither cliques nor jointly occupied positions are inherently robust over changes in system boundaries. In no sense is the analysis of subgroups conducted in "open" systems. Of the social statistics elite jointly occupying position I_1, for example, two have most of their relations to sociologists and two have most of their relations to statisticians. If the system were expanded to include more statisticians, it would be quite possible for position I_1 to divide into two nonequivalent positions, one jointly occupied by the sociologists and the other jointly occupied by the statisticians. In regard to cliques, note that only one expert in Figure 13.1 ties the social psychology leaders and the mathematical sociology elite into a single strong component (expert SPL*). If he had not been included in the system, then there would be two strong components in place of the one observed, one component composed of social psychology leaders and one composed of mathematical sociology elite.

How Robust Are Subgroups Over Measurement Error?

Even the most sophisticated measures of relation are usually based on binary linkages between actors (e.g., see Burt, 1980b, 1982a: 22-29, for review). Random measurement error occurs when binary linkages are occasionally absent/present when they should not be and systematic error occurs when linkages are consistently under-/overestimated. If errors are random, then the ability to test a proposed subgroup statistically makes the subgroup robust over such errors. Accordingly, jointly occupied network positions are more robust over random measurement errors than are cliques.[3] Neither cliques nor jointly occupied positions, however, are robust over easily made systematic measurement errors. Consider the elite experts. If the criterion for an influence citation were set very low (for example, at a level of asking respondents to name experts whose work is familiar to them), then most experts would have a relation to most other experts. In this case, the entire system would be one clique and a single, jointly occupied position. On the other hand, if the criterion were set very high (for example, at a level asking respondents to name the people who directly supervised the respondent's dissertation), then very few experts would have a relation to others. In this case, the system would be composed of individual experts and dyads. Somewhere between these extreme criteria for coding a binary linkage from one expert to another is the criterion appropriate to a specific study. Consequential as this criterion is for the detection of subgroups, little is known about it.

How Are Subgroups to Be Detected Across Multiple Networks?

Actors are usually connected by different types of relations so as to define multiple networks in a system: a network composed of friendship relations, influence relations, and so on. Cliques have usually been defined in terms of a single network, which has meant that developments during the 1970s involving the detection of structurally equivalent actors across multiple networks (White et al., 1976; Burt, 1977b) gave the appearance that the jointly occupied positions were better suited to analyses of multiple network systems. Those developments, however, simply involve adding up comparisons of relations across networks without any regard to substantive differences in the relations being summed (see Burt, 1977b: 110). A corresponding strategy for the relational approach would be to add up the relations from one actor to another across multiple networks to obtain an overall relation. The aggregate relations could then be analyzed to find cliques defined across multiple networks. The concepts of structural equivalence and cohesion are equally well suited to analyses of multiplex relations, i.e., to relations in multiple networks.

How Are Subgroups to Be Analyzed in Large Systems?

One approach to the problem of large systems is to simply spend the funds needed for collecting and analyzing enormous data files. Alba and

Moore discuss some of this work in Chapter 12, this volume. The clique detection algorithms have a clear advantage in analyzing systems composed of hundreds of actors, because no more than a small proportion of all the available network data needs to be in core storage at the same time.

Network analyses of large systems, however, are much more likely to be based on sample data. For one thing, an enormous sum of money is required to obtain and analyze network data on several hundred actors—not to mention the scope of the computer facilities required for the analysis. Further, systems composed of several hundred actors are actually quite small in comparison to the typical systems in which actors will be analyzed (large bureaucracies, cities, regions, and so on), which means that some procedure for sampling actors is likely to be a part of the field work in a network analysis.

As soon as the decision is made to analyze sample data on a network, the concept of structural equivalence offers a decided advantage over cohesion as a basis for network subgroups. Subgroups based on cohesion provide no guide for network sampling other than to indicate where dense spots in the population network are likely to exist (see Granovetter, 1976, for a discussion of sampling to estimate density in a population network, and Erickson et al., 1981, for illustrative application). In contrast, structural equivalence provides a basis for efficient stratified sampling. Where K actors are structurally equivalent, one need not observe all relational patterns involving the K actors in order to describe their relations. Rather, the relational pattern typical of a small number of the K actors can be used to estimate the population pattern for all K actors, since all K actors have the same population pattern; they are structurally equivalent patterns. In order to estimate the density table of relations among jointly occupied positions in the population, therefore, one need only interview a representative sample of individuals occupying each position. In order to estimate the aggregate relations in Table 13.1, for example, I could have interviewed the 14 indicator experts (marked with daggers in Table 13.3) as representative of the seven jointly occupied positions in the influence network—assuming that I knew which experts occupied which positions prior to collecting data. The key idea in this sampling strategy is to divide a large population of actors into strata composed of structurally equivalent actors and sample randomly within each stratum. This theme underlies the network sampling strategy utilized by Beniger (1976) and is developed at length in Chapters 5, 7 and 8 of this volume.

CONCLUSION

Relative to subgroups based on cohesion, those based on structural equivalence: (1) include a broader range of types of network subgroups, (2) extend the scope of types of network subgroups in which homogeneity of attitudes and behaviors can be expected, (3) have a more consistent meaning as operationalized by available computer algorithms, (4) are subject to goodness-of-fit tests, (5) are accordingly more robust over random measurement errors in network data, and (6) provide a basis for sampling population network data in large systems. In short, there is one key assumption to be made. If it is assumed that cohesive subgroups, cliques, are composed of actors with similar types of relations with actors outside the clique, then the idea of a clique is completely subsumed by that of a position. A clique so viewed is a special type of position; namely, it is a position jointly occupied by actors with cohesive ties to one another. Given the advantages of analyzing subgroups in terms of structural equivalence versus cohesion, it seems useful to adopt the above key assumption and altogether do away with the independent concept of network cliques.

NOTES

1. Blockmodels were originally introduced in terms of multiplex network systems and consisted of an image matrix for each network (White et al., 1976), but since I am only considering a single network system for the purposes of this chapter, the distinction between image matrix and blockmodel is empty. I have reviewed blockmodels elsewhere (Burt, 1982a: 65-69), and an illustrative application is provided by Breiger and Pattison in Chapter 16 of this volume.

2. This is a convenient point at which to note the implications of forcing sociometric choices to be symmetric before searching for subgroups in a network. Imposing symmetry in choices usually involves the assumption that expert i chooses expert j if j chooses i (see Alba and Moore in Chapter 12, this volume). Once this symmetry is imposed on choices, there is no difference between strong (equation 13.4) and weak (equation 13.5) components, since z_{ij} equals z_{ji}. Under either definition of clique, when choices are symmetrized, the entire system of elite experts reduces to a single clique. Instead of one triad of experts defining a clique as a maximal complete subgraph discussed in the text, symmetrizing choices would result in six triads as overlapping cliques (see Alba and Moore, Figure 12.1, in Chapter 12 of this volume). In short, symmetrizing choices before searching for cliques will increase the likelihood of all actors being co-members of a single clique, eliminate asymmetric choices as a criterion for clique membership or exclusion, and focus clique definitions on direct versus indirect connections between clique members.

3. The covariance tests referenced in the text, however, only consider random errors in relations after errors and relations have been aggregated into distances between positions. Relations between pairs of actors are not described directly. Recent developments in applying log-linear models to the descriptions of choice data offer a promising approach to modeling errors more directly in observed relations (e.g., see Fienberg and Wasserman, 1981; Holland and Leinhardt, 1981, 1982).

Chapter 14

A Note on Inferences Concerning Network Subgroups

RONALD S. BURT

The substance of social structure is argued to affect the scope, adequacy, and power of conclusions drawn from a network analysis. Substance is therefore a methodological factor to be considered explicitly in justifying conclusions. This chapter is a brief evaluation of an analysis of network subgroups in which these ideas were not considered explicitly.

In a recent series of articles, Russell Bernard and Peter Killworth have presented evidence leading them to the conclusion that the (cognitive) relations in which people say they are involved bear little similarity to the (behavioral) relations in which they are actually involved (Killworth and Bernard, 1976, 1979; Bernard and Killworth, 1977). Their subsequent addition to that series extends the conclusion to network subgroups in the sense that subgroups implied by cognitive relations bear little similarity to the same type of subgroups implied by behavioral relations. Bernard et al. (1980: 208) conclude their analysis with the following statement:

> We are now convinced that cognitive data about communication cannot be used as a proxy for the equivalent behavioral data. This one fundamental conclusion has occurred systematically in a variety of treatment, all as kind to the data as possible. We must therefore recommend unreservedly that any conclusions drawn from the data gathered by the question "who do you talk to" are of no use in understanding the social structure of communication.

Author's Note: *Work on this chapter was supported by grants SOC77-22938 and SOC79-25728 from the National Science Foundation. The data analysis was completed during a leave of absence I spent in the Department of Sociology, State University of New York at Albany. This chapter has been abbreviated from a comment I published with William Bittner in* Social Networks *(Burt and Bittner, 1981). The comment did not go without response from my invigorating colleagues H. Russell Bernard, Peter D. Killworth, and Lee Sailer (1981).*

This is a very general conclusion. My purpose in this chapter is to indicate some problems with the inference leading to the conclusion. Without putting too fine an edge on it, the evidence does not warrant the conclusion. Three methodological problems are discussed here. As illustration, I then offer a reanalysis of one system described in Bernard et al. (1980).

Methodologically, the research question Bernard et al. address is basic in network analysis.[1] How redundant is the structure in two networks? Given two networks of relations, they are redundant to the extent that the structure of one is replicated in the other. At the level of individual relations, this question is captured by multiplexity—the extent to which each nonzero relation in one network corresponds to a nonzero relation in the other. At the level of network subgroups, this question is addressed in terms of the extent to which the same set of interrelated subgroups is implied by relations in either network. Bernard et al. (1980) are concerned with the redundancy of behavioral and cognitive relations, but from a methodological standpoint (which is to say from the standpoint of this note) they could just as well have been concerned with the redundancy of economic and friendship relations, kinship and intimacy relations, or relations in a single network measured at separate points in time.

THE LIMITED UTILITY OF EMPIRICAL GENERALIZATIONS IN NETWORK ANALYSIS

At the outset, the evidence presented by Bernard et al. should be put in its proper perspective. There are no clear epistemic links between the observations they describe and the population social structure about which they make inferences.

Bernard et al. (1980) describe four systems of actors. Although small and conveniently local, these systems are far less esoteric than the system of deaf persons communicating over teletypes that was the basis for their initial evidence (Killworth and Bernard, 1976). The OFFICE data consist of cognitive and behavioral relations among 40 employees of a small social science research office. Behavioral relations were estimated by an "unobtrusive" person walking through the office every 15 minutes for five hours on four consecutive days and coding the frequency with which persons contacted one another. Cognitive relations were obtained in a typical sociometric manner by asking employees to rank order other employees in terms of how often they talked to each employee during a normal working day. The TECH data consist of relations among 34 persons (faculty, graduate students, secretaries) in a graduate program at West Virginia University. Again, a person observed verbal interactions as best he could, and at the end of a week respondents were asked to rank order others in the program from most to least communication that week. The FRAT data similarly consist of behavioral and cognitive relations among 58 residents in a West Virginia University fraternity. An "unobtrusive" observer walked through the fraternity every 15 minutes for 21 hours on five consecutive days in order to estimate the frequency with which people spoke to one another. Cognitive relations were then obtained by asking respondents to code each other resident on a scale from zero (no communication) to five (a great deal of communication).

Finally, the HAMS data consist of relations among 44 amateur radio operators who are members of Monongalia Wireless Association (MWA). As described below in the illustrative reanalysis, frequency of radio contact between operators over a 27-day period provided behavioral relations, and cognitive relations were obtained by asking each operator to code others on a scale from zero (no communication) to nine (a great deal of communication). In short, the observations described in Bernard et al. (1980) are typical network data in the sense that they constitute complete information on networks among all of the sampled members of a small system: all active members of MWA, all respondent members of the graduate program, and so forth.

These data do not provide a foundation for making inferences about the social structure of communication generally. The population (in a statistical sense) to which an analysis of network data on a system can make inferences is the system itself. The HAMS data, for example, can only be used to make inferences about relations among members of the MWA. Network data on one system cannot be used, generally speaking, to make inferences about network structure in another system, particularly in the absence of some argument asserting the two systems to be generically similar. For example, it would be awkward to analyze the OFFICE data in order to make inferences concerning the network structure of the MWA.

This erroneous inference seems obvious, but when an analysis of relations in one system is used to make inferences about all persons engaged in the social structure of communication, a much more serious inferential error is being made, even though its abstraction makes it seem less obvious. Not only do Bernard et al. offer their evidence on these four systems as the basis for a conclusion regarding relations in similar types of systems (other small social science firms, other provincial fraternities, other electronics hobby groups, and the like), but they extend their conclusions to "all persons engaged in the social structure of communication." This includes all systems of community elites, all invisible colleges of elite scientists, all employees in corporate bureaucracies—all systems in short composed of actors who communicate with one another. There is simply no basis for such an inference in network analysis (as it is currently constituted), given the lack of a single clearly defined population in which network hypotheses purport to be true. They concern all types of systems: informal groups, classrooms, bureaucracies, communities, nations, world systems. This means that a large collection of data sets might be treated as if it covered a population. However, the fact that a hypothesis is not useful in describing an arbitrary collection of data sets allows no inference beyond those data. With different types of systems, or different methods of data collection, or different measurement methods, a rejected hypothesis might be quite useful.

Of course, network data on a specific system can be used to suggest hypotheses within that system. But the findings from the analysis cannot be generalized legitimately to all systems of actors. It is perfectly legitimate for Bernard et al. to claim that their results show a lack of generality to the hypothesis that cognitive relations are redundant with behavioral relations in all systems. They claim to present evidence rejecting such a hypothesis with regard to network subgroups in the four systems they consider. But this constraint on the generality of the hypothesis in no sense rejects it for all systems. Even if they obtained data on a great many more systems of actors, their inferences would only pertain to the specific populations from which these observations had been drawn. At first this appears to be an unfortunate restriction, since it severely curtails the usefulness of empirical generalizations in network analysis (more specific comments are given elsewhere, Burt 1980b: 133-134). However, the restriction is common to all research that makes statistical inferences. It serves the useful function of protecting us from exaggerated conclusions and should be applied with a vengeance in network analysis, I believe, up to the limit of developing network theory and our growing understanding of the manner in which different types of systems are representative of social structures generally.

At the very least, then, the above-cited conclusion by Bernard and his colleagues must be restricted in scope to the actual systems of which their data are representative. But even within this considerably more modest scope, their evidence seems sterile and uncompelling.

THE AD HOC QUALITY OF UNTESTED NETWORK SUBGROUPS

Bernard and his colleagues assess the redundancy of behavioral and cognitive relations in terms of three types of network subgroups: those generated by FACTOR, those generated by CONCOR, and those generated by COMPLT. Since their principal concern is the widespread practice of using sociometric data to make inferences about social structure, they are careful to represent "major trends ;among clique-finders," if not substantively distinct types of network subgroups to be found (Bernard et al., 1980: 3-5).

This choice is certainly theirs to make. However, it does not mean that they can ignore the substantive meaning of the subgroups they propose. Bernard et al. (1980: 193) explicitly indicate their familiarity with the substantive difference between cliques and jointly occupied positions. What troubles me is their subsequent statement declaring that: "For our purposes here, the distinction is irrelevant." This is not true. The substantive meaning of network subgroups is never irrelevant to the interpretation of output from computer algorithms purporting to capture those subgroups. For the purpose of assessing the redundancy of two networks (e.g., behavioral and cognitive networks) in terms of the interrelated subgroups each implies, the substantive meaning of subgroups is at least important in regard to testing the adequacy of proposed subgroups.

The meaning of the subgroups the selected algorithms purport to capture was reviewed in the preceding chapter; COMPLT is the only one of the three that purports to generate cliques as primary groups—network subgroups composed of (structurally equivalent) actors involved in similar relational patterns in the sense of having similar relations with all actors in their system.[2] Among the conclusions offered in the preceding chapter is one stating that cliques should be viewed as a special type of jointly occupied position, a position jointly occupied by actors connected by strong relation. In general, the conclusion rests on the less arbitrary nature of subgroups as jointly occupied positions.

Of particular significance is the ability to test the hypothesis that a set of actors actually do jointly occupy a position (this point will be treated in detail shortly). A particularly debilitating feature of network subgroups is the fact that there are so many algorithms available to detect so many types of subgroups that subgroups can be found in virtually any system of actors without being substantively consistent across researchers or even across analyses by the same researcher. This is especially true of cliques, but whenever subgroups are proposed without tests demonstrating their adequacy, they have a nasty ad hoc quality.

Since Bernard and his colleagues do not present evidence on the adequacy of their proposed subgroups, I do not know if their subgroups exist in fact or are merely ad hoc methodological artifacts. In consequence, the reader has little feel for the extent to which they directly address the hypothesis they purport to reject. First, the reader does not know the extent to which a system is actually differentiated in terms of network subgroups. Test statistics applied to the MWA below show that it is not. Second, the reader cannot weigh the import of the evidence available. Under the hypothesis that behavioral and cognitive relations are redundant so as to define the same network subgroups, the fact that different subgroups (demonstrated to be what they purport to be) are defined by the two networks is a serious mark against the hypothesis. To the extent that the hypothesis is true, it is also unlikely to occur. Nevertheless, the fact that different subgoups are generated by two types of networks seems to me to be an unimportant finding in the absence of adequacy tests, since the subgroups could be less a feature of the systems described than they are a feature of the technique used to conduct the description.

THE LOW POWER OF CONCLUSIONS REGARDING NETWORK SUBGROUPS IN COMPLEX SOCIAL STRUCTURES

This brings me to my third and final comment. The lack of tests demonstrating the adequacy of their proposed network subgroups is but one manifestation of the overall lack of concern Bernard and his colleagues show for the substance of social differentiation in the four systems they present as evidence. At no time do they describe the relations within and between their proposed subgroups. If such a description were only useful to increase the reader's familiarity with the systems, then its presentation would be largely a matter of taste. However, the actual structure of a network has implications for the power of the test of the hypothesis that it is redundant with another network in terms of the subgroups each defines.

Consider two systems of actors, each stratified in terms of two jointly occupied positions where relational patterns in each system are characterized by the following density tables:

0.50	0.00	0.50	0.45
0.00	0.50	0.35	0.50

The first system reflects relations among actors polarized into two separate groups. There is some tendency for relations to occur among occupants of a position, but there are no relations between occupants of different positions. In the second system, there is the same tendency for intraposition relations; however, occupants of separate positions have a slightly lower tendency to contact one another. The structure of the first system can be discussed as less complex than the structure of the second. Given random errors in measuring relations, an occupant of position one in the second system is more likely than an occupant of the same position in the first system to be confused with an occupant of the second position. In the second system, the differences between relational patterns defining the two positions are more subtle and accordingly more prone to being confused in empirical research. In general, network structure can be thought of as complex to the extent that there are only minor differences in the relational patterns distinguishing occupants of different positions in the network.

Complexity has implications for the power of conclusions regarding network subgroups. The more complex the structure of a network, the more precisely each relation must be measured in order to describe the structure correctly. If the precision with which relations can be measured is fixed at some acceptably high level, then the probability of errors in describing a network's structure increases with its complexity. Given the hypothesis that the same network subgroups are defined by relations in two networks and a fixed precision of relational measurement, the probability of rejecting the hypothesis increases with the complexity of either network, regardless of the truth in the hypothesis. In other words, the power of the conclusion rejecting the hypothesis is decreased by network complexity. Where the usual alpha level in a statistical test of a hypothesis is the probability of rejecting the hypothesis when it is true, recall that the power of the test is the probability of accepting the hypothesis when it is actually wrong. Where two networks are redundant in terms of subgroups, the power of the conclusion that they are not redundant decreases with the complexity of either network. In other words, the probability of concluding that the two networks are not redundant in terms of subgroups increases with the complexity of either network, despite the fact that the networks are redundant.

Since Bernard and his colleagues do not offer descriptions of the complexity of the networks in the four systems they consider, I do not have a feel for the power of their conclusion, even within the limited scope of their data. If it is the case that the complexity of the systems is low, then evidence rejecting the hypothesis that cognitive and behavioral relations define the same network subgroups is a serious mark against the hypothesis. If the structure of either network in the systems is complex, on the other hand, then the decision to reject the hypothesis has low power since it will be relatively easy to obtain evidence rejecting the hypothesis in complex social structures.

STATUS ROLE-SETS IN THE MONONGALIA WIRELESS ASSOCIATION

It is one thing to criticize someone else's work and quite another to make explicit how the work might be done in light of the criticism. Having done the first, I now offer the second. The four systems considered in Bernard et al. (1980) are not argued to be representative of any more general classes of systems, so for reasons of time and space I focus on the one system providing the best data and strongly supporting their conclusion that different network subgroups are defined by behavioral versus cognitive relations: the MWA. The behavioral relations on this system strike me as the cleanest and probably the most accurate of those obtained on any of the four systems. Moreover, this system strongly supports their conclusion in regard to jointly occupied positions (D is high for this system in Table 5 of Bernard et al., 1980, under the two position-detecting algorithms, FACTOR and CONCOR).

Under the hypothesis that network subgroups defined by behavioral relations are redundant with those defined by cognitive relations, there should be a single set of subgroups defined across the two networks. The subgroups for which I search are statuses—sets of structurally equivalent actors in the sense that occupants of a status are similarly involved in behavioral and cognitive relations with all actors in the system. As discussed in the preceding chapter, cliques can be usefully treated as a special type of status, one occupied by actors interconnected by strong relations. For the situation at hand, statuses offer several advantages over cliques: the ability to consider the overall similarity of both behavioral and cognitive relations involving two actors, the ability to test the adequacy of proposed network subgroups, and the ability to avoid dichotomizing continuous measures of relationship at an arbitrarily set criterion level.

Behavioral and Cognitive Relations

The Monongalia Wireless Association is a system of amateur radio operators scattered across a 30,000 square mile area including West Virginia, western Pennsylvania, and eastern Ohio. Details on these "hams" are given elsewhere (Bernard and Killworth, 1977). Radio contacts among members of the association were monitored for a period of 27 days in order to determine the size of the system and record actual contacts between members. Of the 107 hams eventually located, 53 were only "casual or transient users," leaving the remaining 54 persons as comparatively active users (Bernard and Killworth 1977: 6). Based on their monitoring around the clock, Bernard and Killworth obtained data on symmetric behavioral connections between each pair of hams: z_{jib} is the number of radio contacts between hams i and j during the 27-day period. At the end of the monitoring period, each of the 54 were asked to scale their contacts with each of the 54 from 0 (no communication) to 9 (a great deal of communication). For the 44 hams providing usable responses, the possibly asymmetric cognitive relation from ham j to ham i, z_{jic}, is a rating varying from 0 to 9. The network data therefore consist of two (44,44) matrices, as given in Appendix B of Bernard et al. (1980).

Before searching for statuses as general network subgroups, the relational pattern in which any one ham is involved must be comparable to that in which they others are involved. If the relation from ham j to jam i is in a metric different from that in which the relation from i to k is measured, then z_{jk} and z_{ik} cannot be compared meaningfully as they must be in a search for structurally equivalent hams. This problem deserves brief illustration. Consider the cognitive relations in which hams one and three are involved. Ham one gives a high rating to his interaction with ham two ($z_{12c} = 5$), while ham three gives a low rating to his interaction with ham two ($z_{32c} = 1$). A routine comparison of these relations suggests that ham one values his interaction with ham two more than ham three values his own interaction with two. But hams one and three have different tendencies to acknowledge their involvement in interaction. The highest score ham three gives to any interaction is a one, and he only give two such scores. In contrast, ham one claims to interact with just about everyone in the system, and his cognitive relations range from zero to a maximum of seven—his relation to ham seven. Although z_{32c} is low in an absolute sense, in other words, it is the most intense level of interaction in which ham three is involved—as he sees his network. While z_{12c} is high in an absolute sense, it is two points lower than the most intense level of interaction in which ham one is involved—again, as he sees his network.

A comparison of cognitive and behavioral relations for these two hams is useful. It is not the absolute measurement scale imposed on all hams to express their cognitive relations that corresponds to behavioral relations so much as it is a relativistic scale. Ham one only has a behavioral connection with ham seven. This is the one person to whom ham one acknowledges his maximum cognitive connection. Ham three only has a behavioral connection with ham two, one of the two persons with whom he perceives his maximum amount of interaction. In sum, relations to be compared in order to locate structurally equivalent actors in a network should be transformed into a comparable metric in order to clearly interpret distance measures of similarity between relational patterns in which actors are involved (see Burt, 1976a, for more detail). The metric in which relations are measured must be comparable at least across actors within a network (z_{jk} being in the same metric as z_{ik}). If internetwork subgroups are to be located, then relations in separate networks should be measured in the same metric.

For present purposes I have adopted the expedient metric of each ham's tendency to be involved in interaction. Given the maximum rating ham i gave to any other ham, his normalized cognitive relation to ham j is his expressed rating (z_{ijc}) divided by the maximum rating he gave to anyone (z_{ijc}/[maximum z_{ikc} given by i to any actor k]). His normalized behavioral relation to ham j is similarly his frequency of contact during the 27-day monitoring period (z_{ijb}) divided by the maximum frequency with which he was in contact with anyone (z_{ijb}/[maximum z_{ikb} linking i to any actor k]). These normalized relations then vary from zero (no relation) to one (maximum relation). Diagonal elements have been set equal to the maximum of one, indicating a high level of communication between a ham and himself.

There is a stronger redundancy between the normalized behavioral and cognitive relations than there is between the raw metric relations, but it is slight. Across all 1892 relations, z_{ijb} and z_{ijc} are correlated 0.509 and 0.521, respectively, under the raw and normalized metrics. Since 64 percent of the behavior-cognition relational pairs are both zero, these correlations could be overstating the similarity of the two types of relations when interaction actually occurs. Focusing on the 240 pairs of relations in which both z_{ijb} and z_{ijc} are greater than zero and $i \neq j$, correlations of 0.440 and 0.549, respectively, are obtained under the raw and normalized metrics. These are appreciable correlations for social research, with the shared variance between cognitive and behavioral relations ranging from 19 percent (for the raw metric correlation of 0.440) to 30 percent (for the normalized metric correlation of 0.549) of total variance. However, this still leaves the bulk of variation in either type of relation unexplained by the other type, as stressed by Bernard and Killworth (1977).

Locating Statuses as Jointly Occupied Positions

Structurally equivalent hams jointly occupy a status. If hams j and i are similarly involved in cognitive and behavioral relations with all hams so as to be structurally equivalent across the two networks, the

Euclidean distance between their respective positions (d_{ij}) will be close to zero:

$$d_{ij} = \left\{ \sum_{q=1}^{N} [(z_{iqc} - z_{jqc})^2 + (z_{qic} - z_{qjc})^2 + (z_{iqb} - z_{jqb})^2 + (z_{qib} - z_{qjb})^2] \right\}^{\frac{1}{2}}$$

where d_{ij} is symmetric and its conceptual meaning in defining statuses is detailed elsewhere (as in the preceding chapter).

Figure 14.1 presents a hierarchical cluster analysis of these distances using Johnson's connectedness algorithm and normalized relations. Use of the algorithm in detecting possible subgroups is discussed elsewhere (e.g., Burt, 1982a: ch. 3). Each ham is represented in Figure 14.1 by a column, and two hams are clustered together as structurally equivalent when their columns are connected by Xs. Each row represents a clustering under a different criterion distance, with that criterion increasing from its minimum at the top of the diagram to its maximum at the bottom. For example, hams 23, 36 and 41 are clustered together as structurally equivalent under a criterion distance of 1.9. A status appears in such a diagram as a set of actors clustered together under a strong criterion of equivalence (a row near the top of the diagram) and not combined with other actors until the criterion is weak (a row near the bottom of the diagram where any level of distance is allowed between actors clustered together as structurally equivalent).

Figure 14.1 suggests that there is only one status in the MWA. The hams are not stratified across multiple statuses. Instead, there is one status occupied at its core by hams clustered together under a strong criterion of equivalence (e.g., hams 23, 36 and 41). Beginning with this initial core of occupants, successive hams are clustered into the status by relaxing the level of the distance allowed among its occupants. Eventually, the entire association can be viewed as occupying the status under a very weak criterion of structural equivalence. It is possible for actors to be stratified across multiple jointly occupied positions within each network but to appear to be stratified in terms of a single status across two networks. However, Burt and Bittner (1981: 87-88) show that the same results given in Figure 14.1 are obtained when each network is analyzed separately in terms of raw or normalized relational metrics. In

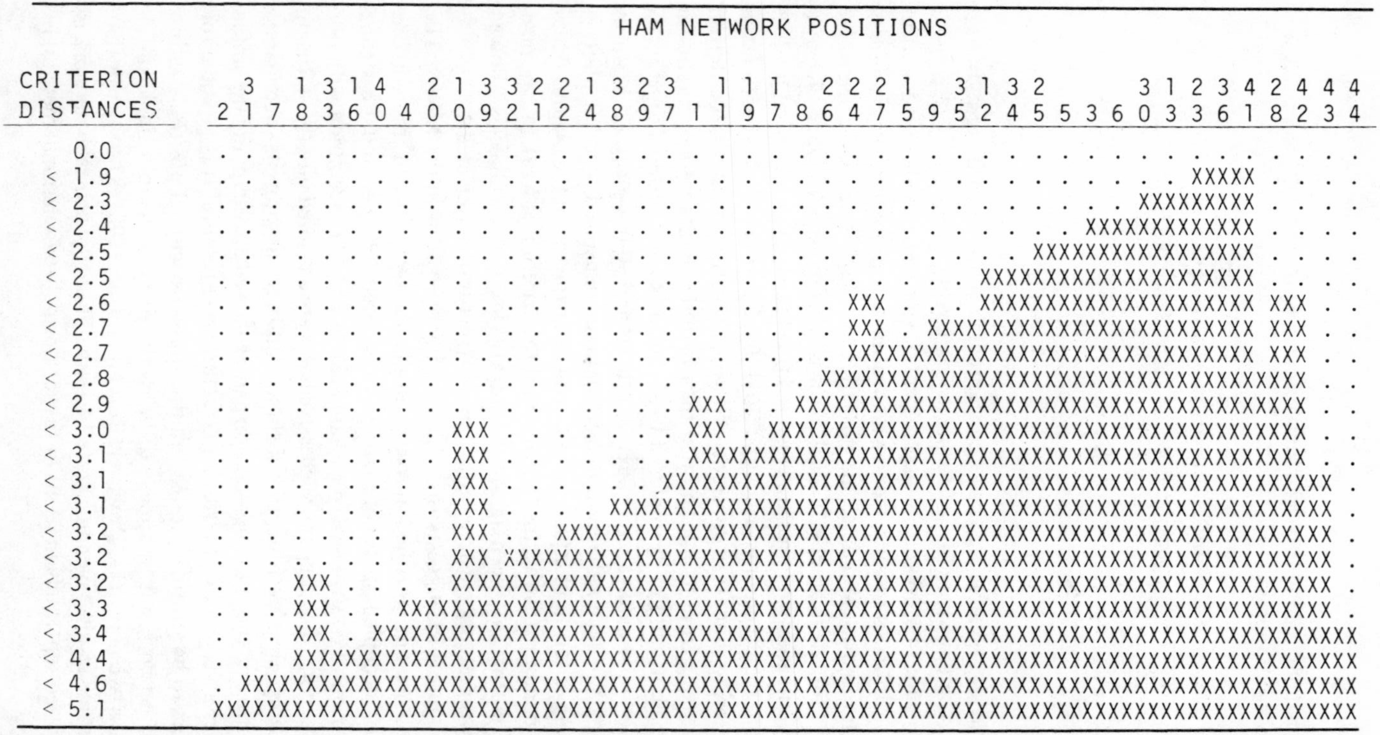

Figure 14.1: Hierarchical Cluster Analysis of Distances within the Monongalia Wireless Association Given Behavioral and Cognitive Relations Among its Members

Network Subgroups 295

short, network subgroups do not appear to be the basis for social differentiation within the Association.

Assessing Subgroups Proposed

Bernard et al. (1980: Table 5) propose five jointly occupied positions in the behavioral network and four such positions in the cognitive network. Since Figure 14.1 does not suggest the presence of multiple subgroups, I was suspicious of their results. Lee Sailer and Russell Bernard kindly provided information on which hams they had assigned to each jointly occupied position. With this information, I have been able to compute densities and assess the extent to which each of their proposed subgroups in fact corresponds to a jointly occupied network position.

Table 14.1 presents the densities of raw and normalized relations among occupants of their proposed five positions in the behavioral network. Table 14.2 presents the densities of raw and normalized relations among occupants of their proposed four positions in the cognitive network. Numerical identification of hams occupying each position is taken from Figure 14.1 and given in each table (for example, Bernard et al. assign hams 23, 34 and 36 to position 1 in the behavior network).

The positions are less distinguished by different types of relational patterns than they are by the extent to which each position exhibits an isolate relational pattern. The pattern characterizing a jointly occupied position is given by the row and column densities for the position. For example, the relation pattern characterizing position 1 in the behavioral network is an isolate pattern. With one exception (cell 4,1), which is itself close to zero, all of the densities in row and column one of Table 14.1 are zero. The separate positions in each network are different principally in terms of the extent to which they reflect this isolate pattern. Positions have been arranged in the two density tables so as to vary from left to right by decreasing isolation. In other words, the right-most column in each table contains higher densities than the left-most column, and the bottom row contains higher densities than the top row. This point is illustrated in Figure 14.2. A jointly occupied position's centrality is given in Figure 14.2 as the proportion of all densities in its network that involve its occupants, i.e., $\Sigma_i(z_{ji} + .z_{ij})/\Sigma_i\Sigma_j(z_{ij})$ is the centrality of position j based on the data in tables 14.1 or 14.2. For the isolate position in the behavioral network (position 1), this score is 0.01, indicating that few of the behavioral densities involve occupants of position 1. As Figure 14.2 shows, centrality gradually increases across the five positions in the behavioral network from 0.01 for position 1 up

TABLE 14.1   Density Table for Behavioral Relations in the Monongalia Wireless Association

Raw Metric

0.00	0.00	0.00	0.00	0.00
0.00	0.08	0.07	0.17	0.03
0.00	0.07	0.74	0.62	1.52
0.07	0.30	0.63	1.26	1.89
0.00	0.03	1.52	2.10	1.04

Normalized Metric

0.00	0.00	0.00	0.00	0.00
0.00	0.05	0.03	0.10	0.02
0.00	0.01	0.06	0.05	0.15
0.01	0.02	0.04	0.07	0.13
0.00	0.01	0.09	0.18	0.07

NOTE: The raw metric is the frequency of radio contact during the 27-day monitoring period, and the normalized metric varies from zero to one as the extent to which z_{ijb} is the maximum frequency in which ham i was involved during the period. Density (A, B) is the average relation from a ham occupying row A to one occupying column B, excluding self relations (z_{ijb}) from the average. Hams are assigned to positions according to the analysis in Bernard et al. (1980). From right to left, position 1 is occupied by hams 23, 34, 36; position 2 is occupied by hams 6, 8, 9, 15, 19, 20, 21, 29, 40; position 3 is occupied by hams 1, 5, 11, 16, 17, 24, 25, 27, 33, 37, 39, 42, 43; position 4 is occupied by hams 3, 4, 12, 13, 18, 22, 31, 35, 44; and the remaining hams occupy position 5.

to 0.22, 0.39, 0.50, and up to 0.60 for position 5. Centrality similarly increases from 0.21, to 0.26, to 0.34, and up to 0.81 across the four positions in the cognitive network.

It would appear that the MWA is characterized by a center-periphery structure in which the structural center of the association is occupied by hams heavily involved in radio communication with one another, and where the structural periphery is occupied by hams largely isolated from other members of the association. Central hams in this imagery occupy the right-most positions in Table 14.1 and 14.2 and in Figure 14.2, while peripheral hams occupy the left-most positions.

However, Figure 14.2 suggests a structure slightly more complex than this center-periphery image. If some hams are structurally equivalent under a strong criterion but random error is responsible for minor differences in their observed relational patterns, then there is a single unobserved dimension of distance from each member of the association to the true position jointly occupied by the set. One measure of the extent to which this is true is the amount of observed variance in distance to actors in the set that can be described by a single principal component (see the preceding chapter). If the actors proposed as

**TABLE 14.2   Density Table for Cognitive Relations in the
Monongalia Wireless Association**

Raw Metric

0.00	0.01	0.04	0.41
0.20	0.16	0.11	1.28
0.52	0.12	0.14	1.06
0.66	0.75	0.91	4.13

Normalized Metric

0.00	0.01	0.03	0.11
0.03	0.07	0.02	0.16
0.09	0.04	0.03	0.25
0.08	0.10	0.11	0.53

NOTE: The raw metric is a questionnaire response ranging from zero to a maximum of nine, and the normalized metric varies from zero to one as the extent to which z_{ijc} is the maximum rating given by ham i. Density (A, B) is the average relation from a ham occupying row A to one occupying column B, excluding self relations (z_{ijc}) from the average. Hams are assigned to positions according to the analysis in Bernard et al. (1980). From right to left, position 1 is occupied by hams 3, 6, 13, 19, 21, 23, 35; position 2 is occupied by hams 10, 26, 28, 29, 32, 37, 41; position 3 is occupied by hams 5, 8, 9, 11, 12, 15, 17, 20, 25, 30, 42; and the remaining hams occupy position 4.

structurally equivalent are equivalent in fact (allowing for random errors), then the ratio of described to observed variance will be close to one. This ratio is plotted in Figure 14.2 for the nine positions Bernard and his colleagues propose.[3] In the behavioral network, this ratio is perfect (1.0) for the isolated position (position one) but decreases from there to 0.75, to 0.69, to 0.68, and down to 0.56 for positions two through five, respectively. Structural equivalence similarly declines from 0.82, to 0.72, to 0.68, down to 0.41 across the four positions in the cognitive network. In other words, only 41 percent of the variance in distances to occupants of position 4 in the cognitive network can be accounted for by a single principal component. Instead of one, ten independent dimensions are required in order to describe 90 percent of the observed variance in distances to hams proposed by Bernard et al. as occupying position 4. Three of these dimensions correspond to eigenvalues greater than one and so might be used to define separate sets of structurally equivalent hams within the proposed position 4. Similarly, there are multiple sets of structurally equivalent hams suggested within the proposed fifth position in the behavioral network.

In short, the network positions proposed by Bernard et al. do not appear to exist in fact, and there is an interesting connection between the centrality of one of their proposed groups and its adequacy as a group.

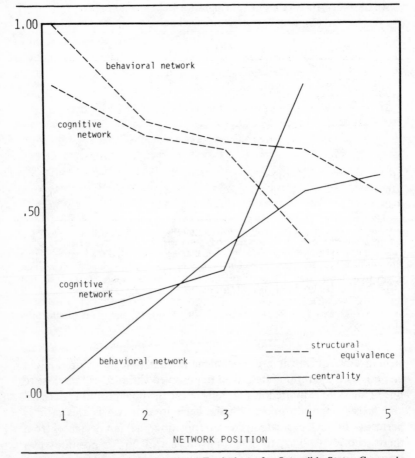

Figure 14.2: Centrality and Structural Equivalence for Ostensible Status Groups in the Monongalia Wireless Association (based on normalized relations)

The more isolated a position is in either the behavioral network or the cognitive network, the more structurally equivalent are its occupant hams. The hams most involved in radio contact within the MWA jointly occupy positions in the behavioral and cognitive networks under the weakest criteria of equivalence.

Social Differentiation in the System

Bringing these results together, I envision the MWA as a single status system in which one status is occupied by isolates as the bulk of the association. Recall that of the 107 hams located as members of the association, 53 were deleted because they were only "casual or transient users," i.e., isolates. Hams vary in their distance from this status according to the frequency of their radio contact with others. However, increased involvement in the association is accomplished in a nonsystematic fashion. Rather than increasing their contact specifically with other highly involved members, hams appear to be increasing their contact with a wide range of other members.

There is no central status jointly occupied by hams who have high contact with one another and similar tendencies to contact hams further removed from the center. There is instead an increasing density of ostensibly random contacts among members as one progresses from the isolate status toward the structural center of the association. Because of their different patterns of contacts with other members, hams at the structural center of the association are less structurally equivalent with one another than hams at its periphery—isolates having more similar relational patterns than hams extensively communicating within the assocation. Instead of the usual elitist center-periphery structure in which actors at the center of the system occupy its core status and jointly define the role of being a leading member of system, the MWA has a pluralistic center-periphery structure. The one clear status in the association is occupied by hams isolated from other members. It is a status for hams who are members more in name than in radio contact activity. There are no statuses within the association in terms of which active members are stratified.

In terms of the general comments I made earlier, the MWA has a complex sructure. The lack of clear distinctions between relational patterns among active members makes it very easy to confuse one actor with another, structurally speaking. This means that the conclusion that different jointly occupied positions are defined by cognitive versus behavioral relations has low power. Moreover, the conclusion itself seems irrelevant here, since active members of the association are not stratified across jointly occupied positions.

In fact, if behavioral and cognitive relations are compared in terms of the actual structure in the association, they appear quite redundant. The system is differentiated in terms of each ham's distance from an isolate status. It is a simple matter to compute ham j's distance from an isolate relational pattern within each network, d_{jic} and d_{jib}, where all the relations in the isolate pattern are zero. The correlation between these distances for the 44 respondent hams is very strong ($r = .825$).

CONCLUSION

In short, the evidence presented by Bernard and his colleagues does not warrant their conclusion. The principal concern in this note has been their lack of concern with the substance of social differentiation in the systems they use as evidence. Obviously, their concern is methodological in the sense of questioning the adequacy of sociometric data as a surrogate for behavioral data. I am not attempting a cheap shot that can be made against any methodological paper, that is, to increase the substantive discussion. Under limits of time and journal space, Bernard et al. focus on technical issues. But I saw this as an opportunity to emphasize the methodological importance of substantive issues for conclusions justified with evidence from a network analysis. The substance of social structure in a system affects the scope, adequacy, and power of conclusions drawn from a network analysis and is accordingly a factor to be explicitly considered in justifying those conclusions. Specifically, I have discussed its effects on a conclusion's:

Scope. The scope of conclusions from a network analysis cannot be generalized beyond the system(s), or their generic types, actually described in the analysis.

Adequacy. Network subgroups should not be proposed without indicators of their adequacy. In other words, it is incumbent upon an author to demonstrate to readers that there is some reason to believe that his proposed subgroups actually differentiate actors in the system being described and are not merely methodological artifacts.

Power. The complexity of a system's social structure affects the power of conclusions from a network analysis of the system. Systems with more complex structures require more carefully justified conclusions, since the power of rejecting hypotheses is lower in such systems.

Bearing these ideas in mind, my reanalysis of the MWA as a system on which good data are available, ostensibly supporting the Bernard et al. (1980) conclusion, illustrates how their conclusion regarding network subgroups in that system is unwarranted.

The authors could seek refuge by saying that they have only done what others appear to be doing. They feel that they have been "fair both to the data and the algorithms." There is something to this. Network analysis is developing rapidly, and the analysis by Bernard et al. could be an artifact of earlier analytical styles. On the other hand, with developments in network analysis technology, it will be increasingly easy for anyone to grind up network data with a computer package without being forced at some time between data collection and publication to think about the substance of social differentiation implied by the data. Casting an eye toward this possibility, the analysis in Bernard et al. appears as an object lesson to network analysts. It is when faulty methodology is used to justify sweeping conclusions that its weaknesses are most apparent.

Of course, rejecting their methodology is not the same as accepting the hypothesis that cognitive and behavioral relations are one and the same. I have argued that the conclusions expressed by Bernard et al. (1980) regarding network subgroups are unwarranted, not that they are untrue.

NOTES

1. Substantively, behavioral and cognitive relations could be argued to have complementary value in describing social structure. The relations in which a person is most often involved (behavioral relations) might differ from the extent to which those relations are significant to him or her (cognitive relations). If a research question calls for a census of interaction among actors in a system, then behavioral relations seem an appropriate data base. If instead it concerns the manner in which interaction affects the behavior of people, then each person's perceptions of relations, i.e., cognitive relations, might provide the most appropriate data base. My analysis of the MWA shows that very similar conclusions will be reached from either data base; however, my principal concern here is methodology.

7. The algorithm called FACTOR is not explained, but since MacRae's early work is the only reference for the algorithm (Bernard et al. 1980: 3), I assume that a principal component analysis has been used. There is no mention of whether actors were assigned to "cliques" in terms of chooser loadings or in terms of chosen loadings. Although the same number of cliques is obtained under either type of loading, clique memberships need not be the same. Memberships based on chosen loadings will be similar to memberships indicated by CONCOR.

3. The ratios in Figure 14.2 are based on correlation matrices. Given the (3,3) correlation matrix among distances to hams 23, 34 and 36 in the behavioral network, for example, the 1.0 ratio means that the eigenvalue defining the first principal component for the matrix was 3.0, the sum of variances in the matrix.

Chapter 15

An Omnibus Test for Social Structure Using Triads

PAUL W. HOLLAND
SAMUEL LEINHARDT

A general or omnibus test of structure in social network data is proposed. The test exploits all of the information contained in the triad census. Analogous to the classical F-test for contrasts among means, the proposed test involves finding a weighting vector which maximizes a test statistic, τ_2 (max), in the context of an empirical data matrix and then determining whether this quantity is statistically significant by reference to a table of the chi-square distribution. An insignificant value of τ_2 (max) implies that the structure of the network data matrix is random, and therefore that the search for a recognizable or substantively meaningful pattern in the data may be subject to artifactual discoveries. Empirical results are presented which indicate that, of the networks commonly studied by social researchers, some have random structure, others have nonrandom structure and exhibit strong indications of transitivity, and still others, with strong indications of nonrandom structure, do not exhibit strong indications of transitivity.

Our purpose here is to present a statistical test for the presence of structure in social network data. The need for such a test rests in the recognition that social network data, like all data, may be subject to uncertainty. The uncertainty may result from measurement error, natural variation, temporal variation, and the like. Its impact is to limit the level of detail that a reasonable analysis can pursue. It affects, among other things, the precision with which parameters are estimated, the ability of the researcher to use the data to distinguish between competing hypotheses, one's confidence in predictions based on the

Authors' Note: *The research reported here is part of an ongoing project that is collaborative in every respect. Consequently, the authors' names appear in alphabetical order. Our research activities were supported in part by grants from the National Science Foundation (SOC73-05489 and SOC77-26821) and from the Foundation for Child Development to Carnegie-Mellon University and a National Science Foundation grant (SOC77-26823) to the Educational Testing Service. Programming assistance was provided by Vinod Khosla. We are also grateful to Christopher Winship, John Dennis, and Stanley Wasserman. An earlier version of this chapter appeared in* Sociological Methods & Research, *November 1978.*

data, and the replicability of conclusions drawn from the data. The approach developed here is to construct a statistical test with which to determine whether the uncertainty contained in a social network data matrix is so great as to render equivocal the detailed analysis of structural features.

CONCEPTUAL BACKGROUND

To motivate our point of view, we begin by discussing a familiar example in data analysis where many of the same issues arise—the analysis of variance. For concreteness, suppose that we are interested in classroom differences in student achievement and that we have collected student scores on standarized tests for several classrooms of a single grade in a large elementary school. A standard application of the analysis of variance (ANOVA) to this situation has two phases. In the first phase, we compute the F-statistic for classroom differences in student achievement. If the F-test based on this statistic is not significant at some reasonable level, then for many purposes it is not worthwhile to proceed to the second phase, which consists of making detailed comparisons of the individual classroom means. The second phase is a "structuring phase" in which the patterns exhibited by the classroom means are organized in various ways to emphasize salient features. For example, they might break into two approximately homogeneous groups. The purpose of the first phase is to insure that the structuring activity of the second phase is meaningful with respect to the uncertainty in test scores as measured by the within-classroom variation. If the F-test is highly significant, then at least one contrast in the classroom means is substantially different from zero. In terms of our example, a highly significant F-value is evidence that the pattern of two approximately homogeneous groups of classrooms is not typical of the patterns formed by random assortment of achievement test scores into sets of values that are the size of the classrooms in our hypothetical study. Hence, armed with a significant F and an interesting pattern, we might pursue the issue further and investigate the possibility that these classroom differences were the result of tracking, or teacher differences, or that they had some other cause.

Now consider the situation faced when analyzing social network data. For example, consider the case where we have a set of individuals and the directed graph of their relationships generated by some criterion. For this situation there are a large number of data-structuring algorithms which have the express purpose of reorganizing the data to reveal interpretable patterns. For example, the sociogram (Moreno, 1934) and the target sociogram (Northway, 1940) are two early techniques whose objectives were to help the analyst visualize the simultaneous sociometric choices of all of the individuals in the group. A number of clique-finding algorithms (see reviews by Alba, 1973; Nosanchuk, 1963; Roistacher, 1974) are based on various criteria for simultaneously permuting the rows and columns of the adjacency matrix of the directed graph to achieve simple blockdiagonal patterns. More recently, White et al. (1976) have proposed simultaneously permuting the rows and columns of adjacency matrices to emphasize blocks of zero entries. In the case of these "block models," several directed graphs on the same set of individuals may be row-column permuted simultaneously to reveal common zero-block patterns across several generators.

All of these algorithms fit into phase two of the ANOVA paradigm described above. They are essentially exploratory data-analytic tools which search for interesting patterns in the data. As far as we know, little work has been done to provide an analogue to phase one of the ANOVA paradigm for social network data. Our own work has focused on the development of tests for specific hypotheses of structural trends in network data, such as transitivity (e.g., Holland and Leinhardt, 1970, 1972). We now present a general or omnibus test of structure which exploits all of the information contained in the triad census (defined in the next section) and which may be used to detect the presence of structural tendencies not limited to transitivity. Like the F-test in ANOVA, our test does not direct one to specific structural features. Rather, significant values of our test statistic indicate that the observed social network data contain some nonrandom features.

USING TRIADS TO SUMMARIZE NETWORK DATA

We will consider social network data in which there is a single binary relationship under study. Simultaneous or multiple relationships may be studied with our methods by applying them separately to each relationship. For expository purposes we shall use sociometric choice ("i chooses j") as a running example, but the methods are generally applicable to any data that may be represented as a directed graph. Thus we assume that the data can be represented as a square matrix of zeros and ones, which we denote by X. The entries of X are defined, as usual, by

$$X_{ij} = \begin{cases} 1 & \text{if } i \rightarrow j(i \text{ chooses } j) \\ 0 & \text{otherwise} \end{cases} \qquad [15.1]$$

We make the convention that $x_{ii} = 0$. This is a minor mathematical convention that is natural in the sociometric context as well as some other social network contexts. We also use an arrow to denote graphically a relationship "going" from i to j. The number of nodes (individuals) is denoted by g.

X is the basic data structure, and important derived statistics of the graph may be expressed in terms of X. As examples, consider the following. For each individual we have

$$X_{i+} = \Sigma_j X_{ij} = \text{out-degree of i} = \text{choices made by i} \qquad [15.2]$$
$$X_{+j} = \Sigma_i X_{ij} = \text{in-degree of j} = \text{choices received by j} \qquad [15.3]$$
$$\text{for } i, j = 1, \dots, g$$

It is natural to summarize the in- and out-degree distributions by their respective means and variances. The means are equal and given by:

$$\bar{X} = \frac{1}{g} \Sigma_i X_{i+} = \frac{1}{g} \Sigma_j X_{+j} \qquad [15.4]$$

The variances are, respectively:

$$V(\text{in}) = \frac{1}{g} \Sigma_j (X_{+j} - \bar{X})^2 \qquad [15.5]$$

and

$$V(\text{out}) = \frac{1}{g} \Sigma_i (X_{i+} - \bar{X})^2 \qquad [15.6]$$

The use of a "fixed choice" sociometric procedure results in the condition that $V(\text{out}) = 0$, whereas $V(\text{out})$ is positive for a "free choice" sociogram. Two other statistics related to X are the total number of choices, X_{++}, and the choice density,

$$CDY = \frac{\bar{X}}{(g - 1)} \qquad [15.7]$$

X is the number of choices made per individual, while CDY is the number of choices made per ordered pair of individuals.

The in- and out-degrees are *nodal properties* in the sense that they describe characteristics of the digraph at each node. The out-degrees reflect individual "expansiveness" or possible experimental constraints, (e.g., when v (out) = 0). The in-degrees are often interpreted as measures of status or of individual popularity. Both expansiveness and popularity are individual characteristics describing properties that individuals may possess regardless of the properties possessed by other individuals.

The distributions of the in- and out-degrees do not distinguish between reciprocated and unreciprocated choices. Many substantively important features of social behavior, such as reciprocation, are properties of *pairs* of individuals. Thus, to use networks to study these properties, we need to go beyond the level of individual nodes. The first level beyond nodes is that of pairs. The numbers of mutual (M), asymmetric (A), and null (N) dyads in the digraph are given by, respectively:

$$M = \sum_{i<j} X_{ij}X_{ji} \qquad [15.8]$$

$$A = \sum_{ij} X_{ij}(1 - X_{ji}) \qquad [15.9]$$

$$N = \sum_{i<j} (1 - X_{ij})(1 - X_{ji}) \qquad [15.10]$$

Although nodal and pair properties of graphs may be substantively interesting in themselves, the essential issue of any notion of structure is how the components are combined, not the components themselves. Thus, in studying structure in social networks, we prefer to focus attention on the next level beyond the pairs, the level of triples of nodes—the triadic level. At this level one can begin to raise the sociologically relevant questions of how the pairs are *combined* in the whole digraph and how this combination is affected by the nodal and pair properties of the digraph.

The *triad census* was introduced in Davis and Leinhardt (1972) to summarize the entire social network given by X.[1] The triad census is obtained by enumerating all of the $\binom{g}{3}$ unordered triples of nodes (i.e., the triads of X) and classifying them into the 16 possible triad types given in Figure 15.1.

Let T_c denote the number of triads in X of type c where c runs over the 16 triad types in Figure 15.1. We set $T' = (T_1, \ldots, T_{16})$ and call T the triad census of X.

The triad census is a summarization of the information in X. It reduces the g(g-1) empirical zeros and ones in X to 16 frequencies. While this is clearly a substantial reduction in information when g is $\geqslant$ 5, T does contain a substantial amount of interesting information about X.

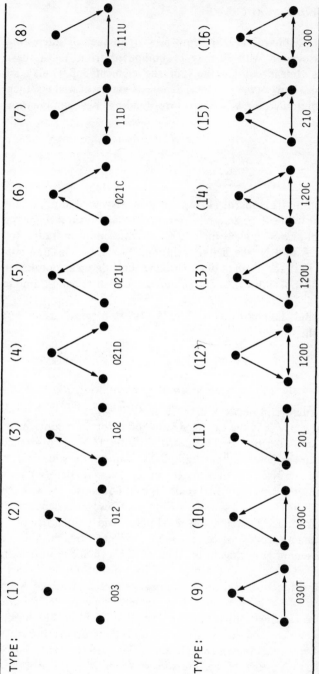

Figure 15.1: The 16 Triad Types for a Digraph

Holland and Leinhardt (1975) show how a number of interesting quantities associated with X may be computed from T. In these computations, linear combinations of the elements of T play an important role. If $w' = (w_1, \ldots, w_{16})$ denotes a vector of weights, then since T is a column vector, $w'T$ is the corresponding linear combination of the T_c:

$$w'T = \sum_c w_c T_c \qquad [15.11]$$

In Holland and Leinhardt (1975), we show that several important features of the data can be determined from the triad census through the appropriate choice of w. These include X_{++}, the total number of edges (or choices), M, A and N (the pairs), V(in) and V(out) (the in- and out-degree variances), the mean in-deree (which equals the mean out-degree or mean number of choices), and the number of transitive triples, among others.

Holland and Leinhardt (1970, 1975, 1979) propose using test statistics of the form

$$\tau(w) = \frac{w'T - w'\mu}{\sqrt{w'\Sigma w}} \qquad [15.12]$$

to test for structure in network data. In 15.12, $\mu' = (\mu_1, \ldots, \mu_{16})$ is the vector whose entry μ_i is the expected value of T_i for a certain type of random digraph distribution. The matrix, Σ, is the 16×16 covariance matrix of T for the same random digraph distribution. Possible choices of μ and Σ will be discussed in the next section. The statistic, $\tau(w)$, tests whether or not the observed triad census is or is not consistent with the predictions of the random digraph distribution. However, it depends on the particular choice of weights in w. Holland and Leinhardt (1975, 1979) proposed a specific choice of w so that w'T measures the number of intransitive configurations in the digraph. This choice of w yields a single degree-of-freedom test for nonrandom deviations in a social network in the direction of transitive or near-transitive structure. Such structure has often been proposed as an ideal-type model for the structure of social relations in small groups (Holland and Leinhardt, 1971). Other choices of w's are possible and reflect interest in other types of structure (see, for example, Davis et al., 1971). If $\tau(w)$ is small relative to the usual cutoff points of the Gaussian or Normal distribution, then one would conclude that the data matrix does not exhibit significant structural tendencies of the type measured by w'T beyond that which is typical of random digraphs.

Because there is little detailed substantive theory to guide investigators analyzing social network data, there is a need for an omnibus test that is capable of detecting the presence of nonrandom network structure no matter what form it takes. Note that the statistic, $\tau(w)$, tests for the presence of structure as summarized by the particular linear combination of triad frequencies given by $w'T$. The omnibus test we now propose is based on $\tau^2(\max)$, which is the maximum of $\tau^2(w)$ over all possible weighting vectors:

$$\tau^2(\max) = \max_w \tau^2(w) \qquad [15.13]$$

Several comments are in order. First, in equation 15.13, w ranges over all possible real weighting vectors and can therefore have negative and fractional components. Second, there is a weighting vector, w_{max}, such that:

$$\tau^2(\max) = \tau^2(w_{max}) \qquad [15.14]$$

In fact, any w that is proportional to w_{max} will maximize $\tau^2(w)$. This maximizing set of weights often is not readily interpreted in terms of easily understood network structure. Third, we maximize $\tau^2(w)$ rather than $\tau(w)$ because of the identity

$$\tau(-w) = -\tau(w) \qquad [15.15]$$

and the fact that the null distribution of $\tau^2(\max)$ is approximately chi-square and therefore easily used.

CHOICE OF REFERENCE DISTRIBUTION

There are actually a number of useful choices of μ and Σ for equation 15.12. Discussions of some of these are given in Holland and Leinhardt (1970, 1975, 1979) and Wasserman (1977) in which the following point of view is taken. First, certain quantities calculated from X are taken to measure features of the digraph which we wish to regard as "givens." For example, the number of nodes, g, the number of directed edges, X_{++}, the number of mutual pairs, M, and the like. Second, we consider a random digraph distribution for which the quantities taken as givens are fixed at the values observed in X and all digraphs with these values of the givens are made equally likely (i.e., random). Third, this digraph distribution implies a probability distribution for the triad census, T. From this distribution we determine the mean vector, μ, and the covariance matrix, Σ, of T. In Holland and Leinhardt (1975) we derive the formulae for components of μ and Σ for the digraph distribution for which M, A and N (see equations 8, 9 and 10 above) are taken as givens. This is equivalent to taking g, $\overline{X}$ and M as givens. In Holland and Leinhardt (1979) we propose an approximate method for adjusting μ and Σ to include additional quantities computed from X as givens. This method allows us to condition μ and Σ on V(in) and V(out) (see equations 15.4 and 15.5 above), as well as g, X_{++} and M. The resulting reference distribution for T takes into account not only the number of choices but also the number of reciprocated choices, as well as the distribution of the in- and out-degrees as summarized by the mean and variance. Controlling for the number of reciprocated choices and for the mean and variances of the in- and out-degrees is important because we wish to have tests for structure that look beyond the often obvious effects of reciprocity, differential attraction, and experimental constraints and which have been known to exist in sociometric data since the inception of sociometry (Moreno, 1934). Feld and Elmore (1977) argue that spurious evidence for transitivity could result from not conditioning μ and Σ on the in- and out-degrees as we have indicated above (and in Holland and Leinhardt, 1975, 1979). For an alternative point of view on the need for conditioning, see Granovetter (1979).

Formulae for adjusting μ and Σ are given in Appendix B of Holland and Leinhardt (1975), and empirical examples in which g, X_{++}, M, V(in), and V(out) are conditioned are given in Holland and Leinhardt (1979). We will not go into the details of these computations here. The statistical justification for the use of conditional reference distributions is based on the theory of uniformly most powerful tests for multiparameter exponential families of distributions (see Lehmann, 1959).

FORMULAE FOR τ^2(max)

In this section we show that τ^2(max) and w_{max} may be expressed in terms of T, μ, and Σ. These results are then applied to obtain the null distribution for τ^2 (max).

One complication of this analysis stems from the fact that Σ is usually a singular matrix. This is due to the fact that the reference distributions we are using are conditional on linear combinations of the elements of T. For example, the distribution used in Holland and Leinhardt (1979) is conditional on g, X_{++}, M, V(in), and V(out). Thus, there is a 5×16 matrix L such that μ and Σ are the following conditional moments:

$$\mu = E(T \mid LT) \qquad [15.16]$$
$$\Sigma = \text{Cov}(T \mid LT)$$

It follows from equation [15.6] that μ and Σ must also satisfy the relations

$$LT = L\mu \qquad [15.17]$$
$$L\Sigma L' = 0$$

Hence we are faced with the following mathematical problem: Find w such that w maximizes

$$\tau^2(w) = \frac{(w'\delta)^2}{w'\Sigma w} \qquad [15.18]$$

where $\delta = T - \mu$ and Σ satisfy equation 15.17.

To show that this problem is well posed, we need the following fact:

Lemma 1: If $w'\Sigma w = 0$ $w'\delta = 0$.
   Proof: $w'\Sigma w = \text{Var}(w'T) = 0$ implies that $w'T = w'\mu = E(w'T)$ so that $w'\delta = 0$.
   QED

Hence the numerator of $\tau^2(w)$ is zero whenever the denominator is so that $w'\Sigma w = 0$ makes $\tau^2(w)$ an indeterminant form. Therefore we may, without loss of generality, study:

$$\tau^2(\max) = \max_{\substack{w \\ \{w'\Sigma w > 0\}}} \frac{(w'\delta)^2}{w'\Sigma w} \qquad [15.19]$$

i.e., we may restrict our attention to the case where $w'\Sigma w > 0$, and we will not omit the real maximum of $\tau^2(w)$.

Lemma 2 is a simple geometrical statement that is the main tool we need for establishing our main result—theorem 1:

Lemma 2: For any vector v, $\quad \max\limits_{\{\|w\| = 1\}} (w'v)^2 = \|v\|^2$

and $w_{\max} = \dfrac{v}{\|v\|}$.

Proof: $\quad \max\limits_{\{\|w\| = 1\}} (w'v)^2$ occurs if and only if the cosine of the angle

between w and v is maximized, i.e., when w is proportional to

$$v \text{ or } w_{\max} = \frac{v}{\|v\|}.$$

Thus

$$\max_{\{\|w\| = 1\}} (w'v)^2 = \frac{(v'v)^2}{\|v\|^2} = \frac{\|v\|^4}{\|v\|^2} = \|v\|^2 . \, QED$$

The remainder of the problem is to reduce the original statement of the problem, equation 15.18, to a form where it may be attacked by applying lemma 2. This is all that is done in the proof of theorem 1. the only complexity of this proof is the need to deal with the aforementioned singularity of Σ.

Theorem 1: (a) $\tau^2(\max)$ *defined by* equation 15.19 *may also be expressed as:*

$$\tau^2(\max) = (T - \mu)'\Sigma^-(T - \mu) \qquad [15.20]$$

where $\Sigma^- = \Gamma D^- \Gamma'$, $D^- = \text{diag}\left(\frac{1}{\lambda_1}, \ldots, \frac{1}{\lambda_p}, 0, \ldots, 0\right)$

where $\lambda_1, \ldots, \lambda_p$ *are the nonzero eigen-values of* Σ *and* Γ *is the matrix of eigen-vectors of* Σ.

(b) $w_{\max}$ *is proportional to* $\Sigma^-(T - \mu)$.

Proof: We begin by using the eigen-system factorization of Σ:

$$\Sigma = \Gamma D \Gamma'$$

where $D = \text{diag}(\lambda_1, \ldots, \lambda_p, 0, \ldots, 0)$ and $\Gamma\Gamma' = \Gamma\Gamma' = I$. Then

$$\tau^2(w) = \frac{(w'\Gamma\Gamma'\delta)^2}{w'\Gamma D\Gamma'w} \qquad [15.21]$$

Since Σ is a covariance matrix, it is nonnegative definite so that the λ_i are positive. Now set $u = \Gamma'w$, then:

$$\max_{\left\{\begin{array}{c} w \\ w'\Gamma D\Gamma'w > 0 \end{array}\right\}} \tau^2(w) = \max_{\left\{\begin{array}{c} u \\ u'Du > 0 \end{array}\right\}} \frac{(u'\Gamma'\delta)^2}{u'Du} \qquad [15.22]$$

Next we partition D into

$$D = \begin{pmatrix} \dot{D} & 0 \\ 0 & 0 \end{pmatrix}$$

where $D_{ii} > 0$, i.e., D contains the nonzero part of the diagonal of D. Similarly, we partition u as

$$u = \begin{pmatrix} \dot{u} \\ \ddot{u} \end{pmatrix}$$

so that u and D are conformable. Then $u'Du = \dot{u}'\dot{D}\dot{u}$ and $u = w + v$, where

$$w = \begin{pmatrix} \dot{u} \\ 0 \end{pmatrix} \text{ and } v = \begin{pmatrix} 0 \\ \ddot{u} \end{pmatrix}$$

Hence we have:

$$\tau^2(\max) = \max_{\substack{\dot{u} \\ \{\dot{u}'\dot{D}\dot{u} > 0\} \\ \ddot{u} \\ \{\text{arbitrary}\}}} \frac{(w'\Gamma'\delta + v'\Gamma'\delta)^2}{\dot{u}'\dot{D}\dot{u}} \qquad [15.23]$$

Now we show that $v'\Gamma'\delta = 0$ for all v of the form

$$v = \begin{pmatrix} 0 \\ \ddot{u} \end{pmatrix}$$

First we compute

$$v'\Gamma'\Sigma\Gamma v = v'\Gamma'\Gamma D\Gamma'\Gamma v = (0,\ddot{u}) \begin{pmatrix} \dot{D} & 0 \\ 0 & 0 \end{pmatrix} \begin{pmatrix} 0 \\ \ddot{u} \end{pmatrix} = 0 \qquad [15.24]$$

Hence from lemma 1, we have:

$$(v'\Gamma')\delta = 0$$

so we are done and

$$\tau^2(\max) = \max_{\substack{\dot{u} \\ \{\dot{u}'\dot{D}\dot{u} > 0\}}} \frac{((\dot{u}',0)\Gamma'\delta)^2}{\dot{u}'\dot{D}\dot{u}} \qquad [15.25]$$

Now, to get rid of $\dot{D}$ in the denominator, we set

$$\dot{D}^{\frac{1}{2}} = \dot{B}$$

and then:

$$\tau^2(\max) = \max_{\substack{\dot{u} \\ \{\dot{u}'\dot{B}\dot{B}\dot{u} > 0\}}} \frac{\left((\dot{u}'\dot{B},0)\begin{pmatrix} \dot{B}^{-1} & 0 \\ 0 & 0 \end{pmatrix}\Gamma'\delta\right)^2}{\dot{u}'\dot{B}\dot{B}\dot{u}} \qquad [15.26]$$

We set $\dot{v} = \dot{B}\dot{u}$ and have

$$\tau^2(\max) = \max_{\substack{\dot{v} \\ \{\dot{v}'\dot{v} > 0\}}} \frac{((\dot{v}',0)h)^2}{\|\dot{v}\|^2} \qquad [15.27]$$

where

$$h = \begin{pmatrix} \dot{B}^{-1} & 0 \\ 0 & 0 \end{pmatrix}\Gamma'\delta$$

Absorbing $\|v\|$ into the numerator of $\tau^2(\max)$, we have the final reduction:

$$\tau^2(\max) = \max_{\{\|\dot{v}\| = 1\}} ((\dot{v}',0)h)^2 = \max_{\{\|\dot{v}\| = 1\}} (\dot{v}'\dot{h})^2 \qquad [15.28]$$

where h is defined by

$$h = \begin{pmatrix} \dot{h} \\ \ddot{h} \end{pmatrix}$$

From lemma Z we know that the maximum value of 15.28 is $\|\ddot{h}\|^2$ and that this maximum occurs when elements of $\dot{v}$ are proportional to elements of $\dot{h}$. This yields the maximum value of τ^2 given μ and Σ:

$$\tau^2(\max) = \|\dot{h}\|^2 \text{ and } \dot{v}_{\max} \text{ is proportional to } \dot{h}.$$

It remains to interpret $\dot{h}$ and its norm. First we note that:

$$h = \begin{pmatrix} \dot{B}^{-1} & 0 \\ 0 & 0 \end{pmatrix}\begin{pmatrix} \dot{\Gamma}' \\ \ddot{\Gamma}' \end{pmatrix}\delta = \begin{pmatrix} \dot{B}^{-1}\dot{\Gamma}' \\ 0 \end{pmatrix}\delta \qquad \mathbf{[15.29]}$$

$$= \begin{pmatrix} B^{-1} \dot{\Gamma}'\delta \\ 0 \end{pmatrix} = \begin{pmatrix} \dot{h} \\ \ddot{h} \end{pmatrix}$$

so that $\ddot{h} = 0$. Hence:

$$\|\dot{h}\|^2 = \|h\|^2 = \delta'\Gamma \begin{pmatrix} D^{-1} & 0 \\ 0 & 0 \end{pmatrix} \Gamma'\delta \qquad [15.30]$$

so that

$$\tau^2(\text{max}) = \delta'\Gamma D^- \Gamma'\delta$$

where

$$D^- = \begin{pmatrix} \dot{D}^{-1} & 0 \\ 0 & 0 \end{pmatrix}$$

is a pseudo-inverse of D defined in the statement of the theorem. Hence we have:

$$\tau^2(\text{max}) = \delta'\Sigma^- \delta = (T - \mu)'\Sigma^- (T - \mu) \qquad [15.31]$$

where $\bar{\Sigma}$ is the pseudo-inverse of Σ given by $\Gamma\bar{D}\,\Gamma'$. This proves part a of the theorem.

For part b we examine

$$\dot{v}_{max} \; \alpha \; \dot{h} = \bar{D}^{1/2}\Gamma'\delta$$

and

$$\dot{v}_{max} = \dot{D}^{1/2}\dot{u}_{max}$$

so that

$$\dot{u}_{max}\alpha D^{-1}\Gamma'\delta$$

But u_{max} can be taken to be

$$u_{max} = \begin{pmatrix} \dot{u}_{max} \\ 0 \end{pmatrix}$$

and

$$w_{max}\alpha\Gamma u_{max} = \Gamma \begin{pmatrix} \dot{D}^{-1} & \dot{\Gamma}'\delta \\ & 0 \end{pmatrix}$$

$$= \Gamma \begin{pmatrix} \dot{D}^{-1} & 0 \\ 0 & 0 \end{pmatrix} \begin{pmatrix} \dot{\Gamma}' \\ \ddot{\Gamma}' \end{pmatrix} \delta$$

$$= \Gamma D^- \Gamma' \delta$$

$$= \Sigma^- \delta = \Sigma^- (T - \mu) \qquad [15.32]$$

This proves part b of the theorem.

Theorem 1 shows how τ^2 (max) may be computed from T, μ, and Σ. Our experience suggests that care must be exercised in the formation of the pseudo-inverse, Σ^-, due to round-off error that yields nonzero values for the zero eigenvalues of Σ.[3]

The null distribution of τ^2 (max) may be based on the form given in equation 15.20 and the assumption that under the reference distribution chosen for T, T has an approximate normal distribution with mean μ and covariance Σ. The adequacy of the assumption of normality is, to our knowledge, not completely resolved, but computer simulation studies (Holland and Leinhardt, 1970) suggest that it is plausible.

Assuming that T is normal with mean μ and covariance Σ implies that (e.g., see Kendall and Stewart, 1963: 355):

$$\tau^2(\text{max}) = (T - \mu)' \Sigma^- (T - \mu)$$

is chi-square distributed with p degrees of freedom where p is the rank of Σ. For example, p = 11 in the case where the reference distribution constrains g, X_{++}, M, V(in) and V(out). Care must be exercised in determining the rank of Σ. If, in this example, the graph were symmetric (i.e., $2M = X_{++}$), then p would equal 1.

EMPIRICAL EXAMPLES

Behavior in the Sociometric Data Bank

Computation of τ^2 (max) requires the aid of a computer. We have calculated τ^2 (max) values for a subset of the sociometric data bank (SDB) gathered by Davis and Leinhardt (1972). This subset of 299 data matrices was drawn at random from a bank containing a wide variety of groups which existed under varying circumstances and which were probed sociometrically with several different criteria. For this example we have made no attempt to insure criterion consistency or similarity in group type. Note, however, that since we used the reference distribution which conditions on g, X_{++}, M, V(in) and V(out), differences in sociometric test procedure, i.e., fixed versus free choice, are of reduced importance.

In Figure 15.2 we present a stem-and-leaf display (see Tukey, 1977; Leinhardt and Wasserman, 1978) of τ^2(max) for the 299 data matrices. Note the range in values from 3.56 to 1297.20 (τ^2(max) has 11 degrees of freedom when the only constraints are those specified[i] in the above-mentioned reference distribution).[4] The median τ^2 (max) is 49.39. In all, 73 groups have τ^2 (max) < 20. The structure of these 73 groups can be explained by reference to the lower order graphical features specified in the reference distribution. The structure of the remaining 226, however, cannot be so explained.

To study the structure of these groups, one might examine the w_{max} vectors associated with each τ^2 (max) and determine whether consistent patterns in the linear combinations were apparent. Another alternative is to calculate a measure for a particular linear combination that refers to a known substantively interesting structural tendency and then determine the proportion of τ^2 (max) that this represents.

One substantively interesting tendency is intransitivity, whose weighting vector, w', is (0, 0, 0, 0, 0, 1, 1, 1, 0, 3, 2, 0, 0, 2, 1, 0). Computing τ (intransitivity) for the 299 SDB groups yields the stem-and-leaf display in Figure 15.3.[5] In 187 cases, τ (intransitivity) ≤ −2. This indicates frequent significant tendencies away from intransitivity (toward transitivity). Note, however, that some values in the display are positive, indicating tendencies toward intransitivity. For purposes of this example, we only considered those values of τ (intransitivity) that were negative, squared these values, and computed ratios of $(\tau(\text{intransitivity}))^2 / \tau^2(\text{max})$. The results appear in Figure 15.4.

The ratio must range between 0 and 1 since $(\tau)^2 \leq \tau^2$ (max). The median of the ratios for the 272 groups is .27, with lower and upper quartiles of .09 and .45, respectively.[6] In 167 cases (61 percent), the tendency toward transitivity accounts for 20 percent or more of τ^2 (max).

Of course, a high value of the ratio may be obtained when both τ and τ^2 (max) are small or when both are large. These two situations, however, provide different substantive information. For example, if most groups have little structure of any kind and are also insignificantly transitive, the ratio may be high. On the other hand, the groups may be extremely structured. If most of this structure is captured by the notion of transitivity, then we would draw very different theoretical conclusions.

To examine this issue we present in Table 15.1 a 2 × 2 table of τ^2 (max) against $(\tau(\text{intransitivity}))^2$ for the 272 data matrices where

```
          (Unit =         10.0000)

73        0   | 0000000000000000000000000000000000001111111111111111111111111111111111111111
120       T   | 222222222222222222222222222222222222223333333333333333
45        F   | 44444444444444444444444444444444444455555555555555
134       S   | 6666666666666677777777777777
108       0.  | 888888888899999
93        1   | 000000000111111111
75        T   | 22222333
67        F   | 44444444455555
53        S   | 667
50        1.  | 8888899
43        2   | 0001111
36        T   | 3333
32        F   | 4555
28        S   | 66


26        HI  |    270.98      278.71      290.55      302.53
                   311.05      323.76      325.78      338.80
                   366.66      368.94      369.21      371.23
                   391.07      395.66      402.23      495.53
                   530.81      533.68      547.94      549.03
                   666.25      668.55      681.07      726.76
                   897.19     1297.20
```

Figure 15.2: Stem-and-Leaf Display of τ (max) for 299 SDB Data Matrices

```
12                      LO |  -21.32      -21.01      -20.29      -17.50
                            -15.66      -14.74      -14.56      -14.30
                            -14.21      -13.70      -13.28      -12.36

                      (UNIT =      0.1000)

14        -11 | 87
20        -10 | 752200
29        -9  | 966553221
42        -8  | 9987654211110
50        -7  | 99775310
63        -6  | 9988765444330
89        -5  | 998887766655543333322211110
121       -4  | 999998887666555544332222111000000
37        -3  | 98887766655554444444433333221111110000
141       -2  | 987777666655544433332100000
112       -1  | 99999888777776666555555444443333321110000
70        -0  | 9999988888877777766655444443332222111111100000
27        0   | 0111222556679
14        1   | 0000002335
4         2   | 224
1         3   |
1         4   | 0
```

Figure 15.3: Stem-and-Leaf Display of τ (intransitivity) for 299 SDB Data Matrices Using the g, X_{++}, M, V(in) and V(out) Reference Distribution

τ(intransitivity) $\leqslant 0$. As can be seen from the table, there are 53 cases in which the triad frequencies are close to those predicted by the random digraph reference distribution. The triad frequencies in these cases can be explained solely on the basis of the pair of nodal properties of the digraph. No resort to hypotheses of tendencies at the triadic level is required and, if made, would be artifactual and nonreplicable. On the other hand, there are 176 cases in which a tendency toward structure

	(Unit = 0.0100)	
49	0	0000000000000000000000001122222222233333334444444444
69	0·	56666666677788888999
91	1	00000011222223333334444
105	1·	55666667777889
131	2	000001111112223333344444444444
19	2·	55666677777777788999
122	3	0000001111222223334
103	3·	555566677778888888889999
80	4	000012222244
68	4·	556666667777899
53	5	0001123444
43	5·	555566677789
31	6	0000122344
21	6·	55669
16	7	11122
11	7·	58
9	8	
9	8·	55679
4	9	013
1	9·	6

Figure 15.4: Stem-and-Leaf Display of the Ratio $(\tau \text{ (intransitivity)})^2/\tau^2$ (max) for the 272 SDB Data Matrices with (intransitivity) $\tau < 0$

beyond what might be expected from the pair and nodal properties of the digraph is present and so, too, are strong tendencies toward transitivity. However, in 32 cases where strong structural tendencies exist, there is no evidence of transitive structure. (One might add to this latter grouping 16 of the 27 data matrices which had τ (intransitivity) > 0 but τ^2 (max) > 20.)[7]

The essential point of this example is as follows: Some of the groups studied by social researchers possess no social structure in the sense that their triadic features do not deviate significantly from what might be expected if only nodal or pair processes determined informal social relational linkages (22.8 percent of the 272). In many cases, though, the groups possess nonrandom structure (77.2 percent of the 272). Often (83.8 percent of 210), transitivity is an important component of this structure and, occasionally, it explains all or most of it (5 percent of the 210 have ratios $\geqslant .75$). Nonetheless, there are some highly structured groups in which transitivity is not strongly indicated (11.8 percent of the 272). It is interesting to speculate about the 32 strongly structured, nontransitive groups. For example, could the classical notions of clustering and hierarchy account for this situation? We think not. Clustering in the sense of Davis (1967), as we show in Holland and Leinhardt (1971), can be viewed as a combination of a tendency toward reciprocation and a tendency toward transitivity. Since the reference distribution conditions on reciprocity, when transitivity is not strongly

TABLE 15.1   Data Matrices with τ (intransitivity) $\leqslant$ 0 Arrayed into High and Low Levels of τ^2 (max) and τ (intransitivity)^2

		$(\tau\,(\text{intransitivity}))^2$		
		Low (<4)	High ($\geqslant 4$)	Total
$\tau^2 <$ (max)	Low (<20)	53	9	62
	High ($\geqslant 20$)	32	176	210
	Total	85	187	272

indicated, neither can clustering be strongly indicated. Hierarchy may also be viewed as a tendency toward transitivity combined with a variation in choices received, i.e., differential attraction (Holland and Leinhardt, 1971). Since the reference distribution also conditions on the variance of the in-degrees, when transitivity is not strongly indicated, neither can hierarchy be strongly indicated. It remains to be determined whether a common substantive interpretation can be given to the structure of the groups. However, before proposing new structural theories, one should first determine whether conditioning on the mean and variances of the degrees effectively captures all of the nodal properties of the digraph.

A Single Group

Here we present results from the analysis of a single group. The example illustrates the effect of using two different reference distributions in the calculation of a measure for intransitivity. We present the entire data matrix (Figure 15.5) with rows and columns permuted on the basis of choices received. The presentation of the data permits investigators with alternative analytic procedures to examine the relationship between results they obtain and the values obtained using τ measures. It can also serve as a test matrix for those constructing computer routines for computing τ^2(max).

These unpublished data were originally collected by Bock of the University of Chicago, Department of Education in 1955. They are the responses of children in a ninth grade general science class at a public high school in Chicago. Bock "first introduced the idea of their working in teams of two and then explained that to help [him] assign partners [in

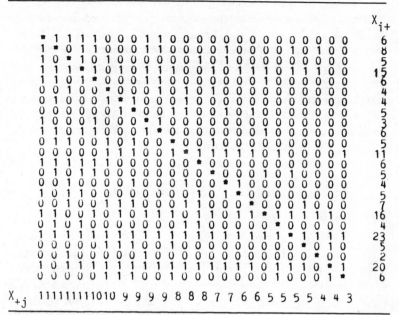

Figure 15.5: Data Matrix Obtained from Bock Row-Column Permuted on Basis of In-Degree (g = 24, M = 41; A = 99; N = 136)

an education task] each pupil was to rank the others according to his or her preferences for them as partners." [8] Since the subjects were also asked to indicate which of their ranks correspond to negative choices, we coded all ranking up to the beginning of the chooser-specified negative cut point as 1 and coded the rest 0. Thus, the sociomatrix is essentially of the free choice variety (see Holland and Leinhardt, 1973, for a discussion of this and related procedures).

We used two reference distributions in calculating τ. First (1) we conditioned on g, $\bar{X}$ and M, and second (2) on g, X_{++}, V(in) and V(out). We computed τ^2 (max) based on the two. Using the weighting vector given above for intransitivity, we obtained values of -13.81 conditioning on (1) and -8.83 conditioning on (2). These results indicate that some of the tendency away from intransitivity detected using (1) is artifactual in the sense that it can be explained by resort to lower-order features of the digraph, namely, the in- and out-degrees. On the other hand, the values of -8.83 obtained with (2) are highly significant and confirm the hypothesis of a strong tendency away from intransitivity in the local structure of this group, one that cannot be explained by resort to well-known nontriadic properties of interpersonal, affective relations.

The value obtained for τ^2(max) was 323.77, indicating that the data matrix evidences significant structural tendencies in general. To gain some feeling for how much the general structure consists of departure from intransitivity, we square the τ measure [continuing to use reference distribution (2)] and form the $\tau(\text{intransitivity})^2 / \tau^2(\text{max})$ which, for this group, is .24. Thus, while the tendency toward transitivity represents a significant structural feature of the group's affective social relations, it does not represent all of the triadic structure present in the data matrix. Fully 76 percent of the network's $\tau^2(\text{max})$ value remains to be explained after taking into account its size, the number of choices being made, the tendency toward reciprocation, the variation in choices made and received, and its tendency toward transitivity.

SUMMARY AND DISCUSSION

Structure in Networks

In sociology, the issue of structure in social relations has received renewed attention of late (Blau, 1975). Two items contributing to this renewal are (1) the development of theories in which the representation of structural issues in terms of network properties seems natural and (2) the development of analytic procedures which permit investigators to explore network data and make inferences about them.

Most often the analytic approach taken by investigators studying network data assumes implicitly that natural social relations are structured in the sense of some straightforward pattern or overall organization. The problem that faces such investigators is the fact that relational data are unorganized and possibly confounded. This is generally true of any set of observational, as opposed to experimental, data and not merely a problem in the study of social networks. The analytic task thus becomes one of reorganizing the data to make the pattern they presumably contain clear and evident to simple visual inspection. This is not necessarily a trivial problem and may involve relatively complicated data manipulations. Ultimately, however, the objectives of such approaches are the same: to find the patterns in the data which are equated a priori with the structure of the social network.

The approach presented in this report and in others we have authored on this topic is in marked contrast to such deterministically based exploratory approaches. We make no assumption that the data possess structure but ask, instead, whether there is sufficient information in the data to reject a hypothesis that no structure exists. This is a conservative view and implies that network data, like all empirical data, must be understood as resulting from an observation made on some underlying and observable process. As with any measurement, the empirical realization may have turned out differently. How differently depends on the precision of the measuring instrument, the inherent or natural variation in the process, temporal variation, and other factors. As is commonly appreciated, empirical data that derive from a random process, one possessing no substantively interesting structure, may appear to be highly structured. In such cases, the presumption that the structure observed in the data is in fact a general characteristic of the underlying process would be erroneous and might lead to invalid theoretical conclusions regarding the natural process under study.

Because of this, the procedures of classical statisical inference are usually conservative in orientation and are designed to aid us in making decisions regarding whether or not the data demonstrate structure beyond that which could be expected in data generated by a random mechanism. Of course, we know that even with this aid, our decisions can still be erroneous, but we are at least able to specify the level or likelihood of such errors and thus minimize them on average.

Tied closely to this framework for decision making is the notion of an appropriate comparison. When we ask how the observation could have arisen in the absence of structure in the natural process, we want to take into consideration as much information as we can about known features of the data, features that we view as theoretically irrelevant because they are prior to the structural features of interest but methodologically important because they can affect the observed structure. To continue the analogy introduced at the beginning of this article, we would not want to contrast outcomes in a classroom consisting of 20 children with one consisting of 5 or 60 unless we felt that, based on prior knowledge, class size has no effect. In the absence of such knowledge we would want to condition on group size, i.e., control its effect on outcome. In the absence of randomization in the experimental design, we would want to introduce into the statistical analysis a control for class size. Thus, in a sociometric context, if we could not hold group size, choice volume, mean choices, variance in choices made and received, and so forth constant experimentally, we would want to introduce them directly into the statistical model.

Some might object here, holding that the introduction as givens of "behavioral" features of the social network represents, in effect, a substantive theory, one which carries with it a bias in the direction of triadic or higher-level organization of social relations. This is one possible interpretation. However, by not introducing statistical conditioning at these levels, one leaves oneself open to an alternative error, that of accepting as structure those features of a network that are implied by known empirical phenomena (e.g., differential attraction and reciprocity). If lower-order features of a digraph explain the triad frequencies, then the apparent triadic structure of the digraph can be understood in their terms. This does not mean that pattern will not be present in the data. There may indeed be substantial pattern. It does mean, however, that a simpler theory of pattern generation will suffice. On the other hand, if after removing the influence of these factors we cannot predict the triad frequencies, then a more elaborate theory that implies structural tendencies at the triadic or even higher level is required.

In this article we have repesented an omnibus procedure which extends current methods and permits us to test whether or not an empirical digraph contains a structural signal sufficiently strong as to warrant further analysis. The test statistic, τ^2 (max), uses all the information in the triad census and corresponds to a weighting vector, w(max), which may be interpretable in substantively important terms. The fact that w(max) is a vector whose components may be fractional or negative indicates that more research is necessary to determine whether this is in fact the case.[9]

In the absence of an easily interpreted w(max), what does a value of τ^2 (max) mean? A large value of τ^2 (max), one much larger than its degrees of freedom, has an interpretation quite similar to the F-test discussed in the first section of the article: There is at least one linear combination of the triad for which the value of w'_{max} T is not likely to have arisen accidentally, i.e., at random. Regardless of whether the weighting vector so determined makes intuitive sense, a high value of τ^2 (max) indicates that there is a structural tendency at the level of triads within the data. It is up to the researcher to determine what that pattern is, in the sense of some identifiable configuration or process, and to ascribe to it some substantively meaningful features, i.e., to construct substantive theory in the face of observed empirical regularities.

In the absence of a significant τ^2 (max), is it sensible to pursue analyzing the data? Certainly there may be structural features which are of substantive importance but which cannot be tapped at the triadic or lower level. An insignificant τ^2 (max) may result when such structure exists. It is unlikely, however, that such higher-order structural tendencies do not also impact on triadic arrangements, in which case τ^2 (max) would detect them (see, for example, Holland and Leinhardt, 1976). Further work on this issue is needed. It should also be clear that if the reference distribution being used to calculate τ^2 (max) is conditional on g, X_{++}, M, V(in) and V(out), then small values of τ^2 (max) strongly suggest that the higher-order structure in the data is explainable by the number of nodes, the number of choices made and received, and the number of reciprocated choices. Pursuing such data more deeply than this may result in nonreplicable findings.

Why Study Triads?

Why are triads the feature of digraphs that we focus on in our approach to studying social structure? On the one hand, we do not focus on triads because we view these configurations as substantively interesting in themselves. Certainly, triads may be of interest to some investigators who may wish to study social behavior as it is revealed when individuals interact in groups of size three. This, however, is not our intent. We use the triad census because it is a conveniently determined summary of the digraph and one which contains a good deal of substantively and statistically important information. The omnibus measure which we have introduced here exploits this information as it bears upon the issue of structural regularities in the empirical frequencies of subgraph configurations.

On the other hand, we have continued to resort to the information contained in triads because of our view of the nature of social organization in the interpersonal relations of group members. This view does not emphasize a broadly based or systemic organization. Rather, we see structure in informal voluntary social behavior as a conglomeration of organizing tendencies which operate locally and which lose strength rapidly over longer paths. Therefore, whatever global patterns exist at the group level, it is our view that they must be compatible with and constructed from the micro processes operating at the subgroup level. (For further discussion of this view, see Holland and Leinhardt, 1977.) We view it to be an important and outstanding problem in sociology to determine what these local structuring properties of interpersonal relations are and to demonstrate their empirical factors.

NOTES

1. "Introduction" occurred when this study was presented at the 1968 meetings of the American Sociological Association in Boston.

2. When X is symmetric—the case of a graph rather than a digraph—T can only have 4 nonzero entries. In this case, reduction to tetrads rather than triads may be more useful. Work on this issue is in progress.

3. FORTRAN routines for producing τ^2 (max) and related quantities are available by writing Samuel Leinhardt, School of Urban and Public Affairs, Carnegie-Mellon University, Pittsburgh, PA 15213.

4. Thus, when more constraints are in effect, as with mutual only sociomatrices, 20 represents a highly conservative cut-off point.

5. Using the reference distribution that controls g, X_{++}, M, V(in) and V(out).

6. Of the 299 groups, 27 had τ (intransitivity) values that were positive.

7. It should be noted that τ^2 (max) is affected by g, the group size. Regressing $ln(\tau^2$ (max)) on group size accounts for 23 percent of the variance in the dependent variable. The regression coefficient is .04 with a t-statistic of 8.9.

8. Private communication. There were no other subject variables provided for these data besides preference rankings.

9. It might be reasonable to constrain w(max) to be a vector of positive integers which are zero as often as possible. Work on this is in progress.

CHAPTER 16

The Joint Role
Structure of Two Communities' Elites

RONALD L. BREIGER
PHILIPPA E. PATTISON

Blockmodel analysis offers a perspective for developing operational theories of role interlock across multiple networks. We identify precisely those features of role interlock that are shared by the elites of two small cities. This joint role structure is then interpreted with the aid of an algebraic model that we formulate on the basis of Granovetter's (1973) "strength of weak ties" argument. Our discussion illustrates the operationalization of substantive and theoretical concepts in the form of idealized role structures and their application via blockmodel analysis to observed network data.

A distinctively sociological conception of social roles emphasizes the interlocking of "role attributes of alters who have in common that they occupy one identical status that places them in a specific role relation to ego" (Blau, 1975: 135). Boorman and White (1976) refer to such alters as "middlemen," conceptualize each role relation as a separate network, and generalize across the positions of all egos simultaneously. The resulting conceptualization of "role structure" exhibits considerable theoretical elegance, is fully operational on multiple network data drawn from observable population, and thus provides one way of developing "the notion of the role-set, [which] at once leads to the inference that social structures confront men with the task of *articulating* the components of countless role-sets" (Merton, 1968: 42, emphasis added).

Authors' Note: *The names attached to this report of joint research are listed alphabetically. We are grateful to Edward O. Laumann, Franz U. Pappi, Joseph Galaskiewicz, and Peter V. Marsden for providing the data for this study and for instructive discussions of the community contexts of their research. John Padgett and Harrison C. White provided constructive criticism of earlier drafts. This research was supported by NSF grants SOC76-24394 and SOC76-24512. An earlier version appeared in* Sociological Methods & Research, *November 1978.*

Editors' Note: *For further discussion of the topics presented here and related issues, see the critiques of Bonacich (1980) and McConaghy (1981a, 1981b), and the replies of Boorman and Arabie (1980) and Pattison (1981).*

In this chapter, an extension of Breiger (1979), we study the role structures of the community elites of two small cities, one West German and one American. The original data were collected by Edward Laumann and his associates, whose evolving analyses are leading to a broad-gauge comparative perspectives on community influence systems.[1] We identify precisely those features of role interlock that are common to the elites of both communities. We then interpret this joint role structure with reference to an algebraic model that we formulate from Granovetter's (1973) "strength of weak ties" argument. This interpretation has the additional purpose of illustrating how a researcher may operationalize general substantive and theoretical concepts in the form of idealized role structures and apply them via blockmodel analysis to observed data.[2]

The American city (pseudonym: Towertown) was selected by Laumann and his associates due to its similarity with the previously studied German community (pseudonym: Alneustadt; see Laumann et al., 1977: 599; Laumann and Pappi, 1976: 31-39, respectively). Both communities are small, but not dominated by nearby larger cities. Both serve as distribution centers of manufacturing plants. A sizable proportion of the labor force of each city is employed by a single large institution (a natural science research center and a university, respectively) that has located there or expanded only recently. Perhaps most importantly, the rapid growth of each of these institutions has attracted new residents of quite different social and geographical origins from those of the long-term inhabitants.

As part of their investigations, the researchers collected data on three networks among the identified influentials in each community, asking each person to indicate the three others with whom he or she had the closest business or professional relations, the most frequent discussions of community affairs, and the most frequent social meetings (see Laumann and Pappi, 1976: 289 for the exact wording; see Laumann et al., 1977: 598-602 on the American data). We label the resulting networks B, C and S, respectively. Each binary matrix is square, indexing all those in the sample as potential senders of ties (rows), as well as receivers (columns). Within each matrix, the initial orderings of individuals in rows and columns are identical but arbitrary. We study 51 influentials in Altneustadt and 58 in Towertown.[3]

For each data set the CONCOR algorithm (Breiger et al., 1975) was implemented, yielding a partition of each elite into four blocks. A detailed discussion of the procedure for the Altneustadt elite may be found in Breiger (1979); our analysis of the Towertown data was analogous. The resulting density matrices for ties within and between *blocks* are presented in the first panel of Table 16.1.

Breiger (1979) also describes a method for identifying a suitable cut-off valued for encoding the density matrices into blockmodel images; the Towertown data were again treated similarly in our analysis. (For definitions of the terms "density matrices," "cut-off density," and "images" widely used in blockmodel analysis, see, e.g., Arabie et al., 1978: 56.) The two resulting sets of blockmodel images are shown in the second panel of Table 16.1. Extensive investigations show that the joint role structure (defined below), as well as its "irreducible structural components" or factors (Pattison, 1982; Pattison and Bartlett, 1982), are reasonably robust under all cut-offs densities in the range $(.75\mu_i, 1.25\mu_i)$, where μ_i is the overall mean density of each set of three matrices.[4]

THE JOINT ROLE STRUCTURE

Consider first the blockmodel images for Altneustadt (Table 16.1, lower panel).[5] Labeling the images for B, C and S (respectively) as 1, 2 and 3, construct the *compound image* 1 * 1. For each ordered pair of blocks, the compound image 1 * 1 shows (in binary fashion) whether the first block has business-professional ties with some "middleman block," which itself seeks business-professional contacts among members of the second. Similarly, the compound image 3 * 2 reports, for each pair of blocks, whether the first has frequent social contact with some set of alters who share location in a block that seeks advice (on community affairs) from the second. In brief: the compound image of any two images (which may themselves be compounds) is simply their Boolean matrix product.

Now imagine forming *all* compounds of *any* length among the Altneustadt images, 1, 2 and 3. These correspond to the "components of countless role-sets" referred to in the first paragraph of this chapter—more precisely, the set is countably infinite—and the fundamental question for role theory becomes how they are articulated. Employing the Axiom of Quality of Boorman and White (1976), equate two compounds if and only if they induce identical block structure (that is, if and only if their associated matrix representations coincide). For example, as the reader may verify, the product of the Altneustadt business professional image composed with itself is equal to the original image; we thus have the equation 1 * 1 = 1. A *role structure* (Boorman and White, 1976) is the set of equations obtained by applying the Axiom

TABLE 16.1   Density Matrices and Identified Blockmodels

Altneustadt Density Matrices

B				C				S			
5.7	3.1	2.4	2.0	14.3	2.2	1.2	3.3	13.8	2.7	0.6	3.3
5.3	11.0	0.0	2.0	8.4	8.1	0.6	0.6	4.0	13.3	0.0	0.6
1.8	0.0	10.0	7.3	1.8	0.0	15.5	5.4	1.2	0.6	15.5	3.6
3.3	2.0	3.6	6.7	7.3	0.0	4.5	3.3	6.0	1.3	1.8	8.9

Towertown Density Matrices

B				C				S			
7.8	6.8	2.9	2.0	11.1	5.8	3.6	0.7	16.7	3.7	2.9	2.0
8.9	6.4	2.6	3.2	8.4	6.7	1.1	4.6	8.9	7.0	1.9	2.5
5.7	3.4	4.4	7.1	5.0	3.0	6.0	7.1	2.1	1.5	9.9	7.1
2.0	6.3	2.4	6.2	3.3	5.6	1.4	9.1	3.3	6.0	1.4	3.8

Altneustadt Blockmodel				*Towertown Blockmodel*		
B	C	S		B	C	S
1000	1000	1000		1100	1100	1000
1100	1100	0100		1100	1100	1100
0011	0010	0010		1001	0011	0011
0001	1000	1001		0101	0101	0100

NOTE: Densities are expressed as percentages.

of Quality to all images (including all compounds derived from these). In brief, the role structure induced by a set of blockmodel images is the *semigroup multiplication table* they generate under the Axiom of Quality. The set of all distinct images and products comprises the semigroup *elements* indexed in the multiplication table.

Figures 16.1 and 16.2 report the role structures and semigroup elements for the Altneustadt and Towertown blockmodels, respectively. As an example of reading Figure 16.1: the multiplication table reports that the products of the second-listed semigroup elements (the image for advice-seeking on community affairs, C) and the first (the image for business-professional relations, B) is the fourth (thus the equation 2 * 1 = 4 reported in the multiplication table). The reader may verify the construction of the entire role table, as well as the semigroup elements 4 through 8, through Boolean matrix multiplication of all combinations of the original images (1 through 3) under the Axiom of Quality.

	1	2	3	4	5	6	7	8
1	1	6	7	8	7	6	7	8
2	4	2	2	4	4	6	8	8
3	5	2	3	4	5	6	7	8
4	4	6	8	8	8	6	8	8
5	5	6	7	8	7	6	7	8
6	8	6	6	8	8	6	8	8
7	7	6	7	8	7	6	7	8
8	8	6	8	8	8	6	8	8

1000	1000	1000	1000	1000	1000	1000	1000
1100	1100	0100	1100	1100	1100	1100	1100
0011	0010	0010	0011	0011	1010	1011	1011
0001	1000	1001	1000	1001	1000	1001	1000
1=B	2=C	3=S	4	5	6	7	8

	1	4	5	6	7	8	2	3
1	1	8	7	6	7	8	6	7
4	4	8	8	6	8	8	6	8
5	5	8	7	6	7	8	6	7
6	8	8	8	6	8	8	6	6
7	7	8	7	6	7	8	6	7
8	8	8	8	6	8	8	6	8
2	4	4	4	6	8	8	2	2
3	5	4	5	6	7	8	2	3

Figure 16.1: Altneustadt Semigroup Multiplication Table, Elements, and Partitioned Table (class (1) = $\{1,4,5,6,7,8\}$, class (2) = $\{2\}$, and class (3) = $\{3\}$)

	1	2	3	4	5	6	7	8	9	10	11	12
1	4	4	8	4	8	4	8	8	8	4	8	8
2	4	6	7	4	5	10	11	8	11	10	11	11
3	5	7	9	5	5	11	11	8	12	11	11	12
4	4	4	8	4	8	4	8	8	8	4	8	8
5	5	5	8	5	8	5	8	8	8	5	8	8
6	4	10	11	4	5	10	11	8	11	10	11	11
7	5	11	11	5	5	11	11	8	11	11	11	11
8	8	8	8	8	8	8	8	8	8	8	8	8
9	5	11	12	5	5	11	11	8	12	11	11	12
10	4	10	11	4	5	10	11	8	11	10	11	11
11	5	11	11	5	5	11	11	8	11	11	11	11
12	5	11	12	5	5	11	11	8	12	11	11	12

1100	1100	1000	1100	1100	1100	1100	1100	1000	1100	1100	1000
1100	1100	1100	1100	1100	1100	1100	1100	1100	1100	1100	1100
1001	0011	0011	1101	1101	0111	0111	1100	0111	1111	1111	1111
0101	0101	0100	1101	1100	1101	1100	1100	1100	1101	1100	1100
1=B	2=C	3=S	4	5	6	7	8	9	10	11	12

	1	4	5	8	2	6	7	10	11	3	9	12
1	4	4	8	8	4	4	8	4	8	8	8	8
4	4	4	8	8	4	4	8	4	8	8	8	8
5	5	5	8	8	5	5	8	5	8	8	8	8
8	8	8	8	8	8	8	8	8	8	8	8	8
2	4	4	5	8	6	10	11	10	11	7	11	11
6	4	4	5	8	10	10	11	10	11	11	11	11
7	5	5	5	8	11	11	11	11	11	11	11	11
10	4	4	5	8	10	10	11	10	11	11	11	11
11	5	5	5	8	11	11	11	11	11	11	11	11
3	5	5	5	8	7	11	11	11	11	9	12	12
9	5	5	5	8	11	11	11	11	11	12	12	12
12	5	5	5	8	11	11	11	11	11	12	12	12

Figure 16.2: Towertown Semigroup Multiplication Table, Elements, and Partitioned Table (class (1) = {1,4,5,8}, class (2) = {2,6,7,10,11}, and class (3) = {3,9,12})

Clearly, the table is closed under the operation of forming compounds (since the product of any two images in the table is itself an image in the table). These comments extend to Figure 16.2 as well.

We now turn to the procedure of blockmodel analysis for comparing the role tables of Figures 16.1 and 16.2. The *joint homomorphic reduction* of these two role tables defined on the same types of images (1, 2, 3) is the unique (largest) table consistent with both original role tables;

that is, the most refined role table which is a homomorphic reduction of both given tables. A *homomorphic reduction* of a single role table is a partition of its rows and columns into equivalence classes such that, for all images e_j in Class C_m and for all images e_i in Class C_n, any product of the form $(e_i e_j)$ equals some element e_k assigned to the *same* class, C_p (where p may index any of the Classes and may equal m or n).

Substantively, the joint reduction is the outcome of abstracting structure common to both original role systems; it is the largest common denominator of the two role structures being compared. In mathematical terms, the joint reduction is the unique intersection (greatest lower bound) of the two given semigroups in the lattice of all homomorphic reductions (Boorman and White, 1976: 1402-1407, 1418-1421). The third panels of Figures 16.1 and 16.2 report partitions of the Altneustadt and Towertown role tables (respectively) into equivalence classes such that Table 16.2 is the joint homomorphic reduction ("joint role structure") of the two original role tables. The reader may directly verify, from the definition stated above, that the joint structure of Table 16.2 is a homomorphic reduction of *both* the Figure 16.1 role table *and* the Figure 16.2 role table. An algorithm of Harrison White (the JNTHOM algorithm) [Boorman and White, 1976], taking the Table 16.1 blockmodel images as input, computes the Table 16.2 reduction as their unique (maximal) joint homomorphic reduction.

INTERPRETATION

Granovetter (1973) presents a persuasive argument for the inference of certain network properties of interpersonal ties from a knowledge of their "strength." His basic contention is that strong ties tend to be densely concentrated within particular groups, while weak ties are less densely concentrated but much more likely to link members of different groups. Thus, for example, "a rumor moving through strong ties is much more likely to be limited to a few cliques than one going via weak ones; bridges will not be crossed" (p. 1366). We will extend Granovetter's argument to a proposition concerning the ways in which strong and weak ties interlock with one another; that is, we will translate Granovetter's hypothesized network properties of strong and weak ties into statements about the structure of the semigroup which they generate.

Let us first consider two individuals A and B connected by a strong tie, S. Granovetter's hypothesis implies that A is weakly tied (by W) to most of the persons to whom B is weakly tied; hence the approximate truth of the statment "acquaintances of friends are acquaintances," and of the equation:

$$SW = W \qquad [16.1]$$

More importantly, it is most unlikely to be true that $SW = S$, or indeed, that SW equals any power of S, since such equations would require violations of Granovetter's "forbidden triad" (p. 1363).

By similar reasoning we have:

$$WS = W \qquad [16.2]$$

illustrated by Granovetter's review of Kerckhoff and Back's study of contagion in a textile plant: The contagion spread through weak ties from marginal members to those in central cliques, then to friends who were themselves only weak contacts (through work relationships) of the original innovators (p. 1368).

Granovetter (1973: 1376-1378) observes that "strong ties breed cohesion" and are likely to be transitive; hence the equation:

$$S^2 = S \qquad [16.3]$$

Equations 16.1, 16.2 and 16.3 describe the action of the strong tie S as a semigroup identity. Equations 16.1 and 16.2 also suggest the absorbing power of W, its functioning as a semigroup zero. In this regard, Granovetter claims (p. 1370) that weak ties are *not* likely to be transitive; nonetheless, the equation:

$$W^2 = W \qquad [16.4]$$

is not inconsistent with the logic of his argument. Boorman (1975: 225) observes that weak ties may in fact be transitive "if people have so many weak ties within some categorical grouping of the population (e.g., workers in a given profession) that the number of ego's weak ties begins to be on the same order as the total population in the category. This situation may . . . lead to positive inbreeding through a version of the small world effect." Moreover, from Granovetter's characterization of weak ties as "diffuse," it follows that the equation $W^k = W$ is likely to be satisfied for suitably high values of k.

We will lend coherence to this argument by proposing that there is a homomorphism from the semigroup generated by the weak and strong relations, which maps S onto a semigroup identity and W onto a semigroup zero. Such a homomorphism may well be induced by

**TABLE 16.2   Joint Homomorphic Reduction of the Altneustadt
and Towertown Multiplication Tables**

	(1)	(2)	(3)
(1)	(1)	(1)	(1)
(2)	(1)	(2)	(2)
(3)	(1)	(2)	(3)

equating all powers of S to S, all powers of W to W, the crucial feature of
the reduction being that equations 16.1 and 16.2 are satisfied. The
resulting semigroup multiplication table is presented in the first panel of
Table 16.3. This abstract role structure encodes the core of
Granovetter's paradox (p. 1378), namely that "weak ties, often
denounced as generative of alienation, are here seen as indispensible to
individuals' . . . integration into communities [due to their absorbing
qualities]; strong ties, breeding local cohesion, lead to overall
fragmentation [due to their functioning as an identity element]."

Return now to the joint role structure derived empirically from two
community elites (Table 16.2). Element number 3, representing the
social relations network, is an identity for the semigroup, while element
number 1 (business and professional relations) is a semigroup zero. By
appealing to the version of Granovetter's hypothesis outlined above, we
argue that the structure *shared* by the Altneustadt and Towertown elites
and encoded in their joint structure may be described in terms of the
relative strength of the three networks linking their members. Social
relations are strong in comparison to links arising from business
contacts or community affairs, with business-professional ties being the
weaker of the latter two. (The strength of the social ties in the
Altneustadt elite also emerged from Breiger's, 1979, analysis, which
motivated the present characterization of the semigroup properties of
strong and weak ties.) The ordering in strength of the relations —B, C,
S—which we claim to exist follows more clearly from a consideration of
the homomorphic images of the joint role structure (Table 16.2). This
structure has precisely two nontrivial homomorphic images, J1 and J2,[6]
whose multiplication tables are presented at the bottom of Table 16.3. In
the first, J1, community affairs relations and social ties are shown to be
strong relative to business-professional linkages. The second
comparison (J2), however, contrasts business-professional and

TABLE 16.3   A Multiplication Table for Weak and Strong Ties

a) Multiplication table to which a semigroup generated by a weak relation, W, and a strong relation, S, is hypothesized to reduce.

	W	S
W	W	W
S	W	S

b) Homomorphic images of the Table 16.2 joint role structure.

J1	1	2
B = 1	1	1
C,S = 2	1	2

J2	1	3
B,C = 1	1	1
S = 3	1	3

community ties with social connection, showing the latter to be strong in relation to the former. The community affairs ties are thus capable of functioning both strongly and weakly—hence their intermediate position in the ordering strength.

Laumann and Pappi (1976: 159) provide a related discussion of tie strength in the form of a discussion of results from a path model predicting distances among pairs of actors in the community affairs network (C) as a function of distances in the other two networks (and several other variables). "The crucial feature of the [path analysis] solution is the impact of informal social ties on the influence structure. Politically relevant information and persuasion tend to flow along friendship ties. Other types of contact and similarity have small and indirect effects, the latter mainly filtered through informal social ties" (compare Laumann et al., 1977: 625-628).

Laumann and Pappi note that the "greatest problem" in pursuing this type of research is "the causal model itself, with its simple additive, linear assumptions. . . . We have postulated a temporal ordering among [variables] that some might find questionable. We have ignored the obvious possibility of mutual feedback effects" (1976: 160-161).

Technically, our analysis and Laumann and Pappi's are strictly noncomparable within any known mathematical context. Preliminary and partial as as our results are, though, we believe that the further development of our approach may lead to a direct solution to the problem of the interrelations among *types* of relations.

CONCLUSION

The homomorphic reduction of a semigroup may be analyzed independently of the particular blockmodel from which it derives, although it can induce useful perspectives on that blockmodel (Pattison, 1982). The separability of a semigroup from the concrete blockmodel images it represents, though, means that the representation is a powerful one. Not only does it permit the change in relational patterns over time to be explored, but it is also a natural means with which to compare relational data from a number of sources. It may even be used to identify the common features of different treatments of the same data set (Breiger, 1979), or—as in this chapter—to capture a substantive interpretation (Granovetter, 1973) of the *abstract* interlock of various qualities of realtionship. A central construction, in all cases, is the joint homophorphic reduction of the semigroups under consideration (Boorman and White, 1976). This "joint structure" is proposed to be a precise record of the relational structure *shared* by the corresponding blockmodels.

NOTES

1. On the German city, see Laumann and Pappi (1973, 1976) and Laumann et al. (1974). On the American data see Marsden and Laumann (1977) and Laumann et al. (1977). This last article includes numerous cross-city comparisons. Laumann et al. (1977) studied two American cities; our analysis includes only the one (Towertown) for which Laumann et al. have generously provided their network data.

2. Burt (1977c) also presents a "role" analysis for one of these cities (Altneustadt).

3. Thus we include all 51 influentials in Altneustadt for whom data are available (Laumann and Pappi's network analysis involves 44 of these), but only 58 of the 77 who were interviewed in Towertown. These 58 include all 53 "positional" leaders who were initially identified on the researchers' questionnaire (see Marsden and Laumann, 1977: 203), as well as the first 5 of 24 others who were added during the course of interviewing. These first 5 "additional" individuals received a very high mean number of choices (15.0) in comparison to the mean number (1.5) received by the remainder of the 24 additions.

4. On a separate issue, the probability of finding at least one mapping from a set of multiple networks to an array of blockmodel images, as well as the expected number of mappings given that there is at least one, see White (1977).

5. For a more detailed treatment of the concepts employed in this section, see White and Breiger (1975) and Boorman and White (1976).

6. Indeed, J1and J2 are "factors" of the Table 16.2 joint role structure, in the sense of Pattison and Bartlett (1982).

References

AGNEW, J. A., L.A. BROWN, and J. P. HERR (1978) "The community innovation process: a conceptualization and empirical analysis." Urban Affairs Quarterly 14: 3-30.

ALBA, R. D. (1973) "A graph-theoretic definition of a sociometric clique." Journal of Mathematical Psychology 3: 113-126.

—— (1972) "COMPLT—a program for analyzing sociometric data and clustering similarity matrices." Behavioral Science 17: 566.

—— and M. P. GUTTMAN (1972) "SOCK: a sociometric analysis system." Behavioral Science 17: 326.

ALBA, R. D. and C. KADUSHIN (1976) "The intersection of social circles: a new measure of social proximity in networks." Sociological Methods & Research 5: 77-102.

ALBA, R. D.and G. MOORE (1978) "Elite social circles." Sociological Methods & Research 7: 167-188 (see Chapter 12 in this volume).

ALLISON, P. D. (1978) "Measures of inequality." American Sociological Review 43: 865-880.

—— (1977) "Testing for interaction in multiple regression." American Journal of Sociology 83: 144-153.

ANDERSON, E. (1978) A Place on the Corner. Chicago: University of Chicago Press.

ARABIE, P., S. A. BOORMAN, and P. R. LEVITT (1978) "Constructing blockmodels: how and why." Journal of Mathematical Psychology 17: 21-63.

AUGUSTSON, J. G. and J. MINKER (1970) "An analysis of some graph theoretic cluster techniques." Journal of the ACM 17: 571-588.

BANFIELD, E. C. (1961) Political Influence. New York: Free Press.

BARNES, J. A. (1979) "Network analysis: orienting notion, rigorous technique or substantive field of study?" in P. W. Holland and S. Leinhardt (eds.) Perspectives on Social Network Research. New York: Academic Press.

—— (1972) Social Networks. Reading, MA: Addison-Wesley.

—— (1969) "Networks and political process," in J. C. Mitchell (ed.) Social Urban Situations. Manchester, UK: Manchester University Press.

—— (1954) "Class and committees in a Norwegian island parish." Human Relations 7: 39-58.

BARTH, E. S. and S. D. JOHNSON (1959) "Community power and a typology of social issues." Social Forces 38: 29-32.

BARTH, F. (1975) Ritual and Knowledge among the Baktaman of New Guinea. New Haven, CT: Yale University Press.

—— [ed.] (1969) Ethnic Groups and Boundaries. London: Allen & Unwin.

BARTON, A. H. (1972) "Sampling and field work for the American Leadership Study." Bureau of Applied Social Research, Columbia University.

BAVELAS, A. (1950) "Communication patterns in task oriented groups." Journal of the Acoustical Society of America 22: 271-282.

—————— (1948) "A mathematical model for group structure." Human Organization 7: 16-30.

BEAUCHAMP, M. A. (1965) "An improved index of centrality." Behavioral Science 10: 161-163.

BECK, M. and P. CADAMAGNANI (1968) "The extent of intra- and extra-social group contact in American society." Unpublished manuscript, John Carroll University.

BECKER, M. (1970) "Sociometric location and innovativeness: reformulation and extension of the diffusion model." American Sociological Review 35: 267-282.

BENDIX, R. and S. M. LIPSET (1966) "Karl Marx's theory of social classes," in Reinhard Bendix and Seymour M. Lipset (eds.) Class Status and Power. (2nd ed.) New York: Free Press.

BENIGER, J. R. (1976) "Sampling social networks: the subgroup approach." Proceedings of the Business and Economic Statistics Section, American Statistical Association.

BERKMAN, L. E. and S. L. SYME (1979) "Social networks, host resistance, and mortality: a nine-year followup study of Alameda County residents." American Journal of Epidemiology 109: 186-204.

BERKOWITZ, S. D. (1982) An Introduction to Structural Analysis. Toronto: Butterworths.

BERNARD, H. R. and P. D. KILLWORTH (1978) "A review of the small-world literature." Connections 2: 15-24.

—————— (1977) "Informant accuracy in social network data II." Human Communication Research 4: 3-18.

—————— and L. SAILER (1981) "A note on inferences regarding network subgroups: response to Burt and Bittner." Social Networks 3: 89-92.

—————— (1980) "Informant accuracy in social network data IV: a comparison of clique-level structure in behavioral and cognitive network data." Social Networks 2: 191-218.

BLAU, P. M. (1977a) "A macrosociological theory of social structure." American Journal of Sociology 83: 26-54.

—————— (1977b) Inequality and Heterogeneity. New York: Macmillan.

—————— [ed.] (1975) Approaches to the Study of Social Structure. New York: Free Press.

—————— (1974) "Parameters of social structure." American Sociological Review 39: 615-635.

BOISSEVAIN, J. (1974) Friends of Friends: Networks, Manipulators and Coalitions. New York: St. Martin's.

BOJE, D. M. and D. A. WHETTEN (1981) "Centrality and attributes of influence in interorganizational networks." Administrative Science Quarterly 26: 378-395.

BONACICH, P. (1980) "The 'common structure semi-group,' a replacement for the Boorman and White 'joint reduction'." American Journal of Sociology 86: 159-166.

—————— (1972) "Factoring and weighting approaches to status scores and clique identification." Journal of Mathematical Sociology 2: 113-120.

BONNER, R. E. (1964) "On some clustering techniques." IBM Journal of Research and Development 8: 22-32.

BOORMAN, S. A. (1975) "A combinatorial optimization model for transmission of job information through contact networks." Bell Journal of Economics 6: 216-249.

—————— and P. ARABIE (1980) "Algebraic approaches to the comparison of concrete social structures represented as networks: reply to Bonacich." American Journal of Sociology 86: 166-174.

BOORMAN, S. A. and H. C. WHITE (1976) "Social structure from multiple networks: II. role structures." American Journal of Sociology 81: 1384-1446.

BOTT, E. (1957/1971) Family and Social Network. New York: Free Press.

BOYER, P. and S. NISSENBAUM (1974) Salem Possessed: The Social Origins of Witchcraft. Cambridge, MA: Harvard University Press.

BRAITHWAITE, R. B. (1959) Scientific Explanation: A Study of the Function of Theory, Probability, and Law in Science. Cambridge, UK: Cambridge University Press.

BREIGER, R. L. (1979) "Toward an operational theory of community elite structures." Quality and Quantity 13: 21-57.

—— (1976) "Career attributes and network structure: a blockmodel study of a biomedical research specialty." American Sociological Review 41: 117-135.

—— and P. E. PATTISON (1978) "The joint role structure of two communities' elites." Sociological Methods & Research 7: 213-226. (See Chapter 16, this volume.)

BREIGER, R. L., S. A. BOORMAN, and P. ARABIE (1975) "An algorithm for clustering relational data, with application to social network analysis comparison with multidimensional scaling." Journal of Mathematical Psychology 12: 328-383.

BRON, C. and J. KERBOSCH (1973) "Finding all cliques of an undirected graph." Communications of the ACM 16: 575-577.

BROOM, L. and F. L. JONES (1977) "Problematics in stratum consistency and stratum formation: an Australian example." American Journal of Sociology 82: 808-825.

BURT, R. S. (forthcoming) Corporate Profits and Cooptation: Networks of Market Constraints and Directorate Ties in the American Economy. New York: Academic Press.

—— (1982a) Toward a Structural Theory of Action: Network Models of Social Structure, Perception, and Action. New York: Academic Press.

—— (1982b) Normative Pressures in Medical Innovation. Monograph 39, Survey Research Center, University of California, Berkeley.

—— (1982c) "Relational contents in multiple network systems," in L. C. Freeman et al. (eds.) Research Methods in Social Network Analysis. Unpublished collection, School of Social Sciences, University of California, Irvine.

—— (1982d) "A note on cooptation and definitions of constraints," in P. V. Marsden and N. Lin (eds.) Social Structure and Network Analysis. Beverly Hills, CA: Sage.

—— (1982e) "Role strain." Presented at the Tenth World Congress of the International Sociological Association, Mexico City.

—— (1981a) "Studying status/role-sets as ersatz network positions in mass surveys." Sociological Methods & Research 9: 313-337. (See Chapter 5, this volume.)

—— (1981b) "Comparative power structures in American communities." Social Science Research 10: 115-176. (See Chapter 7, this volume.)

—— (1980a) "Autonomy in a social typology." American Journal of Sociology 85: 892-925.

—— (1980b) "Models of network structure." Annual Review of Sociology 6: 79-141.

—— (1980c) "Actor interests in a social topology: foundation for a structural theory of action." Sociological Inquiry 49: 107-132.

—— (1980d) "Cooptive corporate actor networks: a reconsideration of interlocking directorates involving American manufacturing." Administrative Science Quarterly 25: 557-582.

—— (1980e) "Innovation as a structural interest: rethinking the impact of network position on innovation adoption." Social Networks 2: 327-355.

—— (1979) "Relational equilibrium in a social topology." Journal of Mathematical Sociology 6: 211-252.

—— (1978a) "Cohesion versus structural equivalence as a basis for network subgroups." Sociological Methods & Research 7: 189-212. (See Chapter 13, this volume.)

—— (1978b) "Stratification and prestige among elite experts in methodological and mathematical sociology circa 1975." Social Networks 1: 105-158.

——— (1977a) "Power in social topology." Social Science Research 6: 1-83.

——— (1977b) "Positions in multiple network systems, part one: a general conception of stratification and prestige in a system of actors cast as a social topology." Social Forces 56: 106-131.

——— (1977c) "Positions in multiple network systems, part two: stratification and prestige among elite decision-makers in the community of Altneustadt." Social Forces 56: 551-575.

——— (1976a) "Positions in networks." Social Forces 55: 93-166.

———(1976b) "Interpretational confounding of unobserved variables in structural equation models." Sociological Methods & Research 5: 3-52.

——— (1975) "Corporate society: a time series analysis of network structure." Social Science Research 4: 271-328.

——— and W. M. BITTNER (1981) "A note on inferences regarding network subgroups." Social Networks 3: 71-83. (See Chapter 14, this volume.)

BURT, R. S. and P. DOREIAN (1982) "Testing a structural theory of perception: conformity and deviance with respect to journal norms in elite sociological methodology." Quality and Quantity 16: 109-150.

BURT, R. S. and N. LIN (1977) "Network time series from archival records," in D. R. Heise (ed.) Sociological Methodology 1977. San Francisco: Jossey-Bass. (See Chapter 8, this volume.)

BURT, R. S., K. P. CHRISTMAN, and H. C. KILBURN (1980) "Testing a structural theory of corporate cooptation: interorganization directorate ties as a strategy for avoiding market constraints on profits." American Sociological Review 45: 821-841.

BURT, R. S., K. L. LIEBEN, and M. G. FISCHER (1980) "Network power structures from informant perceptions." Human Organization 39: 121-133. (See Chapter 7, this volume.)

CAMPBELL, D. T. (1958) "Common fate, similarity, and other indices of the status of aggregates of persons as social aggregates." Behavioral Science 3: 14-25.

CARTWRIGHT, D. [ed.] (1951) Field Theory in Social Science: Selected Theoretical Papers by Kurt Lewin. New York: Harper & Row.

CLARK, T. N. (1971) "Community structure, decision-making, budget expenditures, and urban renewal in 51 American communities," in C. M. Bonjean et al. (eds.) Community Politics. New York: Free Press.

——— [ed.] (1968) Community Structure and Decision-Making: Comparative Analyses. San Francisco: Chandler.

COHEN, A. [ed.] (1974) Urban Ethnicity. London: Tavistock.

——— (1969) Custom and Politics in Urban Africa: A Study of Hausa Migrants in Yocuba Towns. London: Routledge & Kegan Paul.

COLE, J. R. and S. COLE (1973) Social Stratification in Science. Chicago: University of Chicago Press.

COLEMAN, J. S. (1973) The Mathematics of Collective Action. Chicago: Aldine.

——— (1972) "Systems of social exchange." Journal of Mathematical Sociology 2: 145-163.

——— (1966) "Foundations for a theory of collective decisions." American Journal of Sociology 71: 615-627.

——— (1964) Introduction to Mathematical Sociology. New York: Free Press.

——— (1961) The Adolescent Society. New York: Free Press.

——— and D. MacRAE, Jr. (1960) "Electronic processing of sociometric data for groups up to a thousand in size." American Sociological Review 25: 722-726.

COLEMAN, J. S., E. KATZ, and H. MENZEL (1966) Medical Innovation: A Diffusion Study. New York: Bobbs Merrill.

COOLEY, C. H. (1909) Social Organization. New York: Schocken.

COSER, L. A. (1974) Greedy Institutions. New York: Free Press.

CRANE, D. (1972) Invisible Colleges. Chicago: University of Chicago Press.

CRONBACH, B. E. and G. C. GLESER (1953) "Assessing similarity between profiles." Psyhological Bulletin 50: 456-473.

DAHL, R. (1961) Who Governs? New Haven, CT: Yale University Press.

——— (1958) "A critique of the ruling elite model." American Political Science Review 52: 463-469.

DANZER, M. H. (1975) "Validating conflict data." American Sociological Review 40: 570-584.

DAVIS, A., B. B. GARDNER, and M. R. GARDNER (1941) Deep South. Chicago: University of Chicago Press.

DAVIS, J. A. (1970) "Clustering and hierarchy in interpersonal relations: testing two graph theoretical models on 742 sociograms." American Sociological Review 35: 843-852.

——— (1967) "Clustering and balance in graphs." Human Relations 20: 181-187.

——— and S. LEINHARDT (1972) "The structure of positive interpersonal relations in small groups," in J. Berger et al. (eds.) Sociological Theories in Progress. New York: Houghton-Mifflin.

DAVIS, J. A., P. W. HOLLAND, and S. LEINHARDT (1971) "Comments on Professor Mazur's hypothesis about interpersonal sentiments." American Sociological Review 36: 309-311.

DOMHOFF, G. W. (1970) The Higher Circles: The Governing Class in America. New York: Random House.

DOREIAN, P. (1974) "On the connectivity of social networks." Journal of Mathematical Sociology 3: 245-258.

DUNCAN, O. D. (1975) "Partitioning polytomous variables in a multiway contingency analysis." Social Science Research 4: 167-182.

ERICKSON, B. H. (1978) "Some problems of inference from chain data," in K. Schuessler (ed.) Sociological Methodology 1979. San Francisco: Jossey-Bass.

——— T. A. NOSANCHUK, and E. LEE (1981) "Network sampling in practice: some second steps." Social Networks 3: 127-136.

ERICKSON, E. P. and W. L. YANCEY (1976) "Networks and status." Presented to the American Sociological Association, August.

FARARO, T. J. and M. H. SUNSHINE (1964) A Study of a Biased Friendship Net. Syracuse, NY: Syracuse University, Youth Development Center.

FELD, S. L. (1981) "The focused organizations of social ties." American Journal of Sociology 86: 1015-1035.

——— and R. ELMORE (1977) "The spuriousness of transitivity." Presented at the meetings of the American Sociological Association, Chicago.

FESTINGER, L., S. SCHACHTER, and K. W. BACK (1950) Social Pressures in Informal Groups. Stanford, CA: Stanford University Press.

FIENBERG, S. E. and S. S. WASSERMAN (1981) "Categorical data analysis of single sociometric relations," in S. Leinhardt (ed.) Sociological Methodology 1981. San Francisco: Jossey-Bass.

FISCHER, C. S. (1982a) To Dwell Among Friends: Personal Networks in Town and City. Chicago: University of Chicago Press.

——— (1982b) "What do we mean by friend? an inductive study." Social Networks 3: 287-306.

—— R. M. JACKSON, C. A. STUEVE, K. GERSON, L. M. JONES, with M. BALDASSARE (1977) Networks and Places: Social Relations in the Urban Setting. New York: Free Press.

FLAMENT, C. (1963) Applications of Graph Theory to Group Structure. Englewood Cliffs, NJ: Prentice Hall.

FRANK, O. (1981) "A survey of statistical methods for graph analysis," in S. Leinhardt (ed.) Sociological Methodology 1981. San Francisco: Jossey-Bass.

—— (1978) "Sampling and estimation in large social networks." Social Networks 1: 91-101.

—— (1975) "Survey sampling in graphs." Research Report 1975-11. Department of Statistics, University of Lund, Sweden.

FREEMAN, L. C. (1982) "Social networks and the structure experiment," in L. C. Freeman et al. (eds.) Research Methods in Social Network Analysis. Unpublished collection, School of Social Sciences, University of California, Irvine.

—— (1980) "The gatekeeper, pair-dependency and structural centrality." Quality and Quantity 14: 585-592.

—— (1979) "Centrality in social networks: conceptual clarification." Social Networks 1: 215-239.

—— (1977) "A set of measures of centrality based on betweenness." Sociometry 40: 35-41.

—— (1968) Patterns of Local Community Leadership. New York: Bobbs Merrill.

—— D. ROEDER, and R. R. MULHOLLAND (1980) "Centrality in social networks, II: experimental results." Social Networks 2: 119-141.

FREEMAN, L. C., A. K. ROMNEY, and D. R. WHITE [eds.] (1982) Research Methods in Social Network Analysis. Unpublished collection, School of Social Sciences, University of California, Irvine.

GALASKIEWICZ, J. (1979) "The structure of community interorganizational networks." Social Forces 57: 1346-1364.

GANS, H. J. (1967) The Levittowners. New York: Random House.

GELLER, and A., D. KAPLAN, and H. D. LASWELL (1942) "An experimental comparison of four ways of coding editorial content." Journalism Quarterly 19: 362-370.

GLUCKMAN, M. [ed.] (1962) Essays on the Ritual of Social Relations. Manchester, UK: Manchester University Press.

GOFFMAN, E. (1974) Frame Analysis: An Essay on the Organization of Experience. Cambridge, MA: Harvard University Press.

GOODMAN, L. A. (1979) "A brief guide to the causal analysis of data from surveys." American Journal of Sociology 84: 1078-1095.

GRANOVETTER, M. (1982) "The strength of weak ties: a network theory revisited," in P. V. Marsden and N. Lin (eds.) Social Structure and Network Analysis. Beverly Hills, CA: Sage.

—— (1979) "The theory-gap in social network analysis" in S. Leinhardt and P. W. Holland (eds.) Perspectives in Social Network Analysis. New York: Academic Press.

—— (1976) "Network sampling: some first steps." American Journal of Sociology 81: 1287-1303.

—— (1974) Getting a Job: A Study of Contacts and Careers. Cambridge, MA: Harvard University Press.

—— (1973) "The strength of weak ties." American Journal of Sociology 78: 1360-1380.

GRIMES, M. D., C. M. BONJEAN, J. L. LYON, and R. L. LINEBERRY (1976) "Community structure and leadership arrangements: a multidimensional analysis." American Sociological Review 41: 706-725.

GURIN, P., A. H. MILLER, and G. GURIN (1980) "Stratum identification and consciousness." Social Psychology Quarterly 43: 30-47.

HAAS, J. and T. E. DRABEK (1973) Complex Organizations: A Sociological Perspective. New York: Macmillan.

HALLINAN, M. T. (1978) "The process of friendship formation." Social Networks 1: 193-210.

————— (1974) The Structure of Positive Sentiment. New York: Elsevier.

HANUSHEK, E. A. and J. E. JACKSON (1977) Statistical Methods for Social Scientists. New York: Academic Press.

HARARY, F., (1969) Graph Theory. Reading, MA: Addison-Wesley.

————— R. Z. NORMAN, and D. CARTWRIGHT (1965) Structural Models: An Introduction to the Theory of Directed Graphs. New York: John Wiley.

HAWLEY, A. H. (1963) "Community power and urban renewal success." American Journal of Sociology 68: 422-431.

HEIL, G. H. and H. C. WHITE (1976) "An algorithm for finding simultaneous homomorphic correspondences between graphs and their image graphs." Behavioral Science 21: 26-35.

HIGLEY, J., G. MOORE, and D. DEACON (1978) "The national elite network in Australia." Presented at the 1978 meetings of the Sociological Association of Australia and New Zealand in Brisbane.

HOLLAND, P. W. and S. LEINHARDT (1982) "Stochastic blockmodels." Presented at the Sun Belt Social Network Conference in Tampa, FL.

————— (1981) "An exponential family of probability distributions for directed graphs." Journal of the American Statistical Association 76: 33-50.

————— (1979) "Structural sociometry," in S. Leinhardt and P. W. Holland (eds.) Perspectives in Social Network Analysis. New York: Academic Press.

————— (1978) "An omnibus test for social structure using triads." Sociological Methods & Research 7: 227-256. (See Chapter 15, this volume.)

————— (1977) "Social structure as a network process." Zeitschrift für Soziologie 6: 386-402.

————— (1976) "Conditions for eliminating intransitivities in binary digraphs." Journal of Mathematical Psychology 4: 315-318.

————— (1975) "Local structure in social networks," in D. R. Heise (ed.) Sociological Methodology 1976. San Francisco: Jossey-Bass.

————— (1973) "The structural implications of measurement error in sociometry." Journal of Mathematical Psychology 3: 85-111.

————— (1972) "Some evidence on the transitivity of positive interpersonal sentiment." American Journal of Sociology 77: 1205-1209.

————— (1971) "Transitivity in structural models of small groups." Comparative Group Studies 2: 107-124.

————— (1970) "A method for detecting structure in sociometric data." American Journal of Sociology 70: 492-513.

HOLSTI, O. R. (1968) "Content analysis," in G. Lindzey and E. Aronson (eds.) The Handbook of Social Psychology. Reading, MA: Addison-Wesley.

HOMANS, G. C. (1974) Social Behavior: Its Elementary Forms. New York: Harcourt Brace Jovanovich.

————— (1950) The Human Group. New York: Harcourt Brace Jovanovich.

HOROWITZ, A. (1977) "Social networks and pathways to psychiatric treatment." Social Forces 56: 86-105.

HOUSTON, M. J. and S. SUDMAN (1975) "A methodological assessment of the use of key informants." Social Science Research 4: 151-164.

HUBBELL, C. H. (1965) "An input-output approach to clique identification." Sociometry 28: 377-399.

HUNTER, F. (1953) Community Power Structure. Chapel Hill: University of North Carolina Press.

IRVING, A. W. (1977) "Social networks in the modern city." Social Forces 55: 867-880.

JACKSON, R. M. (1977) "Social structure and process in friendship choice," in C. S. Fischer et al., Networks and Places. New York: Free Press.

JANIS, I. L., R. H. FADNER, and M. JANOWITZ (1943) "The reliability of a content analysis technique." Public Opinion Quarterly 7: 293-296.

JOHNSON, S. (1967) "Hierarchical clustering schemes." Psychometrika 32: 241-254.

JONES [McCallister], L. M. and C. S. FISCHER (1978) "Studying egocentric networks by mass survey." Working Paper No. 284, Institute of Urban and Regional Development, University of California, Berkeley.

KADUSHIN, C. (1978) "Introduction to macro-network analysis." Unpublished manuscript, Teachers College, Columbia University.

——— (1968) "Power, influence and social circles: a new methodology for studying opinion makers." American Sociological Review 33: 685-698.

——— (1966) "The friends and supporters of psychotherapy: on social circles in urban life." American Sociological Review 31: 786-802.

KAPFERER, B. (1972) Strategy and Transaction in an African Factory. Manchester, UK: Manchester University Press.

——— (1969) "Norms and the manipulation of relationships in a work context," in J. Clyde Mitchel (ed.) Social Networks in Urban Situations. Manchester, UK: Manchester University Press.

KAPLAN, A. (1964) The Conduct of Inquiry: Methodology for Behavioral Science. San Francisco: Chandler.

KATZ, L. (1953) "A new status index derived from sociometric data." Psychometrika 18: 39-43.

KENDALL, M. G. and A. STEWART (1963) The Advanced Theory of Statistics, Vol. 1. London: Charles Griffin.

KESSLER, R. C. and D. F. GREENBERG (1980) Linear Panel Analysis: Models of Quantitative Change. New York: Academic Press.

KILLWORTH, P. D. and H. R. BERNARD (1979) "Informant accuracy in social network data III: a comparison of triadic structure in behavioral and cognitive data." Social Networks 2: 19-46.

——— (1978) "The reverse small-world experiment." Social Networks 1: 159-192.

——— (1976) "Informant accuracy in social network data." Human Organization 35: 269-286.

——— (1974) "Catij: a new sociometric and its application to a prison living unit." Human Organization 33: 335-350.

KISH, L. (1965) Survey Sampling. New York: John Wiley.

KLEINER, R. J. and S. PARKER (1976) "Network participation and psychological impairment in an urban environment," in P. Meadows and E. H. Mizruchi (eds.) Urbanism, Urbanization, and Change: Comparative Perspectives. Reading, MA: Addison-Wesley.

KNOKE, D. (forthcoming) "Organizational sponsorship and influence reputation of social influence associations." Social Forces 61.

——— and J. H. KUKLINSKI (1982) Network Analysis. Beverly Hills, CA: Sage.

KORTE, C. and S. MILGRAM (1970) "Acquaintance networks between racial groups: application of the small world method." Journal of Personality and Social Psychology 15: 101-108. ,

LANKFORD, P. M. (1974) "Comparative analysis of clique identification methods." Sociometry 37: 283-305.

LAUMANN, E. O. (1973) Bonds of Pluralism. New York: John Wiley.

——— (1966) Prestige and Association in an Urban Community: An Analysis of an Urban Stratification System. New York: Bobbs-Merrill.

——— and F. U. PAPPI (1976) Networks of Collective Action: A Perspective on Communiity Influence Systems. New York: Academic Press.

——— (1973) "New directions in the study of community elites." American Sociological Review 38: 212-230.

LAUMANN, E. O. and R. SENTER (1976) "Subjective social distance, occupational stratification, and forms of status and class consciousness: a cross-national replication and extension." American Journal of Sociology 81: 1304-1338.

LAUMANN, E. O. and P. V. MARSDEN (1979) "The analysis of oppositional structures in political elites: identifying collective actors." American Sociological Review 44: 713-732.

——— and J. GALASKIEWICZ (1977) "Community-elite influence structures: extension of a network approach." American Journal of Sociology 83: 594-631.

LAUMANN, E. O., J. GALASKIEWICZ, and P. V. MARSDEN (1978) "Community structure as interorganizational linkages." Annual Review of Sociology 4: 455-484.

LAUMANN, E. O., L. VERBRUGGE, and F. V. PAPPI (1974) "A causal modelling approach to the study of a community elite's influence structure," in E. O. Laumann and F. U. Pappi (eds.) Networks of Collective Action: A Perspective on Community Influence Systems. New York: Academic Press.

LAZARSFELD, P. F. (1959) "Problems in methodology," in R. K. Merton et al. (eds.) Sociology Today. New York: Harper & Row.

LEAVITT, H. J. (1951) "Some effects of communication patterns on group performance." Journal of Abnormal and Social Psychology 46: 38-50.

LEHMANN, E. L. (1959) Testing Statistical Hypotheses. New York: John Wiley.

LEINHARDT, S. [ed.] (1977) Social Networks: A Developing Paradigm. New York: Academic Press.

——— and S. S. WASSERMAN (1978) "Exploratory data analysis: an introduction to selected methods," in K. Schuessler (ed.) Sociological Methodology 1979. San Francisco: Jossey-Bass.

LENSKI, G. E. (1952) "American social classes: statistical strata or social groups?" American Journal of Sociology 58: 139-144.

LEVINGER, G. and H. RAUSCH [eds.] (1977) Close Relationships. Amherst: University of Massachusetts Press.

LIEBOW, E. (1967) Tally's Corner: A Study of Negro Streetcorner Men. Boston: Little, Brown.

LIN, N. (1982) "Social resources and instrumental action," in P. V. Marsden and N. Lin (eds.) Social Structure and Network Analysis. Beverly Hills, CA: Sage.

——— (1976) Foundations of Social Research. New York: McGraw-Hill.

——— (1973) The Study of Human Communication. Indianapolis: Bobbs-Merrill.

——— P. W. DAYTON, and P. GREENWALD (1978) "Analyzing the instrumental use of relations in the context of social structure." Sociological Methods & Research 7: 149-166. (See Chapter 6, this volume.)

———— (1977) "The urban communication network and social stratification: a 'small world' experiment," in D. B. Ruben (ed.) Communication Yearbook, Vol. 1. New Brunswick, NJ: Transaction Books.

LIN, N., W. M. ENSEL, and J. C. VAUGHN (1981) "Social resources and strength of ties: structural factors in occupational status attainment." American Sociological Review 46: 393-405.

LIN, N., J. C. VAUGHN, and W. M. ENSEL (1981) "Social resources and occupational status attainment." Social Forces 59: 1163-1181.

LINCOLN, J. R. (1976) "Power mobilization in the urban community: reconsidering the ecological approach." American Sociological Review 41: 1-15.

LINDENBERG, S. (1976) "Actor analysis and depersonalization." Mens en Maatschappij 51: 152-178.

LINDZEY, G. and E. F. BORGATTA (1954) "Sociometric measurement," in G. Lindzey (ed.) Handbook of Social Psychology, Vol. 1. Reading, MA: Addison-Wesley.

LINDZEY, G. and D. BYRNE (1968) "Measurement of social choice and interpersonal attractiveness," in G. Lindzey and E. Aronson (eds.) Handbook of Social Psychology, Vol. 3. Reading, MA: Addison-Wesley.

LINGOES, J. C. (1972) "A general survey of the Guttman-Lingoes nonmetric program series," in R. N. Shepard et al. (eds.) Multidimensional Scaling, Vol. 1. New York: Seminar Press.

———— (1965) "An IBM-7090 program for Guttman-Lingoes smallest space analysis-I." Behavioral Science 10: 183-184.

LITWAK, E. and T. SZELENYI (1969) "Primary group structures and their functions." American Sociological Review 35: 465-481.

LIU, W. T. and R. W. DUFF (1972) "The strength in weak ties." Public Opinion Quarterly 36: 361-366.

LORRAIN, F. and H. C. WHITE (1971) "Structural equivalence of individuals in social networks." Journal of Mathematical Sociology 1: 49-80.

LOWENTHAL, M. and C. HAVEN (1968) "Interaction and adaptation: intimacy as a critical variable." American Sociological Review 33: 20-30.

LUCE, R. D. (1950) "Connectivity and generalized cliques in sociometric group structure." Psychometrika 15: 169-190.

———— and A. PERRY (1949) "A method of matrix analysis of group structure." Psychometrika 14: 94-116.

MacRAE, D. (1960) "Direct factor analysis of sociometric data." Sociometry 23: 360-371.

MARKOFF, J., G. SHAPIRO, and S. R. WEITMAN (1974) "Toward the integration of content analysis and general methodology," in D. R. Heise (ed.) Sociological Methodology 1975. San Francisco: Jossey-Bass.

MARSDEN, P. V. (forthcoming a) "Restricted access in networks and models of power." American Journal of Sociology 88.

———— (forthcoming b) Power and Influence Processes: Applications and Extensions of a Model of Collective Action. Greenwich, CT: JAI Press.

———— (1982a) "Brokerage behavior in restricted exchange networks," in P. V. Marsden and N. Lin (eds.) Social Structure and Network Analysis. Beverly Hills, CA: Sage.

———— (1982b) "Methods for the characterization of role structures in network analysis," in L. C. Freeman et al. (eds.) Research Methods in Social Network Analysis. Unpublished collection, School of Social Sciences, University of California, Irvine.

———— (1981a) "Introducing influence processes into a system of collective decisions." American Journal of Sociology 86: 1203-1235.

———— (1981b) "Conditional effects in regression models," in P. V. Marsden (ed.) Linear Models in Social Resarch. Beverly Hills, CA: Sage.

—— and E. O. LAUMANN (1977) "Collective action in a community elite: exchange, influence resources, and issue resolution," in R. J. Liebert and A. W. Imershein (eds.) Power, Paradigms, and Community Research. Beverly Hills, CA: Sage.

MARSDEN, P. V. and N. LIN [eds.] (1982) Social Structure and Network Analysis. Beverly Hills, CA: Sage.

McCALLISTER, L. and C. S. FISCHER (1978) "A procedure for surveying personal Networks." Sociological Methods & Research 7: 131-148. (See Chapter 3, this volume.)

McCONAGHY, M. J. (1981a) "The common role structure: improved blockmodeling methods applied to two communities' elites." Sociological Methods & Research 9: 267-285.

—— (1981b) "Negation to the equation: rejoinder to Pattison." Sociological Methods & Research 9: 303-312.

MERTON, R. K. (1968) Social Theory and Social Structure. New York: Free Press.

MILGRAM, S. (1967) "The small world problem." Psychology Today 1: 61-67.

MILLS, C. W. (1956) The Power Elite. New York: Oxford University Press.

MINOR, M. J. et al. (1982) The California Connection Aftercare Demonstration Program. Berkeley: Pacific Institute for Research and Evaluation.

MITCHELL, J. C. (1969) "The concept and use of social networks," in J. C. Mitchell (ed.) Social Networks in Urban Situations. Manchester, UK: Manchester University Press.

MIZRUCHI, M. S. (1982) The American Corporate Network 1904-1974. Beverly Hills, CA: Sage.

—— and D. BUNTING (1981) "Influence in corporate networks: an examination of four measures." Administrative Science Quarterly 26: 475-489.

MOKKEN, R. J. (1979) "Cliques, clubs and clans." Quality and Quantity 13: 161-173.

—— and F. J.A.M. van VEEN (1981) "GRADAP: graph definition and analysis package." Connections 4: 47.

MOLOTCH, H. (1976) "The city as growth machine: toward a political economy of place." American Journal of Sociology 82: 309-332.

MOORE, G. (1979) "The structure of a national elite network." American Sociological Review 44: 673-692.

MORENO, J. L. [ed.] (1960) The Sociometry Reader. New York: Free Press.

—— (1934) Who Shall Survive? Washington, DC: Nervous and Mental Disease Publishing.

MORGAN, D. L. and S. RYTINA (1977) "Comment on 'Network sampling: some first steps' by Mark Granovetter." American Journal of Sociology 83: 722-727.

MOSTELLER, F. and J. W. TUKEY (1968) "Data analysis, including statistics," in G. Lindzey and E. Aronson (eds.) The Handbook of Social Psychology. Reading, MA: Addison-Wesley.

MOXLEY, R. L. and N. F. MOXLEY (1974) "Determining point-centrality in uncontrived social networks." Sociometry 37: 122-130.

NEWCOMB, T. (1961) The Acquaintance Process. New York: Holt, Rinehart & Winston.

NIEMINEN, J. (1974) "On centrality in a graph." Scandinavian Journal of Psychology 15: 322-336.

—— (1973) "On the centrality in a directed graph." Social Science Research 2: 371-378.

NORTHWAY, M. L. (1940) "A method for depicting social relationships obtained by sociometric testing." Sociometry 3: 144-150.

NOSANCHUK, T. A. (1963) "Comparison of several sociometric partitioning techniques." Sociometry 26: 112-124.

OSGOOD, C. E. (1959) "The representational model and relevant research methods," in I. de S. Pool (ed.) Trends in Content Analysis. Urbana: University of Illinois Press.

OSSOWSKI, S. (1963) Class Structure in the Social Consciousness. London: Routledge & Kegan Paul.

PARSONS, T. (1961) "An outline of the social system," in T. Parsons et al. (eds.) Theories of Society. New York: Free Press.

——— (1951) The Social System. Glencoe, IL: Free Press.

PATTISON, P. E. (1982) "The analysis of semigroups of multirelational systems." Journal of Mathematical Psychology 25.

——— (1981) "Equating the 'joint reduction' with blockmodel common role structure: a reply to McConaghy." Sociological Methods & Research 9: 286-302.

——— and W. K. BARTLETT (1982) "A factorization procedure for finite algebras." Journal of Mathematical Psychology 25.

PERRUCCI, R. and M. PILISUK (1970) "Leaders and ruling elites: the interorganizational basis of community power." American Sociological Review 35: 1040-1057.

PFEFFER, J. (1972) "Merger as a response to organizational interdependency." Administrative Science Quarterly 17: 382-394.

——— and G. SALANCIK (1978) The External Control of Organizations: A Resource Dependence Perspective. New York: Harper & Row.

POLSBY, N. (1963) Community Power and Political Theory. New Haven, CT: Yale University Press.

——— (1960) "How to study community power: the pluralist alternative." Journal of Politics 22: 474-484.

Project in Structural Analysis (1981) "STRUCTURE: a computer program providing basic data for the network analysis of empirical positions in a system of actors." Computer Program 1, Survey Research Center, University of California, Berkeley.

RAPOPORT, A. and W. J. HOVARTH (1961) "A study of a large sociogram." Behavioral Science 6: 279-291.

RICE, R. (1982) "Longitudinal system structure and role occupancy of research groups using a computer conferencing system." Presented at the Second Annual Social Networks Conference, Tampa, FL.

RICHARDS, W. D. and R. E. RICE (1981) "The NEGOPY network analysis program." Social Networks 3: 215-223.

ROETHLISBERGER, F. J. and W. J. DICKSON (1939) Management and the Worker. Cambridge, MA: Harvard University Press.

ROGERS, E. M. and D. K. BHOWMIK (1970) "Homophily-heterophily: relational concepts for communication research." Public Opinion Quarterly 34: 523-538.

ROGERS, E. M. and D. L. KINCAID (1981) Communication Networks: Toward a New Paradigm for Research. New York: Free Press.

ROGERS, E. M. and F. F. SHOEMAKER (1971) Communication of Innovations. New York: Free Press.

ROISTACHER, R. C. (1974) "A review of mathematical models in sociometry." Sociological Methods & Research 3: 123-171.

ROSENBERG, M. (1953) "Perceptual obstacles to class consciousness." Social Forces 32: 22-27.

ROSSI, P. H. and R. CRAIN (1968) "The NORC permanent community sample." Public Opinion Quarterly 32: 261-272.

RUBIN, Z. (1973) Liking and Loving. New York: Holt, Rinehart & Winston.

RUNGER, G. and S. WASSERMAN (1980) "Longitudinal analysis of friendship networks." Social Networks 2: 143-154.

SABIDUSSI, G. (1966) "The centrality index of a graph." Psychometrika 31: 581-603.

SAMPSON, S. F. (1969) "Crisis in a cloister." Ph.D. dissertation, Department of Sociology, Cornell University.

SCHMIDT, S. W., J. C. SCOTT, C. LANDE, and L. GUASTI [eds.] (1977) Friends, Followers and Factions. Berkeley: University of California Press.

SCHUTZ, W. C. (1958) "On categorizing qualitative data in content analysis." Public Opinion Quarterly 22: 503-515.

SCHWARTZ, J. E. (1977) "An examination of CONCOR and related methods for blocking sociometric data," in D. R. Heise (ed.) Sociological Methodology 1977. San Francisco: Jossey-Bass.

SEARLE, S. R. (1966) Matrix Algebra for the Biological Sciences. New York: John Wiley.

SEIDMAN, S. B. and B. L. FOSTER (1979) "SONET-I: social network analysis and modeling system." Social Networks 2: 85-90.

——— (1978) "A graph-theoretic generalization of the clique concept." Journal of Mathematical Sociology 6: 139-154.

SEILER, L. H. and G. F. SUMMERS (1974) "Locating community boundaries: an integration of theory and empirical techniques." Sociological Methods & Research 2: 259-280.

SHOTLAND, R. L. (1970) "The communication patterns and the structure of social relationships at a large university." Ph.D. dissertation, Michigan State University.

SIEGEL, P. M. (1971) "Prestige in the American occupational structure." Ph.D. dissertation, University of Chicago.

SINGER, B. and S. SPILERMAN (1976) "Representation of social processes by Markov models." American Journal of Sociology 82: 1-54.

SMITH, R. A. (1976) "Community power and decision-making: a replication and extension of Hawley." American Sociological Review 41: 691-705.

SNYDER, D. and E. L. KICK (1979) "Structural position in the world system and economic growth, 1955-1970: a multiple network analysis of transnational interactions." American Journal of Sociology 84: 1096-1126.

SONQUIST, J. A. and T. KOENIG (1975) "Interlocking directorates in the top U.S. corporations: a graph theory approach." Insurgent Sociologist 5: 196-229.

STEMPEL, G. H. (1955) "Increasing reliability in content analysis." Journalism Quarterly 32: 449-455.

STEPHENSON, W. (1967) The Play Theory of Mass Communication. Chicago: University of Chicago Press.

STONE, P. J., D. C. DUNPHY, M. S. SMITH, and D. M. OGILVIE (1966) The General Inquirer: A Computer Approach to Content Analysis in the Behavioral Sciences. Cambridge, MA: MIT Press.

SUDMAN, S. and N. BRADBURN (1974) Response Effects. Chicago: Aldine.

TAYLOR, D. G. and J. S. COLEMAN (1979) "Equilibrating processes in social networks: a model for conceptualization and analysis," in P. W. Holland and S. Leinhardt (eds.) Perspectives on Social Network Research. New York: Academic Press.

TAYLOR, M. (1969) "Influence structures." Sociometry 32: 490-502.

THEIL, H. (1967) Economics and Information Theory. Chicago: Rand McNally.

THIBAUT, J. and H. H. KELLEY (1959) The Social Psychology of Groups. New York: John Wiley.

TRAVERS, J. and S. MILGRAM (1969) "An experimental study of the small world problem." Sociometry 32: 425-443.

TUKEY, J. W. (1977) Exploratory Data Analysis. Reading, MA: Addison-Wesley.

TURK, H. (1970) "Interorganizational networks in urban society: initial perspective and comparative research." American Sociological Review 35: 1-19.

USEEM, M. (1979) "The social organization of the American business elite." American Sociological Review 44: 553-572.

VAN de GEER, J. P. (1971) Introduction to Multivariate Analysis for the Social Sciences. San Francisco: W. H. Freeman.

VAN POUCKE, W. (1980) "Network constraints on social action: preliminaries for a network theory." Social Networks 2: 181-190.

VERBRUGGE, L. M. (1979) "Multiplexity in adult friendships." Social Forces 58: 1286-1308.

——— (1977) "The structure of adult friendship choices." Social Forces 56: 576-597.

WALKER, J. L. (1969) "The diffusion of innovations among the American states." American Political Science Review 63: 880-899.

WASSERMAN, S. (1977) "Random directed graph distributions and the triad census in social networks." Journal of Mathematical Sociology 5: 61-86.

WEBB, E. J., D. T. CAMPBELL, R. D. SCHWARTZ, and L. SECHREST (1966) Unobtrusive Measures: Nonreactive Research in the Social Sciences. Chicago: Rand McNally.

WEBER, M. (1947) Social and Economic Organization, trans. A. M. Henderson, T. Parsons. New York: Free Press.

WELLMAN, B. (1982) "Studying personal communities in East York," in P. V. Marsden and N. Lin (eds.) Social Structure and Network Analysis. Beverly Hills, CA: Sage.

——— (1981) "Applying network analysis to the study of support," in B. H. Gottlieb (ed.) Social Networks and Social Support. Beverly Hills, CA: Sage.

——— (1979) "The community question: the intimate networks of East Yorkers." American Journal of Sociology 84: 1201-1231.

WHEELDON, P. D. (1969) "The operation of voluntary associations and personal networks in the political processes of an inter-ethnic community," in J. C. Mitchell (ed.) Social Networks in Urban Situations. Manchester, UK: Manchester University Press.

WHITE, D. R. and K. P. REITZ (1982) "Rethinking the role concept: social networks, homomorphisms and equivalence of positions," in L. C. Freeman et al. (eds.) Research Methods in Social Network Analysis. Unpublished Collection, School of Social Sciences, University of California, Irvine.

WHITE, H. C. (1977) "Probabilities of homomorphic mappings from multiple graphs." Journal of Mathematical Psychology 16: 121-134.

——— and R. L. BREIGER (1975) "Pattern across networks." Society 12: 68-73.

WHITE, H. C., S. A. BOORMAN, and R. L. BREIGER (1976) "Social structure from multiple networks I: blockmodels of roles and positions." American Journal of Sociology 81: 730-780.

WHYTE, W. F. (1955) Street Corner Society. Chicago: University of Chicago Press.

WILLEY, M. M. (1926) The Country Newspaper. Chapel Hill: University of North Carolina Press.

WRIGHT, B. and M. S. EVITTS (1961) "Direct factor analysis in sociometry." Sociometry 24: 82-98.

YANCEY, W. L., E. P. ERICKSON, and R. N. JULIANI (1976) "Emergent ethnicity: a review and reformulation." American Sociological Review 41: 391-403.

About the Authors

RICHARD D. ALBA is Associate Professor of Sociology at the State University of New York at Albany and Director of its Center for Social and Demographic Analysis (Albany, New York 12222). In addition to methodology, his interests lie in the study of ethnicity. His survey of network analysis, "Taking stock of network analysis: a decade's results," was recently published in Samuel Bacharach (ed.), *Research in the Sociology of Organizations,* Volume I.

RONALD L. BREIGER is Professor of Sociology and a faculty research associate of the Institute for Social and Economic Research at Cornell University (Ithaca, New York 14853). His current research is in the areas of social stratification, the evolution of role structure, and the development of network theory and models for the aggregation of social categories.

RONALD S. BURT is Associate Professor of Sociology at Columbia University (New York, New York 10027) and Acting Associate Professor of Sociology at the University of California, Berkeley. His interest is the general development of structural sociology. His recent works concern the social perception of advantage (*Normative Pressures in Medical Innovation,* 1982), the social organization of competition in markets (*Corporate Profits and Cooptation,* forthcoming), and action theory more generally (*Toward a Structural Theory of Action,* 1982).

PAUL W. DAYTON is a research scientist with the Cancer Control Bureau of the New York State Department of Health (16 Martin Terrace, Albany, New York 12205). His major research interests center on the development of new methodologies for analyzing cancer clusters.

CLAUDE S. FISCHER is Professor of Sociology at the University of California, Berkeley (Berkeley, California 94720). He is author of *The Urban Experience* (1976), *To Dwell Among Friends* (1982), and with McCallister and others, of *Networks and Places: Social Relations in an Urban Setting* (1977). His current interests lie in the area of social history and technology.

PETER GREENWALD is Director, Division of Resources, Centers, and Community Activities, National Cancer Institute, and Editor in Chief, Journal of the National Cancer Institute (Building 31 Room 4A32, 9000 Rockville Pike, Bethesda, MD 20205). His research interests center on cancer epidemiology and preventative medicine.

PAUL W. HOLLAND is Director, Program Statistics Research, Educational Testing Service (Princeton, New Jersey 08541). He has been on the faculties of Harvard University, Michigan State University, and Stanford University. He was also on the staff of the National Bureau of Economic Research's Computer Research Center for Economic and Management Science. Stochastic digraph theory is one of his major interests.

DAVID KNOKE is Professor of Sociology, Institute of Social Research, Indiana University (Bloomington, Indiana 47405). With Edward O. Laumann, he is studying the social organization of the national energy and health domains. He is coauthor, with James R. Wood, of *Organized for Action: Commitment in Voluntary Association* (1982) and, with George W. Bohrnstedt, of *Statistics for Social Data Analysis.*

EDWARD O. LAUMANN is Professor and Chair of the Department of Sociology at the University of Chicago (Chicago, Illinois 60637) and Editor of the *American Journal of Sociology.* He has just completed a book with John P. Heinz on the sociology of the legal profession in Chicago and is in the middle of a study of the social organization of the national policy domains of health and energy with David Knoke.

SAMUEL LEINHARDT is Professor of Sociology, School of Urban and Public Affairs, Carnegie-Mellon University (Pittsburgh, Pennsylvania 15213). He has been a lecturer at Harvard University, where he spent a postdoctoral year, and a Visiting Professor of Sociology at Hebrew University. One of his current research interests is the application of stochastic digraph theory to the study of social structure.

NAN LIN is Professor of Sociology at the State University of New York at Albany (Albany, New York 12222). He is studying the relationships between social resources and instrumental action and social support and illness.

PETER V. MARSDEN is Assistant Professor of Sociology at the University of North Carolina at Chapel Hill (Chapel Hill, North Carolina 27514). His interests include stratification, formal organizations, and network analysis.

LYNNE McCALLISTER has recently completed her dissertation, "Planning for mother's work," in the Department of City and Regional Planning at the University of California, Berkeley (Berkeley, California 94720) on jobs, child-care, and homemaking in middle American neighborhoods. She has written and taught about program and policy planning and is interested in networks as alternatives to public sources of services.

MICHAEL J. MINOR is research psychologist at the Pacific Institute for Research and Evaluation (Berkeley, California 94710). He is currently the principal investigator of a panel study on the social networks of former heroin addicts. His interests include social psychological models of health and the design and analysis of longitudinal studies.

GWEN MOORE is Assistant Professor of Sociology at Russell Sage College (Troy, New York 12180). She has just initiated an annual edited volume tentatively entitled *Research in Society and Politics,* to be published by JAI. The first volume will be devoted to empirical studies of national elites. The chapter in this volume is the first of three that Moore and Alba have written together on the American elite. A study on the ethnic origins of the American elite was recently published in the *American Sociological Review* and another on its class and prestige origins will appear in the Sage volume, *Social Structure and Network Analysis,* edited by Peter V. Marsden and Nan Lin.

PHILIPPA E. PATTISON is Lecturer in the Department of Psychology, University of Melbourne (Parkville, Victoria 3052, Australia). Her primary research interest is the development of mathematical theories of social structure and change. Her 1980 dissertation, "An algebraic analysis for multiple social networks," considerably extends the theoretical and operational framework presented in part in her article with Breiger in this volume.

DAVID PRENSKY is a Ph.D. candidate in the Department of Sociology at the University of Chicago (Chicago, Illinois 60637). His interests include political sociology, methodology, and social networks.